ISBN 978-1-331-99144-1
PIBN 10264099

TRANSACTIONS

OF THE

Mississippi Valley Horticultural Society,

FOR THE YEAR 1883,

LI
NE
BO
G

BEING A REPORT OF THE FOURTH ANNUAL MEETING

Compliments of

W. H. RAGAN,

Sec'y Miss. Val. Hort. Society,

CLAYTON,

INDIANA.

Please acknowledge receipt of this.

VOL. I.

BY W. H. RAGAN, SECRETARY.

INDIANAPOLIS:
CARLON & HOLLENBECK, PRINTERS AND BINDERS.
1883.

TRANSACTIONS

OF THE

Mississippi Valley Horticultural Society,

FOR THE YEAR 1883,

LI
NE
BO
G

BEING A REPORT OF THE FOURTH ANNUAL MEETING,
HELD IN THE CITY OF NEW ORLEANS, LA.,
FEBRUARY 21, 22, 23 AND 24, 1883,

TOGETHER WITH

A FULL LIST OF PAPERS READ, WITH ACCOMPANYING DISCUS-
SIONS; ALSO, LIST OF MEMBERS, ROSTER OF OFFICERS OF
HORTICULTURAL SOCIETIES, BUSINESS DIRECTORY,
AND HISTORICAL SKETCH OF THE M. V. H. S.,

WITH

LIST OF PREMIUMS

AWARDED AT THE FIRST ANNUAL MEETING, IN ST. LOUIS, SEP-
TEMBER, 1880.

VOL. I.

By W. H. RAGAN, Secretary.

INDIANAPOLIS:
CARLON & HOLLENBECK, PRINTERS AND BINDERS.
1883.

TABLE OF CONTENTS.

vi   *Table of Contents.*

INTRODUCTORY.

IN presenting this, the first volume of Transactions of the Mississippi Valley Horticultural Society, the Secretary begs the indulgence of members of the Society in any defects that may appear to them. The justice of this request will appear to those who are familiar with the facts in the case, viz., that the Secretary assumed the responsible duties of his office in the midst of the meeting at New Orleans, and, therefore, could not, by any possible means, do full justice to the important trust.

With the exception of the errors that may be due to this cause, and to the inevitable typographical errors that will escape the most careful proof reading, the Secretary flatters himself in the belief that he is presenting to the world, through this publication, one of the most valuable volumes of its kind that has thus far issued from the press of our country. Certainly no similar publication, with perhaps the single exception of the biennial reports of the American Pomological Society, has embraced subjects from a wider range of territory and from a greater list of practical contributors than this volume does.

With this brief introductory this volume is placed before the reader, whose honest verdict will be accepted as justly merited, by the   SECRETARY.

OFFICERS

OF THE

MISSISSIPPI VALLEY HORTICULTURAL SOCIETY

FOR 1883.

———

PARKER EARLE, President..Cobden, Illinois.
S. H. NOWLIN, First Vice President...........................Little Rock, Ark.
W. H. RAGAN, Secretary......................... ....Clayton, Indiana.
J. C. EVANS, Treasurer ....Harlem, Mo.

———

STATE VICE PRESIDENTS.

Dr. Jno. A. Warder, North Bend, Ohio.
T. T. Lyon, South Haven, Michigan.
E. Albertson, Bridgeport, Indiana.
Capt. E. Hollister, Alton, Illinois.
J. M. Smith, Green Bay, Wisconsin.
J. T. Grimes, Minneapolis, Minnesota.
Ex-Gov. R. W. Furnas, Brownville, Nebraska.
Prof. E. Gale, Manhattan, Kansas.
D. S. Grimes, Denver, Colorado.
Prof. J. L. Budd, Ames, Iowa.
Ex-Gov. N. J. Colman, St. Louis, Missouri.
W. B. Clarke, Beebe, Arkansas.
T. V. Munson, Denison, Texas.
Jno. T. Hardie, New Orleans, Louisiana.
Prof. J. J. Colmant, Agricultural College, Miss.
Dr. Chas. Mohr, Mobile, Alabama.
J. E. Porter, Humboldt, Tennessee.
James Decker, Fern Creek, Kentucky.
A. W. Campbell, Wheeling, West Virginia.
Dr. Samuel Hape, Atlanta, Georgia.

CORRESPONDENTS.

Allan, J. T., Sec'y State Hort. Society, Omaha, Nebraska.
Beadle, D. W., Sec'y Fruit-Growers' Association, St. Catharines, Ontario.
Beal. Prof. W. J., Sec'y American Pom. Society, Lansing, Michigan.
Burrill, Prof. T. J., Champaign, Illinois.
Berckmans, P. J., Pres. State Hort. Society, Augusta, Georgia.
Budd, Prof. J. L., Sec'y State Hort. Society, Ames, Iowa.
Brackett, G. C., Sec'y State Hort. Society, Lawrence, Kansas.
Brackett, G. B., Denmark, Iowa.
Bush, Isador, St. Louis, Missouri.
Brayton, Prof. A. W., Indianapolis, Indiana.
Bryant, Arthur, Princeton, Illinois.
Beatty, J. S., Pres. State Hort. Society, Simpsonville, Kentucky.
Barry, Patrick, Pres. Western N. Y. Hort. Society, Rochester, New York.
Baker, F. P., Topeka, Kansas.
Cassell, W. H., Canton, Mississippi.
Colman, Col. N. J., St. Louis, Missouri.
Colmant, Prof. J. J., Agricultural College, Mississippi.
Campbell, G. W., Sec'y State Hort. Society, Delaware, Ohio.
Cowing, Granville, Muncie, Indiana.
Downing, Chas., Newburg, New York.
Evans, J. C., Treas Mississippi Valley Hort. Society, Harlem, Missouri.
Furnas, Gov. R. W., Brownville, Nebraska.
Forbes, Prof. S. A., State Entomologist, Normal, Illinois.
Grimes, J. T., Treas. State Hort. Society, Minneapolis, Minnesota.
Grimes, D. S., Denver, Colorado.
Goodman, L. A., Sec'y State Hort. Society, Westport, Missouri.
Garfield, C. W., Sec'y State Hort. Society, Grand Rapids, Michigan.
Gale, Prof. E., Pres. State Hort. Society, Manhattan, Kansas.
Galusha, O. B., Pres. State Hort. Society, Morris, Illinois.
Hale, J. H., South Glastonbury, Connecticut.
Hape, Dr. Samuel, Atlanta, Georgia.
Hudson, E. M., New Orleans, Louisiana.
Hollister, Capt. E., Alton, Illinois.
Holsinger, F., Rosedale, Kansas.
Hammond, A. C., Warsaw, Illinois.
Ingersoll, Prof. C. L., Pres. State Agri. College, Fort Collins, Colorado.
Johnson, S., Pres. State Hort. Society, Irvington, Indiana.
Johnson, Geo. Y., Sec'y State Agri. Society, Lawrence, Kansas.
Loring, Dr. Geo. B., U. S. Com. of Agri., Washington, D. C.
Lyon, T. T., Pres. State Hort. Society, South Haven, Michigan.
Lazenby, Prof. W. R., Columbus, Ohio.
Lovett, J. T., Little Silver, New Jersey.
Latta, Prof. W. C., Purdue University, Lafayette, Indiana.

Manning, Robert, Sec'y State Hort. Society, Salem, Massachusetts.
Mohr, Dr. Charles, Mobile, Alabama.
McKay, Dr. E. H., Pres. State Hort. Society, Madison, Mississippi.
McWharton, Tyler, Aledo, Illinois.
Munson, T. V., Dennison, Texas.
Minier, Geo. W., Minier, Illinois.
Nowlin, S. H., Little Rock, Arkansas.
Ohmer, N., Dayton, Ohio.
Plumb, J. C., Milton, Wisconsin.
Parry, Wm., Parry P. O., New Jersey.
Porter, J. E., Humboldt, Tennessee.
Roy, Wm., Owen Sound, Ontario.
Riley, Prof. C. V., U. S. Entomologist, Washington, D. C.
Ragan, Z. S., Independence, Missouri.
Roe, Rev. E. P., Cornwal-on the Hudson, New York.
Stuart, W. R., Ocean Springs, Mississippi.
Smith, J. M. Pres. State Hort. Society, Green Bay, Wisconsin.
Scott, D. Wilmot, Secretary American Nursery Association, Galena, Illinois.
Samuels, Wm. M., Clinton, Kentucky.
Stayman, Dr. J. J., Leavenworth, Kansas.
Thomas, J. J., Union Springs, New York.
Teas, E. Y., Dunreith, Indiana.
Tracy, Prof. S. M., Pres. State Hort. Society, Columbia, Missouri.
Vick, Jas., Rochester, New York.
Webber, A. W., Nashville, Tennessee.
Weltz, Leo, Wilmington, Ohio.
Webb, A. D., Bowling Green, Kentucky.
Wilder, Col. Marshall P., Pres. A. P. M., Dorchester, Massachusetts.
Wiggins, S. M., Sec. Gulf States F. G. A., New Orleans, Louisiana.
Warder, Dr. J. A., Pres. State Hort. Society, North Bend, Ohio.

STANDING COMMITTEES FOR 1883.

On Statistics.—O. B. Galusha, of Illinois; Gov. R. W. Furnas, of Nebraska, and Dr. H. E. McKay, of Mississippi.

On Experimental Stations.—W. H. Ragan, of Indiana, F. P. Baker, of Kansas, and J. C. Evans, of Missouri.

On Exhibitions.—S. H. Nowlin, of Arkansas, T. T. Lyon, of Michigan, and J. S. Beatty, of Kentucky.

On Transportation (Northern Section.)—F. A. Thomas, of Illinois, J. M. Smith, of Wisconsin, and Capt. E. Hollister, of Illinois.

(Southern Section.)—Dr. H. E. McKay, of Mississippi, Maj. A. W. Rountree, of Louisiana, and Maj. S. H. Nowlin, of Arkansas.

CONSTITUTION

OF THE

MISSISSIPPI VALLEY HORTICULTURAL SOCIETY.

ARTICLE I. The organization shall be known as the Mississippi Valley Horticultural Society. Its object shall be the promotion of horticulture.

ARTICLE II. Any person may become a member upon the payment of two dollars, and membership shall continue upon the payment of two dollars annually.

ARTICLE III. Its officers shall consist of a President, First Vice President, Secretary and Treasurer, who shall be elected by ballot at each regular meeting; and one Vice President from each State, who may be elected to this position by the several State horticultural societies. Should there be no Vice President elected from any State, the vacancy may be filled by the executive committee of this society. The term of office of the President, Vice President, Secretary and Treasurer, shall begin on the first day of January following their election. No person can act as an officer of this Society who does not maintain his membership by the payment of the annual membership fees.

ARTICLE IV. The regular meetings of this Society shall be held annually on the first Tuesday of September, except when otherwise ordered by the executive committee, and continue for such time as the committee shall determine.

ARTICLE V. The officers of the Society shall constitute an executive committee, at any meeting of which a majority of the members present shall have power to transact business.

ARTICLE VI. Special meetings of the Society may be called by the executive committee, and meetings of the committee may be called by the President and Secretary.

ARTICLE VII. This constitution may be amended by a two-thirds vote of the members present at any regular meeting.

LIST OF MEMBERS

FOR 1883.

A

J. J. Atherly, South Haven..Michigan.
J. Albrecht, 50 Camp street, New Orleans...........................Louisiana.
Dr. F. M. Agnew, Makanda..Illinois.
Mrs. Dr. Agnew, Makanda...Illinois.
George Ames, Michigan City ....Indiana.
Mrs. George Ames, Michigan City..Indiana.
E. Albertson, Bridgeport...Indiana.
Albert Albertson, Canton........................... . ...Indiana.
B. F. Adams, Madison...Wisconsin.
Abner Allen, Wabaunsee...Kansas.
L. F. Adams, cor. Maryland and Penn. streets, Indianapolis...Indiana.
Henry Avery, Burlington.. ....Iowa.
Mrs. Helen V. Austin, Richmond.......................................Indiana.
Geo. G. Atwood, Geneva...New York.

B

Horace Y. Beebe, Ravenna...Ohio.
J. G. Bubaugh, Princeton...................................... . Illinois.
A. G. Brice, 30 Camp street, New Orleans...........................Louisiana.
J. D Baldwin, Ann Arbor..Michigan.
D. W. Beadle, St. Catharines...Ontario.
H. C. Bouton, Anna...Illinois.
Mrs. H. C. Bouton, Anna..Illinois.
A. B. Brown, Villa Ridge...Illinois.
F. P. Baker, Topeka..Kansas.
Prof. T. J. Burrill, Champaign...Illinois.
Benjamin Buckman, Farmingdale.......................................Illinois.
Thomas Bermingham, 131 South Water street, Chicago.........Illinois.
John H. Barnett, 147 South Water street, Chicago.. ....Illinois.
Mrs. J. H. Barnett, Chicago..Illinois.

T. A. Bixby, South Haven..Michigan.
M. H. Bixby, South Haven................................ ....Michigan.
William Britton, Madison................................ Mississippi.
John Buck, Cobden..Illinois.
Mrs. J. Buck, Cobden.................... ....Illinois.
Isidor Bush, St. Louis..Missouri.
J. Bower, New Trenton....................................Indiana.
J. P. Buck, Appleton ....Wisconsin.
Mrs. J. P. Buck, Appleton...Wisconsin.
A. A. Barnes, cor. Maryland and Delaware sts., Indianapolis...Indiana.
George L. Brunton, Centralia................................Illinois.
Fielding Beeler, Indianapolis................................Indiana.
M. Baker, 93 South Water street, Chicago..........................Illinois.
George Booth, 113 South Water street, Chicago...................Illinois.
Mrs. O. W. Brownback, Pendleton................................Indiana.
W. H. Bryan, 12 and 14 Walnut street, Cincinnati................Ohio.
P. J. Berckmans, Augusta................................Georgia.
Phil F. Brown, Blue Ridge Springs................................Virginia.
Prof. J. L. Budd, Ames.......... ....Iowa.
John Blair, Kansas City................................Missouri.
Bloomington Nursery Company, Bloomington....................Illinois.

C

E. N. Clark, Cobden................................Illinois.
Mrs. E. N. Clark, Cobden... ....Illinois.
A. J. Caywood, Marlboro..................................New. York.
C. G. Comstock, Albany................................Missouri.
Prof. J. J. Colmant, Agricultural College...........................Mississippi.
C. D. Colman, St. Louis........................ ......Missouri.
L. Cole, 80 Camp street, New Orleans............................ ...Louisiana.
W. Cook, Bowling Green................................Kentucky.
Mrs. H. Carter, Waverly................................Illinois.
W. H. Cassell, Canton................................Mississippi.
B. O. Curtis, Paris................................Illinois.
L. D. Cassinello, St. Louis................................Missouri.
G. W. Campbell, Delaware................................Ohio.
George Cairncross, Pewaukee................................Wisconsin.
O. D. Clough, St. Louis................................Missouri.
Granville Cowing, Muncie................................Indiana.
John S. Collins, Moorestown................................New Jersey.
Matthew Crawford, Cuyahoga Falls................................Ohio.
E. F. Cadwallader, Louisburg.......... ....Kansas.
A. W. Campbell, Wheeling................................West Virginia.
W. B. Clarke, Beebe........... ....Arkansas.
J. S. Conklin, Sidney. ....Ohio.

Hiram Canfield, 88 West Market street, Buffalo....................New York.
N. J. Colman, St. Louis.......... ....Missouri.
J. K. Cravens, Kansas City. .... Missouri.
Daniel Cox, Cartersburg..................................... ....Indiana.
Phil Chew, St. Louis...Missouri.
Wise A. Cooper, Trenton................................... Tennessee.
Cook & Irwin, Blue Mound......... ....Kansas.

D

M. A. Dunn, Chicago... ....Illinois.
George Davies, 37 Prospect street, Cleveland...... ....Ohio.
Mrs. H. Davies, 37 Prospect street, Cleveland.............. ....Ohio.
H. Daue, Woodland................................... ....Wisconsin.
T. C. Dickinson, Kankakee...................................... .... Illinois.
Mrs. T. C. Dickinson, Kankakee..Illinois.
Dr. T. F. Dryden, Clayton.. Indiana.
D. M. Dewey, Rochester...New York.
C. N. Dennis, Hamilton...Illinois.
Mrs. C. N. Dennis, Hamilton...Illinois.

E

Parker Earle, Cobden. ....Illinois.
Mrs. Parker Earle, Cobden... ....Illinois.
Frank S. Earle, Cobden...Illinois.
Charles T. Earle, Cobden ....Illinois.
G. C. Eisenmeyer, Mascoutah..Illinois.
J. C. Evans, Harlem..Missouri.
G. W. Endicott, Villa Ridge.............. ....Illinois.
J. F. Ewing. Bowling Green......... ....Kentucky.
L. Ellsworth, Milwaukee....... ....Wisconsin.
Mrs. C. G. Eddy, Chicago..Illinois.
James Edgerton, Barnesville..Ohio.
G. F. Espenlaub, Rosedale....... ....Kansas.

F

Frank Ford, Ravenna............ ....Ohio.
Dr. A. D. Finch, Anna ....Illinois.
H. B. Francis, Mulberry. ....Missouri.
Prof. S. A. Forbes, Normal..Illinois.
H. C. Fisher, Memphis ....Tennessee.
E. H. Finch, Anna ....Illinois.
Mrs. E. H. Finch, Anna. ....Illinois.
J. N. Fitch, Cobden. ....Illinois.
Mrs. J. N. Fitch, Cobden.. .....Illinois.
C. W. Faust, Canton......... ....Ohio.

H. H. Farley, Union Springs......................................New York.
C. M. Forbes, Judsonia......................................Arkansas.
C. H. Ferrell, Humboldt......................................Tennessee.

G

A. H. Gilkeson, Warrensburg......................................Missouri.
O. C. Gibbs, Downer's Grove......................................Illinois.
Prof. F. A. Gulley. Agricultural College......................................Mississippi.
Mrs. F. A. Gulley, Agricultural College......................................Mississippi.
W. G. Gano, Parkville......................................Missouri.
L. A. Goodman, Westport......................................Missouri.
J. G. Gilmore, New Iberia......................................Louisiana.
O. B. Galusha, Morris......................................Illinois.
D. S. Grimes, Denver......................................Colorado.
C. W. Gallagher, Meridian......................................Mississippi.
Mrs. A. C. Gallagher, Meridian......................................Mississippi.
Samuel Groenendyke, Eugene......................................Indiana.
D. Ginnochio, St. Louis......................................Missouri.
Col. R. W. Gillespie, New Orleans.......................................Louisiana.
J. H. Gail, Buffalo......................................New York.
M. George, 95 South Water street, Chicago......................................Illinois.
J. T. Grimes, Minneapolis......................................Minnesota.
C. H. Gregory, Altus......................................Arkansas.
John O. Green, New Albany......................................Indiana.
Joseph Gilbert, Terre Haute......................................Indiana.
W. A. Gosnell, Kansas City......................................Missouri.
H. Garman, Normal.......................................Illinois.

H

F. Holsinger, Rosedale.......................................Kansas.
Mrs. F. Holsinger, Rosedale......................................Kansas.
E. M. Hudson, New Orleans......................................Louisiana.
Dr. Samuel Hape, Atlanta......................................Georgia.
J. T. Hardie, New Orleans......................................Louisiana.
E. T. Hollister, St. Louis......................................Missouri.
E. Hollister, Alton......................................Illinois.
Jacob Hileman, Anna......................................Illinois.
Mrs. D. Huntley, Appleton......................................Wisconsin.
A. D. Healy, South Haven.......................................Michigan.
J. H. Hale, South Glastonbury......................................Connecticut.
A. E. Heighway, Cincinnati......................................Ohio.
Dr. Gideon Hunt, Plainfield......................................Indiana.
H. H. Harvey, Gretna......................................Louisiana.
Dr. G. A. Hall, Wabash avenue, Chicago......................................Illinois.
Watson F. Hinckley, Indiana avenue, Chicago......................................Illinois.

Mrs. W. F. Hinckley, Indiana avenue, Chicago......................Illinois.
H. S. Hurd, Burlington...Ontario.
T. S. Hubbard, Fredonia............................... ....New York.
J. J. Harrison, Painesville..Ohio.
W. F. Heikes, Huntsville............................ ....Alabama.
C. G. Hampton, Detroit.............. .... Michigan.
William S. Hubbard, Indianapolis...................................... Indiana.
E. Hollister, Secretary Alton Horticultural Society, Alton.....Illinois.
A. C. Hammond, Warsaw................... ....Illinois.
Mrs. A. C. Hammond, Warsaw.................. ....Illinois.
Heikes Nursery Company, Dayton................ ....Ohio.
W. H. Henry, Beebe..Arkansas.
P. D. Hammond, Indianapolis..Indiana.
John M. Howell, Dallas...Texas.
William M. Hopkins, Kansas City....................................Missouri.
B. B. Hance, Red Bank.. ....New Jersey.
F. L. Houghton, Normal...................... ....Illinois.

I

C. L. Ingersoll, Pres. State Ag. College Fort, Collins............. Colorado.

J

Sylvester Johnson, Irvington.......... .... Indiana.
Edwin Johnson, Clayton................................... ......Indiana.
S. S. Jackson, Cincinnati..Ohio.
Thomas Joannes, Green Bay...Wisconsin.
Z. K. Jewett, Sparta.................................... ....Wisconsin.
Mrs. J. R. Johnson, Sec'y State Hort. Society, Dallas..............'Texas.
Geo. S. Josselyn, Fredonia.............. ....New York.

K

P. M. Kiely, 719 Broadway, St. Louis.............. ....Missouri.
T. W. Kizer, Winchester..Indiana.
E. Kennedy, 190 Josephine street, New Orleans...................Louisiana.
T. J. Knopp, 13 Baronne street, New Orleans......................Louisiana.
A. C. Kendel, 115 Ontario street, Cleveland...................... ..Ohio.
Mrs. A. C. Kendel, Cleveland.................................. .... .Ohio.
C. Kirkpatrick, Anna........ ....Illinois.
Mrs. C. Kennedy, Cartersville...... .... Illinois.
George J. Kellogg, Janesville........ ....Wisconsin.
A. W. Kerr, McKinney..Texas.
E. W. Kirkpatrick, McKinney...Texas.
Wm. Kidwell, Kansas City..Missouri.

L

Wm. Lewis, Kansas City ....Missouri.
Eugene Lindsay, Westport...Missouri.
J. W. Latimer, Pleasanton..Kansas.
J. Van. Lindley, Salem Junction................................North Carolina.
D. W. Langdon, Mobile...Alabama.
V. Litorey, Wartburg.. ......Tennessee.
T. T. Lyon, South Haven...... ....Michigan.
Mrs. C E. Lewis, Madison.. ....Mississippi.
Mrs. H. M. Lewis, Madison ....Wisconsin.
John T. Lovett, Little Silver .. .. New Jersey.
J. E. Lufkin, Anna. ....Illinois.
Robert C. Lee, Madison......... ....Mississippi.
Prof. W. C. Latta, Lafayette.............. ....Indiana.

M

T. V. Munson, Denison.. .... .Texas.
J. C. Miller, Norwich................... ....Ohio.
C. J. Morris, Beebe...... ....Arkansas. ·
V. H. Marshall, Columbus...Mississippi.
J. B. McCranie, Malvern............................... ......Arkansas.
W. P. Minnick, Villa Ridge..Illinois.
L. F. Montgomery, Madison.................................... ......Mississippi.
Dr. H. E. McKay, Madison. ....Mississippi.
Dr. J. H. McKay, Madison..Mississippi.
Mrs. C. P. McKay, Madison......................... ....Mississippi.
Miss F. McKay, Madison.............................. .....Mississippi.
W. P. Mesler, Cobden...Illinois.
Mrs. W. P. Mesler, Cobden ....Illinois.
John Milligan, Rossville. ....Illinois.
S. T. Merrill, Beloit............. ....Wisconsin.
H. C. Minter, Keytsville......... ....Missouri.
Charles W. Mills, Columbus...Mississippi.
A. L. McClay, 95 South Water street, Chicago....................Illinois.
Thomas Mason, 183 South Water street, Chicago.................Illinois.
George W. Minier, Minier.............................. ....Illinois.
J. F. Mendenhall, Indianapolis........... ....Indiana.
M. A. Moore, Greencastle............... ....Indiana.
Malvern Vineyard, Malvern ....Arkansas.
S. G. Minkler, Oswego. ....Illinois.
J. V. Milhouse, Butlerville..Indiana.
T. E. B. Mason, Shenandoah...... ....Iowa.
Wm. Mustard, Kansas City............... ....Missouri.
C. W. Merwin, Medina ....Tennessee.
J. H. Monsees, Beaman... ....Missouri.
J. B. Matthews, Marissa.............................. .. ..Illinois.

N

C. Nordling, Anna..Illinois.
F. Neibauer, Dongola..Illinois.
Mrs. Amy Nicholson, Fillmore..Indiana.
F. Nickerson, Chicago...Illinois.

O

Nicholas Ohmer, Dayton..... ....Ohio.
Gilbert Onderdonk, Mission Valley..Texas.
Ewald Over, Indianapolis...Indiana.

P

Charles Patterson, Kirksville................................ ....Missouri.
W. H. Purcell, Chicago.... ....Illinois.
Charles F. Peirce, 92 Washington street, Chicago ....Illinois.
Amos Poole, Cobden ....Illinois.
Mrs. A. Poole, Cobden.......... ....Illinois.
Elias Powell, Kankakee................................. ....•.Illinois.
Mrs. E. Pow-ll, Kankakee...Illinois.
Mrs. S. M. Phillips, Anna.......................... ....Illinois.
J. E. Porter, Humboldt... ....Tennessee.
M. Phillips, Plainfield................................... ....Indiana.
George P. Peffer, Pewaukee..Wisconsin.
Mrs. G. P. Peffer, Pewaukee.. ....Wisconsin.
Bartlett Presley, St. Paul.................................... ....Minnesota.
Alfred Plant, 812–14 North Fourth street, St. Louis..............Missouri.
G. Poindexter, Blue Lick ....Indiana.
William Parry, Parry P. O. ....New Jersey.
J. H. Priest, Greencastle..Indiana.
F. K. Phœnix, Delavan...Wisconsin.
S. C. Palmer, Kansas City...Missouri.

R

Jesse Ray, Kansas City....... ....Missouri.
William Radam, Austin............................... ....Texas.
William Rendleman, Makanda. ....Illinois.
Mrs. W. Rendleman, Makanda............................... ....Illinois.
A. J. Ritzenthaler, Long Grove.......................... ....Illinois.
M. G. Ritzenthaler, Long Grove..Illinois.
W. H. Ragan, Clayton...Indiana.
John W. Ragan, Fillmore............................... .... Indiana.
T. D. Randall, Chicago.......................... ....Illinois.
Mrs. T. D. Randall, Chicago..Illinois.
William Roy, Owen Sound...Ontario.

2

List of Members.

Prof. J. C. Ridpath, Greencastle..Indiana.
E. C. Reichwald, Chicago ....Illinois.
H. H. Ragan, Salem...Oregon.
Z. S. Ragan, Independence........ ....Missouri.

S

F. W. Strachan, Martinsburg. ....West Virginia.
M. W. Serl, Lebanon... ....Missouri.
H. Shepley, Nevada....... ....Missouri.
Mrs. P. Schweitzer, Columbia ....Missouri.
Dr. W. W. Stell, Paris.. ....Texas.
A. Sambola, New Orleans...Louisiana.
Miss E. Stinson, Norristown ....Pennsylvania.
Mrs. C. Shick, Norristown.................................... ....Pennsylvania.
G. W. Sentelle, New Orleans...Louisiana. .
Dr. J. H. Sanborn, Anna. ....Illinois.
O. P. Stufflebeam, Rossville...Illinois.
Dr. A. L Small, Kankakee...Illinois.
D. Wilmot Scott, Galena..Illinois.
S. W. Salisbury, Kansas City ....Missouri.
Mrs. A. L. Small, Kankakee........ ....Illinois.
J. M. Smith, Green Bay.. ....Wisconsin.
Mrs. J. M. Smith, Green Bay. ....Wisconsin.
W. R. Sprague, 716 North Fifth street, St. Louis..................Missouri.
C. W. Sheller, South Haven... ....Michigan.
W. M. Samuels, Clinton... .... Kentucky.
Mrs. W. M. Samuels, Clinton...Kentucky.
Dr. J. Stayman, Leavenworth ....Kansas.
D. J. Signaigo, St. Louis....... ....Missouri.
Dr. A. M. Strong, Belleville........... ....Indiana
Joseph Spies, 101 South Water street, Chicago. ....Illinois.
A. C. Snyder, Chicago.. ....Illinois.
J. W. Stanley, Gretna...Louisiana.
Mrs. J. W. Stanley. Gretna...Louisiana.
W. R. Stuart, Ocean Springs.................................... ......Mississippi.
Jacob Schopp, St. Louis.. ....Missouri.
E. Schaper, St. Louis. ....Missouri.
Henry Syerup, Indianapolis.................... ....Indiana.
H. M. Simpson, Vincennes ....Indiana.
Dr. H Schroeder, Bloomington....................................... ....Illinois.
I. N. Stone, Fort Atkinson.. ....Wisconsin.
Samuel Smith, Carbondale...... ....Illinois.
Charles A. Stewart, Chicago......................... ....Illinois.
Will P. Stark, Louisiana...Missouri.
Prof. J. J. Schardt, Hot Springs....................................Arkansas.
G. W. Stone, Shreveport.. ....Louisiana.

T

Prof. S. M. Tracy, Columbia... Missouri.
A. Thomson, New Orleans...Louisiana.
H. S. Thompson, Louisville...Kentucky.
T. W. Thompson, Makanda..Illinois.
Mrs. T. W. Thompson, Makanda...Illinois.
M. M. Thompson, Makanda...Illinois.
Mrs. M. M. Thompson, Makanda..Illinois.
L. E. Tyler, New Orleans...Louisiana.
G. A. Tryon, Galesburg...Illinois.
Mrs. G. A. Tryon, Galesburg...Illinois.
J. W. Titus, Villa Ridge. ....Illinois.
T. F. Tunison, Pana. ....Illinois.
F. A. Thomas, Chicago ....Illinois.
Mrs. F. A. Thomas, Chicago...Illinois.
I. P. Tichenor, Milwaukee..Wisconsin.
E. Y. Teas, Dunreith...Indiana.
William Ten Brook, Rockville..Indiana.
Franklin Taylor, Indianapolis..Indiana.
A. L. Tucker, 167 South Water street, Chicago...........................Illinois.
W. K. Tipton, Little Rock...Arkansas.
J. C. Tharp, Gibson...Tennessee
Z. Todd, Kansas City..Missouri.

U

Underwood & Emery, Lake City..Minnesota.

V

D. H. Vancil, Cobden...Illinois.
F. V. D. Voorhees, Detroit..Michigan.
J. C. Vaughan, 42 Lasalle street, Chicago................................Illinois.

W

Jabez Webster, Centralia. ....Illinois.
Mrs. L. R. Wardner, Anna ....Illinois.
S. M. Wiggins, 36 Tchoupitoulas street, New Orleans...............Louisiana.
J. R. Walker, Bay St. Louis..Mississippi.
E. G. Wall, Jackson...Mississippi.
Mrs. N. D. Wetmore, Ponchatoula ....Louisiana.
D. B. Weir, Lacon...Illinois.
H. E. Weir, Lacon...Illinois.
A. D. Webb, Bowling Green...Kentucky.
R. J. Williams, Gadsden..Tennessee.
E. H. Williams, (Mummenhoff & Co.) Indianapolis..................Indiana.

C. L. Watrous, Des Moines...Iowa.
Mrs. C. L. Watrous, Des Moines...Iowa.
Mrs. M. A. Wemple, Waverly,..Illinois.
Mrs. D. Wemple, Waverly..Illinois.
F. H. Wemple, Waverly..Illinois.
A. W. Webber, Nashville............................ ....Tennessee.
C. C. Wright, Cobden..Illinois.
Mrs. C. C. Wright, Cobden...Illinois.
C. H. Weaver, 129 South Water street, Chicago....................Illinois.
D. H. Wright, Minneapolis.............................. ....Minnesota.
Mrs. F. F. Whitehead, New Orleans....................................Louisiana.
A. W. Wells, St. Joseph..Michigan.
Mrs. Nevie Woods, Stilesville..Indiana.
James L. Whippo, Anderson...Indiana.
Leo Weltz, Wilmington ....Ohio.
A. R. Whitney, Franklin Grove...Illinois.
S. D. Willard, Geneva..New York.
Wm. Wesselhoft, 306 North Fifth street, St. Louis................Missouri.
F. M. Webster, Normal..Illinois.
C. B. Warren, Kansas City. ....Missouri.

Y

J. B. Yellowly, Madison.. ....Mississippi.
Mrs. J. B. Yellowly, Madison ....Mississippi.
Dr. Charles Yoke, Bridgeport...... ....Indiana.
Geo. Young (Young & Bro.), Greensburg...............................Indiana.
J. H. York, Fort Scott...Kansas.
A. M. York, Denton..Texas.

PROCEEDINGS

OF THE

FOURTH ANNUAL MEETING

OF THE

MISSISSIPPI VALLEY HORTICULTURAL SOCIETY.

The fourth annual meetiug of the Mississippi Valley Horticultural Society was held in the city of New Orleans, February 21, 22, 23 and 24, 1883.

This meeting was held under circumstances of peculiar interest, the Society being, at the time, the guest of the Gulf States Fruit Growers' Association. The leading railroads of the South and West contributed much to the interest of the occasion by offering very liberal rates to delegates who wished to attend the meeting. The Illinois Central railroad company set the good example by offering very low rates from Chicago and other points on their lines, which, good example, was followed by no less than eighteen other companies, whose lines lead in the direction of New Orleans.

But for the unprecedented floods, extending over the North and West, which rendered railroad travel not only very precarious, but in many instances absolutely impossible, there would have been many more to have enjoyed this pleasant and very profitable meeting in the Crescent City of the South.

Many are the disappointments expressed by hundreds of fruit growers of the North and West at not being permitted, in consequence of the floods, to attend a meeting of so much importance, and especially in a latitude of such peculiar interest to those accustomed to the rigors of a northern climate. As it was, and in spite of the swollen and dangerous condition of the Ohio, the Mississippi and other northern streams, some two hundred or more fruit growers, many of them accompanied by their wives and children, representing twenty-one States and the Dominion of Ontario, found their way to this, the first important meeting of the kind ever held so far in the direction of the noon-day sun. Nor was this meeting exclusively monopolized by the people of the North. The South and South-west, with many from New Orleans and the immediate vicinity, met us on friendly terms in this meeting of mutual interest.

The Society assembled in *Grunewald Hall,* one of the most beautiful and commodious assembly rooms in the country, which had been provided and handsomely decorated and adorned for the occasion by the Gulf States Fruit Growers' Association. Many rare and beautiful semi-tropical plants had been used in the decorations of the hall, which gave to the surroundings an agreeable and pleasant appearance, especially to those of us so recently transported from the icy regions of the North. In connection with the hall were committee rooms and consultation parlors; also, a large corridor fitted up with suitable exhibition tables, all of which were, for the time being, placed at the service of the Society. A very creditable display of fruit was placed on exhibition by members from various sections of our common country.

The agricultural press of the country was largely represented at the meeting, prominent among which the Secretary recognized the following:

Gilbert M. Tucker, of the *Country Gentleman,* Albany, New York; S. M. Tracy, *Rural New Yorker,* New York; John Hyde, *Prairie Farmer,* Chicago, Ill; C. D. Colman, *Colman's Rural World,* St. Louis; Mrs. H. M. Lewis, *Western Farmer,* Madison Wis.; W. H. Ragan, *Midland Monthly,* Indianapolis, Ind.; E. H. Williams, *Indiana Farmer,* Indianapolis; D. W. Beadle, *Canadian Horticulturist,* St. Catherine's, Ont.; O. C. Gibbs, *Chicago Tribune;* A. W. Campbell, *Wheeling Intelligencer,* W. Va.; F. P. Baker, *Topeka Commonwealth,* Topeka, Kan.; S. H. Nowlin, *Rural Southwest,* Little

Rock, Ark.; H. C. Bouton, *Farmer and Fruit Grower*, Anna, Ill.; J. E. Porter, *West Tennessee Argus;* J. Y. Gilmore, *Louisiana Sugar Bowl*, New Iberia, La., and others whose names the Secretary failed to get.

First Day—Wednesday.

EVENING SESSION, February 21, 1883.

At half-past 7 o'clock P. M. Wednesday, February 21, President Parker Earle, of Cobden, Illinois, called the Society to order.

The afternoon of the preceding day had been devoted to the usual preliminary work of such occasions—to the arrangement of fruits for exhibition, and especially to social greetings and to the formation of new acquaintances; and now, at the hour appointed for the first regular business meeting, in the beautiful hall and under the brilliant gas lights, assembled as happy and intelligent a congregation of practical horticulturists as may but rarely be met with, drawn together from far distant points, ranging from almost two thousand miles, to the immediate surroundings.

The following gentlemen occupied seats upon the stage : · Parker Earle, Esq., President ; Prof. S. M. Tracy, Secretary ; Major S. H. Nowlin, Ex-Governor R. W. Furnas, of Nebraska; Prof. J. J. Colmant, of the Mississippi Agricultural and Mechanical College; T. T. Lyon, President Michigan State Horticultural Society, and O. B. Galusha, President Illinois State Horticultural Society, representing the Mississippi Valley Horticultural Society; and Judge E. M. Hudson, Judge A. G. Brice, Major Austin W. Roundtree, Captain J. J. Mellon, Captain A. Sambola, John T. Hardie, Esq., Adam Thomson, Esq., S. M. Wiggins, Esq., and George W. Nicholson, Esq., representing the Fruit Growers' Association of the Gulf States.

Upon taking the chair, President Earle addressed the Society as follows :

"Ladies and gentlemen, members of the Mississippi Valley Horticultural Society, we are assembled to-night in this beautiful hall, in the great commercial metropolis of the South, upon the invitation of the Fruit Growers' Association of the Gulf States, whose President, Hon. E. M. Hudson, of this city, I now have the pleasure of introducing to you."

Mr. Hudson, who is a practical farmer and fruit grower upon a large scale, as well as an eminent counselor at law, addressed the Society as follows:

Gentlemen of the Mississippi Valley Horticultural Society:

It was expected that the Governor of our State would have been present to tender you a welcome and a greeting. He is, unfortunately, kept away by public duties from the city at present, but I am charged by him in his name, on behalf of the State of Louisiana and of the city of New Orleans, to tender you a cordial and hearty welcome. While expressing his deep regret for the circumstances which kept him from participating in your deliberations, he also desired me to say that, should his business engagements allow him, he will try to be here before your adjournment to take some part in your deliberations.

Gentlemen, in the absence of the President of the Fruit Growers' Association (for I am only the Vice President), it devolves upon me, as his exponent, to tender you a welcome; to welcome you here as the representatives of the great Mississippi Valley, a valley which but a few years ago was considered a very inconsiderable portion of these United States, but which, to-day, I think I can say, without exaggeration, when we consider the system of its railway and river connections, extends from the Atlantic to the Pacific slope. We welcome you here as the exponants of an era of peace and prosperity, because it is only with peace and prosperity that art and agriculture can flourish. We welcome you here as our neighbors—neighbors with whom identity of labors and interests have made us acquainted long before we saw your faces.

Yours, gentlemen, is no ignoble mission. The history of the world teaches us that in all ages, where civilization and culture has prospered, horticulture has prospered. It is only when civilization has declined that the cultivation of the soil has fallen into disrepute. In the proudest days of Greece and Rome, when the poets sang, agriculture was at the acme of its prosperity. Afterward, in the decline of the Roman Empire, it fell into disrepute, and it was only when letters were revived by the orders of the monks in their mountain caves that horticulture began again to prosper. Its revival commenced with the revival of letters in the Monastic Period. I said it was no ignoble profession. Charlemagne, himself, was the first who recognized it as a noble one.

And now, if we cast our eyes back over the last fifty years—I will say for the last quarter of a century—and see the wonderful advances which have been made in the United States, having learned all that the older countries of Europe could teach us, we have in our turn become teachers. You are all teachers; by your example, by the organization of such associations as this, you are teaching the young men of the country the art of horticulture; I say art advisedly, for you are teaching them the best method of cultivating the earth and of procuring from it the fairest fruits, flowers and embellishments. Wherever agriculture has flourished, architecture has prospered. We have but to look at a highly cultivated piece of land to-day and note the architectural beauties with which it is embellished.

Gentlemen, I do not propose to detain you to-night. You come here for a grand purpose. The programme shows that you have to consider subjects of importance, and of the greatest importance to the whole land. You have much to do. Our Association, which has not been as active as your own, will take courage from you. We shall listen and expect to be instructed, and we shall take the deepest interest in all the deliberations which shall take place among you.

To which President Earle responded as follows:

Mr. President, Gentlemen and Citizens of New Orleans:

In the unfortunate absence of the gentleman who was to have responded to this most cordial welcome from Mr. Hudson—Gov. Colman, of St. Louis— I can only say, on the part of this Society, that our hearts respond warmly to the welcome which you extend to us. We have come down here from the North, and from the West, and from all parts of the Mississippi valley, to make your acquaintance, to exchange cordial greetings of friendship, to compare views, and to give encouraging words regarding the useful art of horticulture in which the people of all sections of our great country are deeply interested, and to deepen and widen that feeling of a community of interests, and a sincere brotherhood between all of our several sections, without which no permanent prosperity and no high civilization can be maintained. I am glad, Sir, to receive this welcome from you, and to receive it in Louisiana. I am glad we have come down here to this beautiful and historic city, to this memorable and fertile State, where nature smiles perennially in verdure and in flowers; but I am more glad to meet the warm welcome in your faces, than of your mild and sunny skies. Let me assure you, Sir, that every member of this society responds cordially to the generous spirit of your welcome. But I can not trust myself to say more upon a theme which so touches my heart, but will proceed now with my regular address to the Society.

PRESIDENT'S ANNUAL ADDRESS.

MEMBERS AND FRIENDS: The territory which this Society represents, possesses imperial extent and resources. The natural wealth of this great valley surpasses by far that of any existing empire on the globe. The magnitude of our agricultural resources is recognized and commented on the world over with wonder. The markets of the world depend upon the yield of our fields and our pastures. The size of the harvests in the Mississippi valley affects the price of the daily bread of half the population of the globe. The industrial development of this valley has revolutionized the commercial and economic systems of the most powerful nations of the earth. And all of these vast changes have been mostly wrought during the life-time, and by the energy of a single generation of men. It is safe to say that so great a work has never before been done by man. We have in but little more than a quarter of a century converted a boundless wilderness into fruitful fields, spanned it with fifty thousand miles of railway, and made ourselves masters of the world's markets for food and clothing.

But while this wonderful development of the agriculture and commerce of our great valley has swept forward, there has been a minor culture more slowly building itself up, which has not affected the interests of the other nations so deeply, but which has been intimately related to the welfare and prosperity of our own people, and this indispensable thing is *Horticulture.* Horticulture embraces all of those finer products and conditions which, being essential to the best development of men and women, makes a grand agriculture, a fruitful commerce, and a noble civilization possible. A generous horticulture goes hand in hand with an enlightened agriculture, and neither can become great and permanent without the other. As, then, the produce of the garden, the fruits of the orchard, the beautiful growths of the florist, and the grateful shade and shelter of forests, are all indispensable to the growth of the men who grow the crops that feed and clothe the world, we find that the whole great world is, after all, vitally concerned with the success or failure of our Mississippi valley horticulture.

It is then, with great pleasure, that I greet you, fellow-members of this young Society, so young in years, but so great in purposes and in hopes! that I greet you assembled in such goodly numbers in this great and beautiful city of the South, to confer together regarding all those methods by which we may help to perfect our varied work. I am glad, ladies and gentlemen, that we have met here in this Southern metropolis, so near to the mouth of the mighty river which waters and drains the greatest valley of the world; so near to the shore of the great Gulf, whose breezes warm and fertilize all the vast area of our gardens and fields. I am glad that we of the North have come down to meet and shake hands with you of the South, as fellow-members of a noble fraternity, as brotherly citizens of a glorious nation! We come together to-day from widely-separated sections, from more than half of the States of this great republic—but representing one grand community of feeling and purpose—to work out some of the problems which affect the perpetuity of civilized society, and the progress of humanity toward millennial ideals. We come peacefully and joyfully together from a thousand busy communities, where the plowshares and pruning hooks—you remember well from what stern implements they were beaten—are industriously wielded, and all the many arts of life are carried on in glorious peace! God be praised that this is so, and that the firm purpose of our hearts is that this shall remain so forever :

"For humanity sweeps onward ! "

And the men of this country who have mastered their passions and have re-established sincere relations of fraternity may well

> " Stand serene and down the future see the golden beam incline
> To the side of perfect justice, mastered by their faith divine,
> By man's plain truth to manhood, and to God's supreme design."

Perhaps the most satisfactory result of a great gathering of people, who come a thousand miles to see each other—from the great lakes of the North and the coast regions of the tropical Gulf, from the vast plains of Nebraska, Kansas and Texas, the once " Great American Desert," and from the beautiful valleys and hill-sides of the older States, is the great profit we find in a wider and more intimate personal acquaintance. If we were to do no more at this meeting than to shake hands all round, renewing old and forming new acquaintances, engaging in the delightful social intercourse of these days spent together, being warmed by the common sympathy pervading horticultural societies, we should find full repayment for our expense of time and money.

But beyond all this there is, I think, a great work for us to do in perfecting the science and the art of horticulture and contributing to the welfare and happiness of mankind. I have often been asked, " What is the purpose of this Society?" " What is the need of having such a society?" " What is the work you are proposing to do?" It is fitting that these questions should have an answer. If you will indulge me I will briefly give you some of the reasons why, in my judgment, there should be such a society as this, and outline some of the work which it may profitably attempt to do.

A PLEA FOR ORGANIZATION.

We have, in nearly all of the States, Horticultural Societies and a great number of Local Societies, all of which are doing valuable work in educating public taste and extending special knowledge of our business. We have also three great national organizations, each of which is carrying forward a special work of its own. The American Pomological Society has long been doing excellent service in the strictly pomological department of horticultural labor, and its venerable chief, who is the grandest figure which the world's horticulture has produced in any country or in any age, receives the homage of all hearts in the whole realm of our art. We shall gladly be tributary to this great society in its invaluable work. Not less important in its purposes and in the work it has begun to do, is the American Forestry Association. The supreme necessity for the most vigorous labor in this special field is felt by all. With that society we shall labor in perfect sympathy. The American Nurserymen's Association is another organization of great importance to the interests of plant and tree propagation—an indispensable factor in the scheme of horticultural improvement.

But none of these noble societies fully meet a want which many of us have felt, of an organization modeled after the best of our State societies, but embracing a territory almost national in its extent, throughout which commercial horticultural relations are daily becoming more intimate and important.

Inasmuch as local and county societies do not fully meet the desires of the horticulturists of any of our States, but we must have organizations which bring the fruit growers, florists, gardeners and foresters of entire States into more intimate acquaintance and relationships, so it seems that the more comprehensive needs of a great community of States can not be fully answered except by an organization which shall bring us all together in an annual congress, for deliberation as to methods and measures, for the discussion of varieties and principles, and to hear the latest word of science and the best suggestions of art concerning this noble business of our lives.

The horticultural products which enter into the various channels of commerce in this Mississippi valley aggregate not less than fifty millions of dollars of annual value ; while the similar products which pass into immediate domestic use, of which no account is ever kept, are supposed to fully equal this amount. When we consider these vast financial interests, which are subject. more or less, to the influence of horticultural bodies—which have indeed been largely stimulated and developed by the action of these societies —and when we reflect upon the still more vital and weighty questions of the esthetic and moral influences of horticulture upon the daily life and the homes of thirty millions of people in this valley of ours, we shall not disparage the importance of any organized effort to render these great interests more secure, and these beneficent influences more effective.

When we climb to a mountain top and enlarge the horizon of our view, we get a better idea of the relations of the natural features of the country around us ; we see hill and valley, lake and stream, forest and field, all blending into one harmonious landscape. So, when our minds are uplifted to some plane of loftier contemplation of the wide relations of our diversified horticulture, we shall see the lines of our interest reaching out to the utmost boundary of the continent, and we shall find that we are bound one to another, man to man, and State to State, in an intimate business sympathy, as well as in the reciprocity of social relations or the companionship of great ideas. We are engaged not alone in growing apples and strawberries for the market, trees for the orchard, or forests for the lumber there is in them. We have the weightier engagement of making a million homes beautiful, and so more joyful; of ornamenting towns, and roadsides, and fields; of planting groves on treeless plains; of planting flowers in naked dooryards— in a word, of building up the outward forms, and so the inward spirit of a noble civilization. That an organization embracing hundreds of the foremost minds in our profession, coming together yearly from all these States for conference, regarding the multitude of old and new questions ever seeking an answer, can fail to be useful in a large way, I can not believe. Hence I think we need such an organization in addition to all others of a kindred nature, which we now have ; and I believe we have in this Mississippi Valley Society the organization which we need ; and that it should be altogether liberal, far-reaching and national, even continental, in the spirit of its management, if not in its name.

EXPERIMENTAL STATIONS.

That we may consider some matters of moment more particularly, allow me to call your attention to them in detail. One of the greatest needs of the fruit grower, whether in the amateur or the commercial way, is a more competent provision for testing and determining the value in as great a number of localities as possible of the multitude of varieties, new and old, and of new methods of management. The random planting of orchards in our Western States has resulted in losses amounting to millions in the last twenty-five years. Such losses are inseparable from the conditions of a new society, except provisions could be made by government for the early establishment of experiment stations. Our States differ one from another greatly in climate and in soils. The dry climate of the Northwestern plains calls for a totally different planting from that adapted to the moister region around the great lakes, while every condition changes with each degree of latitude, and every successive geological formation, as we travel toward the Gulf. Not only do we need horticultural trial stations in each State, but several of them in each State, to meet the great variety of conditions we everywhere find. A report that a certain variety of apple or pear succeeds well in Illinois, for example, carries very little meaning to those who know the great dissimilarity of conditions existing there. Our agricultural and industrial colleges and universities, and our naturalists working under State appointment, are doing noble work, and they embrace the finest band of experimenters and of practical scientists found in the whole field of scientific labor. Most that we know accurately, and can give a good reason for, both in agriculture and horticulture, we owe to the labors of these noble men. But there are not enough of them.

There is at best but one institution in a State, possessing usually but very limited funds. What can we do toward securing the better endowment by the Nation or the States of these most useful of all our educational agencies? Every one of these State colleges should be liberally equipped for this work of research and experiment, not only at the place where it is located, but should be able to establish branch experiment stations in each State, under the direction of trained experts. Can not this be done? Every State is abundantly able. It is only a question of an enlightened view of what the people need. The European nations are wiser in this respect than we. Not only do they establish these stations at home, but they hasten to build them in their colonies. Says Prof. Budd in a late able report to the trustees of the Iowa Agricultural College: "Dozens of modern instances illustrate this settled principle of political economy. England found Australia, India and New Zealand destitute of hundreds of products for which their climate and soil seemed well adapted. In a brief time numerous experiment stations, under the management of experts trained at the home stations had introduced such a variety of valuable products not native to the countries as to many times quadruple their commerce, and to materially modify the habits and customs of the people. Russia has experimental stations and forestry plantations in every province supported in princely fashion, and she does not

fail to establish such stations as soon as possible in all newly acquired territory." A policy which long experience in many nations has found to be
wise, is surely worthy of the consideration of our several State governments.

FRUIT PACKAGES AND MARKETING.

The growing commercial importance of a horticulture which is having so
rapid an evolution, is constantly bringing up new questions for settlement.
Perhaps as much fruit is now grown for shipment to distant markets as is
sold or used in the immediate neighborhood of its growth. The extension
of our gigantic railway system has revolutionized the commercial features of
American horticulture in all its branches. We not only now want strawberries and peaches that are good in quality and beautiful in appearance, but
which will endure a thousand miles of railway transportation, and still look
well, and taste well. This matter of distant shipment involves the questions
of packages and packing of all kinds of fruits and vegetables. As this matter will be fully presented by one of our most experienced fruit growers and
gardeners, I will here only suggest that a proper thing for this Society to
do is to adopt certain standard measures for packages for each kind of fruit.
It has been often recommended that our legislatures should provide for the
selling of all fruits and vegetables by weight instead of by measure. This is
now done in California. But the practical result does not seem to differ
much from our own method. It is mostly a matter of terms. In California
a box of a certain size is called a fifty-pound box. Here a box of given dimensions is called a third-bushel, a half-bushel, or a bushel box, as the case
may be. There is no weighing in the one case, or measuring in the other.
But we need uniformity in our packages. When a friend speaks to you of
a basket of peaches, what idea of quantity does the expression carry to your
mind?

TARIFF ON HORTICULTURAL PRODUCTS.

Speaking of the commercial aspects of our business, reminds me to call
your attention to the subject of the existing tariff on fruits and other horticultural products. There seems to be no good reason why our government
should tax the importation of horticultural products, possibly excepting
fruits of a semi-tropical character. The tariff averages about 10 per cent. ad
valorem. The government does not need the small income which it brings,
as it is seeking ways of reducing the annual revenue. If the tax was imposed with the idea of "protecting" the horticulturists of these States against
the competition of producers in the British provinces, then it is not called
for, and, in fact, gives us no protection. The planters of orchards and gardens have acted always with entire indifference to the effect of this tariff, if
not indeed in total ignorance of its existence. It is safe to say that not one
tree or plant, more or less, has been planted in these United States on account of the "protection" given by this tariff; that not one day's work, more
or less, has been done or one dime been added to or subtracted from any
day's wages on account of this tariff. This is certainly a case of "protection

which does not protect." But the tariff embarrasses trade. Many hinderances and losses occur on account of it, and the amount of the tax paid to the government is simply added to the cost of the article and is finally paid by the consumer. There is another way in which it affects us as producers unfavorably. The imposition of this tax by our government has induced the Canadian government to impose a similar one about twice as large upon all horticultural products imported from the United States. It is said that these duties would not be maintained long after they were repealed on our side. We export far more fruit to the Canadas than we import from them. And yet the duty against us gives the Canadian producer no protection, for the moment when his crops are ready for the market, our exportation ceases, according to the natural laws of trade. But the producers of the entire country find this tariff troublesome and burdensome. At the last meeting of this Society, in Chicago, in September last, I brought this subject to the attention of members, and resolutions favoring the repeal of our tariff on all horticultural products of Canadian growth were unanimously passed, and a committee was appointed to go before the Tariff Commission, then in session in the city, and present the case to them. This was done. Your committee seemed to carry the conviction of the gentlemen of the commission, and I observe that their report to Congress placed all fruits on the free list, excepting certain kinds of a semi-tropical character. This matter will, in time, come before Congress for action, and I trust that every member of this Society will use his influence to have the report of the Tariff Commission in this particular sustained.

BUREAU OF HORTICULTURAL STATISTICS.

The system of trade in orchard and garden products, which is rapidly growing, with the expansion of our railway interests, has already assumed great proportions. Every day in the year the tides of horticultural commerce are ebbing or flowing over the great area of our country. Car loads and train loads of our various produce begin to move northward every year with the opening spring, over our leading lines of railway, and this continues with the advancing season until the time arrives for the great current to set the other way. Hundreds of thousands of our people are directly engaged in producing or in the distribution of the great harvests of horticulture. And yet no man concerned in this vast production and traffic is guided in his operations by any such carefully compiled knowledge of the changing facts he is dealing with, as the merchant in cotton or the manufacturer of iron would consider of prime importance to an enlightened management. We have no system of collecting the statistics of our business, such as other industries employ. Are they not equally important? We should know the amount of annual planting of berries and vegetables, and the acreage of orchard and vineyard, and the condition and promise of all of these crops, throughout our entire valley not only, but throughout the whole country. Without this knowledge we constantly work in the dark. Every producer who has sought to plant with some reference to the probable demands of his available markets, and every merchant who has tried to follow intelligently the natural laws of trade in his season's transactions, has certainly felt a great want of knowledge of a wide circuit of facts upon which his success or failure must depend. In what way shall we mend this matter? We must in some way have a bureau of horticultural statistics. If we have no machinery ready made for accomplishing this result, then let us invent some. I venture the suggestion, that if there is no more effective way, that this Society can itself organize such a bureau with sufficient completeness to give us great relief from our ignorance. If our secretary could have a salary sufficient to enable him to employ one or more assistants, he could, I think, make a beginning, at least, of this work, which would demonstrate its great value.

EXHIBITIONS.

The question of an annual exhibition of fruits, flowers and garden products, by our Society, is one that some of you have given much thought to. You are aware that we held such an exhibition in St. Louis, in September, 1880, at the time of our organization, which was more attractive and complete, I can say with confidence, than any other similar exhibition ever made on this continent. This magnificent collection was gotten together and managed by a provisional committee, to fitly inaugurate the birth of an organization destined to wield a powerful influence, as we then hoped, and do now hope and feel assured, in molding the industries and the finer culture of human society in the heart of this continent for generations to come. But our experience has justified the belief that no great horticultural exhibition can be made to pay its own way, independently and alone. Such an exhibition as we should make, if we attempt any at all, must cost several thousand dollars. To secure this money, and to secure a sufficient popular attendance to make such a show largely useful, we must, for the present at least, arrange to work in connection with some powerful exposition of other industries. It is for you to decide whether it is desirable to attempt such an exhibition the present year, and also to determine whether in your judgment annual or occasional exhibitions should be considered a portion of the legitimate work of this Society. Of the great educational value of horticultural, as well as of other fairs, there can be no doubt. Of their special value to the professional horticulturist, you are all assured. I commend this subject to your thoughtful consideration.

GENERAL SUGGESTIONS.

Allow me, in conclusion, to call your attention to two or three considerations of a general nature. I desire to have it impressed upon every mind that horticulture is one of the most important agencies for the enhancement of human welfare. Each branch of this profession is useful, dignified and ennobling. It is altogether worthy of the devotion of the best men of the world. It offers a field for the finest powers of the best endowed of mankind. Its problems are sufficient for the best cultivated intellect; its arts will occupy the most cunning mind. We should seek to engage the noblest men and women in its interests. A great need of the times is to make rural life so attractive, and to make pecuniary profit in it so possible, as to hold our boys and young men on the farm and in the garden. Very mistaken ideas of gentility, of ease of life, of opportunities for culture, or for winning fame, draw a large percentage of our brightest boys into the so-called learned professions, into teaching, or into trade. With proper surroundings of the home, with a proper education at school, with a proper administration of the economies of the farm, with a sufficient understanding of the opportunities for a high order of intellectual and social accomplishment in the rural life of this country, this need not, and would not, be so. A bright, high spirited boy is not afraid of labor, but he despises drudgery. He will work hard to accomplish a fine end, when the mind and heart both work together with the muscles; but he will escape from dull, plodding toil. Let our boys learn that rural labor is drudgery only when the mind is dull; that the spade and plow and pruning knife are the apparatus with which he manipulates the wonderful forces of the earth and the sky, and the boy will begin to rank himself with the professor in the laboratory or the master at the easel. There is, indeed, occasion that we should, many of us, feel more deeply the glory of our art; that there is no occupation in life that leads the educated man to more fruitful fields of contemplation and inquiry. The scientific mind finds every day in our orchards and fields new material to work upon, and the cultivated taste endless opportunities for its exercise.

While I desire to see a taste for horticulture become universal in town and hamlet, and country, and believe that every cottage and every palace in the land should have its flower garden and fruit garden, in the window or out of the window, and something of the shelter and ornamentation of trees, yet I would not encourage either amateur or commercial horticulturist to plant one vine, flower or tree more than he expects to take some intelligent care of. There has been too much planting in ignorance and reaping in disgust. Especially should the planter, on a commercial scale, have a better knowledge of the environment of his business. We all need to know more clearly the conditions of great successes, and to understand what difficulties and hinderances are avoidable and what unavoidable. We want more business method in this business. We want scientific knowledge and accuracy instead of empiricism.

But this will come. American horticulture is only in its youthful years. Its splendid maturity shall see every home in this magnificent country sweetened and beautified by its blossoming and fruitful presence. Let us labor cheerfully, my friends, until not only

"The guests in prouder homes shall see
Heaped with the orange and the grape,
As fair as they in tint and shape,
The fruit of the apple tree,"

but the table in every cottage in the land shall be daily filled with an abundance of refreshing fruits and enriching flowers. And let us not rest until we have checked the destruction of the great forests which God has planted, and have restored to the hills and to the plains some portion of that natural shelter without which no land can long be fruitful and no civilization be permanent.

At the close of his address, the President introduced Major S. H. Nowlin, of Little Rock, Ark., as follows:

We have with us this evening Major Nowlin, of Arkansas, the gentleman who first proposed the organization of this Society, and to whom we feel much indebted for many efforts in its behalf. He has been invited to prepare a paper upon the origin and importance of this Society, which he will now present.

ORIGIN AND IMPORTANCE OF THE MISSISSIPPI VALLEY HORTICULTURAL SOCIETY.

BY S. H. NOWLIN.

It has devolved upon me, on the opening of this Convention of Fruit Growers, and the fourth annual meeting of the Mississippi Valley Horticultural Society, to give to you some account of the origin of this Society and to impress upon this assembly the importance of this body to the country we are here to represent, as well as our possible influence in the amelioration and civilization of mankind. In doing this, I must beg the indulgence of my auditory for any appearance of egotism, for the reason that my own personal connection with the origination and organization of this. Society renders it unavoidable. As there are many of you, no doubt, who are not familiar with the history of the Society of which we are members, I will endeavor, in as few words as possible, to recount the circumstances which led to its formation, and the short history connected with it up to the present time.

In the fall of 1879, if my memory correctly serves me, the American Pomological Society held its biennial meeting at Rochester, N. Y. It was my fortune and honor to be sent as a delegate to that meeting by the Arkansas State Horticultural Society. To my surprise (I being a new citizen of my State), I learned that I was the first representative of Arkansas ever in that body. It was also the first time I had ever been sent as a delegate to any association of a national character, and I have no doubt I was personally as much of a novelty to the gray-haired kings of horticulture there assembled as the State I had come to represent; but be that as it may, I had gone there to learn of those wise men of the East, and announced my arrival. (Just here I may be pardoned for reading a little extract upon this incident taken from *Green's Fruit Grower*, of January, 1883):

"Apples grown in Arkansas are selling in Rochester, N. Y., at three to five cents each—splended specimens. Tally one for Arkansas! This reminds us that at the Rochester meeting of the American Pomological Society, at a late hour, bounced in a dark, keen-eyed man, with such a breeze as to suspend the important discussions. Said he in a loud voice: 'Mr. President, I am a representative from Arkansas—hope I am not too late.' They gave a cheer of welcome for Arkansas. We may all cheer now. Arkansas is coming to the front as a fruit growing State."

That same individual is before you to-night. I traveled some 1200 to 1500 miles to attend this meeting at Rochester. I found myself a total stranger to every man I met except Gov. Colman, of Missouri, the editor of *Colman's Rural World*. There were a few representatives in the body from Western States. Missouri was there, so were Michigan, Wisconsin, Iowa and, I believe, Kansas. An exhibition of horticultural products was made in connection with and by invitation of the Western New York Fair Association, and if I remember correctly the West carried off a majority of the prizes, Missouri alone bringing away three of the *Wilder medals*. This was a feather in the cap of Missouri, of which she is justly proud. During the discussions, I observed that there existed a very wide difference of opinion as to the value of certain varieties of fruits, between Eastern and Western men, some, being adapted to and taking high rank in the West, were discarded in the East, and *vice versa*. It was also apparent that there was a wide difference in the mode of culture and general management of orchards and vineyards in the respective localities and climates Taking these things into consideration, and the almost inaccessibility of the meetings of the American Pomological Society to the majority of Western men, it occurred to me that it would not be of any great practical value to us in the West or South; that however important that association might be to the East, where it was first founded, and notwithstanding the very kings of the horticultural world assembled at its biennial meetings, and believing that it gave to the world more wisdom in this particular branch of husbandry than any other body of men on earth, yet it was clear to my mind that it lacked that practical utility to the Western horticulturist that the age demanded.

I wondered, then, why the vigorous, active, wide-awake men of the West did not strike out from their old mother, and with their energy, zeal and independence, establish for themselves a head to their own horticultural empire in the Mississippi valley. The first man, if I remember correctly, to whom the subject was mentioned, was one of those very kings we have just mentioned (and he is no less a king here than there) our esteemed and venerable friend, Dr. John A. Warder, of Ohio, who, since then, said he thought at the time it smacked of considerable impudence. The next man was J. C. Evans, of Missouri, who greatly encouraged the scheme.

When I returned home it was not long until there was a meeting of the Arkansas State Horticultural Society, and while giving in my report this suggestion of forming the Mississippi Valley Horticultural Society was laid before them. Although the scheme appeared rather gigantic for an institution so young and feeble to put in motion, it was determined to make the effort.

A resolution, embodying the ideas of such an organization as we have here to-day, was adopted unanimously, and I had the honor to be appointed chairman of a committee to go to St. Louis and confer with the Missouri State Horticultural Society at its next annual meeting.

That society met in St. Louis on December 20, 1879, and our committee attended the meeting and presented its plans. The proposition met an almost enthusiastic indorsement. It was also our good fortune to meet Mr. Earle, then President of the Illinois State Horticultural Society, now our honored President, who thought he could pledge the fruit growers of Illinois to sustain the movement. There and then an executive committee of nine was appointed, three from Arkansas, three from Missouri and three from Illinois, with power to carry out the programme. That committee waited upon the Merchants' Exchange of the city of St. Louis, and secured the promise of $3,000 as a premium fund. With this backing we went to work in earnest, and in the following September the finest and most comprehensive exhibition of fruit ever held in America was made for four days, in the Merchants' Exchange building, in St. Louis. Twenty-two States were represented at that first meeting, and seventeen entered the organization you have here to-day.

Thus, ladies and gentlemen, you have the origin of the Mississippi Valley Horticultural Society, than which, in my humble opinion, none more important exists on this continent. Three short years embraces its history up to this meeting in New Orleans. The second meeting was held in 1881, in connection with the Exposition held in Cincinnati, and in 1882 the third meeting was held in Chicago, but on account of the failure of the Chicago Fair Association to hold an exhibition, the programme planned the year previous in Cincinnati was not carried out, and to some extent was a disappointment to the Society.

Now, my fellow-countrymen and co-laborers, I have given the origin and history of our Society, and it makes my heart swell with joy and pride to see to what limits it has grown, to see so many of the men who are the vigor, the life, yea the bulwarks of horticulture in our country, assembled here, to mingle together and talk over such subjects as may redound to the good of all mankind. In the past few years the strides made in horticultural pursuits have been rapid and steady, and to-day horticulture occupies a position, in point of scientific development, in the very front of all other branches of agriculture, whilst commercially it is rapidly becoming one of the chief elements of our national greatness.

The men before me represent the richest and grandest country the sun shines upon. Standing here on the shores of the Gulf of Mexico, looking northward we behold a country of more wealth and beauty and grandeur than any other on earth, reaching from the headwaters of the Ohio, and the western slopes of the Alleghanies, over the hills and valleys and plains, to the foot of the snow-clad Rockies; from the burning sands of the Gulf to the ice-ribbed shores of the lakes; from the Rio Grande to the Red river of the

North, from Pittsburg to Denver, from Galveston to Duluth—all, all in one vast body, united by one common interest, are here to-day, enlisted in the cause which brings us together. And while we sit here at the mouth of the great Father of Waters, looking back over this grandest of all countries as our pride and our possession, we should bear in mind that there is no interest more common to all than that which we represent. Every railway and steamboat, every factory and furnace, every village and hamlet, every farm and fireside, every merchant prince and railway magnate, as well as daily laborer and indigent pauper, is directly or indirectly interested in the great cause of practical horticulture which calls us together.

God himself gave to us the fruits of the field and the lilies of the valley, the roses of Sharon, and the vine and fig tree, and told us to cultivate and make glad our hearts and our homes.

The science of horticulture applied to the cultivation and propagation of all these things has wrought wonderful changes in the past half century, and to-day more progressive strides are being made than at any previous period of the world's history, yet we may be only at the threshold of greater future developments in our profession. To the labor of men now living, the world owes more in some particulars than to all generations gone before. Labor and thought and science were their tools, and the same are ours, and we should be equally as diligent in applying them for the benefit of the human race.

Labor, labor, is the watchword of all human greatness; labor of mind as well as muscle. We are all here in the capacity of laborers; in the capacity of men who earn their bread by the sweat of the brow; of men who have built and now uphold one of the great arms of American industry. Why should we not feel proud that we are laborers; laborers from field and prairie, from forest and farm, from mountain side and sunny slope in this great valley of ours, the very vineyard of the Creator, who have come here to talk, sympathize and instruct each other; to bring specimens of luscious fruits and fragrant flowers to exhibit to the world what labor and the Giver of all good gifts have bestowed upon us and our country?

It is through the labor of mind or body, or both, that all the blessings of our civilization flow and life receives its sweetest moments, and it is of ours that we should feel the proudest. No branch of American industry has witnessed more progress or a greater revolution than has horticulture in her varied branches, and I feel in my own heart that no man should feel prouder of what he has accomplished than the American horticulturist.

There is no position so lofty, no calling in life so honorable, as not to bow to this great and honorable avocation. 'Tis labor, labor of mind and body that has made it so.

Standing, as we do to-day, in the midst of the grand achievements of this great American industry, and especially our own Mississippi valley, surrounded by the wealth and magnificence of two hundred millions of fertile acres, and cities and towns whose architecture is often as beautiful as those

2

ncient piles of granite splendor which live and will live forever because of their grandeur, listening to the church chimes, which trill upon the air, blending the devotional whisperings of the heart and stimulating the aspirations of the soul, resting in the shadow of the school-house, from whose doorstep trips the future greatness of our land, and saluted by the thrilling concert of loom and anvil, of forge and furnace, of whistling engines and whirring spindles, which fills with rich melody this great valley and echoes in the far off mountains, it would be an abnormal mind which thinks it can pay sufficient homage to American labor.

The golden harvest surging and rustling over the fields; the wild flower of the hills trained into the laughing, blushing rose of the garden; the delicious fruit that hangs pendant from limb and vine; yea, this magnificent nation itself, with all of her industries and many of her charms, are the fruits of the wear of muscle and the toil of mind. Wherever the adornments of culture and civilization are the most abundant and the comforts of life are the most prominent, there the seal of labor glitters the most proudly.

Yes, my countrymen, the men who sling the sledge and feed the loom, who herd the cattle and hold the plow, who plant the trees and prune the vine, are the ones who feed and clothe this world.

Here in proud America, more than any other country on earth, dotted all over with her cities and villages, the land where Nature has carpeted the valleys and plains with fragrant magnificence and enterprise, has covered her hills and sterile mountains with living beauty, where the birds of the trees strike the key of the anthem of liberty, and fifty millions of people join in the song, it is the man who labors—the man in his shirt sleeves—who is the most important personage who treads the soil or walks the elegant streets of our cities. It is on the great arm of labor that rest the pillars of our government and the prosperity of our nation.

We are, my fellow countrymen and co-laborers, here to represent our great branch of American industry, and from contact and observation, no prouder or more important body of laborers ever assembled in this country. Our position here as members of this Association, representing the richest and most beautiful of all of God's vineyard; aye, the charter members, I may say, of an organization, which, I am led to believe, will live on and grow on when none of us are left to lift a voice in her meeting halls, render it incumbent upon us to don anew the armor of our cause, to add new vigor and life to our work, and delve deeper and deeper into the sciences which render its study and practice so beautiful.

Railroads, grander than the world ever saw, are ribbing our valley, north and south, and east and west, moving the traffic of the millions. The rivers are laden with the riches of our teeming harvests. The hungry millions of the Old World look to our valley as the great granary and store-house from which to draw their supplies. Our orchards are beginning to find a lucrative market on the other side of the Atlantic, and our fruits are sought after in all forms of preservation in European homes. Yet I may say we are only in the beginning. The orchard and nursery of the world is yet to be in our great valley, and the Mississippi Valley Horticultural Society is to be the nucleus around which all the horticulturists of this continent may yet gather and pay homage to the men who are here to-day. Let us go on with all the earnestness and all the zeal of Western and Southern men, with the great work before us; and although adversity and disappointments may come and darkness sometimes take away for awhile the sunshine of our purposes, let us move onward and upward, until we shall become the greatest and best of all horticultural societies on earth.

At the conclusion of Major Nowlin's address, Mr. O. B. Galusha, of Illinois, made a motion in these words:

Gentlemen of our Society: Our President has placed before us matters of the greatest importance. I fear some points which he has presented may be forgotten or passed over in the multiplicity of other matters which shall come before us, unless some action is taken to concentrate our minds upon these important points. I move that three committees be appointed of three members each, upon three of the most important topics presented in his address. First (which I deem of, perhaps, paramount importance), the subject of the experimental stations; second in importance, the establishment of a bureau of statistics to aid in the commercial part of the work of this Society; and third, a committee to consider the subject of the annual exhibition of fruits. I move that three such committees be appointed by the President. (I say the President, because no one else, perhaps, knows as well as he who would be the best persons to put on such committees.)

Mr. W. H. Ragan, of Indiana, rose to emphasize the suggestions of Mr. Galusha in relation to experimental stations.

Motion carried.

Mr. Galusha then suggested that the committees report as early as Friday morning, if possible.

The President then read to the Society the following notice relative to the excursion tendered to them by Mr. Hudson on behalf of the Gulf States Fruit Growers' Association:

At 10 A. M., to-morrow, Thursday, the steamer Jesse K. Bell will leave the foot of Canal street to convey the members of this Society and its friends a few miles up the river, to see the orange orchard of Major Roundtree. All members and visitors desiring to join the excursion are requested to be on board promptly at 10 o'clock. No person will be admitted on board without a badge. These badges can be had of the Secretary of the Society. Ladies accompanying members need no badges.

The invitation was accepted by a standing vote.

Pres. Earle also notified the Society that they had been tendered an invitation to visit the greenhouse and garden of Mrs. Richardson; also, that they had received a communication from the members of the Liedertafel, offering them the hospitalities of their rooms during their sojourn in this city.

After which, the Society adjourned to meet at half-past 2 o'clock to-morrow afternoon.

Second Day—Thursday.

FORENOON SESSION, February 22.

The Society spent the forenoon of this day in a delightful excursion on board the elegant passenger steamer Jesse K. Bell, which had been provided for the occasion by the Gulf States Fruit Growers' Association, first down the river to the Jackson Battlefield, and thence up the river to the extensive orange orchards and vegetable gardens of Maj. A. W. Roundtree, where the party was landed. The *Times-Democrat*, of New Orleans, gives the following graphic description of this pleasant affair:

A DELIGHTFUL TRIP TO THE MODEL TRUCK FARM OF MAJOR ROUNDTREE, IN JEFFERSON PARISH.

Yesterday morning at ten o'clock, according to programme, and upon the invitation of the Gulf States Fruit Growers' Association, the entire delegations of the Mississippi Valley Horticultural Society, headed by their President, Parker Earle, Esq., and lady, boarded the gallant steamer Jesse K. Bell at the foot of Customhouse street, for a trip thirteen miles up the river to the large truck farm of Major Austin W. Roundtree, in Jefferson Parish, right bank.

A committee of the Gulf States Fruit Growers' Association, consisting of Judge E. M. Hudson, Captains A. Sambola, J. J. Mellon, Adam Thomson, Esq., and S. M. Wiggins, Esq., received their guests and did the honors of the day. Besides the delegates and their ladies, several representative ladies and gentlemen of New Orleans, with their friends, participated in the excursion, among them Col. J. W. Glenn, Major Wm. H. Harris and lady, Mrs. Dr.

Hugh Miller Thompson and several of her lady guests, Mrs. E. M. Hudson, Miss Caroline Larose, Miss Regina Prevost, Mrs. Francois Sancho, Mrs. Trezevant, of Memphis, Miss Nora Howard, Miss E. Zachary, Mrs. Gomez, Mrs. E. John Ellis, Mrs. Julia Chamberlain, Mrs. S. M. Wiggins and daughter, Miss Flora Hart, Mrs. Major Davis, and others. Among the excursionists, also, were Dr. Chas. Mohr, of Mobile, United States Government Forester for the Gulf States, one of the most distinguished foresters in the United States, and Col. W. R. Stuart, of Ocean Springs, Miss., who possesses an extensive orange grove of 1,000 trees, and is a well-known importer of Jersey cattle.

The weather was unusually propitious, and the excursionists enthusiastic in their praise of our delightful climate. The old reliable Capt. Dick Sinnot, was in charge of the vessel, and assisted in contributing to the pleasure of all. After first coasting down the front of the city as far as the slaughter-house, in order to give the excursionists a complete panoramic view of the city from the river, the Bell's bow was turned up stream, creeping up close to the city side. The numerous and varied sights, brought out by the civic panorama, elicited as numerous and varied exclamations of delight.

At 12 o'clock the point of destination was reached, and, upon landing, the excursionists were received and welcomed by Major Roundtree in person, assisted by his amiable sisters and household. Under the guidance of the Major a tour of inspection of his model farm was made, the principal features of production, etc., being explained by the Major in the language of agriculture and of horticulture, which, being more or less unintelligible to the *T.-D.* scribe, had to be interpreted to him.

The farm is situated at a point made by a bend in the river, and is a double concession of eighty arpents in length, about 175 acres in all, seventy-five of which are cultivated in oranges. It is the largest truck farm in the State, one of the largest in the South, and the only establishment of the kind devoted to raising early vegetables for the Northern markets, making a specialty of cabbages, cucumbers and tomatoes, the greater portion going to Chicago.

Major Roundtree bought the place in 1870, at that time in bad condition, commenced operations on it in the following year, and in 1873 set out the first orange trees, which at present are 7,200 in number, 6,000 of which will be bearing this year. Besides the ordinary varieties, he has 2,500 mandarin trees. And yet, notwithstanding the extent of the place, and the variety of the products, so admirably is everything arranged and conducted that the entire work is effectually done by a force of not more than twenty or twenty-five colored hands.

Major Roundtree generally makes 800 to 900 barrels of cucumbers and 6,000 to 8,000 boxes tomatoes annually. He will make about 170,000 heads of cabbage this year, grown in a plot covering 40 acres. Besides these staple products, a considerable portion of ground is devoted to the cultivation of strawberries, cauliflower, peaches, grapes, etc., for family use. There is also an apiary with an annual production of eight to ten barrels of honey.

Everything is conducted in the most methodical and economical manner, and yet, withal, imbued by the enterprising and liberal spirit of the proprietor. All of the plants are brought forward under glass, the place having nearly two acres of hot-beds. The plants are set in the open ground as soon as the weather will permit, and in that way these large crops are handled like clock-work and go forward in round lots by the car load.

All the packing, whether of fruits or vegetables, is done in the packing house. situated conveniently near the river. It is a two-story wooden building, 110 feet long and 40 feet wide, the lower floor being devoted to packing, the upper to the box shop or factory.

In order to keep the labor judiciously employed, the first half of the year, from January to July, is devoted entirely to the market garden industry. By the first of July the crops are all gathered and shipped and the whole place sowed down in cow peas as a fertilizer. The only work carried on during the summer is the propping up of trees, making hay and putting the place in order. Then from the first of July to the first of September, in the language of the jovial proprietor, "we all take a holiday, a big rest, and go wandering up and down all over the country, hunting up some fun." These two months comprise the only period of repose in the calendar of the place. By the first of September plowing the pea vines under is begun and everything got in readiness for the spring crops. About the first of October the gathering of oranges is begun and finished by the first of January.

The excursionists examined every point of interest on this admirable establishment, even to the two old houses facing the river in front, built in 1800 and 1802 respectively, and now used as quarters for the hands, the proprietor residing with his family in the city. Every one was charmed with the genial hospitality shown them. A bounteous lunch spread out under the shelter of the beautiful orange grove was partaken of and washed down with a delicious and purely Louisiana beverage made of the juice of sour oranges and claret.

When all had assembled about the festive board, the usual toasts were indulged in, but Major Roundtree was nowhere to be found. Captain Sambola was accordingly appointed a committee of one to find him. The Captain finally found the Major and presented him to the guests in a few eloquent and appropriate remarks, to which the modest host responded most briefly and wittily, deploring, among other things, the want of a Mrs. Roundtree to assist in doing honor to his guests.

The ominous sound of the Bell's whistle admonished the excursionists that the time for returning to the city had arrived, in order to get back in time for the afternoon session of the Horticultural Convention.

The returning party were all laden with souvenirs of their pleasant visit in the shape of oranges, orange blossoms, orange wood canes, moss, etc., and when the Bell made her return landing at the head of Customhouse street, at precisely 2 o'clock, a unanimous regret was expressed that the delightful trip had come to an end.

Second Day—Thursday.

Half-past two was the time fixed for the afternoon session of the Society, but their pleasant river jaunt had so whetted the appetites of its members that it was found necessary to satisfy the cravings of the inner man before proceeding to the discussion of the questions upon the programme for to day. For this reason, it was fully an hour after the appointed time when the strokes of the President's gavel called the meeting to order. President Earle then addressed the Society in the following words:

The hospitalities of the citizens of New Orleans keep raining down upon us. Here is an invitation from the New Orleans Refrigeration Company to visit their establishment at any time during our stay in the city, for which we returned our sincere thanks.

Gentlemen, we are now prepared to begin the serious work of our session. To-day, both the afternoon and evening sessions have been set apart for the discussion of small fruits, beginning with the strawberry.

We have several papers prepared, and the authors are present. They will be read in succession. After a portion, perhaps most of them, have been read, we will have a discussion upon them. Our first paper this afternoon will be by Hon. J. M. Smith, of Green Bay, President of the Wisconsin Horticultural Society. Mr. Smith is one of the largest strawberry growers of the Northwest, and it seems fitting that a man who has succeeded in growing over four hundred bushels of strawberries to the acre should be asked to tell us how to grow strawberries at the North. Your attention is invited to Mr. Smith's paper:

STRAWBERRIES FOR THE NORTH, AND HOW TO GROW THEM.

BY J. M. SMITH.

In the entire list of our small fruits, the strawberry is the only one that can be grown with any certainty from the borders of the torrid zone to arctic regions. It may be said that the north temperate zone is its most favored clime. Yet, with its adaptation to so many different climates and soils, it is only within the last twenty-five years that this most delicious of our small fruits has become at all common.

When I was a little boy and living, as I did, much of the time at the house of my grandparents, my grandmother used to keep a little bed of strawberries of the variety (as I now suppose) known as one of the White Alpines.

They were kept, as far as possible, for extra occasions. The supply, as is generally the case with those varieties, was exceedingly limited.

The largest picking that I remember ever seeing was one of about one pint. I remember that there was company at the time; another thing I also remember very distinctly, was that a taste of them was about all that a little boy like myself could hope for. The idea that I could ever sit down to a table where strawberries were as plenty as potatoes, or bread and butter, was something that had never entered into my childish imagination. Yet I certainly fared as well, and, I think, better than the average of my neighbors. In fact, I do not recollect ever seeing a bed of cultivated strawberries in the days of my childhood except the one above mentioned. They were then a luxury to be enjoyed only by a very few. Now they are, in their season, within the reach of, and enjoyed by, all to a greater or less extent. They have ceased to be a luxury, and are considered one of the necessary articles of food by tens of thousands of our citizens.

It is perfectly safe to say that one hundred bushels of berries are now used at the North where one bushel was used fifty years ago. What has caused this remarkable change? Hovey's Seedling was introduced at an early day, and was a great improvement upon any variety then in cultivation. Soon after the Early Scarlet, sometimes called the Jersey Scarlet, made its appearance and contested the field with the former.

This was not far from 1830, though I am unable to give precise dates. They produced a great change, and were the leading varieties at the North until about 1860, when Wilson's Albany Seedling began to make its appearance. It had been grown by a few for some years previous to the above date, although it was a novelty to many people until 1863. At this time it had about taken possession of our Northern markets, and as a market berry it has virtually held its own until the present time.

New varieties by hundreds have been brought forward, and every effort made to supersede it with something better. None of these have yet succeeded, unless some of the new varieties now upon trial shall prove to be its superior.

No one will claim that the Wilson is in all respects a perfect berry, still it has certainly shown itself to be the most remarkable one for the millions ever yet put into cultivation.

Where and how can it be grown? I believe it is at home in most parts of the Sunny South. In the North, it is safe to say, in general terms, that a fair crop of the Wilsons may be grown wherever a good crop of either corn or potatoes can be grown. It is also perfectly at home upon the shores of Lake Superior and in districts too far north to grow either of the above-named crops with any degree of certainty. If I could just have the soil I preferred for them, I should select a light loam, rather damp than dry, and have it thoroughly drained. Manure it heavily, say from twenty to forty loads of good stable manure per acre.

In my latitude, $44\frac{1}{2}°$, it is not often that the weather will allow us to set our beds before some time in April, and sometimes not until the 1st of May.

If I were upon a farm where a little land, more or less, was of no consequence, and where it is some timesdifficult to get help at a fair price, I should set what gardeners call double rows; that is, to set two rows of plants about 12 or 14 inches apart each way, then leave a space of 3½ to 4 feet, and then set another double row, and so continue until the piece is finished. This plan would allow most of the work to be done with the horse and cultivator. I would allow the plants to fill their intermediate spaces, and about one foot upon each side with their runners.

This will give a nice double row, and if well manured and cultivated would yield a good, though not as large a crop as closer setting and cultivation.

Where land is expensive, worth from $200 to $500 per acre, and labor can be obtained at a reasonable rate, I prefer to set in single rows, say two feet apart, and the plants about twelve or fifteen inches apart in the rows.

This is, of course, a more expensive method of cultivation, but it produces much the largest crop for the ground, and where the circumstances are favorable is, as I believe, much the more profitable.

My own rule is to put my land in the best possible condition and then select nice, thrifty plants of the previous year's growth. Never set plants that have borne fruit.

Set them in rows as above indicated. I have experimented with them (the Wilson) at different distances, and finally settled upon the above as about the best.

Some of the ranker growing varieties, like the Crescent, may safely be set twice or more the above named distances, and they will cover the ground in a short time.

We are careful to set the plants fully as deep, and perhaps a little deeper than they stood in their native beds, still being very careful not to cover the crown of the plants with earth.

The reason for the deeper setting is that the newly plowed land will settle more or less, and although you pack the earth about the plants, as you certainly should do, it will still be very likely to settle from the roots unless the above rule is adhered to; and when this is the case, the plant is always more or less damaged.

If the weather is dry, the newly set plants should be well watered. My own experience tells me that one thorough watering, say one pint of water to the plant, is much better than to put the same amount upon them at two or three different times.

I am also satisfied that it will well repay the labor of picking off all the blossoms the first season, and thus keep the entire strength and growth of the plant within itself, and have it prepared to give us the largest possible crop the following year.

All weeds should be kept down, and the young plants have every encouragement to do their best.

One of the faults of the Wilson is that they do not always throw out as many runners as we desire. I have found the following a good plan with them:

When they begin to throw out runners, go through the beds and distribute them in about equal distances around the parent plant.   For instance, suppose the plant throws out eight runners, perhaps three-fourths of them upon one side, as is often the case.   When they get about ready to commence the formation of new plants, place the runners in equal distances around the parent, and place a little earth upon them, only sufficient to hold them in their place.   In a few days the new plants are formed, and you will have a nice circle of new plants about the old one, all of them preparing to do their best for you the following season, instead of having a cluster of them too thick to do their best upon one side, and few or none upon the other.

They will now go on radiating in all d rections and fill up the ground.   I am speaking now of the Wilson ; this plan may not be necessary with other varieties.

Late in the fall, after the ground freezes, they should be covered with straw, or, what I like better, marsh hay, as the latter has no foul seed in it to annoy us the following season.   Cover the plants sufficiently deep to hide them from view.   The covering should be left upon them until the ground is done freezing in the spring.   One of the greatest benefits of winter covering is the protection given to the plants during the early spring, when the ground freezes more or less nearly every night and thaws during the day.

During this process, the land becomes what we call honey-combed, or in other words, in freezing the top of it rises somewhat from its natural position, and in doing so either starts the roots of the plants from their natural position, or breaks them off a short distance beneath the surface of the earth; either one of these will be fatal to a large crop of fruit.

Hence I leave the covering upon mine until the plants have started beneath it.   After removing the covering, go through the beds and destroy every weed and blade of grass that has hitherto escaped notice.   Put on a good covering of well-rotted manure, say fifteen to twenty loads per acre, or, if you can get it, fifty to seventy-five bushels of unleached ashes per acre.   If leached ashes use twice the amount.   I have almost invariably found it necessary to go through my beds twice during the spring before the picking commences, and occasionally three times.   The beds should be kept free of weeds at any cost.

Both plants and berries need the sun to enable them to do their best.   If, after all other work is done, I find that the crop promises to be an extra large one, I often put on an additional coat of manure, or, if I have used manure in the early spring, put on ashes for the second fertilizer.   This will assist the late berries very much in keeping up their size and firmness, and thus add much to the value of the crop.   During the picking season we sometimes have a very dry time, and unless we can water the beds artificially much of our time and labor will be lost.

For a number of years past I have had no vines out of the reach of artificial watering.   I find one thorough wetting much better than two or three sprinklings.   As regards the amount of expense that may be incurred for this purpose, each grower must be governed by the value to be added to his crop, and the expense necessary to add such value. It is an important question, and should be well considered by those interested in growing this little queen of berries.

If you have had a very large crop, as you are very likely to have if you have followed these directions, examine the beds carefully as soon as the picking season is over, and if the vines look exhausted and are throwing out but very few runners, it is better to plow them under at once and fill the ground with some other crop than to try to care for the plants another year, and then not get sufficient fruit to pay for your time and labor. I refer now only to the Wilson. I have never yet been able to make any other variety bear itself to death the first season, but have repeatedly had the Wilson come so near to it that they were not worth caring for another year. If the yield has been only a moderate one, the second crop will probably be as good, and perhaps better than the first.

Such has, of late years, been about my method of cultivating the Wilson, after more than twenty years of experimenting. I do not consider 200 bushels, or 6,400 boxes, an extra crop. I have repeatedly had much more than the amount named, and sometimes double the amount. In fact, I will not cultivate for any length of time any variety that will not yield at least 6,000 boxes per acre. Still I must confess that I have never succeeded in getting it from any other variety, the Crescent Seedling alone excepted, and this is so soft with me as to make it about worthless for shipping, and not by any means as valuable as the Wilson for the home market.

Of the many other varieties that have been put forward, had their brief day, and then passed away, I scarcely know what to say.

Some of them have doubtless done well in some places and under some circumstances, while for the average grower they have been entirely worthless.

Years ago, when Mr. Knox was, as I doubt not, succeeding well with the Jucunda, I sent to him and obtained some of the plants, and did my best with them for a number of years. I had some magnificent fruit from them, but do not believe that I ever grew one quart of them that cost me as little as fifty cents.

Seth Boyden's No. 30, Triomphe de Gand, Sharpless, and many others that might be named, are large and beautiful to look upon, but with me are worthless for market, or at least for any market in the Northwest. I keep a very few of the No. 30 and the Sharpless, in order to let my friends know that I can grow some large berries.

The Kentucky has done the best of any of the late varieties with me. It is a fair bearer, and the fruit of good quality. For a late berry I like it better than the Glendale.

Captain Jack, Red Jacket, Prouty, Duncan, and possibly some others, have borne with me about one-half of what the Wilson would have done under the same circumstances. I have tried many varieties that were utterly worthless.

For table berries to be used in the home families, I know of nothing better than Burr's New Pine and Downer's Prolific. They are both moderate in size, moderate bearers, and too soft for market, but very choice in quality. Within the last twenty-five years I have picked ripe berries twice upon the 6th of June. Twice it has been the 25th of June when we picked our first ripe fruit.

From the 10th to the 13th we generally get our first ripe fruit. Upon some of the cold highlands about Lake Superior they do not ripen until nearly one month later than in Central and Southern Wisconsin.

The season generally lasts about four weeks, and until about the commencement of the raspberry season. Last season we had our last dish of strawberries and our first dish of raspberries upon the table at the same time.

I employ all of my pickers by the day. Each one has two boxes.

Into one of them is placed all the nice merchantable fruit, and in the other the imperfect berries are put.

The last named are sold at home for what they will bring. The others are of course retained for market.

In advocating spring cultivation as I have done, I well know that I am going against the opinions of some of our large and successful cultivators. In my own defense allow me to say this much: I would not and do not cultivate sufficiently deep to injure the roots of the growing plants. If your lands or strawberry beds were as rich as I make mine, you must of necessity either cultivate in the spring or lose your crop. These are facts from which there is no escape.

It may be asked then, why make the land so very rich? My answer is as follows: My long experience has taught me this. Other things being equal, the richer the land the larger the crop.

The Crescent Seedling may be an exception to this rule. But I can think of no other.

It is often said that the Wilson is failing. I can see no indications of it in the district of country from which I come. On the contrary, I think that the finest and most promising beds of them that I have seen were within the last six months.

Gentlemen, I have thus given you my own views and experience, rather than that of others, not because I wish to boast of what I have done or can do, but simply because my methods have been successful. I have failed but once in more than twenty years to have at least a paying crop, and most of the time they have been not only very large, but very profitable. I believe that I may say, and will only state it because I know it to be a fact, that I have never known any one whose crops have been so uniformly large as my own.

These large crops have by no means been the result of chance or haphazard cultivation, but of very rich land, well drained, heavily manured, thoroughly cultivated, well protected during the winter, surface manured in the spring, and well watered if dry weather came on during the bearing season.

What I have done you may do, provided it is better than the system you are at present pursuing. If it is not, you will, of course, not adopt it.

I make no pretense of having reached perfection, but on the contrary, if I live a few years longer, expect to far outdo anything that I have ever yet done. I do not pretend to know where the limit beyond which we can not pass is, or when it will be reached. But to reach it is an object worthy of our care, our thought, and of our most worthy efforts.

He who wins in this friendly contest will hold a high and an honorable position.

Those who fail to reach the highest point will still have the satisfaction of knowing that they are engaged in a contest that brings no sorrows in its train; but upon the contrary all its tendencies are to elevate and lift up his fellow beings to a higher ideal of home life, and to make homes better and happier, as far as its influence shall reach.

At the conclusion of Mr. Smith's paper the President introduced Dr. H. E. McKay, of Madison, Miss., the President of the State Horticultural Society of that State, who is one of the largest strawberry growers of the entire valley, who read a paper;

STRAWBERRY CULTURE IN THE SOUTH.

BY DR. H. E. M'KAY.

At the request of our worthy President I consented to write a paper, to be read at this meeting, on strawberry culture in the South. In doing so I am most conscious of the fact that I can only present to you a few of the facts and fundamental points upon which the successful culture in the South is based. I am not by any means a "knight of the quill." I have only taken my pen occasionally when circumstances and the necessity of the case seem to demand that I should say something. I have endeavored, so far as possible, to cover the leading points in this paper, and such as we have I will read to you as well as I can. This occasion is very embarrassing to one unaccustomed to either writing or reading for the public, and I hope you will indulge me under these circumstances as kindly as you can.

We do not understand from the above heading that we are limited to the preparation of the land, manner of setting out the plants, and its after cultivation, but all the items necessary to the attainment of successful production are embraced.

With this view, we shall first refer to the different soils upon which it is or may be grown, for both home and commercial use.

Probably no section of our great country, whether we consider the far East, the great and inexhaustible middle belt, or the grand and almost unlimited Northwest, has greater diversity of soils than are to be found in the South; yet, notwithstanding this diversity, if there are places where other southern crops do well, that have failed to give reasonably good results in this fruit, we have so far failed to learn where they are located.

It is true of the strawberry as of other things, that it has its favored localities, where it attains its greatest perfection, and gives its most astonishing results. A few growers fully understand this fact, but many, apparently intelligent, seem not to understand how great these differences really are, and are disappointed when they fail to do as well as others. Too little has been said by many writers on the strawberry, about the soils best suited to the health and growth of the plant, and the perfection and beauty of the fruit. The wonderful ease and facility with which the berry adapts itself to different soils and latitudes, coupled with the fact that even in an imperfect condition it is satisfactory in appearance and taste to most persons, may in part be the cause of this oversight. We do not agree with the generally received opinion, as taught by many writers, that a sandy loam gives either the largest yield or finest fruit. Possibly in the North and West such may be true, but in the South our largest yields and finest berries are obtained from a clay loam.

While it is true that berries grown on a sandy loam are often as large and apparently as firm and well colored as on a clay loam, it is equally true that they are deficient in that solidity, strength of color and general make-up that the same varieties possess grown on the clay loam. All the facts so far as we have been able to gather them, point to the general conclusion, that all other things being equal, the strength, beauty and perfection of the berry is diminished in proportion as free sand exists in the soil; not that any of our good land is without sand, but we use the term free sand where it readily separates and can be seen in the branches and little gullies. By far the larger proportion of all our Southern lands has a liberal amount of free sand in them, whether we take the rich alluvials in the great delta, or the very light, porous, thinner pine lands near the Gulf, or the higher and better grades of the piny sections, this is true. It is also true of the rich "cane hills" or "bluff formations," and nearly all of the high, rolling lands. Besides the above, we have the heavy, waxy lime lands, and the close, compact, retentive table lands. While on these waxy lime lands some of the varieties under skillful and high culture are very fine, the happy medium between the light sandy loams on the one hand, and heavy lime on the other, where all the finer qualities of the berry are brought to their greatest perfection, is on these close, compact, retentive table lands, such as we find in central Mississippi.

While it is a fact that in and around New Orleans, large quantities of berries are grown on the alluvial lands, and on the pine lands adjacent, it is a further fact, understood by first-class dealers and their customers, that they are lacking in that sprightlin- ss and high flavor found in the berries grown on the more compact clay lands at a distance, and can only be shipped to distant markets, under the most favorable atmospheric influences, in the early part of the season, when cool. Many times, in past seasons, when the supply here was large, our berries have won the front rank and sold freely at fair prices, when those grown here can scarcely be sold at any price. On one occasion, when the larger part of our crop had to be sold here or lost, we were told by the autocrat of the market that our fine Wilsons were too crude and sour to be sold in this market; that such had justly been discarded at the North and East, and would find the same fate here. Such wholesale slaughter of our favored variety touched off the lingering Scotch of our nature. We quickly told him we were prepared to test the truth of his assertion; that if he could furnish no better berries than were then in his house, we would force him, within ten days, to buy our berries or lose his trade. In less than ten days he bought freely from our merchant. Last season berries from Madison sold on order, in liberal quantities, in this city, at from twenty to forty cents per quart, when those grown here commanded twelve to twenty cents per quart. It is well understood by St. Louis and Chicago fruit merchants that berries grown on these compact, clay lands in central Mississippi not only command the highest prices in their cities, but can nearly always be safely reshipped to the more distant cities of the great Northwest. It may be asked, how about the berries grown in the sandy regions of Florida, that carry to New York and even Chicago in such attractive shape? We can not explain this apparent exception to what seems the general rule in regard to other sandy soils of the South. Possibly the modifying influence of a salt water atmosphere, together with the cooling process of shipping in refrigerators, may in a great degree account for the facts in regard to their berries.

Fruit completing its ripening process in retarding houses, or a cooler atmosphere than that in which it develops, is known to be not only attractive but of most excellent quality. Reduced temperatures check fermentation, which is the first stage of decay, and the fruit ripening slower and more uniformly preserves all of its good qualities.

The subject of having all of our tender fruits and vegetables transported in reduced temperatures, and our merchants keeping them in such until sold, demands the most earnest consideration of commercial horticulturists. We regard this subject of such vital importance to our material interests, that we ask this Society to give it some attention at a suitable time during this meeting. We have thus alluded to the leading soils of the South, and brought forward some facts bearing on the relative merits of our berry producing soils. To dwell longer in a paper like this on this part of our subject would be to give it undue prominence.

We now come to our second division. What varieties best suit our Southern soils and latitude? This subject is full of interest to all who desire the best success for either home or commercial use. Probably the people of no section of our country have paid out more money for new and unnecessary varieties than we of the South. Growers are mainly divided into three classes: 1. Those ever on the lookout for something new and wonderful, who are good subjects for our annual picture and sample "peddlers;"

2. Those who have such an inherent love of the old that they would not give you a fig for anything better than used to grow on the borders, or in one corner of their good mother's garden; 3. Those who hold fast to all that are good of the old, while they cautiously test those of the new claiming superior merits. During the past ten years we have tested on our grounds about forty varieties, covering many of the old and well tested standards, and such of the new as seemed to give greatest promise; and while we are free to say that among the new there are to be found many charming and valuable acquisitions, we are equally free to say that, up to the present time, we have found no single variety to be trusted so implicitly as Wilson's Albany, and to admit that any other variety yet fully tested deserves to be classed as its rival, is to ignore all the facts that have come under our observation, as well as all that can be gathered from other sources. The great ease and facility with which it adapts itself to latitudes, soils and seasons is wonderful. Wherever other varieties do well, as a rule it does better. Where have we, or where can we find another single variety that has stood the test so long, that has fought and won so many battles, and to-day, after a test of nearly thirty years, with the whole list of new and old, stands grandly and far in the lead of all, with the distinguished position of furnishing nearly, or quite three-fourths of all the strawberries grown and consumed in the United States? No parallel like it can be found in a single variety in any other department of fruit growing.

As we remarked in a former paper on this subject, "banish it from our lists and culture and you remove the 'beacon-light' that lures us on to the goal of success and noble daring in strawberry culture." When allowed to fully mature on our Southern soils, where the saccharine elements are more liberally developed in all our fruits than in higher latitudes, its proverbial acidity is so blended with the sweet that it deserves high rank as a home and local berry.

Next in rank as a commercial berry, we give the place to Newman or Charlestown. It is a hardy plant, a profuse bearer, and first-class shipper. It has, however, the serious drawback of making too many new plants and sending out too large a percentage of its unprotected fruit buds in the early part of the season when liable to be killed by spring frosts. When not damaged by frosts, it gives more early fruit than the Wilson, but fails in good fruit much sooner. After a few heavy pickings, the berries are too small. On the lower Atlantic coast, we understand, it is liked better and grown more liberally than Wilson; we believe it will increase in popularity in localities bordering on the Gulf coast.

Charles Downing, during the past few years, has steadily and justly gained in public favor, and is now grown more generally for home and local use than any other of its class. It seems to possess in a larger degree all the elements that give success to both plant and fruit than any other of the larger and more tender varieties. While in this latitude it is not a profuse plant-maker, it gives sufficient supply for increased culture. It bears large, regular crops of berries, sufficiently large, attractive and sweet to satisfy those who prefer this class of fruit. In and around this city it is preferred by many to any other variety. Were we asked to select two varieties for the South, we say Wilson first and Charles Downing next. In our judgment they represent more completely, and in a higher degree, all the really desirable qualities of their respective types than any others to be found in the whole range of varieties. They can be raised with greater certainty and in larger quantities, with less expense than others—are less fastidious about soils, require less fertilizing, and will continue to bear good crops longer on the same land. Cumberland Triumph deserves high rank for local and home use. The plant is strong and hardy; bears heavy crops of the most uniformly large berries of any variety yet fully tested on our grounds. It only needs to be better known to be more fully appreciated and generally cultivated. Monarch of the West has been, and is still, a great favorite in many sections of the South. It gives a good percentage of the largest and most deliciously flavored berries of any variety we have tested. During spring and fall months, the plant is a strong and vigorous grower, but is tender and hard to carry through the hot, dry summers we sometimes have; but for its great beauty and excellence it deserves a choice spot in all our gardens. Captain Jack, for a time, gave great promise for both home and commercial use, and in some localities it is still a valuable acquisition, but in many localities a complete failure. Beyond the first five above mentioned the field for selection is almost without limit, but we are strongly of the impression that in these five varieties nearly all of the really desirable and valuable qualities of the entire strawberry family, so far as yet fully developed, are well represented. For the ordinary grower to multiply varieties, for the sake of variety, is one of the serious drawbacks to success.

In the undeveloped possibilities of some of the new or future varieties we may find good reasons to modify or even change our present views. On this subject, as we have not, we will not, indulge in a " Rip Van Winkle sleep," or advise our friends to do so.

We now come to the actual field and garden work. For want of something that suits us better on this part of the subject, we shall quote parts of some articles we had published in 1880. Referring to this subject we then said: At this point, too many of our people seem to conclude that the brain work can be suspended, and quite too often the plants are turned over to some one ignorant of their habits and necessities, with instructions to plant them in such a place in rows of a given width, allowing so much space between the plants in the rows. Instructions much of the same careless character are given when the time comes for working. But when it is remembered that the berry is largely composed of water, and that for the health and vigor of the plant, and the full perfection of the fruit, a uniform and abundant supply of moisture is needed; that neither plant nor fruit can bear without injury, and sometimes overthrow an over supply, it will be seen that the brain must still maintain its supremacy.

3

If we can succeed in showing how, by preparation and culture, this most desirable result can be best attained, it will not be without interest, whether for Northern or Southern culture. We care nothing for the opinions of those who give us only the deductions and figures of an imaginative brain, however scientifically they may sound, if they fail to tell us the real facts and figures or what they have done, how and with what they did it, and the results obtained. We are living in an age of real progress, when, to make ourselves a part of it, we must see, understand and utilize the things around us, and harmonize our pursuits with the peculiarities of our own latitude and soil, not relying too much on the advice and teachings that may have given success to other and distant localities, with different soils and very different latitudinal influences. For over ten years we have lived in and of the field, studying and watching this now rapidly growing enterprise. It took us three years to give it respectibility as an occupation, beyond growing for home and local use. It took us five years to convince any considerable number of intelligent fruit growers that it deserved the place of a genuine enterprise.

Asking pardon for these seeming digressions and coming directly to our text, we remark, first, that we find in almost every intelligent agricultural community some fundamental, primary principles, so well settled that no intelligent cultivator will call them in question. This is true of what we call our elevated, circular row system; that is, running our rows in such direction that, while provision is made for carrying off the surplus rain-fall, it is done so gradually, between our elevated, circular rows, that none of the loose earth is carried off, or left by the water before it is fully saturated. Adopting this as a sound central principle, we make no change in the width or direction of our rows, and taking a sharp steel plow and a strong mule, we throw out two deep furrows from the water furrow, one each way, opening twice the width of the plow; then with a subsoil plow run once in the bottom of each turn furrow, just as deep as our mule can pull it. Thus we have the basis for the new bed center, fully eight inches deeper than the general level. Then with the same sharp plow running narrow, deep furrows, we put up our beds on the bed center furrows. In after culture we will show how we finish the plowing so that the new water or drain furrows are deeper by four inches than the furrows under the bed center, and all intermediate spaces between them deeper, by grading down from the bed center furrows to the new and now actual drain furrows. Having thus finished the plow work, we next run the harrow to break the clods and smooth off the beds. Then, with a subsoiler, or long, narrow plow of some kind, we run once in the center of the beds to form a deep, loose and partially open space that serves as a guide to the setters, and enables them to do their work much easier, more rapidly and better than without it. It is not good policy, after your land has been thus prepared, to allow it to be beaten down and packed by the rains before planting. We usually carry on all the work together, and having everything ready, we instruct setters to shake out the roots of the plant sufficiently with one hand to prevent any matting or adhering to each other, and with the other hand a round stick or trowel to open ample space to take in all the roots without twisting or doubling one upon another; then, putting the roots well down, draw the light dirt around them, and with a firm downward pressure finish the work. When we desire to put out small parcels of land, where the plow can not be used, we would have the land deeply spaded and put into beds ten to twelve feet wide, with a drain on each side, and plant in rows two feet wide across the bed. Our plants, in both field and bed culture, stand about twelve inches apart on the rows. For our own part, we have abandoned every form of broad bed or flat culture, because it is more expensive, more uncertain in its results, and in every way less satisfactory than the elevated row system.

To make berries cheap, and at the same time first-class, they ought to be planted so that the plow and subsoiler can be freely used. Our planting season extends from the first of October to the last of March, whenever our land can be found in order for so doing. Plants put out in October or November will, if not lifted by winter freezes, bear more fruit the coming season than later settings. Owing to the fact that this frequently occurs, especially in Central Mississippi, the safest part of the season is the latter half of February and all of March. Owing to the fact that all of our plantings in this latitude bear some fruit the first season, we do not, as a rule, commence our cultivation until the picking season is well near over. If, however, grass or weeds threaten the health and growth of the plant, light surface work with a sharp hoe is given.

It is, in our judgment, not good policy, if it can be avoided, to work either recently set or old stools just before or during the fruiting season, because we not only break some of the attachments, but leave the recently stirred dirt to be thrown on the fruit, to its great detriment. It is better for commercial use to have a half-crop of clean, bright fruit, than a full crop, dingy and soiled. Having come to the working season proper, we again bring into requisition our sharp steel plow and strong mule, with a sufficient hoe force to follow. At this season we must be careful not to break any more attachments than are really necessary to do good work and destroy grass and weeds, hence we do not run the bar of our plow as closely as we do to corn or cotton, but as deep as our mule can pull it. Then, with our hoes as sharp as they can be kept, we cut away all grass and weeds. If to accomplish this we have to cut deep, we return fully as much light dirt as may have been taken away with the grass and weeds. We allow only a few days to pass before we return with our plows freshly sharpened, and run another deep furrow in the bottom of those already run, heaping the dirt high in the middles. We follow immediately with the subsoiler in the bottom of this second furrow, just as deep as our strongest mule can pull it. If we have done our duty with the plow and subsoiler, we will have attained a depth of nearly or quite twelve inches. With such deep and partially open furrows, so near on both sides of our plants, it will not do to rest the work any considerable time, hence we follow very soon with the harrow to level these high middles back into the furrows, after which we can stop the work for a week or ten days, when we should return with the hoes and remove whatever grass and weeds may have come up or been left at the first hoeing, and draw a little light dirt around the plants.   Here we may rest the work for a short time, when we should return with our plows and mold them just as we do corn or cotton, only not quite so close, but as deep as possible, and, following closely with our subsoiler, go down until we are satisfied we are a little deeper than we have run nearer the plant.   After this, whatever remains must be equally spread to the sides, and to complete the work in the middle we run the subsoiler until we are satisfied we are four inches deeper than the bed center furrows described above.   This completes the work of the season, except with the hoe to draw the dirt around the plant, fill up uneven places and put the bed in good shape.   The same principles of cultivation, as far as practicable, should be applied in bed culture; but because they can not be so fully applied is one reason why we dislike this system, and in our opinion the main reason why it is so often a failure.

We have now developed what may be termed our theory and practice.   If you have followed us in our detail with the plow and subsoiler, you will see that we have thoroughly broken and pulverized the soil to an aggregate depth of ten inches, and left our plants on elevated beds or rows, with drain furrows between them four inches deeper than the bed center furrows.   It is thus we propose to furnish the much needed uniform moisture, and avoid the destructive influence of too much.   This work is usually completed about the middle or last of July, and all after grass and weeds are allowed to grow for protection to plants during winter, and the further and more valuable object of a mulch to keep our berries clean and bright.   With such culture we have, during some of our best seasons, gathered one hundred bushels per acre from land that, with the best culture, would not have produced over twenty bushels of corn or half a bale of cotton, without fertilizers of any sort.   If we fertilize in this latitude it must be done with great caution and good judgment.   We have not found the good results from it claimed for it in higher latitudes.   While it may increase the size and yield, the fruit is more perishable and the plant in more danger of overthrow during the hot, dry summer months.   The habits of the plant in this latitude differ in some respects from its habits in higher latitudes.   While it makes large, strong stools, its disposition to send out runners and multiply plants is much less than at the North.   The fruiting season is also much longer, often extending over ninety days, with a strong inclination to fall bearing.   We have a strong conviction that if all the possibilities of some of our varieties were fully understood, and by skillful work thoroughly harmonized with the laws of our latitude and soil, we might have berries, many of our seasons, from March until December.   We have, during three seasons out of the past four, had berries over five months each year from a single variety. Perpetual bearing is more of latitude and skilled culture than of inherent qualities in varieties. This subject, well understood, will form a new departure in Southern culture. But we will close this paper, already too long, by a few quotations from abler pens bearing on the general merits of the fruit and the most remarkable position of the plant to other things in nature.

Mr. A. J. Downing says: "The strawberry is perhaps the most wholesome of all fruits, being very easy of digestion, and never growing acid by fermentation, as most other fruits do. The oft-quoted instance of the great Linnæus curing himself of gout by taking freely of strawberries—a proof of its great wholesomeness—is a letter of credit which this tempting fruit has long enjoyed, for the consolation of those who are always looking for a bitter concealed under every sweet. That ripe, blushing strawberries, eaten fresh from the vine. or served with sugar and cream, are certainly Arcadian dainties, with a true paradisaical flavor, and fortunately they are so easily grown that the poorest owner of a few feet of ground may have them in abundance."

R. G. Pardee says: "It is the most beautiful and delicious of all our early fruits, and so easily cultivated and so uniformly productive, that every housekeeper possessing a few rods of ground can have no excuse for not supplying his table with an abundance."

An unknown writer in one of the old Patent Office reports, speaking of the position of the plant, eloquently says: "When we contemplate the relations which the strawberry plant bears to other parts of nature—to the sun which expands its blossoms—to the winds which sow its seeds—to the brooks whose banks it embellishes; when we contemplate how it is preserved during a winter's cold—capable of cleaving the stones—how it appears verdant in the spring, without any pains to preserve it from frost and snow—how, feeble and trailing along the ground, it should be able to migrate from the deepest valleys to Alpine heights—to traverse the globe from north to south, from mountain to mountain, forming on its passage over prairie and plain a thousand mingled patches of checker work of its fair flowers and scarlet or rose-colored fruit with the plants of every clime; how it has been able to scatter itself from the mountains of Cashmere to Archangel, from Kamtschatka to Spain; how, in a word, we find it in equal abundance on the continent of America, from the bleak fields of Terra del Fuego to Oregon and Hudson's Bay; though myriads of animals are making incessant and universal havoc upon it, yet no gardener is necessary to sow it again—we are struck with wonder and admiration at so precious a gift."

Upon the conclusion of Mr. McKay's address, Pres. Earle stated that before proceeding to the discussion of the questions raised by the reading of the foregoing papers, he would announce the following committees :

On Statistics—O. B. Galusha, Illinois; R. W. Furnas, Nebraska; Dr. H. E. McKay, Mississippi.

On Experiment Stations—W. H. Ragan, Indiana; F. P. Baker, Kansas; J. C. Evans, Missouri.

On Exhibitions—S. H. Nowlin, Arkansas; T. T. Lyon, Michigan; J. S. Beatty, Kentucky.

On Transportation—J. M. Smith, Wisconsin; F. A. Thomas, Illinois; A. W. Roundtree, Louisiana.

On Fruits on Exhibition—P. J. Berckmans, Georgia; J. H. Hale, Connecticut; J. J. Colmant, Mississippi.

On Final Resolutions—O. C. Gibbs, Illinois; J. E. Porter, Tennessee; T. V. Munson, Texas.

The President continued—Having listened with interest to two of our papers upon strawberry culture, one from the North and one from the South, from two of our largest and most successful strawberry-growers, I shall invite a gentleman who is present with us to make remarks upon certain features of these papers, a gentleman who has come almost two thousand miles to attend this meeting of our Society, and one who is a very large and very successful strawberry-grower himself. I introduce to you Mr. J. H. Hale.

Mr. Hale, of Connecticut—I am not going to make a speech or anything of the kind. I was very much interested in Dr. McKay's able essay, but there is one question that I wanted to ask him. He speaks of leaving off cultivation some time in July. Now, I would like to inquire what that is for. Will it not be better to have the cultivation kept up through July, August and September? I would like to know what the doctor has to say on the subject.

Dr. McKay, of Mississippi—This latitude is somewhat different from higher latitudes. When we cultivate our plants thoroughly up to the middle of July we destroy nearly all the noxious weeds. There is then very little that will come up on our land except crab-grass. This is a surface grass, does not root deeply, and on our lands forms a very nice protection for the plants. In the winter and spring it gives us a needed and effectual protection in itself, and also keeps the berries clean.

Mr. Hale, of Connecticut—Does it die, then, in the fall?

Mr. McKay, of Mississippi—Yes, it dies out in the fall and does not come up any more until our fruit is harvested. It is the only thing in our latitude that we can utilize to keep our berries clean.

There is nothing to interfere with the continual growth of our plants when we have destroyed pretty much all the injurious weeds and grasses. Even if the growth is disturbed to a limited extent in the fall months, the protective influence upon the plants during the winter will enable them to regain their strength; and besides, the leaving off of the cultivation after July curtails the expense, while cultivation during the summer months up to November gives us a greater expense, without any corresponding benefits. I have tried very fully fall and winter culture, and I am free to say that the mode of culture we have now adopted at Madison has proved most successful. It will be remembered by gentlemen from the North that land is not such an object here as it is in the North. For if we can by this mode of culture obtain from two acres of land more berries at less cost than we could by continual culture from one, it is good policy to do so.

Mr. Hale, of Connecticut—There was one point in the address of Mr Smith, in regard to the cutting of the blossoms, on which I wish to say a few words. It is a thing which must be done. The greatest mistake is made in planting strawberries in the spring and leaving them to bear what they will. I would as soon think of going without setting out the plants. Mr. Smith has failed to tell us how he waters his strawberries, which is a very important point.

Mr. Smith, of Wisconsin—I have already told you about taking off the blossoms; but I have not followed the practice strictly. I think the finest beds I have ever seen were those where the blossoms were not cut. My plan of watering is artificial. I have a tank that holds from five to six hundred barrels. From the tank I have common gas pipes, running under ground. Upon the ends of these pipes I screw a rubber hose. The water comes through that to my strawberry plants. It costs something, but it often makes a great difference in results. I consider it very essential indeed. The tank is filled by means of a wind engine.

Mr. Hale, of Connecticut—This question of irrigation is a very important one. [Mr. Hale here explained a system of irrigating by means of punctured cans, using ordinary tin cans for the purpose, and said that the result had been to double the size of the berries.] I believe there never was a season with us, so wet that strawberries would not have been benefited by watering. I believe strawberries want water every day; all they can get, and a little more. I have not irrigated my own place yet, but I can tell you what I want to do. Our farm is half a mile long by twenty rods wide, and the house is down at the other end. There is a gradual rise in the ground of some eighty or ninety feet, and by going back half a mile further we can get an abundance of water. We intend to build a reservoir there, and from that lay a pipe right through the center of the farm, carrying branch pipes off to every part of the ground, and we think by carrying branch pipes to every bed on the rising ground, and elevating the water, it will percolate through the soil and so irrigate the whole ground.

Mr. Smith, of Wisconsin, asked whether the last speaker gave his berries sufficient depth of culture.

Mr. Hale, of Connecticut—I don't think we do. I don't think any one does. We plow just as deep as two horses will do it, and then over again with a subsoil plow. I suppose we go twelve or fourteen inches deep. The ground is loosened and then thoroughly cultivated from the first of May until the first of November. This last year was hot and terribly dry, so I took a couple of extra horses and put them to work, and cultivated back and forth between the rows; and that went on for six weeks, and it saved the plants. When the rains came (about the 10th of September), our plants were uninjured, while in the adjoining fields they had been injured; and about the first of November we never had a finer lot of plants.

Dr. McKay, of Mississippi—Don't you think the plants would have greater strength if you did not break off their roots by this deep fall culture? I think that if the gentleman would let his plants stand without breaking off the roots by deep cultivation in the fall, that he would not find the necessity of so much water.

Mr. Hale, of Connecticut—You should understand that in the winter our ground is covered with three or four feet of snow and ice. A letter received from Connecticut this afternoon states, "16° below zero and snowing."

Mr. Galusha, of Illinois—I want to call on the President. He cultivates eighty acres of strawberries. I want him to give us his method. If he don't know how, he ought to expose his ignorance.

The President—That is what I don't like to do.

Mr. Galusha, of Illinois—We want to know from you, Mr. President, how you cultivate your strawberries so as to derive the most profit from them?

The President—I don't think, gentlemen, I cultivate as well as I might, or as well as I intend to do. We (I refer to our firm) have never cultivated as deeply as Mr. Hale has suggested, for various reasons. We intend to deepen our culture. We simply plow our ground in the fall, and then plow it again in the spring, and pulverize thoroughly and roll. Our soil in Southern Illinois is a brownish clay loam, containing a fair percentage of lime and potash. We plow as deeply as we can, and set our plants, and cultivate in matted rows. I don't believe our system is as good as the system of hill culture, where circumstances will permit it. But it is very much a question with us whether we shall be able to carry it (hill culture) out with any great success in our section, on account of the crown borer and the common white grub and other destructive strawberry insects. But for these pests, we should adopt, to a great extent, the plan of hill cultivation. But as we do plant, and have planted mostly, we set in rows three and a half feet and sometimes four feet apart, setting the plants one and a half to four feet apart, according to the variety. This last spring we set a good deal of ground, but the drought of 1881 had nearly ruined our fields; and as strawberry plants all through the West, and perhaps all through the East also, were a very scarce commodity, we set our plants three and half feet apart each way. We cultivated both ways until they commenced making runners, when we discontinued horse cultivation one way. The season proved a very favorable one. We have never cultivated more successfully and obtained completer rows than we did from that sparse setting, of which over one-half the plants were really not fit to plant. Our cultivation we try to make pretty thorough. We keep a cultivator running as often as once a week, the hoes following the cultivator. We continue cultivation until late in September or October, according to the growth of the weeds, and then very soon we commence mulching.

We mulch in the autumn; we do not wait till winter; but we do not cover up the plants. Our mulching covers all vacant ground, but does not cover the plants, except as the mulching will lap over on the rows. We have had some experience in cut mulching, and like it. Cornstalks, cut short, make an excellent mulch; so do forest leaves, if held in place. We use wheat straw mostly, because it is most accessible. I would suggest here that probably the best mulching that can be used, where it can be obtained, is sorghum fiber—"bagasse"—or the waste product of the sorghum mills; but in our country there has been no revival of the sorghum industry. As the case stands, we are compelled to use straw largely; and in many cases there will be, in the spring, a considerble growth of wheat and chess, and this we have to cut out by hand. When the mulching is done, the fall work is done. We do not cultivate in the spring; if weeds come up in the spring, we cut them out with knives. I have had some conflict with clover, and clover has always come out ahead,. We are as careful as possible to avoid land which has been in clover.

Mr. Hale, of Connecticut—What do you use for fertilizers?

The President—We use wood ashes. We used bone dust last spring to a certain extent, but up to this time I am not able to report any specific effect. I can't see that there is any difference as yet between the rows of plants where bone dust was used and those where it was not used. Last spring was our first experience with bone dust.

Mr. Hale—Wait till the crop is gathered before deciding on its merits.

The President—We have used common superphosphate in a limited way. We have used considerable stable manure, and have often regretted its use on account of the introduction of such a quantity of grass seed. If it were properly composted, so as to destroy all seed, it would probably be the best manure for strawberries.

Mr. Hale—What is the quantity of berries to the acre?

The President—I suppose the crop of our country averages forty or fifty bushels to the acre. There have been instances of crops running as high as two hundred and fifty bushels to the acre. We consider two hundred cases (twenty-four quarts each) as a good crop. Much less would not be considered a fine crop. I think good management with good varieties ought to secure two hundred cases, that is, one hundred and fifty bushels to the acre, with considerable certainty. Let me say, I have been greatly interested in the statement of Mr. Hale, both in his remarks here, and in those published by him, regarding the importance of irrigation. I believe in it thoroughly. We have not tried it except in a small way.

Mr. Cassell, of Mississippi—What is the subsequent treatment after the season is over?

The President—We take off one crop of berries and usually let the field stand, doing nothing to it, except that we mow off the weeds that come up, two or three times; and then in the fall, as far as we are able, we manure pretty well with barnyard manure. After the second crop is gone we plow the field; we take but two crops from one field. We pick strawberries as soon as they are colored a light red, and often they are picked at a somewhat greener stage than this; but we don't wait till they are ripe We must pick them as soon as they are colored a good red on top and a full light red underneath. We pick every day—seven days in the week—all of our ground—from the beginning to the end of the season.

Prof. Colmant, of Mississippi—Mr. Smith remarked that a condition of successful planting of the strawberry is, that the plants should be watered. I have never watered a strawberry in my life, and I have planted many acres in the Southern States. Again, Mr. Hale remarked that one of the conditions of success with the strawberry was the pulling of the blossoms. I have planted strawberry plants in February and May and had a crop the same year, and never pulled a blossom. Again, we never mulch our strawberries in the winter. These are the three points that I intended to call the attention of the Society to. Have you ever tried, Mr. Hale, to plant strawberries and not pull the blossoms?

Mr. Hale, of Connecticut—Yes, and it has been almost a failure.

Mr. Evans, of Missouri—I think the question of fertilizing strawberries should not be overlooked. I think it needs more investigation than it has ever had, and I want to state the experience of a neighbor of mine the past season. He fertilized one piece of ground with dried blood. He says that for every dollar's worth of blood he put in, he received five dollars back; that he intended to fertilize all his land in the same way next year.

Prest. Earle—How much did he put on?

Mr. Evans—Four hundred pounds of dried blood to the acre.

Adjournment until 7:30 P. M.

Second Day—Thursday.

EVENING SESSION.

STRAWBERRY DISCUSSION—CONTINUED.

In the temporary absence of the President, Vice-President Smith, of Wisconsin, took the chair. The discussion upon strawberry management was resumed.

Mr. Smith—Some one stated this afternoon that stable manure was not good when applied to strawberry plants. Did the gentleman ever try it when well rotted and well mixed with the soil? I have found it good when used in this way.

Mr. Cassell, of Mississippi—Stable manure burns the plants during the first summer. After that it produces a rank growth and may be beneficial. On account of its burning the plants when first applied it is not used to any great extent in the South. It is thought the plants will not stand drought as well when manured in that way.

Mr. Smith—In Wisconsin well rotted manure is found to be at all times beneficial.

The President—Our next paper is by a gentleman whose name has been for a quarter of a century familiar to all American horticulturists. After more than thirty years strawberry growing, having tested hundreds of varieties, he will tell us something to our advantage about the best kinds for market. I have pleasure in introducing Mr. O. B. Galusha, President of the Illinois State Horticultural Society.

IS THERE A BETTER MARKET STRAWBERRY THAN THE WILSON?

BY O. B. GALUSHA.

Such is the momentous question propounded to me by the President of this Society!

Many other questions equally easy of solution might have been asked such as, " What is the color of the chameleon ? " " Is there a better woman than my wife ? " (or *your* wife, if you please).· Or, " If husband and wife are one, *which is the one ?* " But I will not multiply questions of such easy solution— " the woods are full of them," and the answers are more numerous than the questions.

It is customary, when matters of dispute between neighbors, whether fruit growers, farmers or fist-fighters, are brought into court, to have a jury impaneled to which the case is submitted; but I am denied even this scape-goat in the decision of this matter of dispute between one hundred strawberry growers of Wimbledon and one hundred strawberry growers of Wambledon.

I will do my best, then, without a jury, since I am required to be chief justice and at the same time counsel on both sides! My predicament in this *case* reminds me of that of a worthy German magistrate who, after hearing one side of a case which had been brought before him, ably presented by counsel, said: " Vell, you be rite, anyhow ;" but, after hearing the opposite side of the case adroitly advocated, he said : " Vell, you be rite, too, so I dismish dis gase and sharge de gonstubble mit de kosts for bringing such a gase into goort." So, don't blame me, my friends, if, after considering the arguments on both sides, I shall " dismiss the case and charge the costs upon Constable Earle for bringing it into court."

It would have somewhat relieved the embarrassment of the court had the question been accompanied by some definitions, explanations or limitations, thus marking out a track to be followed in the hunt for a solution. In the absence of these aids we will *assume* that the term " strawberry " includes not only the berry but the plant which produces the berry, taking in all its habits and characteristics; otherwise, were we to be confined to the quality of the berry, the solution would depend entirely upon a census of the eaters of strawberries; for " tastes differ." Were we to attempt to solve the question as to which is the better variety of cheese—Limburger or full cream— we would have imposed upon us the task of taking a census of palates, and this would require a knowledge of the German language, which, unfortunately, we do not possess. Again, the question, " Is there a better *pie* than the pumpkin pie ? " would array the Yankees against the rest of mankind ; and so on through a list of important questions which have agitated the minds or pleased or nauseated the palates or stomachs of civilized man for a century or more.

THE VIGOR OF THE PLANT.

That the Wilson plant is not as robust as many other varieties of the strawberry will scarcely be questioned by any one, certainly by none who have cultivated the Crescent, Piper, Cumberland Triumph, Kentucky, and others of like constitutional vigor. It is now almost universally conceded that varieties of trees, and more especially of plants, deteriorate. Whether this is attributable to a tendency to " revert to the original type," as physiologists claim, or whether it is due to continued stimulation through many successive generations, or any other cause, the fact, in the case of this variety at least, is unquestionable.

The experience of the writer is a fair representation of the general experience of those who have long grown the Wilson and other varieties of strawberries. Upon the same, or adjoining and similar soil, where, fifteen years since, vines of Wilson were healthy and productive, they are now feeble, make but few plants and give but one-fourth, at most, the fruit they formerly gave; and this, too, where the best plants are used in planting, the ground enriched with manure, and good care given in the cultivation.

Samuel Edwards, of Mendota, Ill., a fruit grower of about forty years' experience, says: " The Wilson does not succeed, and I have excused it."

E. C. Hathaway, of Ottawa, Ill., good authority in small fruits and vegetables, says: " Wilson is losing its vitality—'petering out' as it were. I can get no Wilson plants from any source but seem to be in this condition after the first year."

Charles Myers, of Toulon, Ill., writes, in report to State Horticultural Society: "Wilsons have run out. Charles Downing is the most successful berry here."

Geo. J. Kellogg, of Wisconsin, writes: " Captain Jack is best. The leaf of Wilson suffers from rust, while leaf of Captain Jack does not rust at all."

Wm. Jackson, Godfrey, Ill., who grows fruits for market, says: " I have discarded Wilson, except that I keep a few for old acquaintance's sake."

John Howard, of Alton, remarked in the Alton Horticultural Society: " If I were growing berries for fun, I might plant the Wilson." He stated that an acre of Downing produced 2,204 quarts, while an acre of Wilson, on good ground, and well cared for, gave but 240 quarts.

James E. Starr, ex-President Illinois Horticultural Society, wrote: " The Charles Downing is now considered to be ahead in our district (the Alton district)."

Capt. D. Stewart, of Upper Alton, Ill., says: " I will plant no more Wilsons.'

B. F. Smith, of Kansas: " Wilson is the chief variety; the vines have rusted badly."

There are, however, many localities in which the plants are satisfactorily vigorous, and especially in virgin soil not highly stimulated by manures. For instance, we have good evidence that in some localities in Wisconsin, in Western Michigan, and in Southern Illinois, the plants are vigorous and healthy; but these are exceptional.

PRODUCTIVENESS.

The same statement as above may be made relative to the productiveness of the plant. In the long, long ago, when our eyes first read a notice of the berry, in an Albany paper, an order for plants was forwarded, filled, and the plants transplanted into a sandy prairie soil near Lisbon, Illinois; and by special care they and their offspring produced, in fourteen months from the planting, 62½ pounds per square rod, or at the rate of 10,000 pounds per acre, by actual weight! Strawberries were then sold, as they and *all* other *fruit should be, by weight.* This crop, however, was but a few pounds in excess of that of Russell's Prolific and Buffalo Seedling, tested at the same time. Since that time, at least a half dozen varieties have surpassed these in amount of berries produced. It is quite possible to find soils and localities in which, even yet, the Wilson may be made to produce a crop equal to or surpassing this. Yet the general deterioration of the variety, in both vigor, or tenacity of life and productiveness, is plainly to be seen by careful and extensive observation, on nine-tenths of the plantations.

FLAVOR OF BERRY.

A satisfactory conclusion to this point in the problem can not be reached by reason or argument, for the reason just stated. The Wilson strawberry, like the Clinton grape, has, before full maturity, an amount of acid in its juices far in excess of nearly all other varieties of its species; but when allowed to fully ripen upon the vines it becomes a rich fruit. But our question will not admit of taking the fact of its final good quality into the account, unless it can be placed in the *market* and reach the tables of the consumers with this good quality intact. Upon this point a few quotations from the most eminent horticulturists of the West will certainly come in place.

President Lyon, of the Michigan State Horticultural Society, said, in 1881: "The advertisement for the Wilson is, that it gets its color early, before getting anywhere near ripe, and thus can be put upon the market in a firm state, even although when thus thrown upon the market in its half-ripe condition it is hardly fit to eat."

Dr. John A. Warder, of Ohio, said, in the hearing of the writer: "I have never eaten a decent Wilson yet."

Hon. G. C. Lamphere, of Galesburg, Illinois, thus wrote in a report to a horticultural society: "Wilson is solid enough for transportation to the world's end, provided the world's end is in a reasonable distance; but, unless left on the vine till perfectly ripe, when, of course, it has lost some of its firmness, it is sour and somewhat strong in flavor. Acid is a good thing, but one can have too much of it in the temper and in fruit, and a strong, positive flavor can be overdone."

As a member of the Illinois State Horticultural Society, and for many years a recorder of its transactions, whose members have been largely engaged in growing Wilson and other strawberries for market, we can confidently assert that the prevailing and almost universal sentiment of the members is that expressed by Judge Lamphere and President Lyon, quoted above, very few having ever expressed a preference for Wilson, even when well ripened upon the vines, for their own tables.

MARKETING OR " CARRYING " QUALITY.

There remains, therefore, but this single point upon which the great reputation of the Wilson has been builded ; upon which farther, or continued cultivation can be warranted.

That the " Sour Wilson " has been the leading and most profitable berry grown for long shipments, there is no doubt; the only question, then, remaining is, have we convincing evidence or proof that there is any other variety known which is hardy and prolific in plant, and whose fruit is superior in quality, and can be safely shipped *long distances?* I emphasize long distances, for no intelligent cultivator of strawberries will question that there are many varieties superior to it in vigor, hardiness and productiveness of plant, and quality of fruit, which may be grown with greater profit where shipped not to exceed one hundred and fifty miles from producer to consumer, and used within fifty hours from the time of gathering.

We have made many tests of the carrying and keeping qualities of strawberries, and have held quite extensive correspondence with growers of strawberries who have had long experience in shipping them for from two to five hundred miles to market, and find the preponderating testimony to be that, for shipping long distances, say three hundred miles or over, *to reach a distributing point and from thence to be re-shipped,* the Wilson is of greater value than any other variety as yet put to such a severe and unnecessary test. As has been remarked, the facts of its firmness and becoming colored before fully ripe, admit of its being picked green and shipped long distances before ripening and before softening. It perhaps has no equal in these respects. There are, however, other hardier and prolific varieties, producing berries which can be shipped without loss from three to four hundred miles, as has been often proved.

We have received the Bidwell in excellent condition after a journey of three hundred and eighty miles. The Capt. Jack is claimed by many to endure quite as long journeys as the Wilson, if picked at same stage of ripening, though one shipper writes that it loses color sooner than the Wilson. The Sucker State has been shipped a distance of three hundred and thirty miles, through the season, arriving in good order and outselling the Wilson. The Piper Seedling has been put to quite as severe a test as this, in a small way, and proved the superior to any variety ever shipped or received by us ; and, in point of quality, is *far* superior to the Wilson and of much better flavor than either Capt. Jack or Sucker State. After a two days' journey, and being kept nearly five days from the picking, on each of which days the mercury rose to above 90° in the room where kept, berries of the Piper have been placed upon our table and pronounced excellent by all the members of the family. It is quite probable that berries of Wilson, picked as before indicated, could have endured the same handling and high temperature for the same length of time, and preserved their shape, but for educated American palates, would have compared with the Pipers as Limburger to full-cream No. 1 cheese.

Mr. President, you and this large assembly will not be detained to listen to the array of evidence, collected from the records of many State Horticultural Societies, which bear upon this question. We started out in the investigation of this " case " with the supposition that it is a matter of dispute between about an equal number of fruit growers on each side, expecting to find that those who are so located that their berries must be shipped from two to four hundred miles, nearly all place the Wilson first in money value, and are quite unwilling to plant of other reputed good-shipping varieties.

But even this class of growers are not agreed, many of them not being satisfied with the Wilson, and very many casting it aside ; and those who have done so either find a substitute of greater value, or find some modes of picking, handling and transporting other and superior varieties, so that their profits are enhanced rather than diminished by the change. It is a significant fact that the numbers of this class of growers is diminishing from year to year, as the constitutional vigor of the Wilson plant deteriorates and valuable improved varieties, with more robust vigor, are more extensively tested.

In conclusion, allow the writer to protest against the practice of shipping soft fruits long journeys, by ordinary modes of transportation. They can not reach the consumers in a wholesome condition, and with their characteristic flavors unimpaired. The Wilson strawberry, as usually received by the consumer, after a long shipment, a delay, and a reshipment, *is not a healthful article of diet!* It is far better for consumers to content themselves with such species of fruits as can be found in the markets in a wholesome and nutritious state, waiting for the ripening of the strawberries, raspberries and blackberries nearer home, or for those which are placed in the market in a fresh condition, having their flavors unimpaired.

Professor S. A. Forbes, State Entomologist of Illinois, next delivered his address upon the " Insects Affecting the Strawberry," the President introducing him in the following terms:

Most of you know something of what Professor Forbes has done for all of our States—invaluable work in several departments of Natural History. His researches are throwing light upon many obscure questions. He is now Entomologist of the State of Illinois, and we are glad that the whole country will be able to participate in the excellent results of his investigations. Ladies and gentlemen, Prof. Forbes.

4

INSECTS AFFECTING THE STRAWBERRY.

BY PROF. S. A. FORBES, OF ILLINOIS.

At least two dozen species of insects are on record as enemies of the strawberry in the Eastern United States and Canada, and how many more may infest it whose injuries have never got into print, of course no one can tell. Every part of the plant is attacked by them, some limiting themselves to a single structure, and others devouring two or three indifferently. The fibrous roots are eaten by the root-worm, the white grub, and the larva of the goldsmith beetle; the stem or *crown* (as it is commonly called) is gnawed and pierced by the root-worm, and excavated by the crown-borer and the crown miner. At least a dozen enemies attack the leaf, either biting and gnawing its tissues or sucking its juices, and one of these, the strawberry plant-louse, also sucks the sap of the crown and even of the peduncle of the flower. The blossom itself is destroyed by two or three; and finally, the ripened fruit is likewise occasionally injured.

Some find their more usual food in other plants, taking the strawberry only when it comes in their way; still others, limiting themselves to the strawberry field, are doubtless the native enemies of the wild plant, whose multiplication has been immensely facilitated by the enormous increase of the food; and still a few others are believed to be of European origin, imported to this country by accident.

I have herein summarized what is known to me with regard to the most important of these insects, thinking it might be worth while to bring the essential facts together in one place for reference. I have included those found injurious eastward as well as in the limited region covered by the membership of this Society, in order that you of the Mississippi valley may be on the lookout for the invasion of eastern enemies; but I have not noticed especially the strawberry pests of the Old World or of the Pacific Slope. I have drawn freely upon the writings of Thomas, Riley, Packard and Saunders in the preparation of this paper, my own contributions to the subject relating chiefly to the crown-borer, the root-worm and the crown-miner.

It is proposed to treat separately the insects injurious to the root, to the stem or crown, and to the foliage, flower and fruit, taking them up under each head in the order of the classification. Under this arrangement the first to be treated will be those attacking the exposed parts of the plant, namely, the foliage, blossom and berry.

INSECTS INJURING THE LEAVES, FLOWER AND FRUIT.

The Strawberry Worm. *Emphytus maculatus*, Norton.

Order Hymenoptera, Family Tenthredinidæ.

This insect is one of the most destructive enemies of the strawberry in localities where it secures a footing, but is not as widespread and continuous in its ravages as the leaf-roller and some of the various beetle larvæ affecting the root and crown. It is, however, to be placed among strawberry insects of the first class. It has occurred in great numbers throughout Central and Northern Illinois, Missouri and Iowa, and as far east as Ontario, Canada. Prof. Riley's terse description, given in his ninth report as State Entomolo-

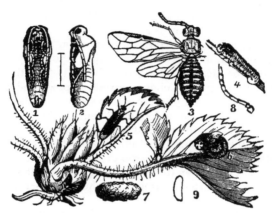

Fig. 1. STRAWBERRY WORM (*Emphytus maculatus, Norton*): 1. Ventral view of pupa; 2. Side view of same; 3. Enlarged sketch of perfect fly, the wings on one side detached; 4, Larva crawling, natural size; 5. Perfect fly, natural size; 6. Larva at rest; 7. Cocoon; 8. Enlarged antenna, showing joints; 9. Enlarged egg. After Riley.

gist of Missouri, can scarcely be improved upon, and I quote the substance of it in his own words:

"Early in spring numerous flies may be seen hanging to and flying about the vines, in fields which have been previously infested. They are dull and inactive in the cool of the evening and at these hours are seldom noticed. They are of a pitchy black color, with two rows of large, transverse, dull whitish spots upon the abdomen. The female, with the saw-like instrument peculiar to the insects of this family, deposits her eggs by a most curious and interesting process, in the stems of the plant, clinging the while to the hairy substance by which these stems are covered. The eggs are white, opaque, and .03 of an inch long, and may be readily perceived upon splitting the stalk, though the outside orifice at which they were introduced is scarcely visible. They soon increase somewhat in bulk, causing a swelling of the stalk, and hatch in two weeks—more or less according to the temperature—and during the early part of May the worms attract attention by the innumerable small holes they make in the leaves. Their colors are dirty yellow and gray-green, and when not feeding they rest on the under side of the leaf, curled up in a spiral manner, the tail occupying the center, and fall to the ground at the slightest disturbance. After changing their skin four times they become fully grown, when they measure about three-fourths of an inch. At this season they descend into the ground, and form a very weak cocoon of earth, the inside being made smooth by a sort of gum.   In this they soon change to pupæ, from which are produced a second brood of flies by the end of June and beginning of July.   Under the influence of July weather the whole process of egg-depositing, etc., is rapidly repeated, and the second brood of worms descend into the earth during the forepart of August, and form their cocoons, in which they remain in the caterpillar state through the fall. winter, and spring months, till the middle of April following, when they become pupæ and flies again, as related."

As the second brood of the larvæ appear upon the leaves in July, after the fruit is picked, and feed entirely upon the foliage of the plant, they may doubtless be destroyed without difficulty by the use of the ordinary poisons.   Paris green, London purple, or powdered hellebore may be safely recommended for this purpose.   It is also not unlikely that fire as applied for the leaf-roller, would be found efficient for the destruction of this pest likewise, if used at the time when the eggs and larvæ are exposed upon the foliage.   It should be noticed that plowing up the field in autumn will not actually destroy this insect, unless the ground be planted for a year to another crop, and that even then it is possible that the adult saw-flies, escaping from the field, will secure a lodgment in other strawberry vines

Mason Bee.   *Osmia canadensis,* Cresson.

Order Hymenoptera, Family Apidæ.

I notice this insect here on the strength of a paragraph by Mr. Wm. A. Saunders, contained in the report of the Entomological Society of Ontario, for 1872.

"This," he says, "is the name of a small hymenopterous insect, a sort of wild bee, which has proved destructive to the foliage of some strawberry plants during the past season, in the township of Oxford.   It was observed by Mr. Johnson Pettit, of Grimsby, who kindly furnished me with specimens of the insect.   In both sexes, the head, thorax, and abdomen is green and more or less densely covered with whitish down or short hairs, those on the thorax being longest.   The wings are nearly transparent, with blackish veins. The female is larger than the male."   The length is .35 inch, and the spread of the extended wings about half an inch.

"Mr. Pettit says: ' The insects were taken in East Oxford, July 2d, on a few strawberry plants in a garden.   The plants, perhaps nearly one hundred in number, had been nearly all denuded of their leaves, and a search in the evening having failed to reveal the authors of the mischief, I examined them again in the heat of the day, and found the little culprits actively engaged in nibbling away the remaining shreds of the leaves.   They appeared to chew the fragments into a pulp and carry it away, but the little time I spent in observing them was insufficient to determine anything further respecting their habits.' Doubtless in this instance the leaves so consumed were used in the construction of suitable nests, in which to deposit the eggs and rear the young of those insects."

If this species should ever become seriously destructive (as is very unlikely), its injuries could probably be checked by the use of insect poison, since the time when it made the attack above described was after the fruiting of the plant.

The Strawberry Span Worm. *Nematocampa filamentaria*, Guenée.

Order Lepidoptera, Family Phalænidæ.

In June, or earlier to the southward, a wood-colored measuring-worm, seven-tenths of an inch in length, with two unequal pairs of long, slender, fleshy filaments, situated on the third and fifth abdominal rings, the posterior pair shorter than the others, curled at the end, and finely tuberculated, may be found feeding on the strawberry and currant. The head is pale rust-red, with some spots of same hue on the body. Half way between the metathoracic legs and the first pair of filaments are two sub-acute tubercles, which are rust-red. When the four filaments are uncurled, they are as long as from the head to the tubercles. The anterior pair of filaments are pale rust-red beneath at base, brown above, but tipped with white. . An oval dark spot occurs behind the last pair of tubercles, and extending into the anal plate. This curious worm produces a little pale ochre-colored moth, measuring about an inch across the wings, with brown lines crossing the wings, and an outer border of dull brown that is continuous across both wings except the apical portion of the anterior pair. They are never sufficiently numerous to cause much injury.

This, like the preceding, if it ever becomes destructive, can doubtless be met with insect poison sprayed or sprinkled upon the leaves.

The Green Strawberry Span Worm. *Angerona crocataria*, Guenée.

Order Lepidoptera, Family Phalænidæ.

This is another of the measuring worms which has been reported injurious to the strawberry; but as it has not been anywhere a serious enemy, as far as I can learn, I mention it here only for the purpose of putting fruit-growers on their guard against it. The larva, which appears on the foliage in May or June, is about an inch and a half long, gradually increasing in size from the head to the first pair of prolegs. The general color is a yellowish green. There is an indistinct dorsal line, and a rather broad whitish line on each side just below the spiracles, bordered above with faint purple, which increases in depth of color towards the posterior rings. This becomes a purple stripe on the anal prolegs, and forms a mark like an inverted Λ. Beneath, same color as above, but with faint, interrupted longitudinal lines. Spiracles white, bordered with purple. Above, on each segment, from second to seventh inclusive, are five minute black dots (four in a square, and one in front towards the head) and all the rings have a yellowish band on the swelled part, where the succeeding segment is inserted; legs pale green.

The pupa is .5 to .6 inch in length, and of a dark olive-green color, with the exception of the abdomen, which is pale greenish yellow, and has a row of black dots on each side, and another dorsal row. The wing-cases are very prominent, and, from their strong contrast with the abdomen in color, make the chrysalis a pretty object. They are fastened by the tail, and rest in a slight net-work of silken threads, with which the caterpillar draws together the edges of the leaf so as to form a kind of cradle.

The moth appears in June or July, and may be found at twilight until September. It expands about an inch and a half; the wings and body are bright yellow, the first spotted with pale reddish brown, and crossed by a broad, broken band of the same color a little beyond the middle. On the forewings, midway between this band and the body, is another band more broken than the outer one, and the spots of which it is composed are smaller. It is one of the brightest colored of the geometrid moths.

The insect is a very prolific one, a single female depositing over two hundred eggs. These are laid soon after the appearance of the moth, in patches or clusters. They are of an oval shape, about one thirty-third of an inch long and one-fiftieth wide. When first laid they are yellow, but in a day or two change to bright red, and afterwards to grayish-brown. They hatch in one or two weeks. The young caterpillar is about a tenth of an inch long, with a large brown head and yellowish green body, with a dark brown stripe along each side. Below this the body is pale, with a whitish bloom on its surface, and a few short, brownish hairs, which are most numerous on the last segment.

If this insect should ever become sufficiently numerous in the strawberry fields to require especial attention, it can probably be destroyed by the same measures which have been found efficient for the leaf-roller.

The Smeared Dagger. Acronycta oblinita, Sm. & Abb.

Order Lepidoptera, Family Noctuidæ.

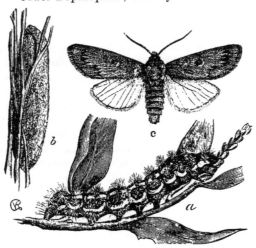

Fig. 2. SMEARED DAGGER (*Acronycta oblinita*, Sm. & Abb.): *a.* Larva; *b.* Pupa; *c.* Moth.

Another minor enemy of the plant, capable, however, of possible mischief, is a caterpillar covered with red bristles proceeding from crimson warts, with a bright yellow band along the sides, which may frequently be found in June and again in August or September. It is about one and a quarter inches long, and the body above is of a dull velvety black. On each side of a line drawn down the center of the back is a row of bright yellow spots, two or more on each segment, and below this and close to the under surface is a bright yellow band, deeply indented on each segment, the indentations being on a line with the rows of tubercles. The spiracles or breathing holes are pure white, and are placed in the indented portions of the yellow band; there are also a few whitish dots scattered irregularly over the surface of the body. The under side is dull reddish along the middle, and brownish black along the sides; the feet are of a shining black, and slightly hairy, while the thick, fleshy hinder legs, called the prolegs, are reddish, tipped with brown, with a cluster of short hairs on the outside of each. This caterpillar is conspicuous from its beauty, and at first one can scarcely believe that such a handsome caterpillar could produce so plain and quiet-looking a moth. It is a general feeder, attacking the strawberry in common with several other plants.

The chrysalis is very dark brown, and with the exception of a smooth, shiny band on the posterior border of each abdominal joint, is rough or shagreened. It has the power of violently turning round and round in its cocoon when disturbed, thereby causing a rustling noise.

The moth has the front wings of an ash-gray color, caused by innumerable dark atoms scattered over a white ground, and there is a distinct row of black dots along the posterior border, a more or less distinct black zigzag line across the outer fourth, and some dusky spots just above the middle of the wing. The hind wings are pure white.

There are two broods each year, the first brood of worms appearing for the most part during June, and giving out the moths in July, and the second brood occurring in the fall, passing the winter in the chrysalis state, and producing moths the following May.

This, like the other late leaf-eating larvæ, may be attacked by insect poisons, if it should chance to become worthy of so much attention.

The Army Worm. *Leucania unipuncta*, Haw.

Order Lepidoptera, Family Noctuidæ.

Passing mention may be made in this connection of this destructive pest, which last year swept through strawberry fields in Southern Illinois, stripping the plants of foliage, and leaving the unripe fruit upon the ground, gnawed from the stems.

The fields might be protected from its attack by the barriers used by grain farmers to arrest its march. The most successful of these is a deep furrow plowed around the field, the inner wall of which may be made slanting outwards from the furrow by the use of a spade. The worms collecting here may be killed by dragging a log along the furrow; or holes may be dug in it at intervals, in which they will rapidly collect, where they may be mashed by thousands. It should be remembered that measures of this sort which will not pay for ordinary farm crops, may nevertheless be employed with great profit for products as valuable as the strawberry.

Cutworms. *Agrotis, sp.*

Order Lepidoptera, Family Noctuidæ.

An illustration of the damage to strawberries which these insects are liable to do under favoring conditions is afforded by the account given by Mr. Saunders, in the article already cited, of the injuries due to a species occurring in Canada, but the name of which he does not mention. He says:—

"This is an insect which has been most unusually injurious during the past season on the fruit plantations of Mr. Mountjoy and Mr. Bunning, on the borders of Lake Huron, near Sarnia. At first its habits were not understood, and it pursued the 'even tenor of its way' uninterrupted night after night; the perplexed fruit-growers not knowing why it was that every day the foliage on their fruit trees and strawberry patches grew slimmer. But soon it was found that the enemy was a night worker, and this knowledge of its habits was at once turned to account, and night watches instituted, with the view of counteracting this insidious foe, and with good results, as many as eighteen hundred having been killed by Mr. Mountjoy in one night.

"Their manner of life may be thus described: The moths from which the worms are produced appear on the wing during the month of August, and soon after pair and deposit their eggs on the ground or on some other plant or other substance near the ground; they probably hatch in the fall, and feed for a time on the leaves of grass and other plants then abundant; and after attaining but a small measure of their growth, they burrow into the earth, and there remain in a torpid state during the winter; but the warmth of spring revives them, and soon they are abroad and active. During the first few weeks, while they are still small, the quantity of food they consume is not sufficient to attract much attention; but as they approach nearer maturity, that is, about the time when the trees first put out their tender foliage, the quantity of food they consume is enormous. In the day time they rest tolerably secure from harm, by burrowing a short distance under ground, and towards night they sally forth from their hiding places to begin their work of destruction. They are extremely active in their movements, and travel over quite a space of ground in a very short time, eating almost everything green in their way; they climb the trunks of trees, and consume not only the young foliage, but the buds also, leaving the limbs almost bare, and before the light of another day dawns they retreat to their hiding places and rest in quiet. When full grown they burrow deeper into the earth, and form for themselves an oval cell or chamber, in which they change to chrysalis, and from which the moths are produced early in the autumn to continue the race. In this instance these caterpillars took a decided liking for the strawberry vines, and in spite of the most vigilant search for them, day after day and night after night, they defoliated a large patch of the vines to such an extent that they were utterly ruined. Nearly all through the month of June they literally swarmed, and scarcely a night passed without considerable damage being done by them."

Concerning remedies for its attack he adds:—

"The battle must be fought with this insect while in the larva or caterpillar state, and then the surest way of disposing of them is to catch and kill them. By searching around the vines just under the surface of the ground during the day, many may be turned up and destroyed, and by inspecting again at night when they are active and busy, their ranks may be still further thinned, and by continuing this treatment, day after day, they may no doubt be kept under. Probably dusting the vines with hellebore would poison them as it does other leaf-feeding insects; this measure is at least worthy of a trial."

It is possible that these cutworms might be enticed and poisoned in the field with cabbage leaves or other foliage laid on the ground and poisoned with Paris green or other arsenical substances.

The Stalk Borer. *Gortyna nitela*, Guenée.

Order Lepidoptera, Family Noctuidæ.

Fig. 3. STALK BORER (*Gortyna nitela, Guenée*): Moth and larva.

Concerning the work in the strawberry field of this well-known and widespread insect, I can add nothing to the mere mention made by Prof. Riley in his third report as State Entomologist of Missouri, that it sometimes bores into ripe strawberries. It is very unlikely that it could do any noticeable damage in this way unless its breeding had been encouraged by permitting the unrestrained growth of thick-stemmed weeds in or near the strawberry field.

The Strawberry Leaf-roller. *Anchylopera fragariæ*, Riley.

Order Lepidoptera, Family Tortricidæ.

Under this name we have to deal with one of the most destructive enemies of the plant, which at one time threatened to put an end to the cultivation of the strawberry over large areas, and which would probably have done so, for a considerable time, at least, if measures of controlling it had not happily been hit upon.

The following description is by Prof. Riley, and is extracted from the *American Entomologist* for January, 1869:—

"The larva or caterpillar measures, when full grown, a little more than one-third of an inch. It is largest on the front segments, tapering slightly towards the hinder ones. In color it varies from a very light yellowish

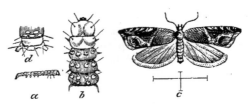

Fig. 4. STRAWBERRY LEAF ROLLER (*Anchylopera fragariæ, Riley*): *a.* LarVa; *b.* Anterior segments, magnified; *c.* Moth; *d.* Last segments. After Riley.

brown to a dark olive-green or brown, with a body soft and somewhat semi-transparent. Its head is of a shining yellowish brown color, with a dark eye-spot on each side. The second segment has a shield above, similar in color and appearance to the head, and on each segment or ring of the body are a few pale spots, from each one of which arises a single hair. The hinder segment has two black spots, while the under surface, feet, and forelegs are about the same color as the body above. In certain parts of Northern Illinois and Indiana this insect has been ruining the strawberry beds in a most wholesale manner. It crumples and folds the leaves, feeding on their pulpy substance, and causes them to appear dry and seared. It most usually lines the inside of the fold with silk. There are two broods during the year, and the worms of the first brood, which appear during the month of June, change to the pupa state within the rolled-up leaf, and become moths during the fore part of July.

"The moth has the head, thorax, and fore wings reddish brown, the latter streaked and spotted with black and white; the hind wings and abdomen are dusky. The wings, when spread, measure nearly half an inch across. After pairing, the females deposit their eggs on the plants, from which eggs, in due time, there hatches a second brood of worms, which come to their growth towards the end of September, and changing to pupæ, pass the winter in that state."

Observations made at Normal show that considerable numbers of the larvæ winter over. The moths begin to fly very early in spring, the first warm days of the opening season calling them forth.

The favorite remedy for this pest is that of mowing the field after the berries are picked, and burning it over when dry. The plants are not hurt, and the leaf-roller is checked at once, and in two or three years reduced to insignificance, if not entirely exterminated. Sprinkling or dusting the vines, in August, with suitable poisons, during the life of the second brood, would probably be equally effectual.

Other Strawberry Leaf-rollers.

Mr. Saunders mentions a second leaf-roller of the strawberry, under the name of *Exartema permundana*, Clemens, which was found attacking strawberry vines in Canada, in immense numbers, in one case destroying nearly half the crop. I quote from the valuable paper already so frequently cited:

"All these leaf-rollers have the habit of rolling up the leaves and fastening them with silken threads, and living within the enclosure; but this little creature prefers taking the flowers, expanded and unexpanded, and, bringing them together with silken threads into a sort of ball, it feasts on their substance. This peculiarity makes its attacks much more annoying and destructive than any mere consumption of leaves would be. It is small in size, of a green color, and with very active habits, wriggling itself quickly out of its hiding place when disturbed. It is the progeny of a small moth, with its fore wings yellowish, varied with brown streaks and patches, and darker hind wings, who lays her eggs quite early in the spring, placing them upon the developing leaves, where the newly hatched larvæ may be sure to enjoy an abundance of tender and juicy food, and these attain to nearly their full growth and are just then capable of most mischief, at the time when the plant is coming into full flower.

"We have found this species attacking the wild strawberry in different localities, and have little doubt but that it is widely disseminated; but why it should so persistently attack the plants in one locality, and multiply so amazingly there, while comparatively unknown in other places, we are unable to more than guess. Possibly they may have been kept under in other localities by parasites which feed on them. The larvæ of most moths are liable to attack from one or more of such enemies, and we know that this species is not exempt, for several of the larvæ which we succeeded in bringing into the chrysalis state, instead of producing moths, yielded specimens of these small parasitic flies.

"This species was described by Dr. Clemens in the Proceedings of the Academy of Natural Sciences, Philadelphia, for August, 1860, where the author states that 'the larvæ bind together the terminal leaves of Spiræa.' Hence it would appear that this insect does not confine itself to the strawberry as a food plant, and may possibly be quite a general feeder. The chrysalides of this species were of the usual dark brown color, from which the moths made their escape from the eighth to the twelfth of July."

Still another species of the same habit, *Loxtænia fragariæ*, from the wild strawberry, has been described by Prof. Packard in his "Guide to the Study of Insects." The larva was found in Maine early in June, in folds of the leaves; the moth appearing about the middle of the same month. The moth is very pretty, and measures, when its wings are expanded, eight-tenths of an inch. Its fore wings are red, darker on the outer half, and with a large triangular white spot near the middle of the front edge; the outer edge of the spot is hollowed out. The outer edge of the wing is pale, especially in the middle, and about the same color as the head and thorax; the hind wings and abdomen are of a whitish buff, underneath they are whitish.

Various other species have also been briefly referred to as enemies of this plant, but it does not seem worth while to multiply descriptions of them, as the same principles must guide us in the destruction of all of them. Fire or insect poisons, either arsenical or vegetable, like hellebore water, must be used, according to the season when the worms or pupæ occur upon the leaves.

The Grape-vine Colaspis. *Colaspis flavida*, Say.

Order Coleoptera, Family Chrysomelidæ.

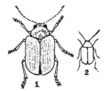

Fig. 5, GRAPEVINE COLASPIS (*Colaspis flavida, Say*): Enlarged, and natural size.

Prof. Riley states in his third report as State Entomologist of Missouri, that this beetle greedily devours the leaves of the strawberry, commencing to appear in June and continuing until autumn, although leaving the strawberry vines for other food, to a great extent, late in July and in August. The following is Say's description of the beetle:

"Pale yellowish; elytra striate, with a double series of punctures. Body densely punctured; punctures rather large and profound, head with two slightly elevated tubercles between the antennæ; thorax tinged with rufous; elytra with elevated lines, of which the inner one curves round at base and descends a short distance to unite with the sutural line; interstitial spaces, excepting the subsutural one and the two exterior ones, with double series of rather large profound punctures; exterior edge blackish brown; venter dusky. Length nearly one-fifth of an inch. Var. *a*. Interstitial spaces of the elytra black; beneath, excepting the feet, black."

Prof. Riley's inference in the article cited, that this beetle is the adult of the common root-worm of the strawberry, can not yet be regarded as established as will be explained more fully under *Paria aterrima*, when treating of species injurious to the root.

The beetle (Colaspis) could, of course, be easily poisoned in the strawberry field; but as it feeds on the leaves of the grape as well, and possibly on some other plants, such treatment might not be a complete remedy.

Until the larva of this beetle is more certainly known, and its life history has been thoroughly cleared up, we can not recommend more effective measures.

The Root-worm Beetle. *Paria aterrima*, Oliv.

Order Coleoptera, Family Chrysomelidæ.

This beetle, probably the imago or adult of the root-worm, will be fully described and discussed under the latter name, and I need only mention here the fact that it appears on the vines in both spring and summer (August), and that it may be poisoned at the latter period without trouble, as has been several times proven by experiment.

Locusts. *Caloptenus spretus*, Thos., *Acridium americanum*, Drury, etc.

Order Orthoptera, Family Acrididæ.

Prof. Riley mentions strawberry leaves as among the favorite food plants of the Rocky Mountain locust (Seventh Report, p. 159), and we have found the young of the second species above mentioned devouring the strawberry leaves in Southern Illinois. Mr. F. S. Earle, of Cobden, Ill., writes in July: "A few days ago I noticed some 'flocks' of young grasshoppers [probably of this species] that were literally eating up some strawberry plants. They were quite small, apparently just hatched, and there were not enough of them to do any serious harm, but they made a clean sweep as far as they went."

The Strawberry Plant-louse. *Siphonophora fragariæ*, Koch.

Order Hemiptera, Family Aphididæ.

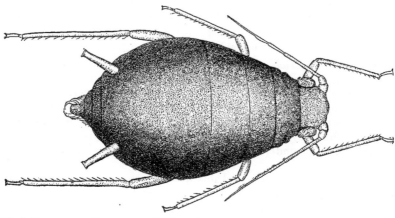

Fig. 6. STRAWBERRY PLANT-LOUSE (*Siphonophora fragariæ, Koch*): Root form (?) from crown. H. Garman.

This species occurs in numbers large enough to attract attention and occasionally to do decided injury, in Kansas and Illinois, * and probably elsewhere also. Like all the plant-lice, it is far more dangerous than its usual insignificance would lead one to suppose. The reproductive rate of these insects is

---

* The form figured above, from Southern Illinois, has the aspect of an Aphis, and it is possible that the Illinois species is not *Siphonophora fragariæ*, as was supposed by Dr. Thomas. Until the aerial forms can be seen, however, I prefer to leave the matter as above.

so enormous that when conditions happen especially to favor their increase, they may suddenly swarm in countless myriads, and utterly destroy the plants which they infest.

In spring and early summer this species occurs on the under sides of the leaves and on the stalks of the growing fruit, causing the leaves to wither, and diminishing the size of the berry. In autumn the lice move to the crown, where they may be found between the bases of the roots. In No-

Fig 7. Egg of above. H. Garman.

vember, the wingless females here lay their eggs, which survive the winter to hatch in the spring.

The winged form probably appears at irregular intervals throughout the summer, as is usually the case with the plant-lice, and this is consequently the time when the species spreads from field to field. The following descriptions are from Buckton's " British Aphides," vol. I, page 125:—

"*Apterous viviparous female.*—Size of body .09 x .04 inch, length of antennæ 1 inch., of cornicles .025 inch. Whole body shining green, except the cornicles, which are tipped with black, and straight. Eyes red. Antennæ long and dark olive. Legs pale, with dark femora and tibia joints. Tail yellow.

"*Pupa.*—Reddish green, with a smoky line down the dorsum. Thorax and ring cases gray. The last with blackish tips.

"*Winged viviparous female.*—Expanse of wings .35 inch, size of body .09 x .04, length of antennæ .1 inch, of cornicles .025 inch. Head, thoracic lobes, antennæ, nectaries, tibiæ, and femoral points black. All the rest of the body green. Abdomen with four round black spots on each side of the carina, and several obscure marks down the dorsum. Eyes red. Cubitus and wing insertions bright yellow, other veins black. Stigma grayish. Tail yellow. Wholly green on the under side. Some specimens are of a redder shade than the rest "

At the time when this insect probably does its principal injuries, namely : previous to the ripening of the fruit, the usual standard remedies for the injuries of plant-lice are impracticable, since the poisonous powders and fluids which are used for the destruction of these insects would render the berries inedible. The proper season to attack this pest by local applications is doubtless in autumn, when the lice are congregated upon the crown. At this time, if desirable, they might easily be exterminated by the thorough application of the kerosene emulsion to the plants. This would have the advantage of destroying both the living insects and the eggs. It is at this time, also, that the fields should be plowed up, if it proves to be necessary to resort to this treatment to arrest the multiplication of the insects. As the eggs remain during the winter upon the crowns of the plants, not hatching until spring, care should of course be taken in forming new plantations, that the young plants are obtained from fields not infested by lice, or else that these and their eggs are destroyed upon the plants before they are set. Although I have not yet had any opportunity to experiment upon this matter, I have little doubt that dipping the plants in the kerosene emulsion or in a simple mechanical mixture of kerosene and water, about three parts to one hundred, would be efficient for this purpose, and secure the new field against infection from the old.

Leaf-Hoppers?

Order Hemiptera, Family Tettigonidæ.

I find in the *Farmer and Fruit-Grower* for June 16, 1880, an item quoted from the "*Examiner and Chronicle*," which probably relates to some one of the above family, known by the name of leaf-hoppers:

"In a field which produced some fine fruit last June, as the plants were set the previous August, there appeared about the time the fruit was gathered a small insect resembling the grape-thrips, only one-third its size, or less than one-sixteenth of an inch long. They are perfectly white, and keep on the under side of the leaves that are nearest the ground. The leaves soon turn black and dry up, and the ground under the plant gets foul, as if soot had been thrown there. As fast as the dead leaves were removed, they would collect on the lowest leaves of the plant as before, and soon cause their decay. So numerous were they that they would fill your eyes and nostrils full when you were cleaning off the plants. I gave them a heavy dose of air-slacked lime, but it did not seem to destroy any of them, and the plants were nearly ruined. Before the season was over I could see some of them on the other plats on my ground, and on some of my neighbors' a mile away, and, if they have not been destroyed by the frost, they may do as much damage this season."

The False Chinch-bug. *Nysius destructor*, Riley.

Order Hemiptera, Family Lygæidæ.

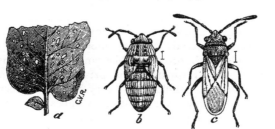

Fig. 8. FALSE CHINCH BUG (*Nysius destructor, Riley*): *a.* Leaf of potato showing injury; *b.* Pupa; *c.* Adult. After Riley.

This little bug is so similar in size, form and general appearance to the notorious chinch-bug, that it is very frequently mistaken for the latter by those not accustomed to observe insects closely.   It often occurs in great numbers in strawberry fields, especially in autumn, when purslane and other spreading weeds have been allowed to grow freely.   It is not usually guilty of any very serious injury to the plants, and yet is worthy of mention. The following item in the *Western Rural* for 1870, by a fruit grower of Centralia, Illinois, probably refers to this insect:—

"A new insect, to us here, has appeared on our strawberries for the first time the past season, damaging the crop very much.   It resembles some- . what the chinch-bug, so destructive to our wheat and corn, and judging from the peculiar odor they emit on being mashed, should think them very nearly related.   Some claim that they are of a different species altogether.   Whether this be so or not, those interested in the cultivation of the strawberry are anxiously looking forward to another season to see if they are to continue their depredations."

From the genuine chinch-bug it may be very readily distinguished by the fact that it is of a rather uniform pale and tarnished brown color, whereas the chinch-bug has a decidedly black head and thorax, with two conspicuous black spots on the front wings, separated by an hour-glass-shaped white blotch.   The genuine chinch-bug does not attack the strawberry.   Prof. Riley's description and figure of *Nysius destructor* are given herewith, somewhat condensed :—

"General color grayish brown.   Head more or less distinctly pubescent; the surface usually brown, with a distinct black, longitudinal line each side, broadening on the crown, but generally leaving the orbit of the eyes pale ; these lines sometimes more diffuse and occupying the whole surface, except a median brown spot at base of crown, and a narrow, paler spot on the clypeus; ocelli piceous; rostrum piceous, paler at base and reaching to hind coxæ; antennæ either pale yellowish brown or darker brown, the torulus and first joint darkest.   Thorax with the pronotum narrowing anteriorly, the sides slightly sinuate, irregularly and more coarsely punctate than the head, more or less pubescent, dingy yellow or brown, with a transverse black band near the anterior edge; also five more or less distinct longitudinal dark lines, the central one most persistent and leading on the posterior margin to a pale, shiny, impunctate spot; scutellum usually dark, coarsely punctate. Legs pale yellow, inclining more or less to brown; coxæ dark at base, pale at tip ; trochanters pale; front and middle femora spotted more or less confluently on the outside with brown; tibiæ ringed with brown at base. Hemelytra either colorless, transparent and prismatic, or distinctly tinged with dingy yellow; shallowly punctate and very finely pubescent.   Venter piceous, minutely and regularly covered with gray pubescence; female dingy yellow, except at base; female paler than male, and generally larger.   Average length .13 inch.   Described from numerous specimens."

The Flea Negro Bug. *Thyreccoris pulicarius*, Germar.

Order Hemiptera, Family Pentatomidæ.

Fig. 9. FLEA NEGRO BUG (*Thyreocoris pulicaria, Germar*). After Riley.

This species is sometimes quite injurious to the strawberry, puncturing the stem with its beak and sucking the sap, thus causing the blossom or fruit to wilt. Wherever it occurs, the nauseous flavor which it imparts to every berry it touches will soon make its presence manifest.

It is about .12 of an inch long, by three-fourths that width; the outline of the head and thorax together triangular; that of the abdomen semi-oval and broadly rounded behind; the scutellum is very large, nearly covering the abdomen. The color is glossy black above and beneath; the edges of the wing covers white; the antennæ, tibiæ, and tarsi brown; the whole surface finely punctured.

Chrysalis Snails. *Pupilla fallax*, Say.

Although these little mollusks are, of course, not properly included in an entomological article, it may be worth while to notice the injury occasionally done by them to the strawberry.

The only mention of this species in this connection, which I have seen, is in Vol. II. of the *American Naturalist*, page 666: A gentleman at New Harmony, Indiana, who found his strawberry plants dying rapidly, on searching for the cause, discovered these mollusks at work upon the stems and crowns of the plants, rasping off the outer coating, and sucking their juices in such a manner as to cause them to decay. He found as many as forty upon one plant, and thinks that they have killed several thousands upon the different beds. Though more abundant on the strawberry, he has found them on a variety of plants. Since attention has been called to the depredations of these minute mollusks, they have been found at work upon the strawberry plants in all the gardens examined.

INSECTS INJURIOUS TO THE CROWN.

The Strawberry Crown Miner. *Anarsia lineatella*, Zeller.

Order Lepidoptera, Family Tineidæ.

Under the above name I have to report the occurrence in Illinois of an insect which, if it has hitherto occurred in this region, has wholly escaped attention until last fall, but which has shown by its performances elsewhere

5

both the ability and the disposition to do serious mischief in the strawberry field. It was detected last September, at Normal, by the roadside, in plants which had escaped from cultivation. About seventy-five per cent. of the crowns of these plants were infested by a small, reddish caterpillar, which had eaten out the interior of the crown, inflicting an injury similar to that done by the crown-borer in Southern Illinois, and certainly equally serious. These caterpillars were about two-fifths of an inch (7 to 8 mm.) in length, reddish pink on the back, fading into dull yellow on the second and third segments. The head is yellow, with the sutures deeply indented. The

Fig. 10. STRAWBERRY CROWN MINER (*Anarsia lineatella, Zeller*): Larva, magnified nine diameters. From strawberry crown. H. Garman.

anterior part of the segment behind the head is smooth and horny, and of a pale, brownish yellow color. On each segment are a few shining reddish dots, or slightly elevated tubercles, from each of which arises a very fine, short yellowish hair. These dots are arranged in imperfect rows, a single one across the third, fourth and last segments, and a more or less perfect double row on the others. The sides and under surface are of a dull whitish color, becoming faintly reddish on the hinder segments. A row of setigerous tubercles, like those on the back, crosses each ventral segment. The feet and false legs are yellowish white, the former tipped with dark brown.

These caterpillars were quite active, creeping rapidly about when their burrows were opened, and often letting themselves drop to the ground by a thread. Mr. Wm. Saunders, of Ontario, Canada, is to be credited with the first published mention of their injuries to the strawberry, and I can not do better than to quote from his account of it, in the annual report of the Entomological Society of the Province of Ontario for the year 1872 :

" This is a very troublesome insect where it occurs plentifully, and takes a liking to the strawberry; but happily this is not often the case. We have never seen it affecting this fruit anywhere except on the grounds of Mr. Luke Bishop, of St. Thomas, Ont., who first called our attention to it about the middle of May, 1869, when he brought us a few specimens. During 1868 and 1869 they played sad havoc with his plants, destroying a large proportion of them.

" On the eighth of June we visited the grounds of Mr. Bishop, and found his strawberry beds badly infested—indeed almost destroyed—by this pest, along with a leaf-roller, to be presently described. The borer eats irregular channels through the crown, sometimes excavating large chambers, at other times merely girdling it in various directions, here and there eating its way to the surface. Whether these various chambers and channels are due to the presence of more worms than one in a single root we were unable to determine with certainty. Most of the larvæ found at this date had eaten their way to the upper part of the crown of the plant, just under the surface, and were found about the center with a hole eaten through the surface. From the fact that a large number of roots were examined, and although almost every one was more or less injured, but very few larvæ were to be found, we inferred that the probabilities were that the larvæ, when mature, usually leave the root, and undergo the change to chrysalis, either under the surface of the ground, or amongst rubbish at the surface. One chrysalis only was found, and that was in the cavity of a root. As soon as Mr. Bishop had discovered the destructive character of this pest, he, with commendable caution, refused to sell any more plants until the insect was subdued, for fear of spreading the evil. He is of opinion that the insect came to him from some part of the United States, with some plants of the Hooker strawberry, as it was in a pitch of these, so obtained, that he first noticed the insect working.

"Specimens of the larvæ gotten late in the season, wintered over, and were examined on the 12th of January following, when they did not appear so plump in body as those examined in July. They appear to spend most of the winter in a torpid state within the silken cases before mentioned. Several were found thus sheltered at this time, and one, whose original abode had been disturbed in the fall, had prepared for itself a similar casing within the fold of a strawberry leaf. In the last instance, the larva seemed quite active, moving itself briskly about whenever touched. The chrysalis of this insect is very small, and of the usual dark reddish brown color. That one which was found on the 8th of June, produced the moth on the 12th of July."

The moth bred from the chrysalis above mentioned was submitted by Mr. Saunders to Prof. Riley, and by him determined to be *Anarsia lineatella*, Zeller. Prof. Riley also says that he has bred the same moth from larvæ boring in peach twigs. The worm has likewise been found by Prof. Com-

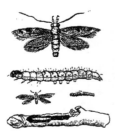

Fig. 11. PEACH TWIG BORER. Larva and perfect insect, natural size, and magnified. Also a bored twig. After Glover.

stock in the fruit of the peach in July and August. These peach and strawberry insects are, however, not certainly the same, as not only their habits but their life histories seem inconsistent as far as known. But, without assuming to pass upon this question now, I have accomplished my present purpose by giving timely warning of the appearance in the Mississippi valley of what may, unless it is closely watched, prove a serious enemy of the favorite fruit of America.

Until the life history of this species is complete, I can only say that the strawberry fields should be inspected in fall and spring for evidence of the presence of this caterpillar; and if it is found, it can be exterminated, as far as we know, only by destroying the plants. It will, of course, be most likely to occur in old and neglected fields, or, as at Normal, in runaway plants in fence corners and by roadsides. I hardly need say that these neglected plants, living from year to year without "rotation," are the best possible breeding places for strawberry pests, and may easily become centers of infection for a whole neighborhood.

Otiorhynchus sulcatus, Schoen.

Order Coleoptera, Family Otiorhynchidæ.

This is a rough, brownish black snout beetle, about four-tenths of an inch long, of whose injuries to the strawberry I only know the fact reported by Prof. Riley in his third report, that it infests the crowns of these plants; doubtless in the larval stage. This species may be distinguished from the other members of its genus by the fact that the femora are provided with a very small tooth, while the rostrum is sulcate, with a bifid carina at the tip; and the elytra are also longitudinally grooved. The thorax is sub-cylindrical, with the sides moderately rounded, widest in front of the middle, and the surface rather closely set with rounded tubercles. Each interval of the elytra bears a row of shining, rounded tubercles, rather closely placed, and small patches of short yellowish hair, irregularly distributed.

The Strawberry Crown-borer. *Tyloderma fragariæ*, Riley.

Order Coleoptera, Family Curculionidæ.

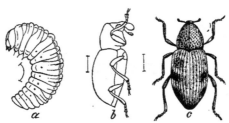

Fig. 12. STRAWBERRY CROWN-BORER (*Tyloderma fragariæ*, Riley): *a*. Larva; *b*. Outline side view; *c*. Back view of beetle. After Riley.

Although it has hitherto done but little harm north of the latitude of Central Illinois, this species certainly occurs as far northward as Minnesota, and there is no sufficient security that it may not become injurious wherever introduced.

It has been known as one of the worst enemies of the strawberry for more than fifteen years, but its life history has only been very lately completed. The first published notice of its injuries of which I am aware occurs in Prof. Riley's third report as State Entomologist of Missouri, published in 1871. "This insect," he says, "has done considerable damage to the strawberry crop in the southern portion of Illinois, especially along the line of the Illinois Central Railroad; and I have seen evidence of its work in St. Louis county, Missouri. At the meeting of the Southern Illinois Fruit-Growers'

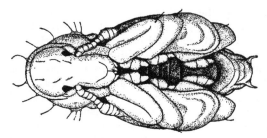

Fig. 13. Pupa of crown-borer. H. Garman.

Association. held at South Pass, in November, 1867, several complaints were made by parties from Anna and Makanda, of a white worm which worked in the roots of their strawberries, and in 1868 the greater portion of the plants of a ten-acre field at Anna, belonging to Mr. Parker Earle, was destroyed by it."

This insect, in the form in which it does its injury, is the grub or larva of one of the snout beetles, belonging, in fact, to the same family as the peach curculio. It was first described by Prof. Riley, in the report already cited, and his description of the beetle is herewith given. The larva and pupa are described from fresh material obtained last fall from strawberry fields in Southern Illinois.

"Tyloderma fragariæ.—*Imago.*—Color deep chestnut-brown, sub-polished, the elytra somewhat lighter. Head and rostrum dark, finely and densely punctate and with short, coarse, fulvous hairs, longest at tip of rostrum; antennæ rather lighter towards base, ten-jointed, the scape much thickened at apex, joint 2 longest and robust, 3 moderately long, 4–7 short, 8–10 connate and forming a stout club. Thorax dark, cylindrical, slightly swollen across the middle and uniformly covered with large thimble-like punctures, and with a few short, coarse fulvous hairs, usually arranged in three more or less distinct longitudinal lines; pectoral groove ending between front legs. Abdomen with small, remote punctures and hairs, which are denser towards apex. Legs of equal stoutness, and with shallow, dilated punctures and uniform very short hairs. Elytra more yellowish brown, dilated at the lower sides anteriorly, and with about nine deeply punctured striæ, the striæ themselves sometimes obsolete; more or less covered with coarse and short pale yellow hairs which form by their greater density three more or less conspicuous transverse bands, the first of which is at the base; between the second and third band in the middle of the elytron, is a smooth, dark brown or black spot, with a less distinct spot of the same color below the third, and a still less distinct one above the second band. Length .16 inch. Described from four specimens bred from strawberry-boring larvæ. The black spots on the elytra are quite distinct and conspicuous on two specimens, less so on one, and entirely obsolete on the other."

Larva—White, except the head, which is pale yellow. The mandibles are dark brown, black at the edges, and bifid at the tip. The labrum is narrowed from behind; broadly rounded, entire and bristly in front, and marked by a transverse suture before the middle. The antennæ, situated outside the upper angles of the mandibles, are one-jointed and excessively minute, being about .02 mm. in length. Just outside each antenna is a black ocellus-like spot in full-grown larvæ, wanting in smaller individuals. The head is smooth, except for about three transverse rows of slender hairs. The body is strongly arched, like that of a lamellicorn, each segment bearing a single row of very short sparse hairs. The first segment of the dorsum is smooth; the remaining segments are divided into three transverse lobes or folds, the first and last of which are interrupted near the end by oblique grooves. Below the spiracles is a row of large, low, triangular tubercles, and beneath these a second row, separated from the former by a longitudinal channel. The ventral segments of the abdomen have the usual form of a single transverse ridge, a triangular portion of each end of which is marked off by an oblique groove. The structure of the segments is, in fact, almost precisely that of the strawberry root-worm, to be hereafter described. The pectoral ridges of the thorax, however, bear upon each side, instead of feet, three large fleshy tubercles, each with two or three stiff hairs at the tip. This larva, when stretched out, is one-fifth of an inch in length by one-half that width.

Pupa.—The pupa is white throughout, with the exception of the eyes, which show through the pupal envelope at the base of the snout. The head and snout are bent against the breast; the second is about twice as long as wide, broadening towards the tip, where it is widely emarginate. The clubbed antennæ extend scarcely beyond the tip of the snout. The middle of the head bears two longitudinal rows of stiff bristles, four or five in each row, and three rows of similar bristles extend transversely upon the thorax, while others surround the margin. The posterior edge of each abdominal segment is likewise bristled, and a pair of incurved hooks terminates the abdomen.

The life history of the crown-borer is now practically complete, thanks to

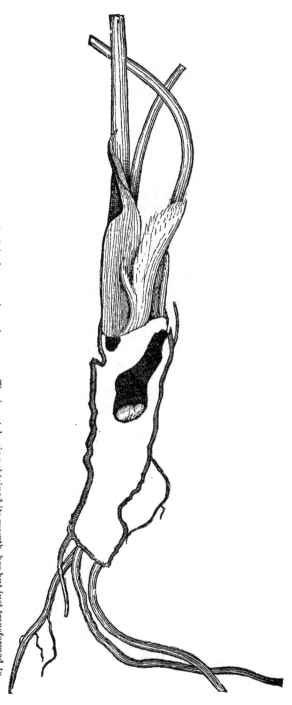

Fig. 14. STRAWBERRY PLANT, showing work of single crown-borer in crown. The insect, having obtained its growth, has but just transformed to the adult stage. H. Garman.

the early observations of Prof. Riley, and to some contributions to the subject which I have been able to make since last August.

The eggs are laid on the crown in spring (this year certainly not earlier than April), being pushed down among the bases of the leaves. The larvæ penetrate the crowns soon after hatching, and excavate the interior all summer, until they get their growth.

It is worthy of note, however, that a single larva does not wholly destroy a plant, as it matures by the time a quarter or a fourth of the substance of the crown is devoured. (See Fig. 14.) Frequently two or three or more beetles will attack a single stool, and they then leave behind them only a hollow shell, to which the roots are attached. (See Fig. 15.) Still in its subterranean cavity, the worm transforms to a pupa, and in the same safe retreat effects also the final change into the mature beetle, this last transformation occurring all the way along from August to October, during a period of about two months. These beetles all escape from the crowns in autumn, but are not known to lay any eggs until the following year. That they pass the winter as adults in the fields infested by them as larvæ, I have proven by finding a number of them there alive this year as late as November 29, and also by finding them in the fields this spring. None of these insects, in any stage, occur in the crowns later than the latter part of October, and none were to be found there in Southern Illinois as late as April 25, although the adult beetles of last year's brood were occasionally encountered on the crown among the leaf stalks and leaves. A pair of these were seen there *in copulo*, on the 12th of that month.

This is a shy and sluggish insect, rarely seen outside its burrow, *and incapable of flight*, the membranous wings being reduced to useless rudiments, as shown by several dissections which I made last fall. As it does not leave the field in which it had its origin, it feeds of course, while a mature insect, on the tissues of the plant.

The effect of this borer varies according to the variety of strawberry, and the condition of the field. Wilsons are said to be destroyed by a single attack, but some more thriftily-growing varieties will form new crowns year after year to replace those excavated by the borer, and will thus resist its injuries for some time. Our observations show that this process is considerably facilitated by hilling up the plants, or throwing dirt against the rows.

I do not know that this insect has been found injurious anywhere except in Illinois and Missouri, although we have specimens collected in Minnesota. It doubtless originated in the wild strawberries of our prairies, and its work could probably have been foreseen, and its ravages prevented, if a proper study had been made, in time, of insect injuries to the wild plant.

As these beetles spend their entire time in the field, and feed, of course, as adults, upon the foliage of the strawberry, it is not impossible that they might be poisoned in the fall. Except by this method, it is difficult to see how the insect can be destroyed without sacrificing the plants. To kill both together, the ground should be plowed late in June or early in July, when the crowns are full of half-grown larvæ.

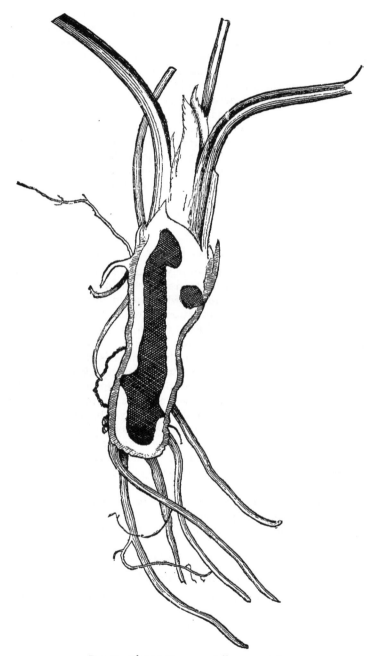

Fig. 15. Plant with crown fully excavated.

It is not in the life history of this insect, but in its structure, that we find a clue to its subjugation. The rudimentary condition of its wings, and its conse-quent lack of the power of flight, taken together with its sluggish movements, suggest the value of the isolation of new fields as a preventive measure, or at least the policy of separating them from infested areas by a considerable in-terval. Just how wide this interval should be, it is impossible to tell without experiment; but from the observed rate of progress of the pest during the year from one patch to another adjacent, it seems probable that a few rods would suffice. To obtain plants from an old field in which the crown-borer has prevailed without serious risk of transporting the insect with them, it is evidently necessary that the stools selected should be transplanted as early as possible in spring. After the beetle commences to stir, the danger will daily increase that the crowns will be infested with its eggs.

INSECTS INJURIOUS TO THE ROOT.

Ants.

Order Hymenoptera, Family Formicidæ.

Although these enterprising and nearly omnipresent insects of various species often occur in strawberry fields in noticeable numbers, I have never learned personally of any serious injury which could justly be attributed to them. For the purpose of calling attention to them, however, I quote the following note from the *Farmer and Fruit-Grower* for June 16, 1880, and cred-ited therein to the *Examiner and Chronicle:*—

"The next pest that we have to contend with here is the ants, and so de-structive are they in this locality that some growers think of turning their attention to other pursuits. They honeycomb the ground right under the plants, eat off the fine roots, and as fast as new ones are put forth they share the same fate, and the plants soon lose their vitality. If the grass and weeds are allowed to grow among the plants, they will not suffer so much, as the ants will work among the weeds as well as the strawberry plants; but to grow fine fruit the ground must be kept clear of weeds and runners."

It is proper to say, however, that the difficulty of determining exactly what as small a creature as an ant is doing under ground, makes it not impossible that the writer of this article was deceived as to the real business of these insects. Only a dissection of specimens and a study of the contents of their alimentary canals could determine this matter with certainty.

The White Grub.   *Lachnosterna,* sp.

Order Coleoptera, Family Scarabæidæ.

Doubtless I can say little or nothing concerning this species which is new to the readers of this article, so familiar is the insect to every one who has anything to do with agriculture or horticulture in any of their depart-ments. All know that the name is commonly applied to the larvæ of several species of the chestnut-brown May beetles, or June beetles or dor-bugs, as they are variously called ; that the grub lives in the ground, feeding on the roots of vegetation for about three years; that it emerges as a beetle in May or June, and that in this stage it feeds on the leaves of various fruit and ornamental trees, often defoliating them when it becomes very abundant. All fruit-growers know, too, that the strawberry is not exempt from its attacks, but that the roots of this plant are often destroyed by it to a degree to impair seriously the value of the plantation.

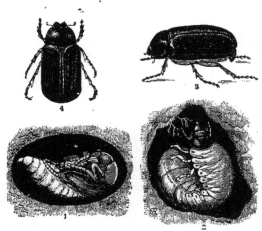

Fig. 16. MAY BEETLE, WHITE GRUB (*Lachnosterna fusca, Frohl*) : 1. Pupa in its earthen cell ; 2. Larva ; 3, 4. Beetle, side and back view.

This is perhaps the most unsatisfactory insect with which the strawberry-grower has to deal, offering the fewest opportunities for effective attack. It is true that in the beetle stage large numbers may be destroyed by the use of lights and reflectors, placed above tubs of water into which the beetles may fall, this trap being rendered more efficient if the water is covered with a thin film of kerosene ; but unless this method is generally and continuously used by an entire community, and throughout a term of years, it can have no great effect upon the crops of the individual fruit farmer. In the egg stage this species is beyond our reach, and as a larva it can be attacked only by repeated stirring of the ground, or by digging out the individual grubs as their presence is manifested by the withering of the plants. No applications to the soil have established more than a temporary reputation, and all are probably nearly ineffective. A single preventive measure may, however, be taken to advantage. In a region where the grub is prevalent, ground should not be set to strawberries until these insects have been pretty well cleared out of it by two or three years' cultivation in some hoed crop. Further than this, reliance must probably be had, as far as we now know, upon the rather crude and expensive method of the destruction of the grubs by hand.

The Goldsmith Beetle. *Cotalpa lanigera*, Linn.

Order Coleoptera, Family Scarabæidæ.

This beetle is also a white grub in the larval stage, distinguished from the preceding only by trivial characters, but widely different as an adult. The beetle is about of the same size as the common "June bug," bright yellow above, with a golden metallic luster on the head and thorax, while the un-

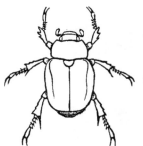

Fig. 17. GOLDSMITH BEETLE (*Cotalpa lanigera, Linn*): Adult. After Packard.

der side of the body is copper-colored and densely covered with long white hairs. The life history of this species is almost identical with that of the true white grub, and the beetle feeds, like the June beetle, upon the leaves of a variety of fruit and forest trees. It also appears at about the same time of the year, namely, in May and June. For practical purposes, consequently, these two insects may be treated as one.

The following comparative description of the larva of the goldsmith beetle is quoted from Prof. Packard:—

Fig. 18. GOLDSMITH BEETLE (*Cotalpa lanigera, Linn*): LarVa. After Packard.

"*Larva.*—The larvæ are whitish grubs, about one inch and three-quarters long and over half an inch thick, with a yellowish brown scale on the part corresponding to the thorax It so nearly resembles the young of the May beetle that it requires a close examination to tell them apart The proportions of the two are much the same; if anything, the Cotalpa is slightly shorter and thicker, and its body is covered with short stiff hair, especially at the end, while in the May beetle the hairs are much finer, sparse, and the skin is consequently shiny. They a'so differ in the head, it being fuller, more rounded in Cotalpa, the clypeus shorter and very convex, while in the May beetle it is flattened. The upper lip (labium) is in Cotalpa longer, more rounded in front and narrower at the base. and full convex on the surface, while in the young May beetle it is flat. The antennæ are larger and longer in the goldsmith beetle, the second joint a little over half as long as the third, while in the May beetle grub it is nearly three-quarters as long; the third joint is much longer than in the latter grub, while the fourth and fifth are of the same relative length as in the May beetle, but much thicker. The jaws (mandibles) are much alike in both, but not quite so acute in the Cotalpa as in the other, nor are the inner teeth so prominent. The maxilla is much longer and with stouter spines, and the palpi are longer and slende er in the grub of Cotalpa than in the other, though the joints have the same relative proportion in each; the basal joint is nearly twice as long as in the May beetle. The under lip (labium) is throughout much longer, and the palpi, though two-jointed in each, are much longer and slenderer in the grub of Cotalpa than in that of the May beetle. The feet are much larger and more hairy in the Cotalpa. Both larvæ are about an inch and a half long, and a third (.35) of an inch thick at the widest part."

This grub has been reported extremely destructive to strawberry roots in New Jersey by Dr. S. Lockwood, and doubtless occurs in strawberry fields in other parts of the country wherever the beetle is known, probably having been generally confounded with the larva of Lachnosterna. Certain fields, according to Dr. Lockwood, in Monmouth county, New Jersey, were badly thinned out by it, the plants being dead on the surface and easily pulled up, the roots having been eaten off below.

The remarks made respecting remedies for the previous species will apply equally, as far as we know, to this.

The Strawberry Root-Worm. *Paria aterrima*, Oliv., and *Paria sexnotata*, Say.

Order Coleoptera, Family Chrysomelidæ.

The strawberry root-worm, not less abundant than the crown-borer, and certainly not less destructive where it occurs, is very similar to it in general appearance, but may be easily distinguished with a hand-glass, or even with the naked eye, by the fact that it has three pairs of short jointed legs just behind the head, while the crown-borer proper is footless, the legs being replaced by three pairs of bristly warts. It devours the roots of the strawberry and also penetrates the crown, not hollowing out the interior, but boring from side to side in any direction, and often riddling it as if it had been peppered with fine shot.

This insect has been previously noticed several times in the literature of horticulture, but its habits and life history have not been fully made out. It ranges throughout Illinois, and occurs at least as far northward as Michigan, having been reported in destructive numb rs at various points in this area.

In the adult, or beetle stage, this species may be readily distinguished from the crown-borer beetle, to which it bears a slight superficial resemblance, by the fact that it has no snout or "bill" like the latter. It also flies readily, while the other is wingless.

.The genus Paria,* to which this beetle belongs, was first described by Dr. J. L. Leconte, in 1858, in volume 10 of the *Proceedings of the Philadelphia Academy*, page 86, in the following terms:—

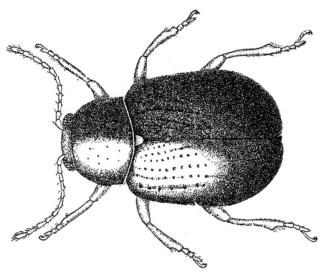

Fig. 19. STRAWBERRY ROOT WORM (*Paria aterrima, Oliv.*): Adult, magnified 16 diameters. H. Garman.

"*Beetle*—Oblong, short, yellowish, or brownish red, varying to black, usually with the ventral segments and three spots in each elytron black; head and thorax slightly punctate, the latter margined; sides slightly rounded; elytra with deep punctures arranged in rows, which are obsolete before the apex: interspaces smooth; L. .12—.16 in."

Paria sexnotata is described as follows: "Oblong, short, yellowish red, ventral segments and three spots on each elytron, black; head coarsely punctate; thorax margined, sides slightly rounded, sparsely punctate; elytra deeply punctate-striate, interstices smooth, striæ obsolete before the apex. L. .12—.16 in." Varieties occur in which the spots on the elytra mentioned above are variously enlarged in breadth until in extreme cases the whole individual is black, with pale legs.

---

*I have taken in this article that view of the life history of the root-worm which seems to me to be on the whole most probable, although it must be admitted that we have not yet absolutely demonstrated that this is not the larva of *Colaspis flavida*, as stated by Prof. Riley in his second and third reports as State Entomologist of Missouri. It is scarcely worth while in this place to give the reasons pro and con, since the question will be very soon decided by the transformation of the larvæ we are now rearing.

To whichever species the larva may prove to belong, the remedies suggested will be equally applicable.

Paria aterrima is extremely like the preceding, of the same size, and similarly variable, but the head is commonly said to be much less punctate, and the thorax less punctate and minutely wrinkled. I am inclined to doubt, however, the distinctness of the two species

Larva—The larva is about four mm. long by two mm. wide; white, excepting the head and first segment, which are pale yellowish brown. The segments are twelve in number behind the head, the first leathery and smooth,

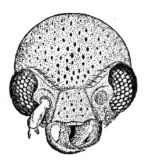

Fig. 20.   Head of same, front view.

and as long as the two following. Each of the remaining segments is marked by about three transverse dorsal folds, and bears a transverse row of ten or twelve long slender hairs. The spiracles are nine in number, the first larger than the others, and situated between the first two thoracic segments, the remainder on the abdominal segments from the first to the eighth. They are situated in a longitudinal groove, separating the ends of the dorsal segments from the first of two rows of prominent tubercles which extend along

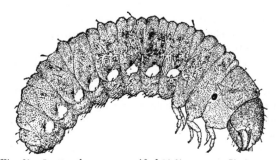

Fig. 21.   Larva of same, magnified 16 diameters.   H. Garman.

the sides, one tubercle of each row corresponding to a segment of the body. The summits of these tubercles are smooth and slightly shining, and each bears usually two or three scattered hairs. The two rows of tubercles above mentioned are separated from each other by an irregular longitudinal groove, about half the width of one row. The second, or inferior row, is separated from the ventral segments by a similar, but narrower and shallower longitudinal groove. Each ventral segment bears a single transverse ridge, somewhat thickly set with short stiff hairs, a little longer towards the ends of the ridge. The terminal portion of each ridge is cut off by an oblique groove, which extends from before backwards and inwards, thus giving to the end of the ridge the appearance of a tubercle of triangular outline, the apex of which is inward, and the length of which is about twice its depth. This row of triangular prominences is in a line with the coxæ of the legs on the thoracic segments. The skin of the entire body, with the exception of the upper surface of the first segment, is minutely roughened, as is usual with soft-bodied subterranean larvæ. The tubercles and processes described are not in any way retractile, being simply lobes or divisions of the transverse folds of the skin. The head is smooth, somewhat flattened in front, with a few slender scattered hairs, pale yellowish brown, with the exception of the usual frontal incisures, which are white, and the anterior margin of the clypeus, which is dark brown. A single ocellus occurs a short distance behind the antennæ. The labrum is narrowed forwards, and rounded in front, the posterior part of it membranous, and the surface bearing a few long hairs. The antennæ are white, three-jointed, the third joint being double,—consisting, that is to say, of two short parallel appendages, the outer of which is cylindrical and blunt at the tip, and the second tapering. The maxillæ are stout, and fringed with strong spines within, the palpi prominent and four-jointed, the three basal joints thick and short, the fourth slender. The labium is thick and quadrate, and bears on its under surface two slender, cylindrical, unarticulated palpi, each about three times as long as wide. The mandibles are dark brown, and black at the tips, where they are slightly excavated.

The legs are about as long as their corresponding segments, and are white, with the exception of the claws at the tips, which are dark brown. They are provided with a few slender white hairs, becoming shorter and more spinelike towards the tip of the leg.

Described from several alcoholic and living specimens obtained from the ground about strawberry roots, in November, 1882.

This species is at least two-brooded, the beetles of one brood commencing to appear early in spring, a few sometimes occurring upon the vines in the previous autumn. They feed during their lives as beetles upon the leaves of the strawberry, a fact already mentioned when treating of the insects injurious to the foliage. In June, according to the observations of Prof. Cook, of Michigan, the beetles disappear, and at this time larvæ of various sizes and pupæ nearly ready to emerge, may be found in the ground about the roots. The beetles of the second brood occur in Southern Illinois in August, probably commencing to emerge in July. They continue until September, but disappear before cold weather. The larvæ, which in the meantime have been working upon the plant, now form oval cell-like cavities in the earth, in which they hibernate, commencing to emerge again in April and May, as already related.

The eggs have not yet been observed, and it is not certainly known whether they are laid on the crowns or in the earth about the plants.

The fact that the adult of this species feeds upon the leaves after the fruiting season is over, gives us a ready means of controlling its ravages; as it can at that time be easily poisoned by the use of Paris green or other arsenical compounds.

If a field infested by these worms is to be plowed up, it is probably best that this should be done late in August or in September, after the beetles of the second brood have disappeared, as at this time the larvæ have not progressed far enough to make it likely that they can complete their development. The next best time is probably June, in the interval between the appearance of the first and second broods of the beetles.

As two sets of eggs are probably laid each year, one in spring and the other in midsummer, it is evidently important that young plants from fields infested by this insect should be taken up for resetting as early in spring as possible; the later transplanting is postponed, the greater is the probability that the eggs of this pest will be transferred with the plants.

GENERAL DISCUSSION.

Having now treated separately all the species of insects injurious to the strawberry which it seems worth while to notice in this paper, and having given under each species the most practicable or promising remedies for its ravages, it now remains to summarize the essential facts, especially those relating to remedies and methods of prevention. In order to present what I have to say on these topics as compactly as I can, let us imagine the worst case possible. Let us suppose that we have to deal with a large field infested by every known insect enemy of this crop, and then let us see what can be done with it. Let the roots be eaten by the root-worm and the white grubs, let the crowns be bored by both kinds of crown-borers and punctured by the crown weevil (*Otiorhynchus sulcatus*), let the foliage be devoured by grasshoppers and leaf-beetles and carpenter bees and leaf-rollers of all sorts, and by its various saw-fly and caterpillar enemies, and let the plant-louse and the false chinch-bug and the negro-bug and a variety of other hemipterous insects drain away the life-supporting sap of the plants, and then let us see what will be the effect of such measures as we may be able to devise; first, to destroy the insects without injury to the plants; or, failing in this, second, to destroy insect and plant together; and, third, to establish a new plantation, which shall be free from danger of infection by the old.

The first thing needful will evidently be a calendar of the injurious species, such as will enable us to tell in what condition every insect infesting the field will be at each season of the year. With this we may see at once what will result to each species from each measure proposed.

I have consequently prepared a table of dates and stages of the insects treated, by consulting which one may see at a glance the periods of the transformations, and the stages in which each species occurs at any time. This table is of course far from complete, since the life histories of but few species have been made out in full. In some instances it is not impossible that it may be found incorrect, although all possible pains have been taken to select the data from the best authorities, as far as they were not derived from our personal experience. Observations made in those years when the seasons are very much accelerated or retarded, will possibly, also, be found to differ somewhat from the particulars of this table, and differences due to latitude may likewise occasionally be noticed. This must therefore be taken merely as a general statement of the truth, subject to future correction, but understood with these limitations, it will be found useful for guidance in practical work.

CALENDAR OF STRAWBERRY INSECTS.

INSECTS.	WINTER.			SPRING.			SUMMER.			AUTUMN.		
	Dec	Jan	Feb	Mar.	Apr.	May.	June.	July.	Aug.	Sept.	Oct.	Nov.
Strawberry Worm	L 1	L 1	L 1	L 1	P1, I2	I2,E3,L4	P1,I2,L4	I2, E3,L4	L 1	L 1	L 1	L 1
Crown Miner	L 5	L 5	L 5	L 5	L 5	L 5	L 5, P 5	I 6	......	L 5	L 5	L 5
Leaf-roller	P 4	P 4	P 4	......	......	I 6	L 4, P 4	I6,E4,L4	L 4	L4,P4	P 4	P 4
Cutworm	L 1	L 1	L 1	L 4*	L 4*	L 4*	L 4*	L 1, P 1	I6,EL	L	L 1	L I
Angerona	......	......	......	......	......	L 4	L4, I6,E	L 4. I 6	I 6	I 6	......	......
Smeared Dagger	P 4	P 4	P 4	P 4	P 4	P 4, I 6	I6, E, L4	I 6, E	L 4	L 4, P 4	L4, P4	P 4
Stalk-Borer	I	I	I	I	I, E	E, L	L	L	L, P, I	I	I	I
Crown-Borer	I 8	I 8	I 8	I2?E5?	I2,E5?	L 5 ?	L 5	L 5, P 5	I5, L5	I5 L5 } P 5 }	I 6	I 6
Root-Worm	L 1	L 1	L I	L1,P1	L1, P1 I 4	I 4	L 1, P 1	P1, I 4	I4,L1	L 1	L 1	L 1
White Grub	L 1	L 1	L 1	L 1	L1, P1	L1,P1,I6	L 1, I 6	L 1, E 1	L 1	L I	L I	L I
Goldsmith Beetle	L 1	L I	L 1	L 1	L I	L 1, P 1	P 1, I 6	I 6, E	I 6, E	I6, L 1	L 1	L I
False Chinch-bug	I 8	I 8	I 8	I 8	......	......	......	......	......	I 6	I 6,L 6	I 6,L 6
Plant-louse	E 9	E 9	E 9	E 9	I 4	I 4	I 4	I 4	I 4	I 9	I 9	I 9,E 9

E, egg; L, larva; P, pupa; I, imago, or perfect insect; 1, in ground; 2, on vines; 3, in petiole; 4, on leaves; 5, in crown; 6, free; 7, on flowers; 8, on ground; 9, on crown; *, nocturnal.

The principal modes of fighting insects may be classified under three heads; modes of culture, barriers to progress, and topical applications. The modes of culture may be directed either to the destruction of the insect, or to the support of the plant under insect injuries, enabling it to rally against them. They are commonly the simplest, most convenient, and cheapest methods of controlling insect depredations, when they *do* really *control*, and should consequently be treated first. As a crop *must* be cultivated at any rate, if by varying slightly the times and modes of our culture we can take advantage of our insect enemies, this is of course to be preferred as a general rule to any method requiring special labor, apparatus, and material.

The favorite method of strawberry culture in Illinois is that of growing the plant in rows, between which the ground is regularly cultivated for three years, after which the whole field is plowed up and reset with young plants. Of course, where this method is followed, if proper care be taken to set the ground again with plants free from noxious insects, few injurious species can make much headway; and if to these precautions we add that of taking measures to prevent the spread of insect enemies from an old field to a new one, we should certainly have the matter pretty well under control, as far as those species are concerned which pass their whole lives during all their stages in the strawberry field.

As an example of the use of barriers to progress, we may refer to the practice of opening new fields at a distance from the old, in order to prevent the passage of the crown-borer from one to the other—a practice to which I shall again refer farther on, while topical applications may be illustrated by the use of Paris green on the vines, or even the fire cure, as applied for the leaf-roller.

Little can be done for the direct destruction of insect enemies until the fruit is picked, unless it be the hand picking of grubs and cutworms, where they are very numerous, or the use of harmless insect poisons, like pyrethrum, for some of the minor larvæ which may perhaps require attention. In June, after the crop is harvested, some things may well be done. The field may be mowed, covered lightly with straw if necessary, and fired when dry, thus destroying the leaf-rollers, and probably the plant-lice also, and perhaps the strawberry worms, and the eggs and larvæ of the Angerona and of the "smeared dagger." Some other insects would probably likewise be exposed to extermination at the same time by these means.

The summer months (June, July and August), are the proper ones for the application of poisons, which will take effect at this time upon the strawberry worm, some, at least, of the leaf-rollers, the Angerona (if it should happen to be in the field), and the beetle of the root-worm. Some other species, less common and destructive, would probably also be reached if present.

If, as is not unlikely in a badly infested field, such measures as the above are found after all ineffective, and the strawberry farmer finds himself reduced to the last desperate expedient of destroying the plants and their enemies together, he should carefully study the calendar in order to determine at what season the greatest number of the species actually infesting his fields may be exterminated by that means. At whatever season the plowing is done, if the ground is planted to another crop the following year, the crown-borer will be destroyed, since its feeble migratory power will not enable it to save itself by retreat. Still, plowing soon after berry-picking would most certainly affect the entire destruction of the brood, since at that time no adults are living, and few if any larvæ would be far enough advanced to transform in the dead crowns. Plowing in spring (March or April) would probably destroy such cutworms as occurred in the fields; would certainly exterminate the plant-lice, which at this time would be found upon the crowns, either as eggs or as newly hatched young; and would probably kill the crown miner also, which is at this time still in the crown, lacking some weeks of its full development. The strawberry worm, however, being imbedded in the ground, prepared for its final transformation, would not now be injuriously affected. Neither would the leaf-roller, nor the smeared dagger, nor the root-worm, nor the white grub, nor the larva of the goldsmith beetle, be prevented from completing their development. True, these insects on emerging would find no breeding places in the field, but this fact would simply force them to scatter to other situations, thus transferring, but, perhaps, scarcely mitigating their attack. If plowing be postponed until September or October, the crown miner would doubtless be destroyed, and many if not all of the root-worms would be prevented from reaching maturity, especially if the field were plowed early in the first month mentioned or late in August. At this time, also, the young white grubs hatched from the eggs laid in June and July would perhaps also perish, and the plant-lice, collected upon the crowns, would share the same fate.

If it be desired to exterminate the crown-borer and the root-worm without changing ground and without alternation of crops, I see but one way in which this can be done. If the vines are thoroughly treated with Paris green or some other equally effective insect poison from the middle of June to the middle of August, when the beetles of the root-worm are on the leaves, and there will probably be little trouble from these worms the following year; and if on this next year, the field be plowed up immediately after picking, it will be impossible for the crown-borer to survive until the following spring, when I believe that the ground may then be safely reset.

But I need not ring the changes on all possible methods of treating the field at each season of the year, as, with such an insect calendar as that herewith given before him, every intelligent fruit-grower, knowing the species with which he has to deal, can decide for himself what measures are best suited to meet existing conditions.

I will add only a few words on the establishment of new plantations in a way to escape infection by insects from old fields. Of course two points are to be considered; first, that of securing young plants free from noxious insects in any stage, and second, that of guarding the newly planted fields from invasion. Here, again, everything depends on the insects occurring in the field. If it is the strawberry worm or the cutworm, or the root-worm, or the white grub which is to be guarded against, the young plants may be taken up at any time before April, but every care must be taken that none of the hibernating larvæ or pupæ are transferred among the roots. If the field should happen to be infested by the crown miner, only the stools which formed in autumn would be certainly free from this pest, and the difficulty of distinguishing these from those of earlier growth, which might consequently contain the eggs of the moth, would make it imprudent to take young plants from a field where the insect was known to occur. Substantially the same remark must be made respecting the leaf-roller. Unless the field has been fired the previous year, all leaves of stools forming earlier than August will be liable to harbor the hibernating pupa, and it is prudent to get plants for a new stand elsewhere.

Concerning the crown-borer it is safe to say that the earlier in spring plants intended for setting can be removed from a field previously infested by this insect, the less will be their liability to contain the seed of future generations of this most destructive pest. If it is the strawberry plant-louse which we wish to exclude, the case is still more difficult. As already noted, this insect occurs on the plants either as egg or female, at every season of the year, and no security can be had against transferring it unless the plants be dipped, before setting, in some insecticide which will destroy both the lice and eggs. I know of nothing more likely to effect this than the kerosene emulsion, the use of which for horticultural purposes has been so widely and emphatically recommended by Prof. Riley.

For the protection of the new fields from invasion, I know of no resource but isolation. Either the entire plantation should be renewed at once, with proper precautions to destroy the insects existing, so that no old fields will remain to infect the new, or else fields of different ages should be separated from each other by areas devoted to other crops. If one grows raspberries and strawberries both, for example, and wishes so to manage his strawberries that he shall have about equal areas in bearing every year, the two crops might be arranged in alternating belts. If these belts were only a few rods wide, the spread of the crown-borer from patch to patch would probably be prevented, and the other insects can be managed by other methods.

To summarize in a word what may be done, according to the best of our present knowledge, in the case of our hypothetical field infested by all known strawberry insects, I would say that we shall have to depend chiefly on insect poisons in June and July, and on burning in June, to exterminate all insects but the crown-borers, and that to rid the plants of these, we must plow up the field in the following June, resetting with young plants as early as possible in the spring. If the field is not exposed to immediate infection from others near by, we have fair reason to believe that these measures would be found efficient against the insects affecting the strawberry.

President Earle, of Illinois—It seems to me, gentlemen, that I have never heard a paper read which possessed more value for us than the one we have just listened to. But before we enter upon the discussion of it we will hear a paper from Mr. A. D. Webb, of Kentucky. Mr. Webb is the originator of several noted varieties of the strawberry, among others, of the Longfellow and the Warren. Perhaps no gentleman in this country is better qualified from a long and intelligent experience to tell us what are the best varieties for home use, and which are best for market. I invite your attention to Mr. Webb's paper.

THE BEST STRAWBERRIES FOR HOME USE AND FOR MARKET.

BY A. D. WEBB, OF KENTUCKY.

Ever since I attached myself to a horticultural society I have endeavored to make myself useful by complying, to the best of my ability, with every request made of me in the interest of horticulture. Permit me to say I could but feel highly complimented on receipt of a request to have my name appear in the programme of business as one of the contributors to this meeting.

Permit me to say further, that my presence on this occasion is coupled with a double pleasure, being the first meeting of this Society it has been my privilege to attend, also my first visit to the Crescent City. Consequently I expect to be abundantly rewarded for the sacrifice of a few days' time and a few dollars, in what I may see of interest and what I may learn and profit by in the future.

The subject I am billed for is, "The Best Strawberries for Home Use and for Market," a very difficult one to handle satisfactorily to any one but myself. There being such a variety of soils and localities to accommodate, so many tastes to please, that an effort on my part to name a half dozen varieties as the best for family use, expecting my list to meet with general approval, would be an effort to accomplish an impossibility. I doubt if two parties representing the same locality would be a unit on a similar list. Therefore, I merely propose to exercise my own judgment in my selection, based upon practical experience and close observation, as to the best for my locality, as well as others where they have or will prove equally successful.

Allow me to further preface by saying, that I have been engaged in growing strawberries, both for home use and for market, for the last twenty-five years (more, however, in the capacity of an amateur than as a large commercial grower), during which time it has been my pleasure, and I might add misfortune, financially, to fruit on my own grounds not less than one hundred and fifty varieties, a very large per cent. of my investments ranging in price from two to five dollars per dozen plants—went back on their good record, or rather what was claimed for them, and proved not worth a nickel. I merely refer to this to show that I have had quite a long list from which to skim the cream.

I now name the following varieties as the best for family use, viz.: Cumberland Triumph, Mt. Vernon, Warren, Longfellow, Monarch, Chas. Downing, and last, though not least, Sharpless.

I do not propose them to stand in the order named, as, in a few instances,

I have not been expert enough to discriminate so as to give one preference over another.

These named varieties have been carefully selected from the many I have fruited, after a thorough test (except Mt. Vernon*), through a series of years embracing favorable as well as very unfavorable seasons, with an eye especially to hardiness and vigor of plant and reliable bearing; with a single exception, (Sharpless), fruit of the largest size and of superior quality forming a succession from early to late. While I do not claim perfection in any one of these, I doubt if an equal number could be selected from our present long list that would rival these in number of desirable merits, or with as few faults.

The Sharpless is all that could be desired in plant and fruit when one can get it, but it has not proved wholly reliable with me, being easily touched by frost and liable to rot of a wet season. Yet, I would recommend it in every family collection and trust to Providence for protection against frost and rot.

THE BEST STRAWBERRIES FOR MARKET.

This heading necessarily calls for two lists: one for a near market and one for distant markets.

We often see varieties recommended for home use or a near market. What are we to understand by the term near market? My idea is, this should be governed by circumstances. Where shipping facilities are favorable, a near market may be at one's door, or two hundred and fifty miles distant, or any distance our fast trains can make, receiving the fruit late in the afternoon of the day it is picked and putting it on an early market next morning. For this purpose, I can only improve on my family list by adding Crescent.

My principal market is Cincinnati, distant about two hundred and fifty miles, to which I have shipped more or less of all these named varieties, except Mt. Vernon; even when fairly ripe had them to arrive in good condition and bring the top of the market.

THE BEST STRAWBERRIES FOR DISTANT MARKETS.

The list under this head is very short, and not very sweet, namely, Wilson and Glendale. Since the introduction of the Wilson it has outranked all others as a shipper, has proved nearer a success everywhere than perhaps any other, has been, and doubtless is yet, more extensively grown for commercial purposes than any other. "Why so?" Simply on account of its coloring two or three days before it is ripe. Picked as soon as colored, which it generally is for long shipments, it will carry hundreds of miles and be in good condition for a few hundred more. This premature coloring and its

---

*The Mt. Vernon is of recent introduction—not so thoroughly tested as the others. From its good record, so far, I feel warranted in giving it a place in my list.

general success are the only two great merits I can see to the credit of the Wilson.

Glendale, of more recent introduction, has justly acquired some reputation as a good shipper; seems to succeed wherever tested; a late variety, of large size, and shows well in patch and on the fruit stands, when free from dirt. When dirty it is a hard-looking berry. Will bear washing almost equal to Irish potatoes. It is pronounced by some of very inferior quality. I say ditto to the Wilson. When thoroughly ripe I regard the Wilson of fair quality; the Glendale in same condition is not as bad as some would have us believe. I regard these two as the best adapted to long shipments of any that have proved generally successful. Am sorry we have no better with which to supply our distant markets. I can but feel great sympathy for the consumers of any half-ripe fruit, especially such as Wilson and Glendale, unless they are the happy owners of a sugar plantation and a registered Jersey cow. Except for this class, they are only desirable for hotels and boarding houses, where they are served in limited quantities. A second plate is never called for.

Quite a number of new varieties are now under test, for which every desirable merit in the strawberry is claimed, viz: Jas Vick, Bidwell, Big Bob, Manchester, Finch's Prolific, Phelps' Seedling, Piper's Seedling, and Sucker State. From this list we may possibly get one or more varieties worthy to be added to our shipping list. So far as I have tested them, my present judgment is that the first four named will prove of no real value in my locality, while they may be all that is claimed for them in others. I have some faith in the future success of the other four. Further time, however, is necessary to fully determine this, and might also change my opinion as to the others.

I refer to these new varieties for the purpose of comparing notes with others who may have, like myself, given them a partial test.

DISCUSSION ON STRAWBERRY GROWING.

Mr. Samuels, of Kentucky—I don't feel competent to lead this discussion; I have not had experience enough. But I asked several questions, about which there seems to be a difference of opinion. One was in regard to fall cultivation. The strawberry makes new roots in the fall; hence, fall cultivation should produce a better profit than in the spring. I only want to have the point discussed.

Mr. Galusha, of Illinois—I remarked this afternoon that I would like to say a few words on the cultivation of the strawberry, and particularly in connection with what was said in regard to manuring. No one in the North, I think, would object to manuring the ground for strawberries. In a paper read here objection was made because, in the South, on account of the greater heat of the sun, manure causes the plants to burn. It seems to me that would depend on the character of the manure. I think the very fact of supplying that in which the soil is deficient, enables the plant to resist any deleterious influence of the sun. I think the application of ashes to a certain extent is calculated to encourage plant growth and also fruitage. I can not see the philosophy of not applying to the soil elements in which it is deficient, or which the needs of the plant may require. With regard to watering, that point has been before you, and some experience given. I have had some experience in watering. I can not irrigate, owing to there not being sufficient inclination to my grounds. I, consequently, have elevated tanks, and a wind engine to pump the water from a very large well, which no pump can exhaust. I laid out my ground in tracts of one hundred feet broad, and the rows are planted at right angles; then, with a portable tank of about two barrels, and one hundred feet of hose, I water my beds. This is a more economical way, to me, than using pipes, as I first intended. My modes of cultivation are very similar to those which have been given. Thirty-five years ago it was the doctrine that, to stimulate strawberries, would make them run to vine, and you would not get the fruit. It has been a stumbling block to a great many strawberry growers. I believe I would have been worth twice as much as I am now if I had not followed this theory.

Mr. Smith, of Wisconsin—Do you believe the Crescent Seedling can be damaged by over manuring?

Mr. Galusha—I question if it can. My practice has been a little different from our President, in one regard. He spoke of applying stable manure; I have done that with Crescents every fall, and they have not deteriorated a particle for the last five years.

Prest. Earle—You don't have crown borers?

Mr. Galusha—No, sir; the President and I are three hundred and forty miles apart. I apply, however, such manures as have no seeds in them—from livery stables where only prairie hay is used. White clover and blue grass can not be eradicated. These two are the worst weeds we have to contend with. Strawberries must not be put upon ground that has had white clover in it. I once took a piece of ground that I knew had been clean for ten years. I plowed it deeply. The next year what was my surprise to find it perfectly stocked with clover. I went to the owner and asked a solution. He said, "Thirteen years ago that land was in clover. I got the clover plowed under so as to get rid of the seed, just as deep as a team could plow it." You must know the history of your soil.

Dr. McKay, of Mississippi—As I have started this discussion, it will be well for me to make a statement. I have tried fertilizing with almost everything within reach. When I commenced strawberry culture in this latitude, I commenced with the idea that high fertilizing was the proper mode to be pursued, and would give the best and most satisfactory results. I did it with this idea, it having been impressed upon me in Kentucky. There, fertilizing was a success. I therefore commenced in this State with high manuring. While I was pursuing this system, I had other plants growing upon very thin lands. I did not look upon these as being very profitable. When the time came for the fruit, however, I found that my best fruit was upon the thin land. It was better in color and had more solidity than that grown on the richer lands. I had three patches; one was very heavy, another was good sand land with some fertilizing, the other was very poor—land that would not produce, under good cultivation, over fifteen bushels of corn per acre. When I came to gather fruit from the highly cultivated patches I sometimes had to pay the shipping expenses from the fruit grown on the thinner land.

Mr. Smith—What was the condition of your manure when put upon that land?

Dr. McKay—It was such as we get from our cows pens. It was what we would call manure deprived of its fermenting properties. Then we used bone dust. We could see no benefit to the plants or increase of the fruit. Afterwards I used cotton seed, some sixty bushels, plowing in with a deep subsoiler. This increased the yield, but I could see no difference in the price obtained for the berries. I afterwards tested cotton seed ashes, then cotton seed meal. This increased the size of the plants but did not increase the yield nor the quality of fruit, and, I think, to a certain extent, damaged the keeping qualities. The fruit has not the solidity or permanent color that we find when grown on land without fertilizers. I will state that I shipped 11,500 quarts one season from three acres and a half of just such land as I have described (which would not produce over twenty bushels of corn to the acre) besides all consumed at home and given away. I have tried various other manures, but always with the same result, increased growth of the plant, but no advantage to the fruit. We are compelled, in spite of the teachings, to accept the facts. The relative cost of production and selling price shows a greater profit when we don't use fertilizers. Two years ago we had a peculiar experience. We have great variety in our Southern lands—red clay, loam with clay beneath, gravelly land, rich land making forty or fifty bushels of corn per acre, and other grades. Two years ago we had a most disastrous drouth; so much so that the berries on all kinds of rich land were almost totally ruined; so much so that we fell back on our poor red land, and by the application of a little fertilizer that is taken up mainly in the production of the fruit proper, we succeeded in making a good crop; but on the rich land we made no crop.

Mr. Galusha, of Illinois—Mr. President, I do not question the facts. I merely suggested that perhaps he didn't use the right kind of manure for the soil. Stable manure, well rotted, as Mr. Smith uses it, is one of the best fertilizers. The only objection is that it encourages an excessive plant growth the first season. I recommend bone dust. As you all know, the strawberry plant is a gross feeder. It will feed on anything in its reach. I do believe if the gentleman would try bone dust under favorable conditions he would find it would well repay him.

Prof. Colmant, of Mississippi—Why is it that the Monarch of the West has not been mentioned; it is one of our best varieties?

Mr. Galusha—Monarch of the West originated about fourteen miles from me. It is a magnificent berry. It has the drawback of not ripening well at the tip end, and also of not producing enough to the acre. I couldn't get enough out of it and I plowed it up five years ago.

Prof. Colmant—Monarch of the West loses the green tip by cultivation. Besides it is the earliest berry in the market.

Mr. Cook—I endorse everything the gentleman has said in regard to the Monarch. In southern Kentucky it is certainly one of the best of our varieties. I wish to call the attention of the gentlemen to the form of fertilizers to be used. Last year, from a suggestion I saw in an Eastern paper, I procured some bone dust, the best I could find in the Louisville market. It cost me some $34.00 per ton. Acting upon the suggestion I went to a neighboring steam mill that burned wood and bought fifty bushels of ashes at five cents per bushel. That made $36.50 for about two tons of fertilizer. I mixed the bone dust and wood ashes, half and half. As I mixed I applied water. After this I put it in barrels. In a few days fermentation set in; the heat lasting two or three weeks, and then it cooled off. Then it was ready for use, and I used some of it on some plants, mixing it thoroughly with the soil. I set the plants out four feet each way. I tell you, Mr. President, you never saw fruit superior to that raised under these circumstances. Our soil is heavy, dark clay, very well adapted to the strawberry. The people of the country said that forty or fifty years ago it was one vast field of wild strawberries. It is the natural home of the strawberry. The Downer, Longfellow and Warren originated in our neighborhood. There are wild strawberries around our fences now. The fertilizer I have described is, in my judgment, superior to the commercial fertilizers that we pay for at the rate of $50 or $60 a ton, and mine didn't cost me $20 a ton. If we can mix our fertilizers at such small prices let us keep our money in our pockets and not squander it by buying these high-priced fertilizers, many of which produce very questionable results.

Mr. T. T. Lyon, of Michigan—In our State we have entirely abandoned the Monarch of the West. There is another portion of the subject I would like to hear discussed. We have the Wilson all over our country. Out of the Wilson and some other varieties growers can just make a livlihood, and the fruit they send to market is in the way of other fruit. It seems to me that more can be made by cultivation of strawberries in very narrow rows than can be made by any system of broadcast culture, which always encourages slovenliness. With the great majority of growers it is almost impossible to keep the land in good condition, clear of weeds, and get crops such as we should have. Now, if you keep your plants six inches apart, or in hills, cutting off the runners, you can at least succeed in educating your market so that it will pay four prices for what you produce in that way. It seems to me that this is well worth our consideration. It can be done. There are plenty of men in most of our markets who are willing to pay for a good article. I believe in educating the markets, but I would not educate them at our own expense; I believe in making money while we educate the public taste. People like quality when they find it, and the better class of our buyers will soon learn that one berry is superior to another.

Mr. E. T. Hollister, of St. Louis—I would like to say a few words in favor of an old friend of mine who has been very much abused to-night. Its name is Wilson's Albany strawberry. Now, if I am not mistaken, we all want to raise a berry that customers will come up and pay for; out of which they can get the greatest profit from the smallest investment. I have handled a great variety of berries, and almost invariably, when people come into my store, they first ask for the Wilson. You may say to them, "I have the Downer and many others better than the Wilson," but they will tell you, "The Wilson is good enough for me." There is a berry called the Crystal City which comes in early and brings a good price. It is very successful in Arkansas. I am sorry to hear the Wilson so much abused. The Wilson sells the best, and that is what we raise berries for. The best results in strawberry culture have been realized with the bone dust and blood fertilizers.

Mr. Galusha, of Illinois—I agree entirely with the last speaker. As I said in my article, for shipping any distance the Wilson is a berry that will sell and bring money. The Wilson strawberry is like the Ben Davis apple, in this respect; but I want to sell my Wilsons and buy strawberries good to eat.

Mr. Hollister—I have shipped Wilsons one hundred and fifty miles and put them along side of Crescents, and the Wilsons would be sold first.

Mr. Goodman, of Missouri—I have shipped berries from Kansas City to Denver, a distance of six hundred miles, and they would arrive in good order.

Mr. Williams, of Indiana, asked for the President's experience in shipping.

Prest. Earle—I will call on Mr. A. C. Kendel, of Cleveland, Ohio, to tell the story for me. He has handled my berries for a dozen years, many of them soft kinds, and he knows how they ship.

Mr. Kendel, of Cleveland, Ohio—My experience is, that people like the best quality of berry, and those that keep best, and are willing to pay the highest price for them. When the Wilson is larger, they take the Wilson ; when others are larger, they take them. It all depends upon the variety, and the care with which the fruit is shipped. It is the shipper's fault, in a great many instances, when the berries don't sell. I agree with Mr. Hale, the gentleman from Connecticut, as to making our own fertilizers. If every gentleman here took what was needful for his soil, and mixed it in the proper proportions, he would get his manure for half price. I believe in putting the fertilizers down among the roots, and not on top.

Mr. Galusha, of Illinois—We want to know whether other varieties than the Wilson have been shipped long distances and with what success.

Mr. Kendel—We have had berries shipped from Southern Illinois to us at Cleveland, about seven hundred and fifty miles. The Sharpless and the Wilson keep equally well. I think it is not so much the distance as the time, and whether the berry is kept warm or cold during the passage. Mr. Galusha said we should develop the public taste ; we should grow the most profitable varieties, and to practice those modes of shipment which would give to consumers these palatable varieties. This is what our President has done. He has shipped those very varieties which are called soft a distance of seven hundred and fifty miles, and they arrive in good order. We ought to put better berries on the tables of our consumers. This is what we should do as cultivators of the public taste and as suppliers of the public tables.

Mr. Smith, of Wisconsin—My experience in shipping berries, with the exception of the Wilson, is this : Wherever they have been thirty-six hours on the road, I have received a letter saying, Don't send me any more. Crescent don't ship well.

Mr. O. C. Gibbs, of the *Chicago Tribune*—It seems to me that this discussion can be narrowed down to one or two points. One is that with a cooling house such as our worthy President has, the berries can be thoroughly cooled and then shipped in refrigerating cars almost any distance and arrive at the market in a good condition. But few of the growers have their cooling arrangements; so that if we were dependent upon fruit shipped under such conditions, we should not get a great deal of it. The practical question with us in the city is to get fruit, and if we are to have strawberries at all we are to have those which will come to us under ordinary conditions, and the Wilson is the berry that fulfills these conditions. The Wilson is the berry that the laboring man will eat. I never had my heart more touched than on one occasion in Chicago. I found a very respectable woman locked up in jail. I asked her how she came there. She said for stealing a basket of peaches. Said I, " did you steal them?" " Yes," she says, " I did." "What did you steal them for?" " Well," she said, " I wanted them so bad and hadn't the money to pay for them." I am glad the Wilson strawberry is a berry that can be grown cheap enough for poor people to eat.

Mr. Lyon, of Michigan—I have a word for these gentlemen who can't sell any thing but Wilsons. I recollect a few years ago when a man could hardly sell a single berry. But people have got acquainted with them and now they sell with any other berry in the market. I am not at all disposed to question the merits of the Wilson as a shipping berry, and if we can only induce our growers to put it in the market ripe, the objection will be removed.

Pending a motion to adjourn—

President Earle said: It is understood, I believe, that to-morrow morning we proceed immediately to elect officers for this Society for the coming year. Will you take any measures to-night preparatory to this election in the morning?

Mr. Smith, of Wisconsin—I move that a committee of one from each State represented here be appointed to suggest names for our various officers. Motion carried.

The President—Before putting the motion to adjourn, allow me to express my own great pleasure that we have had such a very profitable and interesting meeting as we have had this evening. We are certainly progressing finely. We are having a very rich session to-day, and I hope it will be even better to-morrow and Saturday.

Adjourned to meet at 9 o'clock to-morrow morning.

Third Day—Friday.

FORENOON SESSION, February 23.

At half past nine o'clock A. M. the Society was called to order by President Earle.

Pending the report of the Committee on Nominations, which, according to programme, was the first thing in order, President Earle read the following letters, saying: I will embrace this opportunity of reading to the Society certain letters from distinguished friends of the Society and from members who found it impossible to be present. The first letters I will read you are from the Hon. Marshall P. Wilder, of Boston, President of the American Pomological Society. The name of our venerable friend is one blessed and reverenced by all horticulturists the world over, and should never be mentioned in a horticultural assembly without applause. (Very hearty applause.)

DORCHESTER, MASS., December 11, 1882.

My Valued Friend:

Thanks for your circulars and kind letter. How I wish I could go with you to New Orleans; but at my time of life it would be too dangerous. I must husband my strength so as to make it hold out as long as possible. You will have a grand time, and do your country great good yet. Let your Society and the old American Pomological Society go along arm-in-arm together in the good cause, and posterity will rise up and bless the men who founded them and are carrying them on for the public good.

Please have a large delegation appointed to the American Pomological Society, at Philadelphia, September 12, 13, 14, 1883.

As ever, yours,　MARSHALL P. WILDER.

DORCHESTER, MASS., January 30, 1883.

My Good Friend:

I still live and keep up my official relations, but dare not go from home at this season of the year. O, how I wish I could be with you and our friends at New

Orleans, and rejoice with you in the wonderful progress of American Pomology in our own day. It is a glorious cause. Let it go on prospering and to prosper, and generations yet unborn shall rise up and bless the memory of those like yourself and others of our pioneers who are, one and all, doing so much for its advancement. Yours, as ever, MARSHALL P. WILDER.

Now, my friends, I will give you a letter from one of the founders of this Society, who was unable to leave his beautiful home on the bluffs of the Ohio to come to this meeting, on account of the deluge which filled the Ohio valley. As our first letter was signed by the greatest name in America or the world's pomology, so this one bears the most honored signature in our Western horticulture, and in the great movement for American forestry—that of Dr. Warder, of Ohio.

NORTH BEND, OHIO, February 18, 1883.

Parker Earle, Esq., Mr. President and Dear Friends:

As apprehended, so has it eventuated. The pleasure of joining you and your confreres at New Orleans this week must be one of the unrealized anticipations, after having been so long looked forward to as a charming release from the grip of winter. The floods, almost Noachian, have confined us to our hill-tops, whence, as from Ararat, we could survey the waste of waters, as two mighty seas on either haud, Ohio and Miami, dash their angry waves toward our eminence and cut off communication with the world. For eight days our mails have been suspended, the railway trains are abandoned, and I know not when this may reach you, if ever, or its predecessor, written on receipt of your kind card of last week; nor am I informed as to the others, who were to have started to-morrow, probably via Cincinnati Southern Railway, having heard nothing, but apprehend the party will be small, so great has been the derangement of travel. For an oldish person, no longer strong, the journey at this season would have been hazardous, but be pleased, for yourself and your worthy associates, to accept the best wishes for your success.

With sincere regrets on account of his absence,

From your and their earnest friend,

JNO. A. WARDER.

Let him hear soon of your success.

Mr. Earle continued: And here I have a letter from an old friend—Robert Manning, of Boston—whose handwriting, in the absence of his genial face, I am glad to see. Mr. Manning is, as you know, one of the most learned pomologists in this country. He was many years Secretary of the American Pomological Society, and is now Secretary of the Massachusetts Horticultural Society, which is, I believe, the model horticultural society of the continent. Here is Mr. Manning's letter:

BOSTON, December 18, 1882.

My Dear Sir:

Your favor of the 7th came to hand a week ago, and was communicated to the Society at the meeting last Saturday. Mr. Wilder spoke of the meeting to which you kindly invite the members of the Society, as giving unusual promise of a good time, both horticulturally and socially, and it was voted that the Secretary return the thanks of the Society for the invitation.

So much for the official part; but I can not omit to thank you for your very kind invitation to myself particularly. No doubt you are right in thinking it would prove a pleasant vacation, and that a vacation would not hurt me. I do wish I could go with you and attend your meeting; but here I am, in the busiest part of the year—from the 1st of December to the 1st of April is when the heaviest pressure of work comes on me, and I do not see how I can possibly get away. * * *

Yours truly,

ROBERT MANNING,

Sec. Mass. Hort. Soc.

And here I have a letter from a most indefatigable horticultural worker—Prof. J. L. Budd, of the Iowa Agricultural College. Prof. Budd has done more than any other man to introduce such European fruits as seem likely to endure the extreme vicissitudes of your northwestern climate. The Professor has but just returned from a long journey through Eastern Europe and Western Asia in search of valuable new fruits for the West.

AMES, Iowa, December 1, 1882.

My Dear Sir:

Your kind letter at hand. * * * I would like to talk about Russian fruits, even so far South as New Orleans, as my observation in the hottest portions of Europe and the United States convince me that the thick foliage apples and pears of Eastern Russia and Central Asia bear summer heat better than the South of Europe fruits. But I will have to defer this to a more convenient season, for which I am sorry.   Yours with respect,

J. L. BUDD.

And here I have a note from one of the busiest men in the country, who, both through his newspaper and his experimental farm and gardens, is doing so much for rural interests—Mr. Carman, editor of the *Rural New Yorker.*

NEW YORK, December 10, 1882.

My Respected Sir:

Nothing would delight me more. How I wish I could be with you! We shall have a representative, I think, and give a good report. All should feel indebted to you for your enterprise.   With heartiest, best wishes,

E. S. CARMAN.

I have the following from the earnest pomologist and genial gentleman, J. S. Woodward, of Lockport, N. Y., who seems to have temporarily left the management of the Niagara grape interest for the even more golden management of the " Niagara Mining Company," away off in the wilds of New Mexico. But he carries with him to the mountains the spirit which made him so successful a horticulturist, and we are glad to hear from him:

PYRAMID, GRANT CO., NEW MEXICO, December 18, 1882.

My Dear Sir:

Your favor of the 5th inst., containing programme of the Mississippi Valley Horticultural excursion and meeting, and your very kind letter of same date, has been forwarded to me. I had fully intended to have attended your meeting, and to have gone in company with the very distinguished and pleasant gentlemen who will leave Chicago Feb. 19, but I have got switched off into this far-away country, and hardly expect to be able to do so now. While I am for the present isolated here, I have lost none of my interest in fruit-growing. I may possibly have business that will take me over part of the way to New Orleans, and if so I shall most gladly avail myself of the opportunity to meet with the fruit-growers of the West and South. One of the greatest regrets I had in leaving the management of the Niagara Grape Company, and coming here, was the loss of the great opportunity I had to meet with these generous, open hearted fruit-growers, East, West, North and South.

Very Respectfully Yours,

J. S. WOODWARD.

I have here a letter from one of those horticultural pioneers who have had to re-create horticulture as a new art, under new and very extreme conditions, on the great plains and among the mountains of the far West. One of the most energetic of these men is our Vice President for Colorado, Mr. D. S. Grimes, of Denver. He writes me as follows:

DENVER, COL., February 11, 1883.

My Dear Sir:

On account of the entire management of our nurseries, both here and four hundred miles west of here, falling on me, I regret to say that it is impossible for me to attend the meeting in New Orleans.

It hurts me all over to be thus deprived of this great treat, and I submit with the greatest reluctance. But as I can not go, I will give you this brief report of our horticultural condition :

The State of Colorado is making rapid progress in all branches of horticulture. Our altitude, climatic influences, and manner of cultivation, all differ widely from those of the Eastern States. On account of these peculiar features our experience may be of interest to our Eastern brethren. Fruit growing is an industry very profitable to those engaged in it. The people of Colorado are great fruit eaters.

Around Denver there are over one thousand acres in market gardens, but they fall far short of supplying the markets. Last summer as many as one hundred car loads of fruit were received in Denver in a week from abroad. The alkali taken into the system in the water we drink requires the acid of fruits to counteract its effect; hence, we will have fruit, let it cost what it may.

When I read the list of papers booked for your meeting, the temptation to attend is almost greater than I can bear, but the press of business says no, and I must submit this time, but you may look for me next time. Wishing you every success,

I remain truly yours,

D. S. GRIMES.

My friends, my pile of letters is a pretty large one, and very interesting; and they come from representative horticulturists from all sections of the country, and all of them are full of the most cordial sympathy for our Society and our meeting. I must read you two or three more.

Here is one from that able horticultural writer and experimenter, Mr. D. Redmond, editor of the *Florida Dispatch:*

JACKSONVILLE, FLA., November 29, 1882.

My Dear Sir:

I regret that severe illness has prevented me from replying earlier to your kind favor. If it were at all possible for me to do so, it would give me very great pleasure to prepare the paper you suggest, and also to attend the meeting in New Orleans in February; but my duties and engagements here are so pressing that I am very regretfully obliged to forego the gratification which a visit to old scenes and a reunion with old friends could not fail to afford me. If I live until your next annual meeting, I shall certainly try to be with you.

Thanking you very cordially for the kind and courteous manner in which your invitation was tendered, and trusting that your coming meeting may be a grand and influential one—a success in every way, I remain,   Most truly yours,

D. REDMOND.

Mr. Earle continued: Knowing full well that a meeting, where small fruit culture was to receive great attention, could not be a complete success without some voice from New Jersey, the greatest small fruit State in the whole world, I endeavored to secure two papers from distinguished gentlemen in that State concerning that interest. I succeeded so far as to get a promise of attendance and a paper from Mr. Jno. T. Lovett, which severe illness in his family has prevented him from keeping*; and I have also this kindly letter

*Since writing this we have been favored by a valuable paper by Mr. Lovett, which may be found in the body of this report. [SEC'Y.]

from Mr. P. T. Quinn, saying why he could not come. As you know, no name stands higher than Mr. Quinn's, in all matters horticultural, all along the entire Atlantic coast:

NEWARK, N. J., November 20, 1882.

My Dear Mr. Earle:

I am glad to hear by your letter of the 17th inst. of your prospects for a first-class meeting of fruit men at New Orleans in February. I don't know of a better place to hold a winter meeting; and nothing would afford me more pleasure than to join you at Chicago, on the 19th of February, and take an active part in the proceedings. But I am afraid I can not spare the time. My duties as Secretary of the State Agricultural Society, and of the State Board, and as Controller of Newark, together with my farm business, leave me little spare time at present. I can not now promise to write you the paper on the "Growth and Importance of Small Fruit Culture," but should I find time between now and then will do so with pleasure.

The last two years have been bad ones for small fruits with us in New Jersey. We were almost burned to a crisp in 1881; and for six weeks last summer not a drop of rain fell on my farms, with a scorching sun the whole time. I had belief that lightning would not strike in the same spot twice, but alas! it did; and you know what that means in receipts.

With very kind regards, I am cordially yours, P. T. QUINN.

All Western men will recognize in the name of Geo. W. Minier, of Illinois, a venerable horticulturist who has had no superior for zeal and ability in promoting all good works for the benefit of mankind. Until within a few days he expected to be with us here, and it is a matter of regret to all of us that he at the last could not come.

MINIER, Illinois, February 14, 1883.

My Dear Sir:

Your circular and generous invitation is duly received. I have been from home this entire month, and have been constantly promising myself the great pleasure of meeting that host of good men, and *thinking* men, which will assemble at New Orleans on the 21st instant. But it is possible I may not meet with you. A man of my age—my next birthday will be my seventieth—must not promise too firmly. Should any contingency debar me, you will have my most cordial good wishes.

Most respectfully yours,

GEO. W. MINIER.

Our venerable friend and fellow member, Mr. Isador Bush, of Missouri, the enthusiastic advocate of all that relates to the interests of American grape culture, writes me as follows:

ST. LOUIS, February 17, 1883.

My Dear Sir:

You know how cordially I desire, and firmly contemplated, going with you to New Orleans. But sickness in my family, and the bad condition of the railroads, made my wife and myself, though very reluctantly, give up the long-anticipated trip. Our Mississippi Valley Horticultural Society is struggling under adverse circumstances; the floods will of necessity hinder many members from coming, and I had almost hoped that I might get to-day yet a letter from you that the meeting had been postponed! As this has not come, I can only wish you and the meeting best success, and you all an enjoyable trip and safe return. Again assuring you of my sincere regrets, I am   Truly yours,

ISIDOR BUSH.

I will close the reading of this list of eloquent letters with a note from the distinguished gentleman who presides over the Department of Agriculture at Washington:

WASHINGTON, D. C., December 17, 1882.

My Dear Sir:

My engagements are such in the month of February, in the States of Massachusetts and Ohio, that it will be impossible for me to attend the meeting of the Mississippi Valley Horticultural Society, to be held at New Orleans. It would give me great pleasure to accept your invitation and to listen to discussions upon the horticultural wealth of one of the most important agricultural districts of this or any other country.   Very respectfully,

GEO. B. LORING,
Commissioner.

After the reading of the letters, Dr. Samuel Hape, of Georgia, expressing a regret at his State being outside of the geographical limits of the Society, moved that a committee be appointed to consider the propriety of so amending the name of the Society that it might become national in its extent.

Mr. T. T. Lyon, of Michigan, seconded the motion, and said that he hoped that the Society might become national in name as well as in fact.

Mr. Nowlin, of Arkansas, said that he felt proud that this Society, with which he had been so long connected, and which had been so small in the beginning, had so enlarged as to be able to take into consideration the admission of other parts of the Union; that, while he was willing for the Society to stretch out its arms so as to take in the whole country, from the Atlantic to the Pacific, at the same time he wished to see the identity of the Society preserved.

Mr. Galusha, of Illinois, opposed the motion on the ground that he thought there was danger that, in thus seeking to cover so large an area of country, so different in climate and soil, that the objects for which the Society was formed would be frustrated and its utility impaired.

Mr. Lyon, of Michigan, said : The objection seems to be urged that there is danger of our falling to pieces from being too much expanded, but I remember that there were once only thirteen stars in our nation, but since then we have extended to the Gulf coast, and to the Pacific, and I don't see but we are as closely knit as we were then.

Mr. Yellowly, of Mississippi, moved that the committee should consist of a member from each State represented.

The motion, thus amended, was adopted.

The President then announced that he had received a letter from the manager of the Mobile and Ohio Railway, extending the courtesies of the road to the Society. He said he would take the liberty, on the part of the Society, of returning thanks for this very magnanimous offer, and that the business portion of the letter would receive due consideration.

On motion of Mr. Baker, of Kansas, a committee of three was appointed to take charge of this matter.

The Committee on Nominations then reported :

For President—Mr Parker Earle, of Illinois.

For Vice-President—Maj. S. H. Nowlin, of Arkansas.

For Secretary—Hon. W. H. Ragan, of Indiana.

For Treasurer—Maj. J. C. Evans, of Missouri.

On motion, the report of the committee was unanimously adopted, and the above named gentlemen declared duly elected to serve for the ensuing year.

President Earle returned thanks for the honor conferred upon him, in a few well chosen words. He then called attention to the fact that Prof. Tracy, the present Secretary, had been compelled, from the pressure of other duties, to decline the re-election to the position he had filled with such honor to himself and advantage to the Society, and suggested that the thanks of the members were due him for the efficient manner in which he had performed his duties.

Mr. Davies, of Ohio, moved that some more substantial mark of esteem from the Society should be conferred upon Prof. Tracy.

The motion was unanimously carried, and a committee appointed to decide upon a proper testimonial.

The Committee on Experimental Stations reported the following :

REPORT OF COMMITTEE ON EXPERIMENTAL STATIONS.

WHEREAS, The agricultural colleges established under the congressional land grants, for the encouragement of industrial education in the several States of this Union, are, with some honorable exceptions, managed in such a way as to seriously pervert the original purpose for which they have been so liberally endowed ; and,

WHEREAS, The friends of horticulture, who were first to urge upon the general government the importance of the said appropriations for the establishment of practical schools of agriculture, and kindred sciences in the several States, are seriously disappointed in the management of many of said institutions, especially in the fact that there is so little of the strictly practical and useful taught, and so much that differs so slightly from the curriculum of ordinary literary institutions; and,

WHEREAS, It has at all times been the earnest hope of the true friends of practical industrial education that these institutions were to devote a larger share of their energies to practical experiments in agriculture, horticulture, etc.; therefore be it

Resolved, That it is the sense of this convention that the management of the several state industrial institutions, above referred to, should divert from the ordinary literary work, in which they are now so largely engaged, a sufficient amount of the liberal endowment fund as may be necessary to fully establish and endow, in each of the States, Experimental Stations, to be placed under the immediate control—not of politicians, or simply scholars, but of thoroughly practical agriculturists and horticulturists, for the specific purpose of testing and disseminating new and untried varieties; of testing the practical value of fertilizers; of making experiments in entomology and ornithology, so nearly related to our every-day operations upon the farm and in the garden, etc., and that such results as may thus be reached should be freely disseminated amongst the class directly interested.

Resolved, That until the management of these several State industrial institutions shall be made to conform more fully to the above ideas, it is the judgment of the Mississippi Valley Horticultural Society, embracing in its extensive area a large proportion of the strictly agricultural portion of this country, that the original purpose of the liberal bequests for the encouragement of industrial education is being diverted from its original purpose, greatly to the detriment of agriculture and its kindred branches.   W. H. RAGAN.
                                                                                    F. P. BAKER.
                                                                                    J. C. EVANS.

After a spirited discussion, participated in by several gentlemen, the report was recommitted to the committee, to which four additional members were added, viz., Lyon, Furnas, Galusha and Now-lin, and the committee was instructed to report at a subsequent session of the Society.

Mr. O. B. Galusha, Chairman of the Committee on Horticultural Statistics, then reported the following, which was adopted:

REPORT OF COMMITTEE ON HORTICULTURAL STATISTICS.

MR. PRESIDENT—Your committee, to whom was referred the subject of the practicability of arranging for the collection of statistics relating to horticultural work and products in the Mississippi Valley, beg leave to report that they appreciate the great importance of such a work as set forth by the President of this Society in his address.

We see but one objection to successfully carrying out the views of the President, viz., the want of funds to defray the necessary expense of collecting such statistics; but in view of the general liberality of the fruit growers and shippers of this great valley, we are confident this objection can and will be overcome, and present the following:

Resolved, That our Secretary be and hereby is instructed to secure, if possible, the co-operation of the several State horticultural societies in collecting these statistics, and arrange with them for furnishing a portion of the funds necessary to defray the expense of printing, postage, etc.; and he is further instructed to supply them with a *pro rata* number of copies of the reports.

—Resolved, That the Secretary is hereby instructed to issue and collect three sets of statistics during the year, viz: one in the spring, as soon as the general planting season has closed, of the areas of old and new plantations; the second during the growing season, giving statements of condition of trees and plants, and prospects for crops; and the third, at the close of the season, giving amounts of crops, where marketed and average prices obtained.

O. B. GALUSHA,
R. W. FURNAS,
H. E. McKAY,
Committee.

S. H. Nowlin, from the Committee on Exhibitions, then made the following report, which was adopted:

MR. PRESIDENT—Your Committee on Exhibitions beg leave to make the following report:

That in order to render this Society of greater practical utility to the country, and to stimulate an active interest in the production of superior horticultural products, we deem it essential to hold exhibitions at least once in two years; and as the Southern Exposition will hold an exhibition of agricultural products in the city of Louisville, Ky., beginning on the 1st of August next, and continuing one hundred days, we deem it advisable to hold an exhibition of horticultural products on that occasion. We think, in order to make the exhibition a success, and render

justice to all parties, it will require a premium list of at least $5,000, and we have reason to believe that the amount will be placed at our disposal. We further recommend that the executive committee take the matter in charge, and arrange, if possible, to hold in September next, or at such time as they may find most convenient, at Louisville, Ky., the grandest exhibition of horticultural products ever yet held anywhere.   S. H. NOWLIN, *Chairman.*
                                                                T. T. LYON.
                                                                J. S. BEATY.

The President—Our next paper considers a subject of growing importance in all portions of this country—irrigation in horticulture. You have already given some attention to it in the strawberry discussion, and I think you are inclined to consider this question in its more general aspects. The Hon. F. P. Baker, of Topeka, Kansas, who is the United States Commissioner of Forestry for the Mississippi Valley, has given this matter much attention. You will be glad to hear Mr. Baker.

IRRIGATION IN HORTICULTURE.

BY F. P. BAKER.

From the earliest dawn of primeval history, in the opening records of the life of man on earth, water has been artificially applied in the cultivation of the soil. The earliest records of all nations, the poetical imagery, of every people living, far back in the gray dawn of antiquity, indicate no mean appreciation of their "larger and smaller streams" in the success of their tillage or grazing. No more beautiful description of this kind can, perhaps, be found than the picture drawn by a Hebrew poet when he speaks of the provision God has made for the people of Eastern climes: "He sendeth the springs into the valleys which run along the hills; he watereth the hills from his chambers and the laughing abundance by which the mountains are crowned in consequence of it. The little hills rejoice on every side. The pastures are clothed with flocks; the valleys also are covered over with corn : they shout for joy; they also sing."

The cradle of the human race, and their first settlements being in the East, where the temperature is similar to that of our great western plains, the care of the first tillers of the soil was to securing that supply of water for their fields which might yield food to their families, flocks and herds. For this purpose, in case the natural supply of water was scanty, they dug wells and canals and sought to lead out streams and rivulets to spread over their lands.

To guard against the effects of heat, in drying up their fields, was an object of great desire. Artificial means of various kinds were adopted. Among the ancient Assyrians, Babylonians and Egyptians a variety of methods was resorted to for this purpose. Herodotus mentions the fact that canals were constructed at great expense, and sometimes lakes and large reservoirs were prepared, by means of which the natural deficiencies might be remedied. Even in modern times travelers speak of the remains of ancient traces of structures as in existence, which indicate on how large a scale aids to agriculture of these ancient people must have been conducted

Sir Henry Rawlinsin says: "Rain is very rare in Babylon during the summer months, and productiveness depends entirely on irrigation."

Mr. Layard, in his researches in Assyria, says: "The Assyrians used machines for rais ng water from the river or from the canals when it could not be led into the fields through common conduits."

Herodotus refers to a machine or mode of raising water for purposes of irrigation, called the handswipe. Representations of the handswipe have been found on the monuments of Assyria.

Through Persia and Syria, and all the more Eastern countries, irrigation is practiced even to this day. In China and India, as is well known, it has had an important place among the agricultural practices of these nations, and dates back to remote antiquity.

On this continent, in ancient Peru, the Spaniards found the most costly works for irrigating lands. The Aztecs, of Mexico, also made use of irrigation. Cato, the earliest of writers in Roman agriculture (150 years before Christ), recommends to his countrymen to form water meadows. Pliny says that meadows ought to be watered immediately after the spring equinox, and the water kept back when the grass shoots up to stalk.

Virgil, in his well known Georgics, thus alludes to irrigation:

> "Of him who on his land,
> Fresh sown, destroys each ridge of barren sand:
> Then instant o'er the leveled furrows brings
> Refreshful waters from the cooling springs.
> Behold, when burning suns of Syria's beams
> Strike fiercely on the fields and withering streams,
> Down from the summit of neighboring hills,
> O'er the smooth stones he calls the babbling rills.
> Soon as he clears whate'er their passage stayed,
> And marks their future current with his spade,
> Before him scattering they prevent his pains,
> Burst all abroad and drench the thirsty plains."

The practice of irrigation prevailed likewise in the various parts of the Roman empire, while the Moors seem to have introduced or prosecuted it with vigor in Spain when they held possession of that country. Fraas, one of the most recent German writers on agriculture, remarks that in modern times certainly no question has more engaged the attention of the learned agricultural public than that of extensive irrigation, wholly different from the primitive systems of the people of the southern regions, or, indeed, of the people who, in the gray antiquity, conducted the civilization of the world. He states that in all parts of Germany such preparations exist. Fraas comes to the conclusion that it is evident that irrigation will soon dissipate the old relations, and in view of the facts of the disappearance of the forests and lack of rainfall, a higher culture will come in and the benefits of such a cultivation will be fully realized.

Thaer, the most noted German writer on agriculture, lays down the proposition that irrigation "is one of the most useful and important of all the operations within the province of the agriculturist." Moisture is essential to vegetation; and water, either directly or indirectly, or by decomposition, contributes materially to the nutrition of plants.

Von Lengerke, replying to sixteen questions proposed by the German Royal College of Rural Economy, says that river or lake water which contains a sediment is more advantageous than water from springs or wells. The highest degree of heat that water can obtain in the open air, by means of the sun, is the best; a warm rain being more beneficial than a cold rain ; and, as a complete refutation of the argument against irrigation in western Kansas, Nebraska and Colorado, that the hot winds will prove injurious, he says, "irrigated in the greatest warmth of the atmosphere, so the fields receive the necessary quantity of water, properly distributed, such crops have a more luxuriant growth than others." His experience is, that if there is plenty of sand in the soil, irrigation on the surface is preferable. The advantages of irrigation are presented by many French writers on agriculture·

In the south of France and Italy, and in Spain, six to twelve irrigations are bestowed on gardens per month, six being more frequent than twelve, meadows being watered once per week. One writer says the sole object in the use of water is to keep up the moisture in the heat of summer, and especially is it valuable when the water contains a slight slime. .

The orange groves, orchards and vineyards of Southern California are only made to yield bountifully by irrigation. Although living streams are few, the whole country seems to be well supplied with vast reservoirs of water a few feet below the surface of the ground. The farms are to be found on the low lands, embracing from two to ten acres each. Wells are dug, windmills erected and reservoirs for retaining water are built on the elevated lands adjoining. Iron pipes are laid from the reservoirs through the orchards or gardens. The wind furnishes the motive power, and each day some portion of the farm is flooded with water. If a tree, an embankment six or eight inches is thrown up around it twenty feet in diameter, and in this inclosure the water is turned. Trees do not need, as a rule, but two applications of water during the year. Potatoes and garden vegetables are watered by trenches or with the hose. Thus every farmer is his own thunder shower. The fruit is rich and juicy, the grapes the finest in the world, while the vegetables are as tender and crisp as those grown in the best gardens of the eastern States.

In New Mexico and Arizona water is applied in the cultivation of the soil in the most primitive way. Windmills are not used, the cultivated lands being found along the streams. The Pueblo or the Mexican digs an acequia or ditch for conducting the water from the stream near by. At sundown he takes his hoe and proceeds to the field, followed by all the members of his household, and for several hours the work of irrigation goes on. The wheat and corn fields are flooded, the water containing a rich sediment, which is thus deposited at the roots of the growing grain. The yield is enormous, although the cultivated area is not great. For hundreds of years the farmers of the Rio Grande have turned the water from that stream upon the adjacent lands, producing fruit, grapes and garden vegetables of superior quality. When the lamented Horace Greeley advised the young man to "go west and grow up with the country," he had already traversed the upper tributatries of the Platte river, and had seen with his own eyes the wonderful crops grown at the foot of the mountains by half-civilized inhabitants; and when he embarked in the scheme to establish a colony on the "Cache La Poudre," to forever bear his historic name, he had years before witnessed the successful operation of farming by artificial water supply carried to a considerable state of perfection in that far-off region. It is needless for us to say here that one of the most prosperous farming communities in the world is to be found at Greeley, Col. Trees grow upon the sandy soil in beauty and grandeur when fed and nourished from the waters of the streams, while the products of the farm attain their highest degree of perfection. The tiny acorn falling upon the leaves that thinly cover the barren rocks, germinates and sends its rootlets into the very crevices, and will live and flourish in spite of the rocky barrenness beneath, if only supplied with water. The tops of the highest mountains in Arizona are covered with timber, while the sides of these great peaks are as dry as the ashes from a volcano and as barren of trees as the desert of Sahara; the clouds condense and give forth the refreshing shower on the top of the mountain, while the heated air of the desert prevents the rain upon the mountain sides. The low, sandy streams that flow from the mountain reservoirs across the great arid plains of the West, on their course to the Gulf, are skirted on either side by the cottonwood and the willow, while back from the stream, upon the broad plain, the buffalo grass and the sage brush only withstand the climate where there is no rain. Three years ago farming was first attempted in Western Kansas by irrigation. Beyond the rain belt and far beyond the timber line, in the very heart of the great desert, a few hardy pioneers pitched their tents and made the beginning. The low banks of the Arkansas river enabled them to turn the water upon the broad plains at little cost. A ditch three miles long was constructed, and small patches of land on either side broken up. Fruit and forest trees were set out, vegetable seeds were planted, and the ground thus prepared was occasionally flooded, and the result was beyond expectation. Onions yielded 600 bushels to the acre, turnips 1,000, sweet potatoes 600, Irish potatoes 400, while the fruit trees blossomed the second year. Behold what a change. To-day hundreds of farmers are engaged in tilling the soil in that region. Miles and miles of ditches have been constructed; capital has been drawn thither, so that a government homestead, that could be had for the taking, if favorably located, now sells readily at $20 per acre.

Carping critics asserted that as the mythical rain belt never reached the great plains, and the cloudless sky and never-failing sunshine throughout the spring and summer months precluded the possibility of the growth of cereals or vegetables, yet here, in the midst of these impossibilities, is a broad expanse of valley, embracing many thousand acres, which is being rendered more certainly productive than the richest bottoms of the Mississippi or the Missouri. The wisdom of man has overcome the seemingly insuperable difficulties of nature—has set aside the natural laws and caused this hitherto trackless waste to smile with the richest harvest. Every man is his own thunder storm, and while nature too often floods the fields or withholds the needed rain at a critical period in the life of the crops in other regions, here the water is turned on at pleasure, the sediment of the stream furnishing an extra amount of richness to the soil. Prejudice and unbelief have given place to knowledge and absolute conviction. The scheme of irrigation in Western Kansas is to-day a magnificent success. Here, beyond the rain belt, on these lands redeemed by the skill of man from the desert, are to be the happy homes of thousands, prosperous communities, wholesome laws and the reign of wide-lapped plenty. Quietly the great work has been accomplished. A system has been established, the fertility of the valley of the Nile imparted to tens of thousands of acres, that not a decade of years hence will be pointed to as the crown of Kansas, and will endure for centuries as the most economical mode of farming known to man. A distinguished engineer shows conclusively, from a record of observations extending over a long series of years, in one case 142, that the annual discharge of water from the Danube, Rhine, Oder, Elbe and Vistula, five of the principal rivers of Europe, has been continually decreasing, as the area drained by these rivers has been brought more and more under cultivation. The decrease of water discharge has been most rapid during the last twenty years. Means should be taken to retain the water falling from the clouds within the area upon which it falls. This could be accomplished by the building of dams in water courses, and by the construction of reservoirs near the streams which overflow. The draining of existing lakes and ponds should be prohibited. A net-work of navigable canals should be constructed wherever practicable.

This is substantially the policy that has become so successful in China. A large part of Western Kansas and Nebraska, of Eastern Colorado and New Mexico requires irrigation before the soil can be cultivated and made to produce the usual variety of farm products. At present the land is used, when used at all, for grazing only. The big stock men control the land lying along the Arkansas, and the few other water courses, "freeze out" the small owners, and keep the greater part of the land idle and valueless. The rainfall in that region is from ten to fifteen inches annually, which amounts to perpetual drought. Engineers and geologists began last year to spend a national appropriation for sinking artesian wells. One experiment was partially made near Fort Lyon, and then the hole was abandoned. Something may yet come out of this project; it was a scheme worth trying. The soil in this territory is good ; it only lacks water to make it very productive. In some way, somehow, and at some time, this water will be found and set free, and when this is done a new empire will be opened for settlement and cultivation—a land already penetrated by several railroads into the lap of the East and the West. When that country is watered, groves will spring up as they do now in Denver and San Francisco, and the climate further east will be ameliorated, and the rainfall will be greater and more evenly distributed, less drought and fewer torrents and tornadoes. A tornado, or a " twister," let us define it now for the first time, is a loafer and an assassin, the dead beat and the Guiteau of the plains, born of idleness on a parched, empty and lazy prairie, and nurtured in the same hot and hellish air that makes the whisky-fed cowboy a devil incarnate. Irrigate the plains and you gibbet both the human and the atmospheric fiend, and the plains will be irrigated; if not this year, then ten years hence, as Damascus, and Palestine, and India have been irrigated—millions of acres, and by " Pagans " thousands of years ago. Damascus is called the " Eye of the East," and a thousand other poetic names. The cyclopedia says the river Abana "is the life of Damascus, and has made it perennial." Its system of irrigation is "apparently of high antiquity; canals are led off from it at different elevations above the city, and carried far and wide over the surrounding plain, converting what would otherwise be a parched desert into a paradise." Are we less wise, less enterprising than that remote people whom we now call barbarians?

It may be objected that this paper and the subject matter embraced in it refers exclusively to the arid regions of the West, but every region of our country is embraced within the domain of this Society. If he has been called a benefactor to the race who makes two spears of grass grow where one grew before, what may be said of him who makes not only grass but flowers and fruits grow, where nothing but grass grew before? I regard my subject, even with the thus limited application of it, as of the first importance to this Society and every member of it. To extend our view, however, is irrigation of value only on the great Western plains and mountains? Is it not worthy of investigation and experiment everywhere? Most certainly; and nothing stands in the way of that investigation and experiment except, first, ignorance of the results of irrigation elsewhere, and in other ages; and, second, a sort of superstition akin to that which led some of the Scotch covenanters, who opposed the introduction of fanning mills, because it was the province of the Lord, and him alone, to raise the wind. We are prone to think that it is the Lord's business to also raise the water, or rather let it fall. But on the same principle, why not depend on nature for fertilizers? Irrigation is the art of saving and applying water in quantity to cultivated ground when it is needed. It is, therefore, of value in every country where water does not fall from the clouds when and where it is needed. And where is the country that rain can always be depended upon? Irrigation is needed in those semi-tropical regions where the year is divided into a wet and a dry season, and it is needed in countries where what should be a wet turns out to be a dry season. Every portion of the United States is subject to a drought. Kansas can not be reproached alone in that regard. Droughts have attacked Maine, Michigan and heavily forested regions of the United States, so that the woods and the very earth out of which they grew burned up like tinder.

The work of man on the earth is to make the most of the bounty of nature, and one of the forces he is to apply is water, wherever he can find it, and to the best advantage, and it makes no difference where that may be. While it is objected that irrigation by the ditch and feed system can not be applied to great tracts of land and extensive agriculture, no such objection lies against its employment in horticulture, where comparatively small areas are and must be employed. Let me urge your attention then to the employment of irrigation in horticulture, in the nursery of trees, in the management, care and propagation of orchards. The finest fruits on this continent are raised by its aid. The Mission grape, which has called forth the encomiums of Spaniard, Mexican, American and Indian, grows in irrigated vineyards. Water is the life-giving principle of vegetation everywhere, and the little ditch flowing along at the base of the trees in the streets of Denver would be of like value during the parched summer in every city in America. It must be remembered that we have nowhere a climate like that of England, nowhere moisture is at all times superabundant.

Ponds should exist on every farm for fish culture, which some day will be as common as chicken raising; for watering stock in many instances, and for furnishing a supply of water for irrigation in the season of gardens and orchards. The stream which plunges down the mountain side, casting its spray on nothing but rocks, might well be directed into the thin soiled fields and orchards on the lower slope, which are so susceptible to the drought as are the plains of the West. The South has vast areas which should be devoted to horticulture and small farming with the advantage of a great supply of running streams, which need only to be diverted into needed channels. Traveling through the most barren regions of the South given over to sand and pines, almost as deserted by man, note what a mass of tangled vegetation, what trees and vines are found as soon as water appears. Nature gives a hint here that ought to be taken. Much of this may seem fanciful to you, but remember that all knowledge is at first some man's fancy, which grows into steady thought, then experiment, then application; but the subject of irrigation was thought out, doubtless, by the first horticulturist, Adam, in the first garden, Eden. It is as old as man on the earth. It only remains for us to add in this matter, as we have in many others, to the accumulated and accumulating wisdom of the ages.

DISCUSSION ON IRRIGATION.

Dr. Hape, of Georgia—I have been very much interested in the paper read by the gentleman who has just taken his seat. I was also quite interested last night in the matter of the irrigation of strawberries. It is a subject of particular importance as regards strawberries. They are composed of about ninety per cent. of water, and if not watered in the proper season they become soft and deteriorate.

Mr. Smith, of Wisconsin—It is about twenty years since I commenced irrigating in a small way. I described the machinery last night—a tank filled by a wind engine supplied from Lake Michigan, the rubber hose being in sections of fifty feet. The ground being dry, the watering should be done as often as twice a week. The cost of preparing for this irrigation was about $1,000, to keep thirteen acres of berries in good condition. It has been the general opinion that watering in the hot sun in the early part of the day is not beneficial. The only difference I have found is, that it takes probably fifty per cent. more water on account of evaporation. My rule is, for this reason, to water at night.

Mr. Hale, of Connecticut—Do you know how much this increased your crop?

Mr. Smith—No; but it has on some occasions made the difference between no crop at all and a very good crop.

Dr. Hape, of Georgia—Do you water with a hose, or sprinkle it?

Mr. Smith—I sprinkle it. My soil is a light, sandy loam, and never bakes under any circumstances. My experience has been that I have never put on enough water, and if I had used a sufficient quantity the berries would have been much larger and finer. It might be possible, of course, to put on too much water.

Prof. Gulley, of Mississippi—I have had something to do with the garden department. We had a windmill which did not furnish sufficient water for an acre of ground. At the same time we succeeded by steam-power in watering four or five acres per day. I don't believe it is possible to water with a windmill on any large area of ground.

Mr. Peffer, of Wisconsin—Mr. Smith's garden is located, perhaps, very little above the source of water supply. He says his land is better than sand. I don't consider it so.

Mr. Hale, of Connecticut—A gentleman in the eastern part of

8

Connecticut owned a small tract of land, little more than half an acre, that lay a little lower than a small brook, and by tapping this brook he let the water in on his land. He planted two varieties of berries, one of which was the Wilson, keeping the runners cut. The next year he let in the water from the time the plants were in blossom, letting it in at night, and cutting it off at 2 o'clock in the morning. The whole field was saturated every night, and he picked and delivered over 7,000 quarts of Wilson strawberries and sold them at 35 cents a quart.

Mr. Smith—We have had one or two dry years since I put up my waterworks, and I have no doubt that they paid me in those years.

The President—My friends, our programme calls for a paper, which I know you are all anxious to hear, from the Rev. E. P. Roe, of New York, a gentleman whose "Success with Small Fruits" has not only fascinated the thousands of readers of his very sumptuous and valuable book, but the many visitors to his finely cultivated berry farm. You will all regret, as I do deeply, Mr. Roe's unavoidable detention at home by sickness; but you will both hear and read his too brief paper with satisfaction and profit.

SMALL FRUITS IN THE SOUTH.

BY E. P. ROE, OF NEW YORK.

There has been a vast deal of disappointment and useless expense incurred in Southern small fruit culture, and all from the lack of due consideration of a few essential facts and principles. An enterprising Southerner sends to a responsible nurseryman for his catalogue, orders and sets out the most approved varieties, gives them careful culture, and, in many instances, is rewarded by utter failure. The foliage of certain kinds of strawberries shrivels and disappears during the long hot summer; the most vaunted raspberries lose their leaves and perish; gooseberries and currants maintain a sickly existence if they survive at all. What is the reason?

The explanation, and also the secret of success, is found by going back to first principles. Let us begin with the strawberry, the small fruit best adapted to the South, and the most valuable everywhere.

In the first place, strawberries of commerce, and ninety-nine hundredths of all that appear on our tables, are wholly American in origin. What are termed foreign varieties were originally imported from North and South America, propagated in France and England and disseminated to other parts of the continent. Varieties were obtained from, (*a*) the species known as the

Fragaria Chilensis, which is native to the great mountain system extending through Western, North and South America; and (*b*) from the other most valuable strawberry species of the world, *Fragaria Virginiana*, found wild from the extreme north to Florida, and westward to the Rocky Mountains. The first importations of these two American species disappointed French and English gardeners because of their non-productiveness; but as time passed more plants were brought over the sea which did better. Eventually the fact (so well known to us), was discovered and appreciated that the seeds of these American strawberries produced widely differing varieties, and by this method of propagation there was scope for very great improvement. It is not strange that European gardeners should have been slow in learning this fact, for the two species hitherto known to them, the Alpine and Hautbois, reproduce themselves from the seed without material differences. In time, foreign horticulturists vied with each other in producing new and celebrated varieties, and it would seem that the strain derived from the *Fragaria Chilensis* took the lead as promising the best results abroad.

In the earlier stages of horticulture in this country almost all of our cultivated fruits were imported from Europe, and the leading strawberries in our gardens bore foreign names. In the North, and under high and careful culture, many of these succeeded well. Some have justly maintained their popularity in many regions to the present day, as for example the Jucunda and Triomphe de Gand. But the great majority were soon found not to be adapted to our climate. It is a fact which is now very generally recognized by well informed fruit growers that the *Fragaria Chilensis* strain, of which the Jucunda is the best type we have, is an element of weakness in all varieties when planted on light soils and under a Southern sun. But just here we face our chief difficulty. How are we to detect this *Chilensis* strain, this element of weakness? In the first place, it was for generations crossed or breeded into our hardy Virginian species, that was also imported into England; and in our own land the same process has been continued indefinitely, sometimes by a direct cross, like that made by President Wilder, between Hovey's Seedling and La Constante, but more often by sowing the seeds of fine berries of fine varieties whose pedigree could not be traced, and whose blossoms had been fertilized from other untraceable kinds growing near. Hereditary traits will continue in strawberry plants as well as in peoples to the end of time, and the ancestor of some variety that we set out this spring may first have received its dash of the *Chilensis* strain a century ago, and have been crossed with it a score of times since. Therefore in the majority of the cultivated strawberries of to-day we find the two great species of the world, the *Chilensis* and the *Virginiana*, inextricably blended and, as has been said, that to the degree that the *Chilensis* element abounds in a variety that kind will falter and fail under a Southern sun. Even at the cooler North, on rich loamy land, many varieties in which this foreign strain abounds will not thrive. The fruit-stalks mildew or rust and the foliage burns or scalds. How often we have seen this of late in varieties, that, like the Great American and Forest Rose, were superb in a few localities but which failed utterly, after wide dissemination, to maintain their fame.   For a long time the success or failure of the vaunted kinds introduced seemed but a question of chance. I am now satisfied that in the foregoing paragraphs I have suggested the causes of failure and made it clear that our best success in this country; especially at the South, will be found in developing on hardy native Virginian species.   Nine-tenths of the new kinds set out are chance seedlings, or else are the outcome of long generations of cultivated varieties in which *Chilensis* strain abounds.

The Southern fruit grower should seek to develop a class of varieties suited to his climate, and, to a certain extent, this has been done, as for instance in Neunan's Prolific or the Charleston Seedling.   The trouble, however, with this berry is, that it is only fit to ship, not to eat, unless dead ripe on the vines.   If I were growing strawberries in the South I would order only such varieties as had shown in their foliage the highest degree of endurance of summer heat, as for example, the Bidwell, Sharpless (staminate), and the Golden Defiance, and Champion (pistillate).   Here are five male and female varieties from which new kinds could be obtained, and they might be crossed with vigorous and productive plants growing wild in the vicinity. Thus in time there would be a class of strawberries that had originated in Southern soil and under Southern skies.   I have never seen a plant that maintained its foliage so perfectly from year to year, until dying of old age, as the Bidwell.   It is also enormously productive, setting more fruit in many localities, it is said, than it can mature.   Admitting this fault fully, yet it has been well proved that the Bidwell possesses superb qualities in the hardness of 'its foliage and its tendency to stool out into enormous fruit-crowns.   It therefore should become the sire of new varieties in which the one weakness of the parent might be breeded out.   My advice to Southern growers would be to buy charily of kinds heralded at the North, to test them and discover through adequate trial how far they are suited to the region, then propagate those most vigorous and productive and make them the parents of new varieties.

To a very great degree the same principles that we have already considered apply to the red raspberry.   Until recently the kinds chiefly cultivated at the North were imported from Europe, and, as a rule, they exceed in excellence our native varieties.   Many seedlings have also been introduced but they were of foreign parentage and possessed the same lack of adaptation to even the southern part of the Middle States, and, with few exceptions, required covering everywhere.   They well repay it where they can be grown. We are learning, however, that our native raspberries well deserve cultivation, and specimens found growing wild have been propagated to very great advantage.   As, for example, the Turner or Southern Thornless (they are identical), the Brandywine and others.   In the Southern woods and fields may be found other prizes, and from the seeds of these new and still better kinds might be obtained.   There is no use of trying to raise foreign blooded raspberries even in Southern New Jersey, and as we advance towards the extreme South the possibility of growing even the most vigorous of the red or black raspberries steadily diminishes except on the upper mountain slopes. I can see no reason why the mountain regions of North and South Carolina and Georgia should not be one of the finest fruit growing localities in the world. The origin of the Cuthbert raspberry is obscure, but the native element predominates so largely that it endures the heat of summer remarkably well. If it would thrive in the vicinity of Norfolk it would prove remarkably profitable.

The character of the black cap family (*Rubus Occidentalis*), is too well known to need discussion. A certain degree of moisture and shade, and cool northern exposures add essentially to the prospects of success with all kinds of raspberries in the South. If placed on the north side of fences and buildings they would often thrive when they would fail utterly in the open field or garden.

The currant and gooseberry are not found growing wild along our higher latitudes; but when we remember their cold, moist, shaded, native haunts it will be understood at once that they are fruits not adapted to a sunny clime. Only as the grower can supply in some degree the conditions of coolness and moisture can he hope for any return from them.

In closing I suggest that the best success will be found in conformity to the principles of adaptation and acclimation. Nature can neither be tricked nor forced, and our aim should ever be to work with, not against her.

Mr. Earle then reminded the Society that there had been a committee ordered, consisting of one member from each State, to consult as to the enlargement of the sphere of the Society and the change of its name. He appointed the following gentlemen to serve upon said committee: Messrs. Furnas, Hape, Lyon, Smith, Holsinger, Tracy, Nowlin, Wiggins, Mohr, Colmant, Porter, Ragan, Jackson, Hale, Galusha, Campbell and Munson.

The Society then adjourned until 2:30 P. M.

Third Day—Friday.

Afternoon Session.

The Society met at 4 o'clock, Mr. Earle in the chair.

Ex-Governor Furnas, of Nebraska, from the committee appointed to consider the advisability of enlarging the field of work of the Society and a change of its name, reported, that, after mature consideration of this subject, they had decided to recommend that the subject be laid on the table till the next annual meeting. This report was adopted.

The President—Ladies and gentlemen, we are happy to have with us a gentleman of world-wide reputation as a pomologist, who has prepared a paper upon the new peaches, and other new fruits. We extend our greetings and our welcome to Mr. Prosper J. Berckmans, President of the Georgia Horticultural Society.

THE NEWER PEACHES AND NEW FRUITS FOR THE COTTON STATES.

BY P. J. BERKMANS, OF GEORGIA.

When we take a retrospective summary of the varieties of fruits known to Southern fruit growers of ten years ago, and compare these with our present resources, we may, without presumption, take the heading of this essay as a suitable subject.

The advent of the Hale's Early peach was such a great step in the advance of maturity of our earliest peaches, that by many of us this wonderful freak was supposed to be an exaggeration from interested tree growers. As the variety, however, sustained all that was claimed by the originator, this supposition gave place to another, that the earliest limit of maturity had been reached.

Again a change of opinion had to take place when the Beatrice, Louise and Rivers proved to be still more precocious; thus upsetting all previous theories, and leaving the undeniable evidence that a still greater step in early maturity was not impossible. This was instanced by the almost simultaneous introduction of the Alexander and Amsden.

We have thus advanced the period of earliest maturity of the peach, within the short space of twenty years, from twenty-five to thirty days. Twenty years ago the Early Tillotson, our best good early peach, seldom began to ripen before the end of June; now we are disappointed if our Alexanders are not ready for use by the 20th of May.

Although the Alexander and Amsden originated about the same time, but at considerable distances apart, I was struck with the similarity of the specimens of the ripe fruit which I received from the original trees at their second production. This evidently denoted their origin to be from the same parentage. Subsequent experience leaves no doubt as to this, and furthermore that the Hale's Early was their common parent.

We have, again, sufficient evidence that from this variety have originated the many seedlings, whose characteristics have so much similarity that to name one is to name nearly all.

The regularity of bearing of the Hale's Early is due to its lateness in blooming, as well as the thickness of the calyx, which, remaining upon the young fruit for several days after the petals have dropped, acts as a great protection against cold weather. But this late blooming has also the effect of causing the flowers of the Hale's to be self-fertilized. As very few other varieties being then in bloom, cross-impregnation is less frequent than in varieties blooming at the same time. This explains the great similarity in all the offsprings of this variety, and so long as it is used as a parent so long will the list of the so-called distinct new early peaches remain without variety, and increase the already numerous synonyms and confusion in our nomenclature.

Those of our peach growers present at this assembly will bear me witness that, although they may have a large number of names, still they have but one or two peaches that can be said to differ more or less in the main. It will not do to rely upon one or two seasons of fruiting, or upon one tree, to form an opinion that a seedling peach is earlier, better or larger than others of the same class; but if, after three or four crops, and these from different localities and soils, no material difference can be detected, it is then useless to retain the names of new comers, as it results really in a distinction without a difference.

Some of the offsprings of Hale's have serrated leaves, others are with glands; in this, and in a very slight difference in the texture of the flesh, count all the variations which I have been enabled to detect between the Alexander and its sub-varieties, such as Amsden, Governor Garland, Waterloo, Saunders, Downing, Musser, Wilder, Brice's, Early Canada and perhaps a dozen others.

Some of these sub-varieties ripen a few days after Alexander, but from an experience of six years in fruiting the latter, and a host of others, none are earlier or last any longer in average seasons. So far as their carrying capacity is concerned no difference has been perceptible.

It is a notable fact, that while seventy-five out of one hundred of the pits of the Early Beatrice will produce strong and healthy seedlings, not above 10 per cent. of the pits of the Alexander will germinate.

The varieties maturing immediately after the Alexander, such as Early Louise and Early Rivers, have given but occasionally satisfactory results in shipping to a distance; their skin is so thin as to prevent distant carriage, unless shipped under the most favorable concomitants of weather and rapid transit.

The Chinese strain, of which the old China Cling was for years the only representative, has of late years produced a large number of sub-varieties; some are free-stones, others clings, some with yellow flesh, others retaining the color of the old variety, but all possessing the peculiar finely grained and melting texture which characterizes this type. While a few years ago we had the China Cling in maturity during two weeks, we now have a regular succession of both free-stones and cling-stones to ripen from the first week in July until the beginning of September. First we have the General Lee, next the Stonewall Jackson, Spottswood, Albert Sidney, Thurber, Elberta, Sylphedi and many others.

The Elberta is, however, a well defined hybrid of the Chinese type, and a yellow-fleshed variety of the Persian type; it has proved a remarkably large and excellent variety, one which, at its season of maturity, from the middle of July to beginning of August, has commanded the highest prices in the Northern markets.

Perhaps the most valuable new peach adapted to the sub-tropical zone of Florida and Louisiana is the Peen To, or Flat Peach of China. A description of this fruit appeared in the earlier editions of "Downing's Fruits and Fruit Trees of America," but the genuine variety seemed not to have been introduced in this country until a zealous horticultural friend from Australia sent me some of its pits in 1868. From these originated this variety, which, although of no value for what is termed the peach growing belt of the United States, owing to its blossoming very early, it has proven to be well suited to sections of Florida where the varieties of the Persian strain are unsuccessful, and given there material for a new source of fruit producing.

This peach is, however, only a variety of a type, and the latter is also somewhat distinct from both the Persian and Chinese, as it is almost an evergreen tree, the old leaves remaining upon the tree until after the middle of December, while the new growth begins at the end of January. The fruit is very flat, flesh of a melting and fine-grained texture, juicy and of excellent flavor, cling-stone; has matured in Middle Florida as early as the 10th of April, when shipments were made to Philadelphia, where the fruit sold at 75 cents each.

It is hoped that experiments will be made by our Forida friends in raising seedlings from it, as new and distinct varieties will no doubt be obtained, thus giving them a race of peaches which will be as profitable to them as the orange.

Many of the members of this Society have doubtless fruited some of the varieties of the Japanese Persimmon, and become somewhat acquainted with this new fruit; others, however, may only know of the fruit from descriptions.

The limits of this paper forbid dwelling at length upon these new comers, and I must therefore only give their salient points.

1. The trees of nearly all the varieties are of rather dwarf habit of growth, and, so far as our experience goes, all produce fruit at a very early age. Imported trees usually yield a crop the year following transplanting. Those grafted upon well established native stocks grow more rapidly, and are apt to make larger trees; they also usually produce fruit the second year from graft.

2. Nearly all the round-shaped varieties have a tendency to overbear; thus the fruit requires thinning when set.

3. The trees are hardy in the cotton belt, but more reliable in good results below the 32°.

4. The fruit is very attractive, of a bright vermilion or deep orange. The flesh is soft, and, when fully ripe, of the consistency of jelly; the flavor is sweet, with an aroma partaking somewhat of the apricot and date.

5. Some varieties are round, others oblong, and some conical; but, although mention is made by several growers of from ten to fifteen varieties, we have so far only found six to be quite distinct. There is confusion in their nomenclature as well as in the varieties received at various times from Japan; it will require one or two more fruiting seasons to correct the many synonyms under which we now grow these varieties.

Four consecutive years of fruiting have enabled us to name the following as distinct, and determine some of their synonyms.

Among—Round, somewhat flattened, and with well marked corrugations at the apex. Average diameter, 3 inches. Ripens in October.

Kurokumo—Round, nearly globular, diameter $2\frac{1}{2}$ inches, very productive, tree affects a dwarf growth. Matures October and November.

Hyakume—Large, sometimes 4 inches in diameter, seedless. Keeps until February. Its synonyms are Minokaki, Tanenashi, Die Die Mawrn, etc.

Hachyia—Conical, $2\frac{1}{2}$ inches by $3\frac{1}{2}$. This variety seems to be predisposed to drop its fruit before maturity. Its synonyms are Tomato, Imperial, etc.

Mikado—Oblong or obtuse. Diameter 2 inches by 3.

Zingi—Small, diameter 2 inches. Quality best. Matures early in fall.

6. All the varieties can be successfully grafted upon our native persimmon, but the best results are obtained by inserting the graft upon the colar of the root, two or three inches below the surface. Top grafting, or budding, has with me nearly always proved a failure, but I learn that in Florida budding is quite successful.

7. Seedlings are unreliable. They usually produce male flowers only while young, the female flowers not appearing until the tree has reached six to eight years. The fruit produced, so far, by our seedlings, has been small, inferior in quality, and matured in September.

8. As a commercial product little can be said because of the small amount of fruit produced. In San Francisco the fruit has sold in market at ten cents per pound. We may, however, confidently expect our markets to be soon supplied with this fruit from October until February, but, as with all new fruits, a ready sale will not be secured until the supply is ample.

Some twelve years ago there came from South Georgia a very distinct fruit known there as the China Sand. As this name belonged to a well known ornamental variety, pomologists gave little belief to the wonderful reports of its yield of fruit and growth. As it became apparent that it was, however, entirely distinct from the China Sand Pear, and there was no exaggeration in what was claimed for it, there began an incredible demand for the trees.

The original tree was sent from New York to Liberty county, Georgia, by Major LeConte, and by giving the fruit the latter name it was placed in a better light before the horticultural public. This original tree is now still standing, and although some forty years old has never shown any sign of blight, and, I am told, never failed to yield a crop of fruit.

No variety of the European type can compare with the LeConte in growth or productiveness. A peculiarity of this pear is, that, like its congener, the China Sand, it can be grown from cuttings. But while the latter may, during winter, grow quite readily in Lower Georgia, nearly all attempts of propagating by this method have failed in Middle and Upper Georgia. Where trees can only be propagated with certainty when grafted upon pear stocks, worked upon quince gives bad results; the buds grow rapidly the first year, but gradually die off afterward. Its apparent resistance against blight is, doubtless, attributable to a peculiar thick epidermis which prevents fungii from obtaining a foothold. Admitting that pear blight is caused by the attacks of a fungus, which destroys the tissue of the bark, it becomes evident that so long as a tree is grown from a graft below the surface, its immunity from blight will be equal to that of a tree grown from a cutting, as the stock is not exposed to the atmosphere and thus protected from the fungus. However, when top-grafted the liability to blight is increased, the graft must suffer should the body of the tree become affected. The theory of blight being generated from lack of affinity between graft and stock and carried through the circulation receives, in this instance, a practical refutation, as the wonderful vigor infused in pear stocks, when grafted with the LeConte, is conclusive evidence of the affinity, and if effected by blight it is only when top-grafted, because fungus growth makes its appearance only upon that portion of the tissue of the pears of European type, which is exposed to the atmosphere.

As a market fruit the LeConte has proven valuable. Although without being of superior quality, it is sufficiently good to be desirable. But its good market points consist in its even size and smooth skin, combined with its great fertility. We may, in the near future, obtain better varieties of this type, as several are already quite prominent, such as Keiffer's, Garber's and other hybrid varieties; but even should we make no further advance in point of quality, the advent of the Leconte has made pear culture possible and profitable where it was a failure before.

DISCUSSION ON SOUTHERN FRUITS.

The President—Several topics suggested in Mr. Berckmans' admirable paper will certainly elicit valuable discussion, and he will doubtless be willing to answer any questions that you may desire to ask him.

Mr. Smith, of Wisconsin—Why is it that certain varieties of peaches ripened in certain sections of the country earlier than in regions lower down?

Mr. Berckmans, of Georgia—That is one of those climatic freaks that we can not account for. The nearness to the sea is thought to have a great influence upon varieties. I was told that about Mobile it is almost impossible for them to grow figs, except the Celesti, whereas at Norfolk, which is five hundred miles further north, I have seen half a dozen varieties uninjured for years.

Mr. Baldwin, of Michigan—Do you find the LeConte pear as good upon its own root as when grafted?

Mr. Berckmans—I find it better upon another root. I think it is better suited to the light lands of the Southern States than any other pear they can grow. It has matured in Connecticut and New York. They find it there not so desirable as some other varieties. In the Southern States you can grow it where you can grow no other pear.

Mr. Smith, of Wisconsin—It has been represented to me that the pear would not be valuable except upon its own root.

Mr. Berckmans—Certain ideas obtain with certain men. We can not take stock in all these things.

Mr. Baldwin, of Michigan—I came down to attend this meeting a little in advance, wanting to make a trip into Florida. On my return I stopped at what was supposed to be the headquarters of the LeConte pear. I got some very valuable information by going to the parties who grow them largely near Thomasville, Ga. One fact they impressed upon my mind, that they never graft it upon another stock.

Mr. Berckmans, of Georgia—That does not agree with my experience.

Mr. Baldwin, of Michigan—In going through one of the orchards the owner showed me a row that were grown on their own roots, and several grown on other stocks. They were about five years old, and those grown on their own roots were fully twice as large. I ascertained that they began planting their trees twelve or fourteen feet apart, then eighteen or twenty. They have now found that they must not plant them nearer than thirty feet. They have about three thousand trees in orchards from two to eleven years old. The average yield of the ten years old trees was about fifteen bushels to the tree. The first shipments sold in New York at $5.00 a bushel.

Mr. Berckmans, of Georgia—At our last meeting we classified the LeConte not very high in quality. Afterwards Mr. Albert Manning told me that in 1876 the LeConte sold in Boston for $16.00 a barrel.

Mr. Baldwin, of Michigan—Several barrels that sold as low as $2.00 a barrel were sent to the evaporator, in North Georgia, and they made eight pounds to the bushel. The owner was offered 30 cents, but he declined. They were afterwards sold in New York at 40 cents a pound. They make as fine fruit as I ever saw A gentleman I know is president of a company that is now planting one hundred acres of trees of this variety. There are some LeConte pear orchards which I would not give anything for, but they had been neglected. The gentlemen I saw, however, were thorough cultivators. You can stand and look down a row of one hundred trees and you can hardly tell the difference, they are so nearly alike. One of the ten years old trees bore last year thirty-two bushels. Mr. Sandford told me that there were thirty bushels of these marketable. A gentleman has twelve trees which have netted him a little over $400 in one year.

The President—What is it that makes it sell, its beauty or its quality?

Mr. Berckmans, of Georgia—I am unable to say exactly.

The President—What is its quality as a table fruit?

Mr. Berckmans—It is about good.

The President—Is it a very handsome pear?

Mr. Berckmans—Yes, sir. It is smooth and fine. This year my opinion of the LeConte has undergone a favorable change. I used to be prejudiced against it, but the quality this year was so much sweeter that I changed my opinion of it.

The President—Will it be successful to any extent in the latitude of Cincinnati and St. Louis?

Mr. Berckmans—If I can judge from the results in New York and New Jersey, I would say, yes.

The President—If all of these premises are correct, we ought to plant a great many LeConte pears.

Mr. Baldwin, of Michigan—These gentlemen told me that they had never had a tree blighted.

Mr. Berckmans, of Georgia—They say it is blight-proof, but I do not believe that. I do not believe that any pear is blight-proof. The LeConte may be more nearly so than any other kind. I believe that it has been reported blighted in Southwestern Georgia.

Prof. Colmant, of Mississippi—I have had a few hundred LeConte pears in cultivation, and my opinion has been about the same as Mr. Berckmans'. I have seen it blighted, but I have seen it resist blight. It is different from all the other pears in its habits. Our experience has been that the strongest growing pears were subject most to blight. The LeConte has been less subject to it than any variety I have ever cultivated.

Col. R. W. Gillespie, of the Mobile and Ohio Railroad, was then introduced to the Society, who said that he came on the part of his own road and the Louisville and Nashville road to extend an invitation to the Society. The L. & N. offered them an excursion to Mobile and back, or transportation to Mobile, if they accepted the invitation of the M. & O., which was to give them a special train from Mobile to Cairo.

The President said that this was the most generous hospitality he had ever heard tendered to a society, and thanked Mr. Gillespie therefor.

After some discussion upon these proposals, Mr. W. H. Cassell, of Mississippi, a gentleman of long experience in growing pears at the South, read the following paper on "Pear Culture":

PEARS AND THEIR CULTURE IN THE SOUTH.

BY W. H. CASSELL, OF MISSISSIPPI.

In the discussion of this subject, we are met first by the questions of latitude and longitude, and suppose that the Society will generally construe these to embrace that part of the United States between the Rocky Mountains on the west, and the Atlantic on the east, for longitude, and extending, in latitude, from the southern limits of the United States to the northern limits of the Cotton Belt, embracing some six or seven degrees of latitude. This opens up a large territory, varied considerably as to climate, and greatly as to soil, embracing almost every variety of the latter. But we find this (the favorite fruit of the writer) adapting itself, with considerable success, to the different conditions which these diversities of soil and climate necessarily impose upon it, so that from all quarters comes the report that some varieties of the pear are grown successfully, unless it be on lands too low and wet for fruit culture generally. The best results, however, are on well drained soils; and here at the outset I would like to ask if any one in the South has tried growing the pear on lands artificially drained, either by tiles or otherwise, and, if so, with what results?

There is a difference in the adaptation of the varieties to different soils, while the Duchesse d'Angouleme seems to adapt itself to all soils. The Vicar of Winkfield, or Le Cure, is a most miserable failure everywhere. A wide field is open here for experiment, and a careful comparison of notes by growers in different sections, and on different soils, is necessary to determine the exact status of most kinds. The lack of horticultural societies generally over the South has been a great hinderance here; and it is hoped the meeting of this Society, by bringing together prominent growers from different sections, may be of decided benefit in this direction. As far as my observation extends, if I could choose a soil more suited than any other, it would be represented by a fresh piece of land on the Chickasaw bluffs, or line of hills extending from Vicksburg to Natchez, east of the Mississippi river, and where it was not too rolling to admit of cultivation without the soil being soon washed away. Here growth is strong and vigorous, wood ripens well, and fruit well developed in size, appearance and quality. At the same time I have seen fine results on pine lands, where there was considerable clay in the subsoil. Next in order comes

CULTIVATION.

I believe it is conceded on all hands that all young pear trees should be cultivated, at any rate, up to the point where fruiting begins. Here cultivators differ; some preferring to continue stirring the soil with the plow or spade several times during the growing season, while others would sow in grass, and top-dress with manure during the winter, while still some others would allow the trees to take their chances without manuring. In the opinion of the writer, good judgment would determine a modification of these practices according to circumstances, the end to be gained being vigor sufficient to develop strong, healthy fruit buds, and carry to maturity a fair crop of fruit without an excessive stimulation of wood growth, which tends to make the tree cast its fruit and become more susceptible to attacks of the blight. In this, soil and variety must be considered together. For instance. a standard Bartlett on rich or strong soil, if highly cultivated, is exceedingly liable to blight; on a poor soil, uncultivated, it would not have vigor sufficient to perfect a full crop of fruit; *per contra*, a standard Seckel would be benefited by generous cultivation, on a fair soil, and is a comparative failure on poor soil, even with moderate cultivation, and completely so if uncultivated. Right here, the seasons too, exert a manifest influence and present sometimes a nice point to the anxious cultivator. If fertilized or cultivated to an extent sufficient to perfect a fair crop of fruit in an average season, and an extremely wet season should occur, the tree may cast its fruit and an excessive growth of unripe' wood may follow, predisposing to blight. Again, a dry season may occur, retarding the growth of the fruit and hindering its perfect development. As he can not control the seasons, however, the judicious cultivator will adapt himself to the average, as nearly as possible, and then cultivate or not, according to variety and strength of soil.

DISEASES AND INSECTS.

The one great disease (if I may so call it) of the pear in the South, as in some other places, is the blight. · It is a terror to cultivators, whether as amateurs or market growers, discouraging success, and hindering or preventing the planting of thousands of trees annually in the South, that but for this would be grown. I will not attempt to discuss its nature, whether it be the effect of frozen and vitiated sap, of fungoid growth, or insect enemies. That will probably be done in other papers during this meeting. Nor can I announce a specific against its ravages. I have tried the application of linseed oil to the trunks and larger limbs, as high up as it could be conveniently applied, with encouraging success; others have used carbolic acid in various forms with some degree of success, but a specific that shall be practicable in its application has not, in my knowledge, been reported. Such a discovery would be an inestimable boon to the South. Give us immunity from blight and an impetus would be given to pear culture, measured for years to come only by the ability of nurserymen to supply the trees. Give us immunity from blight, and in their different forms we can supply the world with choice pears. All other diseases and hinderances sink into insignificance compared with the blight.

An insect that sometimes affects the dwarf tree is the borer, especially in old orchards and where the quince stock is exposed. Deep planting, placing the entire quince stock some two or three inches below the surface, will prevent the attacks of this insect. Another still is the curculio, which stings some kinds of pears considerably in some seasons. The Duchesse is especially liable to its attacks. The larvæ bore out generally before the fruit falls or ripens, causing it to rot prematurely. While I do not certainly know how to prevent injury by this insect, I wish to offer a suggestion for experiment. Salt is, I believe, generally destructive of insect life. Some years since I noticed a statement in White's Gardening for the South, concerning the cutworm, that when salt had been applied in the fall, at the rate of eight bushels to the acre, no cutworms made their appearance the following spring. May not the same application destroy this pest of the orchard, saving not only pears, but peaches and apples as well? Has it been tried? or, if not, who will try it and report?

Another insect infesting the pear sometimes is the girdler, that cuts off the hickory limbs in the fall. I've known them occasionally to cut off the leading shoot of half an inch or more in diameter. Such injuries, however, are not very frequent, as far as my information extends. Some of our entomological friends can probably suggest a remedy for this.

PRUNING.

For this fruit the pyramid or cone more properly is suited, this being the natural form of the tree, as in the Urbanite, though some, as the Julienne, will assume a spreading or rounded form, like the apple tree. I prefer to shorten in annually until the tree commences bearing or the head is well formed; afterwards, merely thinning out shoots that cross or interfere with the proper shape of the tree. From two and a half to three feet high I like to form the heads of standard trees, but on the quince from twelve to eighteen inches is high enough If a tree is exhausted from overbearing it may be resuscitated by close pruning, thinning of the fruit spurs and generous cultivation. Should wood growth be excessive and fruiting retarded, the former may be checked and the latter hastened by summer pinching and root pruning. Right here let me mention a practice which I might denominate quackery in the management of trees. I have repeatedly heard statements like the following: "Mr. A. had a pear tree that had grown twenty years without producing a pear. Some one told him he ought to whip it. Accordingly, he got a lot of brush and stout switches and literally wore them out in thrashing the tree. Next season it produced a fine crop of fruit." Another will say: "My neighbor B. had a tree that would not bear and he drove nails in the trunk, numbers of them, and the tree afterwards bore good fruit." Others will bore holes in the tree, some putting in calomel, some sulpher, and so on, and then drive in a plug to stop the hole, and the tree afterwards set a crop of fruit. Ignorant of the principle that underlies these practices, some suppose that if from any cause they have trees that fail to bear, such trees must be whipped, pierced with nails or bored, and dosed with drugs, when in many cases manuring and generous cultivation are what the tree really needs; reminding one of the man who asked his neighbor what he should do to fatten his horse; he had tried every tonic he could hear of and none did any good, when his neighbor surprised him with the question, "Did you ever try corn and fodder?" The principle is this: Whatever tends to check excessive wood growth, will hasten the production of fruit. Whipping, boring, etc., check the sap by mutilating the sap vessels of the tree. The sap then, of course, flows more slowly through them, is better elaborated, becomes richer, and in the condition necessary for the formation of fruit buds. Root pruning lessens the supply of sap, and with summer pinching will accomplish the end with least injury to the tree, and is the only proper practice. I do not suppose that any intelligent cultivator before me would be guilty of such practices as I have mentioned; but these papers contributed here are likely to reach some who are not so intelligent, and it is one of the missions of this Society to correct popular errors in fruit culture.

VARIETIES.

Here cultivators are likely to differ considerably, each estimating a fit variety by its value in his locality for certain purposes. If I were asked what variety stands at the head of the list for cultivation in the South, for general purposes, taking into consideration vigor, health and productiveness of tree, with quality, size and appearance of fruit, I would most unhesitatingly say Duchesse d'Angouleme. It is par excellence the pear for the South, well tested and succeeding everywhere. It combines more good qualities than any other of the tested varieties. What our new kinds, LeConte and Keiffer, may do in this way remains to be seen. I have often said that if I planted but one pear it should be the Duchesse. It ripens rather late for the northern market, and does not bring the highest figures, but the yield is so great, the size so large, and the crop so reliable, that I consider it profitable as a market variety.

For market purposes only, no pear has so far been able to compete with the Bartlett, when properly grown, and there are many who call it the best table pear. Unfortunately, it is liable to blight; but so great is its popularity that many will plant it and take the risk. If it has any rival in market it is the Howell. Maturing about the same time, not differing greatly in size or form, excellent in quality, it has the advantage of the Bartlett in a smooth and glossy skin, giving it a waxen appearance. Last season I shipped this variety with the Bartlett, and it sold for the same price, while others dropped below. It is, however, by no means blight-proof, and on the quince will overbear and soon lose its vigor.

Beurre d'Anjou is quite a favorite in many parts of the South for table use, and some grow it for market. With me it has hardly color enough, and many specimens have lumps in the flesh, while the flavor is not altogether acceptable to my taste. It sells for moderate prices, as it ripens rather late for the Northern market and when our Southern markets are stocked with fruits of all kinds.

The Seckel, standing at the head of the list for quality, from its small size and season of ripening (August, in latitude $32\frac{1}{2}°$), together with its tardiness in bearing, is only moderately profitable, and not largely planted except for family use. It is, however, among the healthiest of any of the older kinds.

Doyenne Boussock is a fruit of good size and appearance, while the quality is fair. It lacks a little in sweetness. It comes in rather ahead of the Bartlett. I notice that some Southern catalogues place it as late as August, or after the Bartlett. It may be considered a profitable variety. Tree is moderately healthy and vigorous.

The Julienne is a profitable variety in the South, has a bright yellow color, and excellent quality, while its season (early July, here) helps it to sell. It is of medium size, hardly large enough. It costs more to gather and pack a box of small fruit than large ones. Tree of moderate health and vigor, with a spreading form.

Winter Nellis ripens at a season that ought to make it profitable. Its quality is very fine when in perfection, but the tree so often sheds its leaves, and then the fruit fails to ripen well, so that I can hardly call it a success with me.

9

Buffum is a good pear, of medium size, or below, comes in rather later than the Duchesse, after fruit begins to grow scarce, and generally sells well in the Southern markets. The trees bear heavy crops, but are rather tardy coming into bearing.

Lawrence—beautiful in tree, of moderate vigor and health, fruit above medium size, excellent in quality when perfect, but with me generally has blisters or watery places in it, especially at its base, which appear just as the fruit begins to ripen. It is recommended highly, in some sections of the South. Would like to hear a general expression of its merits in different places.

Easter Beurre—fine in size, very buttery, but rots badly with me. Tree, a rather crooked grower.

Doyenne d'Alencon—I have kept until February, but it was hardly worth the keeping, medium size, rough, green skin, and granular or gritty in its flesh Of little value.

Doyenne White, or Virgalieu, when in perfection, it is perfection to my taste, but, unfortunately, mildews and cracks so badly as hardly to be worth cultivating with me. Tree of moderate vigor, subject to blight. The Gray Doyenne is said to do better. I have not fruited it.

Dearborn's Seedling—a very good little pear, too small for market. Tree, a strong, upright grower, moderately healthy.

Beurre Giffard grows vigorously, of spreading habit, early and handsome if perfect, but cracks so as to be worthless here. In some sections it succeeds well, and there it ought to be profitable.

Rostiezer—a sweet and rich little pear, second early, but subject to those blisters or watery spots, that increase until sometimes the whole fruit is affected and worthless. Tree strong and vigorous, of straggling habit, bears heavily in clusters.

Urbansite is an excellent fruit of mid season, or rather later, rather large, buttery and rich. Not color enough for a market fruit. Tree grows dense, makes a fine pyramid.

Heathcot—juicy and buttery, but lacks sweetness. Greenish yellow in color, of full medium size, obovate form, mid season. Tree grows well.

Skinless—small, pyriform, second early, in clusters, sweet, but has a peculiar flavor I don't like. Tree, a rapid grower and good bearer.

Fondante d'Automme—approaches the Seckel in quality, larger in size, greenish yellow in color. Tree, a heavy bearer, but not healthy with me.

Beurre Clairgeau—large size, pyriform, firm flesh, sweet, but spots and cracks badly. Valueless, or nearly so, here.

St. Ghislain is an excellent fruit, rather small but regular and perfect in form, yellow color, rather firm, though very palatable, will ship anywhere, and, I believe, will sell well where once known. Tree, upright, vigorous, healthy.

In Alabama I learn the Kirtland is a very profitable variety, of very good flavor, golden russety color, and comes in just ahead of the Bartlett. It is also quite a healthy tree, with short jointed wood of moderate vigor.

Louise Bonne of Jersey bears early and enormous crops. If not fed sufficiently high the fruit is quite astringent next the skin : if on generous soil and highly fed, the fruit is of fair quality and much handsomer, but the tree is sure to blight

Flemish Beauty is a handsome fruit, of good size and quality, but the tree is not hardy enough to warrant its cultivation.

Zepherin Gregoire bears heavy crops of fruit rather below the medium size, but with me the flesh has lumps in it and is so gritty as not to be desirable. This fruit is very sweet.

Forelle, a beautiful speckled French pear of moderate quality and medium size, but the tree too tender here.

Onondaga is a very sweet, delicious pear, of good size and rather handsome but the tree will not last.

Sheldon is a fine, handsome American pear, but I do not see it in any of the Southern catalogues. I have some trees, six years planted, on pear stock, that look healthy and promise well—will probably bear this year.

There are several of the older varieties of good repute generally in the South as table fruits, but of which I do not know the market value, such as Beurre Superfin, St. Michael, Bloodgood, Tyson. For a market pear, other things being equal, earliness is of great consideration. We want a good fruit of fair size and appearance that shall precede the Bartlett, as it is generally conceded that while the Bartlett is on the market it takes precedence of all others. Among the earliest kinds are Madeleine and Doyenne d'Ete, which, in latitude $32\frac{1}{2}°$ begin to ripen from the 27th of May to the 1st of June. The former is the larger of the two but hardly of medium size, of a pale or greenish yellow color Tree, a rapid, upright grower, very liable to blight as soon as the tree has borne one or two good crops. The latter is smaller but rather handsome, frequently with a red cheek; of fair quality for an early pear, and sells moderately well. Tree healthier than the Madeleine. But these are too small to fully meet the views of a grower for market.

I will now mention one that is rather a curiosity in its way, viz., the Jefferson. It is a native Mississippian, originating in Hinds county, I believe, some forty or fifty years ago. To use brevity, I should call it the earliest, largest, handsomest, meanest pear I know of. It begins to ripen with me the latter part of May or early June. It will average about the size of the Bartlett, or nearly so. I have grown an occasional specimen that would weigh a pound. It is obovate pyriform in shape, of a bright yellow color, and on many specimens, where exposed to the sun, a rich crimson cheek, giving it altogether a remarkably showy appearance. It has, moreover, a delicious perfume. The flesh is coarse, brittle sometimes, at others tough, corky and insipid. It rots badly at the core, and must be eaten before it seems fully ripe in order to have it perfectly sound. The tree is quite hardy, almost ironclad, rather tardy coming into bearing, but yields heavy crops. One pear will satisfy the average customer, less than one a critical connoisseur. I think it would be an excellent variety to use in hybridizing, and offers superior inducements for experiment in that direction. If it possessed the one element of fine quality, I would, unhesitatingly, call it the most desirable pear known. But this defect is a most serious one.

At present, however, it is my most profitable variety, having little or no competition on account of its earliness: but it takes the tree some time to come into profitable bearing, and a pear of good size same season, and even moderate quality (which in this progressive age we are likely to have soon), would drive it at once from the market, so that I can not recommend it for general cultivation. There are several new candidates for public favor, conspicuous among which are the LeConte and Kieffer, represented as being blight-proof, and coming early into bearing. LeConte is planted extensively in Southeastern Georgia and with encouraging results. There is an old adage concerning pear culture. that "He who plants pears, plants for his heirs," and when a variety comes forward claiming to bear even earlier than the apple, almost as early as the peach, and add to this the other important merit of being blight-proof, thus covering the two leading defects of pears generally, it is likely to be hailed with enthusiasm. Both LeConte and Kieffer set up these claims, and are being tested pretty generally over the South; with what results we shall soon know. There may, however, be wisdom in the application here of the advice of Polonius: "The friends thou hast, and their affections tried, grapple them to thyself with hooks of steel, but do not dull thy palm with each new-hatched, unfledged comrade." I see before me many who are interested in fruit growing as a business, and the question of interest to them is, will pear growing in the South pay? I answer, yes, if a judicious selection of varieties is made in the beginning, and the same care and attention given which is essential to success in growing other fruits, such as the apple, peach, etc.

Beginning as an amateur some twenty-five years since, I began some five years later to grow for market; not a man of my acquaintance could tell me what to plant. Among other kinds I grew Vicar of Winkfield, or Le Cure, seeing it recommended in Europe, and some parts of this country, as a profitable late pear. I cultivated some five hundred trees of this, mostly as dwarfs, and a few standards.· They grew of will, and after five or six years began to bear heavily. In August or September, however, the fruit commenced·rotting and I never obtained a single perfect specimen. A year or two afterwards they were swept off by the blight. Some other kinds fared not much better. I would, if possible, save others such a costly experience. The grower for market does not need many varieties; five or six being generally sufficient, and a smaller number might do even better. I have already given my experience with the Jefferson. For six kinds of the older and better pears I would name, for my locality, Duchesse d'Angouleme, Bartlett, Julienne, Howell, Buffum and, perhaps, Kirtland or Doyenne Boussock, as profitable in the order mentioned. Another Southern cultivator of large experience would select Bartlett, Duchesse, Doyenne, Buffum, Beurre d'Anjou and Beurre Giffard, giving large prominence to the Bartlett. The next most important point is to cultivate without excessive stimulation, which predisposes to blight, and yet grows enough to produce a fair growth of wood and carry the fruit to its full development. On these two conditions hang the law and the prophets of successful and profitable pear culture in the South.

DISCUSSION ON PEAR CULTURE.

Dr. Hape, of Georgia—I have my serious doubts whether the Le-Conte pear is going to succeed in northern latitudes. Near Atlanta I have never been able to procure a single perfect specimen in ten years. It blooms out too early, and of course it is more liable to be killed by spring frosts. I have never been able to procure a perfect one myself. I have tried it on its own root and otherwise. I may be mistaken about it succeeding further north—I hope I am. I am going to plant it in a moderate way. I have succeeded best with the Bartlett, although it blights considerably.

Mr. Beatty, of Kentucky—The Chambers pear is grown more extensively around Louisville than any other. There is more profit in it. It is true it grows very slowly, but when it does fruit it sells for twice as much money as the Bartlett. It is pretty to look at, fine size, and ripens with us about the 1st of July. But we have to wait a long time for the fruit. I have three hundred trees of it. They were planted six or eight years ago and last year they began to show some fruit buds. About Middletown, where the original tree is still standing, it is the popular pear. They sell from $10 to $20 per barrel. I never knew them to blight until this year. This year has been the most destructive year for blight I ever knew. In my three hundred Chambers trees I think there are three that have shown some blight in the top limbs.

The President—What is the peculiarity of the Chambers that makes it command such a price?

Mr. Beatty, of Kentucky—Its fine size, fine appearance and earliness. It has a beautiful red blush.

Mr. Cook, of Kentucky—I have planted a great many varieties to throw them away after trial, but for the last three or four years I have only been planting about three varieties and have discarded all others. I have discarded the dwarfs, coming to the conclusion that they will not pay. In my experience the Seckel, Lawrence and Beurre d'Anjou are the best varieties. All others blight badly.

The Lawrence is the most healthy, and it very seldom blights. As a general thing, it grows very perfect. It does not bear as well as we would like. We would like to get hold of a pear that we can raise, but this abominable blight is doing more damage than any thing else. If we could get rid of that, we could raise pears cheaper than any other fruit.

Mr. Hollister, of Illinois—I am glad to know that some of our friends are able to raise pears with little or no blight. I had hoped we should hear something that would help us to get rid of the blight. I had, two years ago, as nice an orchard as one would wish to see. We had a bad blight year, and there was not a single LeConte tree left. It was the first to show blight. In proportion, I had more Bartletts left than anything else. The Sheldon is the only one that remained sound. They have stood for fifteen years, and have been cultivated every year, which I did not dare do with my Bartletts and other kinds. They have yielded me some pears almost every year. The Bloodgood is another variety of which less than 25 per cent. survives.

Dr. Hape, of Georgia—In planting my orchards, I have noticed that those trees which are planted on a northwestern exposure, and are protected against the evening sun, which I have found injurious in almost every instance, are exempt from blight. The ground in my neighborhood is rolling. Other gentlemen have made the same tests. Their experience has corroborated mine. I believe our pear trees, and I am sure our cherry trees, would be benefited by boxes around them, protecting them from the rays of the evening sun. The sides of the trees with the southwestern exposure show a blighted surface, indicating a mischievous influence. If I were to plant an orchard of any size I would box every tree.

Mr. Baldwin, of Michigan—My opinion is that the use of salt about pear trees will prove useful in preventing blight. In our county there is an old tree that bears pears, and has borne them for thirty years. The owner told me, not long ago, that he had for several years strewn salt around his tree, and ever since he had good crops. However, we are not troubled with that so much so far north.

Mr. Beatty, of Kentucky—I have tried the salt remedy. It appeared to me that it did some good at the time; but the succeeding year the blight appeared as bad as ever. I have lost so much confidence in pear culture that I have planted a peach tree in each space, when my trees are twenty feet apart.

Adjourned to meet at eight o'clock, P. M.

Third Day—Friday.

EVENING SESSION.

The Society met at 8 o'clock, Mr. Earle in the chair, who announced the reception of a most cordial invitation from the Continental Guards to visit their armory. He also stated that the Louisville & Nashville Railroad Company invited the Society to make a trip to Mobile over their line, and the Mobile & Ohio Railroad Company had placed a special train at the disposition of the Society to go to Cairo, or to stop at any point along the route. He further said it was necessary that immediate action should be taken on these offers, and the members desiring to avail themselves of this means of returning home should signify their wishes. In the case of both roads the members would be guests of the companies. This is an exceedingly generous offer.

Upon motion, about fifty members indicated their desire to go home via the Mobile & Ohio Railroad.

Tuesday was determined on as the date for the departure of the excursion party via the Louisville & Nashville and Mobile & Ohio railroads.

The President—Ladies and gentlemen, our first paper to-night will be upon "Systematic Progress in Horticulture," by Mr. T. V. Munson, of Texas, who is one of the founders of this Society. Texas is a giant among States, and furnishes a vast field for horticultural effort. It is fortunate that they have in this great young State a few horticultural men of notable energy and intelligence, prominent among whom is our friend Munson, who will now address you.

SYSTEMATIC HORTICULTURAL PROGRESS.

BY T. V. MUNSON, OF TEXAS.

It may be inappropriate in me, and Eutopian in character, to consume time in presenting the following proposition. My excuse is, my great desire to see more rapid and true development, and that I believe that the great majority of horticultural societies cost their members more than they return, and that simply from lack of making them a strictly business concern. From this do not infer that I think primarily of selfish gain, but just the contrary. Nor that I should dare cast a reflection upon the organizers of these useful, fraternizing institutions. Far be it from me, but I wish to help with my little mite to press forward the good work. Believing there is wealth and happiness enough in the earth, water, air, light and life for us all to make a heaven here, if we but harmoniously and intelligently press nature more closely, more extensively, for her hidden treasures, I beg your indulgence in a few hasty thoughts.

The business has been, and yet is almost universal for these societies to content themselves with the collecting and printing the heterogeneous re-countings of the hap-hazard workings of persons from every section. Their exhibitions have been huge and burdensome displays, chiefly of old or comparatively worthless varieties, as though the mammoth collection and pumpkin-like samples therein make the calling a success.

Gentlemen, as much as we all love a grand display and forty feet columns of Ben Davis apples, yet what horticulturist would not rather come here to see and learn of the origination of a single variety of grape, apple, pear, plum or potato, superior in every point to anything yet produced, than to behold mountains of old and well known kinds? 'Tis well we have planted largely of the standard varieties for market, but must we never try to elevate the standard? This Society can do us no good by piling great tables full of these same old kinds from year to year for us to stare at vacantly, or attend with languid minds the old tale of their growing. We want something new here, yet something better than the old; if possible, something which will profitably produce in soils and localities where others fail. In a word, we want this Society to be one of systematic, profitable progress. How shall we make it so? Others here can far more ably suggest than myself, but I will venture an idea to start the discussion. Let us *organize progress itself* not merely report chance progress, though that is well in its place. Suppose that each member of this Society to-day, if he or she has not already done so, choose a field for systematic experimentation most appropriate to his or her peculiar acquirements and circumstances. One may take soils and manures, and find the classes of fruits and vegetables best suited to each; another may take Rupestris or Sugar grape, the Post Oak, Mustang, Scuppernong, Frost grape, and, by selection and hybridization, fill the "Sunny South," as should be, with the largest, most delicate and lucious grape fruit on earth, upon never-failing vines. Who knows but that the despised little Frost grape may be made to put on the fruit of a Hamburg, and ripen it here in October and November!

Now our grape crop in the South, excepting the Scuppernong, passes away in August, when we scarce can relish such fruit, and are compelled to convert into wine or make no profit. Some one else can take our fine native persimmons, and lodge the grand, luscious Kaki in their tops, and have them hardy enough to succeed at the northern bounds of the native species. Thus each can have some special vegetable, fruit, shrub, tree or flower. The field is illimitable, both in variety and degree of development. Yes, even new trees may be originated of great value. For instance, Teas' Hybrid Catalpa now seems to be the most promising of all trees for forest planting. .

Above all things, we must avoid falling into "ruts," in our experiments, as our able member from Michigan, President Lyon, has so well illustrated. Don't all raise seedling strawberries, "picked up from some weedy fence-corner."

Let each report to the Secretary his chosen field for experimentation, that his name may be entered in its proper class. Then each year the President and Executive Board can, in making up their programme of exercises for the annual meeting, call in order upon this army of experimenters to bring forward, in a concise, methodical form, the results of their work, with samples of all their new products of special promise. Medals or premiums can be awarded by the Society for very worthy papers or varieties (or a special committee report would be better); not as a reward for excelling his brother horticulturist in producing the biggest potato of a certain kind, but for his triumphing over the elements in extorting from them some new secret or luscious product. The fund of new knowledge thus brought together would enable the Secretary to compile a year-book of our work, which would be sought eagerly by all enterprising horticulturists, and thus large editions might be sold, and. with the increased membership-fees which would come to such a progressive society, funds would accrue to compensate over-zealous, faithful officers, who should be paid well for doing their irksome work in the best manner.

The horticultural professors, especially in all the State agricultural colleges, should be enlisted in the work to give more thorough systematic investigation and compilation of data. In time such a society would become, so to speak, the University of American Horticulture, and could make just claims upon the general government for large appropriations to push forward its more complete organization, the acquirement of library, halls for meetings, exhibitions and collections of samples.

Instead of issuing a few hundred copies of its reports, to remain silent in the hands of its own members, who already know its contents before publication (as I am sorry to say is too true of the reports of the American Pomological Society), hundreds of thousands should go broadcast throughout the land.   There is one plant which should be our chief study and object of culture, and that is the brain of every man or woman who owns a foot of soil.

The publication of reports could be placed with some substantial firm, like Orange Judd & Co., Gardener's Monthly, Rural New Yorker, or better, some house nearer home with a national reputation.

In this way, when any of our members should originate a truly valuable variety, it would at once be set before the world in its true light, and the producer, who often is too poor to alone bring before the public the results of his labors, be able to secure a just compensation for his patient toil to improve for the good of all.

Likewise, the Society could do good service in guarding the public against horticultural frauds, by establishing experimental stations, where all advertised novelties should be thoroughly tested before receiving its approval or condemnation.   To aid in this, a committee of its ablest veterans might be appointed to investigate these matters and make an annual report.

Let every department of its work be then organized on the progressive idea, and then, instead of merely marking time, we shall make a grand, triumphant march, all over the fertile plains, the sunny slopes, the nestling vales, the lowlands and highlands, and even the barren, gullied hills and rugged crags and cliffs, we may clothe in ruddy fruits, protecting vines, grand trees and fringing flowers.

In fifty years more of peaceful growth this land will swarm with people of every clime and nation, and the struggle for the necessities and comforts of life will wax hot.   We hope it may not come down to a mere question of "survival of the fittest" upon the brutal basis of physical endurance, but, as we come nearer together, we may have learned how to grow two blades, with double the nutriment in each, where but one grew before; and, instead of being proud to boast that we are "monarchs of all we survey," be glad to have near neighbors with whom we can mutually enjoy the new flavors, perfumes, tints and forms we have coaxed from the earth.

It well behooves us to-day to anticipate by finding out and making known the capabilities of every variety of soil and situation, every development of vegetable, vine, tree, shrub and flower, that the future great throng may feed, enjoy and commune in peace and love.

To-day we see our forests fading before the ruthless ax.   Fruit and provisions of every class go higher and higher in price.   Our virgin soils are swiftly fleeing through Eads' jetties before our very eyes into the depths of the ocean, leaving our once fertile fields pale and sickly, and India's inevitable lot staring us boldly in the face but a few years hence, when a severe drought may sweep away by starvation hundreds of thousands.

Then he, who has learned best how to save his rod of ground and reach into it deepest, will be fittest, and *he* will survive.

Nature, here, has been lavishly generous in soil, climate and variety of products, but even these may be exhausted by a great, wasteful, unprogressive population, as may shortly occupy this country, unless societies, as this, lead on in the right direction.

Great praise is due our Northern brethren for their early foresight in these matters, and the numerous well regulated County, State and general societies to meet the emergencies of the times. There has been formed even a most extensive, intelligent " American Nurseryman's Association," an " American Forestry Congress," an " American Agricultural Association," an " American Pomological Society;" but these, in the great West and South, are heard of only as holding forth away in the Northeast, from which the Mississippi Valley, especially its western slope, is looked upon as "a wild, unsettled country." It remains for this Society to rise in her might, and, as her territory is great, also become truly great and beneficent, and join hands with true progress everywhere, and make every rod of western soil a teeming hot-bed of usefulness. Looking over the programme of exercises for this meeting, as published by our worthy President and Secretary, the themes discussed indicate that they, too, were inspired with the same sentiments which brought forth these remarks.

Thank Providence, the ship sails in the right direction. Her name is Progress; her rudder, Prudence ; her beacon light, Investigation; her cargo, the products of skilled Horticulture from all the world; her banner, " Peace and good will among men." Brothers! Sisters! speed her on her blessed mission. Fill every sail with wind of fact. To her speed add wings of steam and electric flight, that she may sail swiftly into the port of humanity, strong and bright, in reason's broad light, under a smiling heaven.

The President—The name of President T. T. Lyon, of Michigan, is as widely known as horticultural newspapers circulate. I esteem it fortunate that we have been able to secure Mr. Lyon's presence here, and an excellent paper from him—he never writes any other kind—upon so suggestive a subject as

HORTICULTURE VS. RUTS.

BY T. T. LYON, OF MICHIGAN.

If we may accept the demonstrations of the mathematician and scientist, and their theories as well, we will be almost unavoidably brought to the conclusion, that the great congeries of planets, designated as the solar system, as well as that intangible and apparently illimitable aggregation known as the Universe, in which immense worlds maintain their apparently permanent positions, or wheel their ceaseless rounds, obviously in obedience to the fiat of definite and unvarying laws, are to be considered as a congeries of ruts, devised by the great Author of all things, including, here and there, the erratic track of a comet, apparently thrown in to quicken our apprehensions by the possibilities, real or imaginary, of collision and destruction, upon a scale too grand and calamitous for mere human conception, but whose path may, nevertheless, be only ruts, so complex and involved that we are unable to trace them.

As in the Universe, so upon our lesser planet the laws of chemical affinity, as well as those controlling animal and vegetable life, are, in an essential degree, inflexible; so that the constant changes occurring about us proceed in regular and recurring cycles—in other words, in ruts, with only an occasional erratic case, consequent, possibly, upon the influence of that disturbing factor in the problem—man, who would seem, in various ways, to have proved an element of discord, or a modifying factor, in the otherwise fatalistic problem.

The lower animals, as well as birds and insects, are infallibly guided, in the selection of their proper food, in the location and construction of their nests, and in the preparation for their periodical changes, as well as for the changes of the seasons, by laws apparently inherent in their natures; of whose mode of operation we can have no real conception, except as exemplified by their acts in obedience to such behests. These are, therefore, merely ruts, devised by the great Author of all things, to direct them infallibly in the fulfillment of their mission.

Although it often seems difficult to draw the line of demarkation between the results of what we are pleased to designate as instinct, and those attributable to the operations of reason, man does not hesitate to arrogate to himself the sole possession of the latter; failing, doubtless, as the rule, to realize how much of grave responsibility hinges upon such assumption.

It is, doubtless, this capacity to devise and establish premises, to draw conclusions therefrom, and to apply these to the working out of valuable or otherwise important results; in other words, to devise new systems of ruts, as guides to the working out of new processes that entitles man to the post of honor; at the same time imposing upon him the more strongly the obligation to "act well his part." He is reputed to have initiated his six thousand years sojourn upon the earth as a horticulturist; but, alas! either from not having yet acquired the habit of rut-following, or because he chose rather to be guided by his wife, he was very summarily thrown out of this groove, and assigned the alternative of trying his fortune in the then undeveloped general field of agriculture, from which, during this long period, he has been able to win the sustenance of the race; although it is, sometimes, very distinctly charged (and with warrant, if we consider certain modern discoveries), that he has wasted even more than he has succeeded in utilizing. Be this as it may, it is clear that, during his long occupancy of this field, he has succeeded in withdrawing the grains, the domestic animals and various other products of nature, from the grooves in which they were originally wont to exist, and in very greatly increasing their capacity to minister to his support. Whatever credit may be due the race, in this direction, to our apprehension, one of its constant and distinguishing characteristics has been a persistent and thoughtless following in ruts previously worn by others.

It has ever been a peculiarity of agricultural ruts that, while yet comparatively few in number, they are, by consequence, the more deeply worn, and hence the more readily followed. Indeed, the time is hardly yet past when the remark, "my father did so. and he knew," was, with very many persons, the most conclusive possible defense of the rut in which they chanced to be traveling; while the effort to search, by reading and thought, for a better way, was sneered at as book-farming.

In the horticultural field, on the other hand, while ruts may be found in greater numbers, they are, by consequence, less clearly defined, and hence the more readily avoided, and less likely to be persistently followed. Notwithstanding these facts, it is believed to be the besetting sin of horticulturists, in common with others, to accept conclusions at second hand, and drop into one convenient or seductive rut after another, following them implicitly, oblivious of the known and conceded fact that eminent success is only gained by taking prompt and intelligent advantage of circumstances as they arise, aided by a thorough and comprehensive grasp of all the conditions of the problem to be solved.

In horticulture (of which modern pomology may be considered as a branch), more than in most rural pursuits, success lies, very largely, in the thorough mastery of a variety of not very obvious, although essential, particulars, and in the ability to intelligently apply them, at the right time and in the proper manner.

The recognized existence of this fact would seem to give force to the assumption that, more than most other tillers of the soil, horticulturists are men who do their own thinking, and hence are the more inclined to devise each his own independent system of ruts. True as this may be, they, in common with others, have to do with ruts that must be followed, as well as with yet others which they sometimes unconsciously, and perhaps improperly, follow.

To illustrate: Nature has provided for certain forms of cacti a special rut, out of which they are obstinately unsuccessful. Many years since an English plant grower, an expert in his calling, received one of these then novel and curious plants, to be nursed and developed into bloom. Following the stereotyped plant grower's rut, he nursed, watered and watched over it with the most solicitous care, but all in vain. It persistently refused to honor his efforts, till at last wearying with the trial, he, in disgust, cast it under the stage of the green-house, where, thrown upon its side, it was abandoned; when, presto! the obstinate plant found itself in the rut marked out by nature, and soon developed into bloom! It had, under neglect, acquired the arid condition indispensable to its prosperity.

The fuchsia is one of the most attractive of ordinary conservatory or parlor plants; but nature has located its rut in coolness and shade, and the follower of ruts who, in our climate, oblivious of this peculiarity, attempts to compel its adaptation to a warm, sunny exposure, will need but a short time to become assured that it will not take kindly to these conditions.

We trust that no one but the *farm*-horticulturist will either plant an orchard in a field of grain, or sow grain in an orchard, with the hope to secure a double crop from the same land; and *he* will surely learn that, to do so, is

like the attempt of two railroad trains to pass each other upon a single track
—not a success.

The very self-sufficient, young horticulturist may imagine that nature is
mistaken in placing a ligature of outer, fibrous bark around the cherry tree
to restrict its growth, and he may attempt to remedy the error by slitting it
vertically, or by even peeling it wholly away; but the outcome will surely
convince him that her mistakes are fewer than he had supposed, and that
she rarely exchanges ruts with even the most expert horticulturist.

The immigrant from the cool, humid climate of old England, whose subdued temperatures and mellow lights are born of the tepid waters, tempered
by the torrid suns of our tropic gulf, and thrown upon her shores by our
wonderful ocean river, will have, under these conditions, worn for himself a
rut in which he will possibly essay to travel on this side the water—telling
us to use the knife freely upon our orchard trees—" open their heads and let
in the air and light;" but time and experience will surely teach him that
this rut accords not with the general law of nature, but is, instead, a merely
local sequence, and not to be tolerated here—especially not under the
brighter and more arid skies of the West, with its extreme alternations of
temperature.

On the other hand, there are those among us, even "to the manor born,"
who assert that, at the period when the horticultural afflatus may be expected
to inspire them to action, and when their impulsive jack-knives marshall for
the fray against the persistent efforts of nature, possibly for the repair of
earlier mistakes, they manage to lose these, in their estimation, objectionable
implements; intimating their opposition to all pruning; and thus, in dissent
from the previous idea, vibrating, pendulum like, to the opposite extreme;
and making to themselves a counter-rut, possibly quite as far aside from the
true and proper mean.

This very human tendency to draw conclusions and fall into practices,
based upon an inadequate conception of principles or facts, often, if not, indeed, usually accepting the conclusions or practice of others, at second-hand,
lies, very largely, at the foundation of the faulty practice and unprofitable
rut-following, even of those engaged in horticultural pursuits, to say nothing
of others.

Of all those who grow the peach, how few have learned that nature has
established for it the invariable law; that neither foliage nor fruit can be produced from wood of more than a single year's growth; and hence, that the
life of a shoot, beyond the second year, except by an extension of its growth,
is impossible. Upon this fact, or in this rut, lies the basis of all successful
management of the peach tree. Its strong tendency, at least in our Northern
climate, to the continuous elongation of its stronger shoots, to the detriment
of the weaker ones, justifies, if indeed it does not necessitate the adaption of
the "shortening in system of pruning;" as a means of forcing the weaker
shoots into annual growth, supplying to them a renewed crop of buds, for
the production of foliage and fruit, and thus rescuing them from otherwise
inevitable death.

Let us for a moment contemplate the not infrequent attempt to ignore the fact that nature has, in some sense, devised a special law, obedience to which is essential to the highest success and the most perfect development of each family of plants; and the tendency of man, on the other hand, to apply his own Procustean ideas alike to all. An assumed expert of this school, having devised a model to which he would conform the growth of his trees, shortens the growth of his peach trees; and, with the eye of an artist, brings them to the form of the model. Satisfied with the result in their case, he proceeds next to bring his pear trees, and anon the apples also into the same favorite rut; only to learn, possibly after years of misdirected effort, that with some varieties of these fruits, at least, while his trees may become assimilated, in form, to the chosen model, the process involves the removal, in whole or in part, of all possibility of fruit.

Pausing at the vineyards, he shakes his wise head at their rampant disregard of his model, and, in sheer disgust, leaves them to their trellis, the Thrips and the Philloxera; and wends his way to the small fruit plantation, where he deftly licks the raspberry and blackberry plants into satisfactory form, while nature smiles upon his labor. Emboldened by success, he next attacks the currants and gooseberries; whereupon Dame Nature compromises the matter, with decided indications of disapproval, by perhaps giving him large and beautiful fruit, but very little of it.

But the afflatus is still strong upon him, and impels him, next, to the lawn, where, in the working out of his model upon the shruberry, he is ultimately made to comprehend that trees and plants which bloom from the last season's wood yield but a partial and dissatisfied assent to the application of his straight-jacket, which despoils them of very much of their incipient bloom, while most of the Spireas, with many other plants of corresponding habit, can only be shortened or sheared, with the entire loss of the season's bloom.

In certain pursuits involving a division of labor, an operative, by continuous manipulation of a single process, may become so expert that thought respecting it ceases to be a necessity, since the deeply worn rut comes to be an unerring guide. Unfortunately, doubtless, for the perfection of the manipulations, but, fortunately for the mental status of the operative, in horticultural pursuits, this condition of affairs very rarely becomes possible. On the other hand, in this specialty, we have to do with trees and plants, brought together from dissimilar climates, and from varying conditions even of the same climate, as well as with dissimilar habits of growth and fruitage, all which particulars must be studied, both separately and associated, in the case of each class of plants, before we can determine the rut in which it will most surely and perfectly respond to our treatment, while the neglect of any of these essentially modifying particulars will, quite possibly, as with the inconsiderate artist, who selected a grazing cow as the standpoint for a picture, cause his plans to fall into confusion, to the ruin of his work.

Besides the agricultural ruts, of which we have heretofore spoken, horticulture seems to be essentially complicated with other ruts, almost innumerable, one class of which may be designated as botanical ruts, by the careful study of which we might, perchance, become expert enough to be able to determine authoritatively whether the pulp or the pit of a peach is the fruit— whether tomatoes, potatoes, melons and pumpkins are, in fact, vegetables or fruits, while it may even be found possible to discover the true reason why the fabled pumpkin did not grow upon the oak.

In one of these ruts we might, if only blest with the requisite acuteness of vision and perception, follow in the track of Professor Burrill, and be able to finally and authoritatively determine the question whether bacteria are really vegetables or insects, and whether they are the cause or only a concomitant of blight and yellows.

Yet another system of ruts, which add greatly to the complications of horticulture, may be denominated entomological ruts, in the study of which, some very acute plant-grower might succeed in winning the gratitude of his compeers by the discovery of some means of propagating thrips, phylloxera, red spider and scale insect, short of a resort to his pet plants for the purpose. And if, moreover, our honored President could, after a critical survey of this field, tempt the lachnosterna, the crown-borer and the leaf-roller with forage more to their liking, and, at the same time, more economical than strawberry plants, there would no longer be a peg on which to hang a doubt of the appropriateness of his recognized title of strawberry king. The orchardist and nurseryman might, doubtless, with equal reason, hope to discover some other pasture so satisfactory to the aphis and his reputed dairyman, the ant, that it would be accepted in place of his trees, to his great relief and gratification. And if, furthermore, he could succeed in persuading the curculio, and even the codling moth and borer, back into the ruts occupied by them prior to their discovery of the plum and the apple, he might be almost, if not altogether, prepared to hail the advent of the millennium of horticulture, though he will hardly be able to felicitate himself upon the actual arrival of that much-to-be-desired era, till (after investigating the ruts of commerce) he shall discover a way to turn out a thoroughly honest package from the faced ones which reach our markets through the back door, minus a sponsor, and seem to serve, most appropriately, as a bait to catch gudgeons, who may be ready to bite at an apparent offer of something for nothing, and until he shall find himself able to measure out a full quart from a one and a half pint box, and an honest peck from a six quart basket. These accomplished, he will need, next, to provide the inevitable tree peddler a school in which he may be taught how to realize the many wonderful facts which now find an existence only in his fertile brain; and in such school there might be a department in which the sanguine and ambitious originator and disseminator of novelties may learn just how far he may venture to impose his wares upon a credulous public without endangering his reputation for honesty, and even how the nurseryman may most effectively conduct a paper at the expense of the public, to be used in "blowing his own horn" and in belittling his rivals.

In this investigation he may perchance be brought face to face with the question—so long an ogre to the grangers—what percentage of his income the "middle man" may reasonably sweat out of his produce "en passant," and whether, as the electric current waits not in its passage, so produce may not be made to pass from producer to consumer direct. And he may even find occasion to consider whether he or the commission merchant is the better judge as to the most desirable varieties of fruit to be grown for his own use, and even for market purposes.

Nor can he, even yet, drop quietly down upon the milennial couch of rose leaves, till, after inuring his olfactories to the mal-odors of the political arena, and acquiring a mastery of the system of ruts governmental, he shall be able to impress upon the mind of the public, and, through it, upon the legislative mind, the fact that, as horticulture is older than agriculture, of the practice of which it is rather a dilution than an improvement, the most direct and effective method by which to improve and elevate the latter must surely be to place the leading ideas and the highest practice in horticulture in the forefront, as a sublimation or intensification of the best, most productive and profitable possible practice in agriculture, needing mere amplification to adapt it to practice on a broader scale.

Having studied these, and multitudes of other ruts and combinations of ruts, and settled, to his own satisfaction, how far it may prove pleasant or profitable to follow their guidance, and having also assured himself of the probable consequences of following them too implicitly, it may be supposed that this graduated student of ruts will find himself at full liberty to settle quietly down to the life work of growing the best possible crops of vegetables, fruits and flowers, and of "paddling his own canoe," generally. Bless you! nothing of the kind! He has become too conspicuous a mark for newspaper pellets, and will not be spared from sitting with gatherings of horticulturists, while his lucubrations are being deliberately picked in pieces by his associates; and he will be required to employ his pen, and, perchance, a writing machine or two, in responding to the thousand and one queries of correspondents who may lack the facilities, the time, or, perchance, even the disposition to elaborate them for themselves. In fact, he will now, pretty surely, find himself settled down in the deepest of horticultural ruts, with no alternative but to go straight forward, unless, perchance, he shall succeed in making a qualified or partial escape by assuming the role of horticultural editor, and, in so doing, acquire the right (by courtesy) to impose a share of the burden upon his friends or acquaintances.

The President—The last topic and paper for this evening is one upon forestry—a subject that ranks all others in importance to our interests all over this continent. The success of our horticulture, the prosperity of our agriculture, and the permanence of our civilization even, all depend upon the wisdom with which we manage this paramount interest of forestry. I am glad that so able a man as Governor Furnas, of Nebraska, has undertaken to discuss this subject here, and am very sorry that Dr. Warder was not able to get here to present his paper upon this question in person.

Before introducing Governor Furnas, allow me to say that I hold in my hand this handsome gavel—A beautiful emblem of my office— which was, at the beginning of this meeting, presented to me by my esteemed friend, the Governor. It is made of three varieties of native timber from trees planted and grown by the Governor on the great plains of Nebraska, once known as the Great American Desert. And a very suggestive commentary it is upon the old theories concerning the sterility of these magnificent plains of the Northwest.

Ladies and gentlemen, the Hon. Robert W. Furnas, of Nebraska.

FORESTRY ON THE PLAINS.

BY R. W. FURNAS, OF NEBRASKA.

" With every successive year the depletion of the lumber forests is deplored, and the cry raised that only a short time will intervene before the vast timbered districts will be barren areas. Owners of pine lands materially differ as to when this famine will occur, some placing the limit at seven years and others as far off as twenty-five years. It is a subject, although closely studied, still not demonstrable as an absolute certainty. No one knows just how much timber there is in the Northwest, though perhaps a pretty fair approximate can be arrived at, and from such an estimate is based the reasonable deduction that in about seven years, at the rate timber is now being cut, the market here will have to seek new fields of supply.

" Michigan forests are being thinned out more rapidly than those of Wisconsin and Minnesota, chiefly because the timber is more plentiful and attracts more dealers. It was estimated by lumber dealers and owners of pine lands that the main lumber region of Michigan, that is, the main peninsula, contained in 1880 about 29,000,000,000 of feet. Since then an average of 4,000,000,000 feet a year have been cut, thus making 12,000,000,000 feet subtracted from the 29,000,000,000, leaving 17,000,000,000 standing. The upper peninsula was estimated at the same time to contain about 6,000,000,000 feet, of which something like 1,500,000,000 have been cut. Thus, in the two districts or peninsulas of Michigan, the standing timber at present is estimated at 21,500,000,000 feet of lumber.

" In 1881 Michigan contributed 4,500,000,000 feet, and 1882 about 6,000,000,000 feet. The total amount of feet of lumber cut in Michigan, Wisconsin and Minnesota in 1881 was 6,768,886,749 feet. The figures for the year 1882 have not yet been completed, but an approximation places the yield at nearly 10,000,000,000.

" It is readily perceived, therefore, that the day is not far off, if the cutting continues at this rate, when the lumber fields of the Northwest will be things of the past. Fully alive to the inevitable result, capital is being invested in the South, particularly in Mississippi and Alabama, where the pine belts are enormous in extent and apparently inexhaustible. Unlike the white pine of the Northwest, the yellow pine of the South grows rapidly and is not killed by civilization. The young pines of the Northwest are not reckoned in the calculation, as maturity is too indefinite, and growth is stunted by the smoke and camp-fires of the lumbermen. The hardy yellow pine of Southern Mississippi, Arkansas, portions of Tennessee and Alabama, grow, the smoke of settlers to the contrary notwithstanding. The Mississippi pine lands, which have recently attracted the attention of a wealthy syndicate of western men, are seemingly inexhaustible. Their richness is no new discovery, and billions of feet have been cut from them and transported to every port in the civilized world."*

With these figures before us, together with the well-known constantly increasing consumption of timber, and consequent growing demand, there is well founded solicitude, not only on the part of the United States, but of the whole civilized world, as to future timber supply.

Solicited by this Society to prepare and read a paper on this occasion, and the subject, "Forestry on the Plains," designated, the object will be, not so much a treatise, as to present as briefly as may be practical what has been done, what is being done, and what may be done, converting naturally timberless portions of country into tree-growing regions. The presentation is substantially the experience and observation of the writer during a residence of twenty-seven years west of the Missouri river, in what is now the States of Nebraska and Kansas, familiarly known as "Twin Sister" territories, organized under the same act of Congress.

Taking the geography of boyhood days, together with official reports of Captain Miles, U. S. A., and the western explorer, Colonel Fremont, relating to that portion of the national domain situated between the Missouri river and the Rocky Mountains, as a basis for conclusions, there was at date of extinguishment of Indian title to these lands, in 1854, nothing enticing to enterprising adventurers seeking new homes in the Far West, especially in matters of tree-growing. The thought that the then naked plains would ever be transformed into groves of valuable timber was not entertained.

Those who first came, during the years 1854-55-56, soon discovered, however, that, particularly along the borders of streams and where prairie fires were kept out, there was promising spontaneous indigenous growth of valuable varieties of timber: Oaks, black walnut, hickories, elms, ash, red mulberry, honey-locust, hackberry, linden, soft maple, sycamore, Kentucky cof-

---

*Chicago Times, January, 1883.

fee tree, red cedar, cottonwoods, willows and others. Still later, it was found by experiment, that native seedlings transplanted into carefully prepared soil, did well on high uplands—out on the open prairie. Not only did well, but grew with remarkable vigor and rapidity, showing characteristics of excellence in quality. To those of indigenous growth were added in time varieties of foreign origin: Hard, or sugar maple, American chestnut, white walnut, poplar, beech, birch, black locust, larch, pines, catalpa, black cherry and others. While success followed efforts in this direction, only the most sanguine, adventurous experimenters had faith in ultimate practical results. In further time, through an act of the Territorial Legislature, creating a board of agriculture, the labors of the board organized under its provisions, and afterwards, liberal legislative appropriations, keeping out annual fires, and other aids and precautions, tree growing in Nebraska and Kansas is universally conceded a success. There is now no hesitancy or risk in predicting in the near future, that this region will be known and characterized as a timber-producing division of the country.

EXTENT OF TREE PLANTING AND GROWING.

It may be safely stated that but little tree planting was done in the district designated, and by reason of annual fires sweeping very generally over the country, spontaneous growth was exceedingly meagre, for at least ten years after organization of the territories and first efforts by settlers to improve and develop. Statistics here presented in connection with Nebraska and Kansas commence with date, passage of Kansas-Nebraska act, 1854. From that time up to, and including the year 1882, covering a period of twenty-eight years, official statistics, with some reliable estimate to cover dates not thus provided, it is found there have been planted within the borders of what is now the State of Nebraska, 244,356 acres of forest trees. This includes seedlings, seeds and cuttings, planted in permanent forests, groves, and along highways and streets in cities and villages. Spontaneous indigenous growth, since fires have been kept from borders of streams and ravines, is estimated equal to half the area planted. Personal observation would warrant a larger proportion. Not a few informants contend for an equal extent; some higher—even to double. James T. Allan, Omaha, Ex-Secretary American Forestry Association, now in employ of the U. P. R. R. Co., traveling extensively over the West, responding to inquiries on this particular point, writes: " I have watched the spontaneous growth of young elms, walnuts, oaks, ash, hickories, etc., along the Missouri, Wood, and other rivers in the West, since fires have been kept back, and seen their growth among the hazel brush, which is the fringe on the border of native timber, dividing it from the prairie. I hardly think I am out of the way in setting it at double the amount of timber planted." A majority, however, in various parts of the State, place the estimate as stated—at one-half.

It is safe to say a majority of the planting is made, originally, four feet by four, with view to cutting out first one-half, as growth demands space, and eventually another half of that remaining; three-fourths in all. Some plant six by six; others eight by eight. Planted four by four, we have 2,622 trees to the acre; or a total of 640,701,432. Eight by eight, 682 to the acre, or a total of 166,680,790. Average the totals and there is shown 403,676,112; add to the average the spontaneous estimate, one-half, and the grand total is, planted and grown in twenty-eight years, 605,514,168 trees. The number of trees per acre, spontaneous growth, will more than equal one-half the acreage planted. It is estimated one-fourth of the trees, seeds and cuttings planted did not grow, and therefore not now occupying the ground. Spontaneous growth, except where the weak have been crowded out by the strong, and such as may have been destroyed by occasional fires, it may be said all are growing.

FRUIT TREES

Planted in Nebraska, since 1854 to 1882 inclusive, 12,038,112, of which 1,714,442 were planted in the year 1882; 2,906,754 grape vines have been planted, fully 30 per cent. of that number planted in 1882.

KANSAS.

From statistics on file with the State Board of Agriculture, Kansas, the following figures are obtained:

There have been planted since the first settlement in that State, 139,995 acres of forest trees. Walnut, 9,512 acres; maple (mostly soft) 13,545; honey locust, 1,916; cottonwood, 47,363; other varieties, 67,659. Planted four by four, or 2,622 plants to the acre, the total is shown, 376,066,890 trees, or eight by eight, 682 to the acre, the total is 195,376,590 trees. Average the totals and we have 231,221,710. Add for spontaneous growth 115,610,870, and the grand total is 346,832,640 trees. These estimates for spontaneous growth in that State range from 20 to 50 per cent.

As a rule, trees planted were put out under provisions of the national timber culture act. Of course many thousands of acres were planted by farmers who have not timber claims.

The number of fruit trees planted in that State during the same time, as shown by State records, is:

	Bearing.	Non-bearing.
Apple	3,028,100	3,590,333
Pear	97,369	164,302
Peach	5,983,140	4,089,803
Plum	293,474	339,516
Cherry	776,498	756,576
Totals	10,178,581	8,940,430

Grand total, 19,119,019.

NATIONAL TIMBER ACT.

Justice to the West, where this act originated, and where most of the work under its provisions has been done, would seem to demand at least a passing notice in this paper, especially when so eminent a personage as Prof. Sargent has publicly declared through the pages of the *North American Review,* October issue, 1882, the act a "disgrace to the statute books," " has not accomplished what was expected," " has given rise to gigantic frauds," " worthless as a means of forest growth," "encourages planting trees where trees can not grow unless artificially irrigated, and thus entails losses upon honest settlers." Great personal regard for Prof. Sargent, and high estimates of his ability and standing as a scientist, lead to the belief that he has made these assertions without proper consideration, or having in his possession reliable information. Facts known to myself, and many others in the West familiar with them, lead to different conclusions.

Brief reference is made to the professor's assertion relating to arid characteristics. Personal knowledge is had of over five hundred quarter sections of land west of the hundredth meridian in Nebraska, where groves of from five to thirty acres are planted on each, and growing well without any irrigation whatever. This planting was done under the act, all growing well and now thirty to forty feet in height. One man in this "arid region" commenced planting in 1875, and now has 45,000 flourishing trees—maple, ash, walnut, box-elder and cottonwood, some thirty inches in circumference.

Since the passsge of the timber culture act, there have been entered in Nebraska and Kansas, under its provisions, 5,932,520 acres of timber land, as shown by official statistics. The general land office books show 39,617 entries, or 396,170 acres planted in detail, as follows:

YEAR.	NEBRASKA.		KANSAS.	
	Acres.	Entries.	Acres.	Entries.
1873	21,858	137	9,642	60
1874	312,712	2,164	282,479	1,954
1875	130,894	1,061	168,269	1,265
1876	106,499	834	185,596	1,354
1877	90,812	706	238,020	1,666
1878	195,306	1,408	593,295	4,031
1879	465,968	3,183	1,167,582	7,776
1880	475,275	3,202	408,261	2,891
1881	240,306	1,682	268,575	1,924
1882	298,520	2,086	273,053	1,933

There may be frauds perpetrated under this act. It would be strange rather than otherwise, were there none. Frauds are, or can be perpetrated under almost any act and for any purpose. Those who know practically of the workings of the timber act do not favor its repeal. Possibly it can be advantageously amended in certain respects, but as it stands an incalculable amount of good has grown out of it and will so continue.

DEMONSTRATED USEFUL AND VALUABLE VARIETIES.

It has been practically demonstrated the following valuable varieties of forest timber can be successfully and satisfactorily grown, both planted and of spontaneous growth. Only the most valuable are named in this list. Those designated with a * are indigenous:

Ash, Fraxinus Americana.*
"   "   virdis.*
"   "   quadrangulata.*
"   "   pubescens.*
"   "   platy carpa.*
"   "   sambucifolia.*
Oak, Quercus alba.*
"   "   obtusiloba.*
"   "   macrocarpa.*
"   "   primus.*
"   "   tinctoria.*
"   "   rubra.*
"   "   nigra.*

A dwarf chinquapin oak—prinoides—of shrub character, grows in abundance, particularly on the bluff lands adjacent to the Missouri river, and in places in profusion on prairie lands, many acres in a body. It is a profuse bearer; nuts equal almost to chestnuts. In early days it was considered a " Munchausen story " when old settlers talked of hogs eating acorns from trees. The small growth, often not over a foot high, was loaded with nuts, and, therefore, easily eaten from by swine. Deer and antelope fatted on them.

Black Walnut, Juglans nigra.*
White   "   "   cinerea.
Hickory, Carya alba.*
"   "   sulcata.*
"   "   tomentosa.*
"   "   porcina.*
"   "   amara.*
Pecan nut,   "   olivæformis.*
Elm, Ulmus, Americana.*
"   "   fulva.*
"   "   racemosa.*
"   "   alata.*
Hackberry, Celtis occidentalis *
Honey Locust, Gled'a triacanthus.*
"   "   "   monosperma.*
Kentucky Coffee Tree, Gym's canadensis.*
Linden, Tillia Americana.*
Sycamore, Acer pseudo platanus.*
Black Locust, Robinia pseudo acacia.
Soft Maple, Acer dasycarpum.*
Sugar Maple, Acer saccharinum.

Sugar maple grown thus far, little else than for ornamental purposes, lawns and street trees. There is no reason why it may not be grown successfully for forest purposes, as it thrives well where introduced and planted.

> Poplar, Liriodendron tulipifera.
> Wild Black Cherry, Prunus serotina.
>   "   Red   "   "   Pennsylvanica.*
> Catalpa Hardy, Speciosa.
> Cottonwood, Populus monilifera.*
>   "   "   heterophylla.*
> Willow, Salix purpurea.*
>   "   "   cordata.*
>   "   "   longifolia.*
>   "   "   nigra.*

Valuable characteristics are noted of a willow, growing spontaneously along the Missouri river, from the mouth of the Big Nemaha south, to the Yellowstone north, familiarly known as " Diamond Willow." Prof. Sargent names it *Salix cordata,* var. vestita. Experience demonstrates it as durable almost for underground uses, posts, etc., as red cedar. Northern Indians seem to have known of its valuable characteristics. They call it " Twat," which interpreted signifies *durable.* It grows readily from cuttings, either in its natural home—the bottom lands—or out on high upland prairies.

> Box Elder, Negundo aceroides.*
> Chestnut, Castanea Americana.
> Pine, Pinus, Sylvestris.
>   "   "   Austriaca.
>   "   "   strobus.
> Red Cedar, Juniperus Virginiana.*
> Larch, Larix Europæa.
>   "   "   Americana.
> Mulberry, Morus rubra.*
>   "   "   alba.
>   "   "   monetti.

Many varieties of less value than the foregoing, embraced in a complete sylva of the States, are here omitted, as not of practical value for forest purposes.

GROWTH OF TREES.

The following actual measurement of tree growths, of known ages, are made, showing circumference in inches, two feet above ground:

	Yeaas old.	Inches.
White Elm*	15	24¾
White Elm*	24	63
Red Elm†	24	36
Catalpa*	20	48½
Soft Maple†	18	54¾
Soft Maple*	18	69¼

	Years old.	Inches.
Sycamore*	16	43½
Pig Hickory†	14	37½
Shag-bark Hickory†	24	30
Cottonwood†	23	78¼
Cottonwood*	11	93
Cottonwood*	25	98
Chestnut*	14	24½
Box Elder†	14	25¼
Box Elder*	14	31⅛
Honey Locust†	22	40¼
Honey Locust*	22	41½
Kentucky Coffee Tree†	14	25½
Burr Oak†	22	36⅛
Burr Oak†	26	43½
White Oak†	22	29
Red Oak†	22	37⅛
Black Oak†	22	38½
White Ash†	22	32¼
Green Ash†	22	30
Black Walnut†.	22	48
Black Walnut*	16	18
Black Walnut*	16	50¼
White Walnut*	16	49¼
Osage Orange*	25	26¼
Larch*	10	24
White Pine*	20	36¼
White Pine*	12	29
Scotch Pine*	15	23
Scotch Pine*	10	36
Austrian Pine*	11	22½
Balsam Fir*	12	26
Red Cedar*	12	26¼
White Cedar*	12	22
Mulberry*	18	43
Mulberry†	18	39¼
Russian Mulberry*	6	24
Linden†	14	35
Poplar*	4	12
Silver Leaf Poplar*	12	67
Black Locust*	24	60½
Red Willow*	20	58
Gray Willow*	15	26¼
Yellow Willow*	21	132

*Planted.
†Spontaneous growth.

I give no measurements as to height of trees, as all this depends on the
distance apart they are planted. Isolated, they are low headed; close together, they run upward, as all well know.

ORDER OF VALUE.

The order of ultimate value of deciduous varieties, while there may be difference of individual opinions, it is safe to arrange: White, burr and chestnut oaks, black and white walnut, white, green and blue ash, black cherry,
catalpa, black locust, honey locust, Kentucky coffee tree, elms, hickories,
larch, soft maple, hackberry, mulberry, cottonwoods, willows, box elders.
For present or near value, cottonwoods—especially the yellow—are almost
universally conceded preferable. There are, as shown, two varieties: yellow and white—*monilifera* and *heterophylla*. The yellow makes excellent lumber, particularly for inside uses, not exposed to weather. For shingles, only
pine, cedar or walnut are superior. Both make good fuel, after reasonable
drying or seasoning. Old steamboat and mill men prefer half seasoned cottonwood to any other obtainable in this region, claiming they get more
steam from it. Also much used in burning brick. No other wood holds
nails so well. Recently the white cottonwood is attracting attention for use
in manufacturing paper, the pulp from which is pronounced superior. This
may, some day, become a feature in cottonwood culture.

Evergreens stand in order of value: Red cedar, white, Scotch and Aus-
trian pines.

ORDER OF PLANTING.

The order of tree planting, numerically speaking, of deciduous varieties,
is, as near as may be: Cottonwoods, box elder, soft maple, elms, ashes, black
walnut, honey locust, catapla, oaks, hickories, Kentucky coffee tree, black locust, larch, sycamore, hackberry, mulberry, black cherry and willows. Two-
thirds of the whole are cottonwoods, from the facts: They are more easily
obtained, cost less, are of more rapid and certain growth, and from which
realizations are more speedily and certainly secured. And in addition, succeed almost anywhere planted.

Evergreens are planted in order: Scotch pine, red cedar, white and Aus-
trian pine.

Spontaneous growths range in order of value: Oaks, red and black perhaps predominating; hickories, more shag bark than others; black walnut,
elms, linden, white ash, mulberry and hackberry, on higher lands. On bottoms, cottonwoods, box elder, willows, sycamore, soft maples, green and water
ash.

PRICES FOREST TREE SEEDLINGS.

Prices of forest tree seedlings are such as to place them within reach of
the very poorest. In fact, as the great bulk planted are of a spontaneous origin, they are to be had for mere gathering, in regions where found. When
trafficked in, prices range, owing to variety and size, from six inches to four

feet, all along from fifty cents to three dollars per thousand. Nursery grown, range grades higher. Many millions are now planted annually.

COST OF PLANTING

Depends much on circumstances, price of land, labor, varieties planted, skill in planting, and many other minor details. Cottonwood seedlings can be furnished in quantity, from fifty cents to one dollar per thousand. Box elder and soft maple, from one to two dollars. Oaks, ash, walnut, hickory, çatapla and chestnut, from five to ten dollars. Robert Douglas & Son, Waukeegan, Illinois, are contractors for planting timber on the plains. From a letter on the subject, I quote:

"We plant this section for the railroad company. They pay the actual cost of breaking and cross-plowing the prairie, which costs four dollars an acre. We prepare the land, furnish the trees, plant them four by four feet, and grow them till they are four to six feet high, and shade the ground till they require no further care or cultivation, and are to deliver two thousand trees, four to six feet high, on each acre, for which we receive thirty dollars per acre. In taking contracts for the future we will charge five dollars per acre for breaking and cross-plowing the land, as the cost of getting the teams together, seeing that it is properly done, measuring for the different plowmen, paying them, etc., costs considerable, and actually stands us about five dollars per acre.

"Then labor has advanced since three years ago, so that we shall add $5 per acre, thus making, including breaking the raw prairie and everything, till the trees are delivered over, $40 per acre, getting the $5 per acre at the time of breaking, $20 per acre when the trees are planted, and $15 per acre when they are delivered over.

"When the trees are delivered over they are to be four to six feet, but most of them are much taller, and two to two and a half inches in diameter at the butt, perfectly free from weeds and not the least particle of danger from fires, as the catalpa leaves are very much like pumpkin leaves, and rot down. They need no pruning, as 100,000, four years planted, ten to fifteen feet high, are now shedding their under branches, or at least they are dead and will soon shed off.

"I was to select land for another plantation when I was out last month, but the land that could have been bought three years ago at $2.80 per acre is now worth $12 to $15 per acre, and on this account we concluded not to purchase. This would not make so much difference as it appears to, as the land will keep on increasing in value.

"We think this a reasonable price, taking all the risks and care ourselves, and if any railroad companies or forest planting associations should undertake it, it would certainly cost more. Of course we would take the contract to plant without the further care—that is, $20 an acre for the trees and planting, or $25 if the prairie is unbroken."

This will afford an approximate estimate of cost where all is done by contract. Most planting, however, at present, is done by individuals for individual use, and when done by one's own labor and teams, the cost is much less, at least the outlay.

ENCOURAGING ENACTMENTS AND PROVISIONS.

The Nebraska State constitution provides that "the increased value of lands, by reason of live fences, fruit and forest trees grown and cultivated thereon, shall not be taken into consideration in the assessment thereof." A State law "exempts from taxation for five years, $100 valuation for each acre of fruit trees planted, and $50 for each acre forest trees." Also makes it obligatory that "the corporate authorities of cities and villages in the State shall cause shade trees to be planted along the streets thereof." Further, "any person who shall injure or destroy the shade tree, or trees, of another, or permit his or her animals to do the same, shall be liable to a fine not less than $5 nor more than $50 for each tree injured or destroyed." To encourage growing live fences, the law permits planting "precisely on the line of the road or highway, and, for its protection, to ccupy, for a term of seven years, six feet of the the road or highway."

ARBOR DAY*

Originated in Nebraska through the action of the State Board of Agriculture. It is a day designated by the Board, during planting season, each spring, usually about the middle of April. The Board annually award liberal premiums for greatest number of trees, cuttings and seeds permanently planted on that day. The Governor annually, by proclamation, recognizes the day for the puposes indicated, urging the people to devote it exclusively to tree planting. It is very generally observed, and millions of trees planted that day.

MODES OF PLANTING AND TREATMENT.

The usual distances apart are by multiples, 4–8–12–16, etc., that intermediate ground may be utilized, by being cultivated in other crops until trees are sufficient size to protect themselves, when, in farm parlance, they are permitted to "take the ground."

Most experimenters at first planted tree seeds where they were to remain permanently. Experience has shown this a mistake, for numerous reasons. Principally, by this mode, uneven stand, growth, grade, size and vigor are to contend with. By planting seeds, first in beds, and say, at one year's growth, assorting, grading and transplanting permanently, each grade to itself, better results are secured. Same grades as to size and vigor do better together; grow more evenly; the weak are not crowded out or overshadowed by the stronger—a practical illustration of "survival of the fittest."

---

*Hon. J. Sterling Morton was the originator of "Arbor Day," not only in Nebraska, but in the United States. It originated by the introduction by him of a resolution adopted by the Nebraska State Board of Agriculture, since which many other States have adopted it, as well as foreign countries.

By this plan small plants, if healthy, do about as well in the end as the large. No variety is known not readily transplanting at one year old. Even varieties of tap-root characteristics, oaks, walnuts, hickories and chestnuts, are really better, I am convinced, for tap-root pruning. By it, laterals or fibrous feeding roots are induced. Or, if larger sizes are desired before transplanting, root-pruning, by running a tree-digger under the rows and allowing them to remain a year or two longer, good results are obtained. As a rule, however, better success is had by transplanting young trees when, as near as possible, all roots are preserved. Small trees cost less to purchase, transport, handle and transplant.

Alternating—especially certain varieties—has not given satisfaction. Trees in some respects are not unlike mankind—will not fraternize. For instance, oaks, walnuts and hickories will not fraternize with maples, cottonwoods and elms. When planted near each other, the latter will invariably lean away from the former, assuming crooked, gnarly appearance, and in the end virtually die out.

INCIDENTAL ILLS.

Thus far few ills have attended timber culture on the plains. The great losses or failures have been from careless handling, planting and after neglect. Black locust was planted extensively in earlier days, but being so badly affected by borers, its cultivation, until of late, was almost entirely abandoned. The pest, which almost universally destroyed in the beginning, suddenly and without known cause disappeared, and that valuable variety of timber is again receiving merited attention. In certain portions of Nebraska, during one or two years, a large green worm—name not known—defoliated most soft maples, for a time checking their growth. In a few instances the same borer attacking black locust, to a limited extent, injured soft maples and cottonwoods. They being of such rampant growth, injury was not material.

Trees attacked were principally those used for ornamental purposes—those on streets in cities and villages. Where ground has been well and deeply prepared. good healthy plants used, care exercised in handling and planting, followed by attention and proper cultivation, until able to care for self, there has been no good cause for complaint.

IMPORTANCE OF SPONTANEOUS GROWTH.

Too much importance can not attach to spontaneous timber growing. Nature, in this respect, is both accommodating and bounteous in her provisions. Waste places, as a rule, are utilized. Lands, which, if at all adapted to other uses, could only be prepared at extra expense, are those nature occupies and renders of value. This growth comes of its own accord, so to speak, without preparation or labor by man, other than to guard against fires along broken and often precipitous bluffs and ravines, in nooks and corners of tortuous and meandering streams, incident to prairie regions.

A friend, writing from the Republican Valley, three hundred miles west from the Missouri river, says: "Oak timber begins to be noticeable, and there are so many little burr oak saplings creeping along up the hill-sides that I marvel how they got there. This oak is strangely typical of the white pioneer of this section. At first there were a few scattering trees of large size along the banks of the streams, where natural protection from fire enabled them to grow and spread their limbs in rugged strength and healthfulness. A few years more, and bushes of the same kind sprouted up in sheltered nooks and dells and about the bases of the bluffs. Before these were so high as a man's head, other germs of oak life broke through the sod further away from the parental stem. And so it went on, until now this sturdy tree promises to possess all uncultivated land, if spared by the ax. Here and there the brown verdure is relieved by a speck of green, denoting the presence of a clump of small cedars, or, mayhap, a patriarch that escaped the prairie fires of aboriginal days. These, sharply defined against the gray bluff or blue sky, and relieved by the brown and leafless arms of the oak or elm, make a dot of landscape that would secure immortality to the artist whose pencil could reproduce it with fidelity to nature."*

A belief is freely expressed that greater proportionate successful tree growing, and at compartively no expense, has been done by nature, than by man planting. As stated before, by far greater proportions such planting and growing stands and succeeds than that of artificial processes. Losses are rare, and only from occasional invading fires, and where too thick on the ground the stronger kill out the weaker—no loss in fact, simply adjusting or equalizing.

Personal knowledge is had, in many instances, where lands twenty and twenty-five years ago were considered worthless, have grown to be valued at from twenty to one hundred dollars per acre, solely for the timber value nature planted and grew.

In conclusion let it be remembered, " Man's conquest over nature is not for a generation, but for all generations. One bequeaths its work to the next. The old builders knew, or rather limitations on them, compelled observance of this law. They attempted not to complete a great work in a single lifetime. They laid foundations broad and strong. They built as though they meant endurance. They did what they could, and left that unfinished to their successors. So the great walls of the masters remain to-day a wonder to the world—solid in fabric and rich in ornamentation." Let these truisms point the way to those who aim to rehabilitate the denuded, or invest naturally treeless domain.

Notwithstanding Dr. Warder was prevented from attending the meeting by the floods in the Ohio river, he has kindly supplied the following paper, which the Secretary deems appropriate to follow the valuable paper by Gov. Furnas on the same topic. Dr. Warder is so well and so favorably known that the Secretary presents this paper without further introduction or apology.

---

* J. D. Calhoun, in State Journal.

INFLUENCE OF FORESTS ON HEALTH.

BY JOHN A. WARDER, M. D.

A medical friend*, who has strenuously advocated the preservation of forests for their hygienic influence, in a recent paper presented before the American Forestry Congress, took for his thesis the following proposition : " Trees conduce to health, and the more trees the more health."

He takes and maintains the position that trees notably modify the climate by arresting the currents of air, the winds, which constitute an important element in climate, the influence of which, he thinks, has been far too much overlooked by writers on hygiene. He asserts that " a windy climate is a bad climate—wind interferes with health as well as comfort; it punishes hearty persons and is ruinous to invalids; it interferes with good ventilation, and with the moderate, uniform warmth that should prevail in our houses. A windy climate is a climate of shivers and snuffles, and colds and consumption. Therefore, I say, the more trees the less wind, the more trees the more health."

He also advocates the effects of forests on the score of temperature. Admitting that the mean average temperature may be the same in wooded as in open regions, he claims that " the annual means have little to do with health. What concerns the physician and the sanitarian most is the extent and the rapidity of the oscillations of temperature; here the influence of forests is eminently conservative." From which the writer will not demur, but proceeds :

CLIMATIC INFLUENCES OF FORESTS.

While it will not be insisted upon that the general rainfall will be increased, as is so generally supposed, the forests do undoubtedly exert an important influence upon the climatic conditions. The general storms of our country may be dependent upon the relative configuration of land and water, as well as upon the lines of elevations. These are conditions that are arranged on a plan of grand proportions. They cover continental areas; still, it may safely be asserted, that the fortunate or judicious distribution of forests in prairie regions, and even on our great western plains, can not fail to exert a controling influence of vast importance and of greater or less extent. Certainly the local climate will be affected by the woodlands, which act upon it in the following manner:

First—By checking the force of the currents of air, woodlands will, in a great measure, prevent excessive evaporation, and the moisture thus permitted to remain in the soil will prove as valuable as an equal amount in rainfall.

Second—The forests are of great value in a similar way by the influence of their shade, which prevents the fierce rays of the sun from exercising an ad-

*Dan. Milliken, M. D., Hamilton, Ohio.

ditional power in drying the soil by evaporation. This has been fully demonstrated by the long continued experiments of Prof. Ebermeyer, of Bavaria.

Third—The trees are of great value by their agency in the same direction through the action of their leaves, which cause a more copious condensation of the atmospheric humidity than will occur in closely adjacent lands bare of such vegetation. This fact has been abundantly proved by the experiments of the same careful observer, whose results have been confirmed by others.

Fourth—It has been found, moreover, that the atmosphere within a forest of some extent is always more humid than that of open lands in the same neighborhood. So also the temperature of the forests and of the soil itself is always lower in summer and higher in winter than that of the open lands, cultivated or waste; the climate is rendered more equable.

Fifth—Another very important matter must be apparent to the most casual observer, to-wit: That the moisture precipitated on forest lands is, in a great measure, retained and allowed to percolate quietly into the loose and mellow soil, and even to reach the subsoil and fissile rocks beneath. Its flow is obstructed by fallen leaves, twigs, branches and logs, by mosses, roots and herbage; whereas, the same amount of rain, when falling upon the compact turf of a grassy pasture or upon the bare surface of arable lands, especially when these are firmly trodden, sun-baked or frozen, will at once flow off by every depression, carrying with it the best elements of the soil, suddenly swelling the streams, and eventually cutting the fields into frightful gullies and chasms so as to destroy their usefulness as farm lands.

Sixth—Most especially is it important to preserve forest growths upon declivitous lands, hillsides and river banks, particularly in those regions where our streams take their source. Mountain regions, emphatically those of an Alpine character, should be largely, nay, almost exclusively devoted to forests, and these should be sacredly preserved, for in this condition alone can such tracts of country most perfectly fulfill the destiny for which they seem to have been designed by an all-wise Creator.

The mountains are the sources of the streams which fructify the earth. They intercept the floating clouds, laden with vapor, that is precipitated upon them; when forested, this is retained and furnishes perennial springs, that combine their many contributions to fill the streams which unite to form the world's rivers, and thus, after enriching the earth and turning the busy wheels of manufactures, they open to us channels of commerce of the most valuable and economical character.

If these elevated regions be chiefly covered with trees, they are in the best possible condition to fulfill their admirable function of receivers and reservoirs of pure and healthful waters, which they slowly, but regularly and faithfully, give up for our use and for the continued fertility of the earth.

EFFECTS OF EXPOSING THE MOUNTAINS.

But it has been again and again demonstrated that where the cupidity of man has ruthlessly destroyed the natural arboreal covering of such regions, that the perennial and gently flowing rivulet has, at frequent intervals, become the uncontrollable mountain torrent, which, in its rapid course to the lower levels, bears everything before it. It first takes away the accumulated soil, produced by ages of decay, from the action of the elements upon the rocks, and mingled with the moldering remains of vegetation, long since gathered from the atmosphere by nature's chemistry. Then the rocks themselves yield to the impetuous current, the mountain sides are scored and gashed, rent into frightful fissures and canyons, that are filled for a few hours in every storm with a turbid stream laden with the debris which floods the fertile valleys. This spreads ruin among the villages, destroying bridges, roads, houses, cattle and even human beings, while at the same time the once fertile plains and intervales are covered with obnoxious debris and rendered unfit for culture. So terribly have certain portions of Europe suffered from this cause, even in enlightened States, that it has become necessary to meet the evil by government interference, requiring the reforestation of large tracts of such mountains. Already we may see the happy effects of the reboisement of Alpine heights in many of the provinces of France and other countries. The same terrible results are in prospect as a consequence of the ruthless destruction of the timber in the mountain regions of our own Western territories.

SHELTER BELTS.

Even the richest arable lands of our country are found to be very generally enhanced in productiveness by judicious planting of forest trees, arranged as shelter belts. These break the force of the blasts which sweep over any great extent of open country that lies in broad plateaux, unbroken by any considerable line of elevation. This effect is equally marked in summer, the season of growth, as in the period of wintry storms.

This sheltering influence of trees is well understood by the Chinese, with their dense population, and where every rood must maintain its man, for while the whole surface is cultivated with sedulous care, we are told by intelligent travelers that the lines of trees scattered here and there give the impression at some distance that you are in a wooded country.

A somewhat similar appearance is presented in the highly cultivated and densely populous regions of portions of Holland and some other countries, where these wind-breaks have been planted, and are fully appreciated for the shelter they afford.

But we need not look abroad for illustrations of the great value of such plantations. In portions of our own prairie regions there are many intelligent cultivators who have learned the value of such shelter-belts around their farms. Judge C. Whiting, of Monona county, Iowa, asserts that since he has planted and grown such barriers against the winds, he has realized more profit from the crops produced upon the remaining four-fifths of his land than formerly, when it was open prairie, he was able to harvest from the whole farm in the same kind of crops.

11

PROTECTION TO MEN.

In the western half of Minnesota there is a large tract of very fertile land (10,000,0C0 acres), said to be capable of becoming the granary of the Northwest, on account of its wonderful adaptation to the wheat crop. This region is estimated to possess but one acre of natural timber to the section (or square mile of 640 acres). Immigration into this region was attempted, but the terrible severity of the winter's winds drove back the distressed settlers, until it was shown, by the successful efforts of Mr. L. B. Hodges, that shelter could be cheaply and quickly furnished by tree planting. This demonstration was followed by a large influx of an industrious population.

But every gardener understands the great benefits he derives from shelter hedges, even where they are kept trimmed down to a moderate height. This is especially the case when these wind-screens are composed of evergreens. Such lines of living plants not only check the driving winds, and thus ward off constant accessions of cold air, but they at the same time prevent, to a certain extent, the increased evaporation that would result, and its attendant depression of temperature. Besides this, the living plants themselves appear to have an amount of specific heat within them, as has been proved by observations made at some of the forest experiment stations in Germany. A series of observations made in the neighborhood of St. Louis, by Mr. Tice, showed the protecting influence exerted by an evergreen hedge which extended for several rods to the leeward, before the thermometers indicated the same degree of cold as those on the windward side. [Mr. Tice's experiments, reported in Ills. Hort. Trans.]

WOODLANDS RETAIN MOISTURE.

But another fact in reference to the influence of forests upon climates and its results is too important to be overlooked. Woodlands are not only receptive of snows and rains, but they are also remarkably retentive of these treasures from the skies. Beneath the trees we usually find the soil loose and open; the surface is more or less covered by the debris of decaying vegetable matter, all of which must receive, absorb and temporarily retain the rains and melting snows until the fluid may quietly settle into the soil and subjacent rocks, and thus the forest regions become reservoirs for supplying springs that pour forth the runlets, rivulets and streams which eventually form the rivers of the continents.

SAND-WASTES—SAND-DUNES.

While considering the relations of forestry, we should not overlook the immense value of tree plantations upon low, sandy lands. These sometimes occur in the interior of a continent, though they are more frequent in situations exposed to the sea, where the combined influence of the waves and the winds pile up the sands into great dunes that are often mercilessly wafted about, overwhelming agricultural districts. and obstructing once navigable rivers, destroying commerce, and often injuriously affecting the sanitary condition of the country adjacent to the streams.

Such instances are common in various parts of the world, and their management becomes an important problem in forestry. All must be familiar with the disastrous effects produced by the removal of the forests in regions thus situated. Such results have occurred in Northern Germany, on the shores of the Baltic, and in Holland and Belgium, where the coast-line is exposed to the lashing storms of the North Sea. Similar conditions have been observed in the Province of Cadiz, Spain, where the coast-line is open to the winds of the broad Atlantic, which seriously affect the flow of the Guadalquiver, as is forcibly set forth in a recent pamphlet by Don Salvador Ceron.

The condition of the country in Gascony, upon the shores of the stormy Bay of Biscay, has become familiar to all modern readers who have seen the graphic accounts of the Hon. Geo. P. Marsh.

There the mouth of the River Levre has been dammed up by drifting sands, and the whole region, known as Les Landes, is a waste of successive dunes and lagoons.

This whole region has been much improved by the persevering application of practical skill, directed by the scientific knowledge of Messrs. Bagneris and Bremontier, who succeeded, under the most unfavorable circumstances, in producing valuable forests upon these sand-wastes. The *Pinus maritima* has here proved most successful on these lands.

. We have similar tracts in our own country that should receive the attention of scientific forestry before it be too late—though we must not be misled by those who would advise us blindly to follow the practice of France in its details and species, regardless of the climatic conditions of our country as compared with those of the regions lying on the western shores of Europe, between the same parallels. Indeed, one of the most intelligent and extensive cultivators of nursery trees admits that he was so taken with the accounts of this same *Pinus maritima* that, many years ago, he imported a large quantity of seed. These vegetated readily and grew apace, in promise exceeding all others, and he was delighted until, at the close of the following winter, he was made a wiser and also a sadder man, by finding that all his beautiful little trees had died. And yet we have again heard this tree recommended for planting on the sandy shores of Massachusetts!

Excuse this digression, Mr. Chairman. It has been introduced simply as an illustration of the great need which exists among us for real and practical knowledge upon almost every point connected with forestry.

We should not despair, however, for we have many other plants that are equally capable of fixing the blowing sands of these wastes, which exist in many parts of our own country, though generally in limited areas. By observing the natural growths upon such sandy regions, we shall meet with the indications of the means to be applied for the preservation of adjacent lands from the inroads of these moving sands. First in importance, let it be remembered, such dunes should never be stripped of their natural growths, nor should they ever be cut, torn or plowed; keep them covered with vegetation and they may be controlled.

On coming to the discussion of this branch of the subject, the first impression was that it might be difficult to see wherein the sanitary differed from the hygienic, since both words are derived from radicals that convey the idea of health.

The difficulty was solved, however, by a more careful study of their derivation. Sanitary, or that which pertains to health, from *sanitas*, health, appears to be a more generic term, since it is applicable to all that relates to health, whether good or bad, as it is sometimes used in the sense of depreciation— thus the sanitary condition of a place may be esteemed bad, and capable of amendment.

Hygienic, from *Hygeia*, the Goddess of Health, or health itself, may be said to refer to that which produces and protects our health—it is preservative and should not be used in a bad sense.

Thus the hygienic relations of forests must refer solely to the influences which trees may contribute to the healthfulness of a community or country, while the sanitary relations may also include all those results connected with our health or disease that are traceable to the influences exerted upon the animal frame by the presence and proximity of forests.

That forests do exert an important influence upon the sanitary conditions of a country can not be doubted, and it must be admitted that their relation to public health is not always favorable.

It is especially true that too much shade in the immediate vicinity of our dwellings, so as to exclude the direct access of sun and air, is productive of insalubrious results.

Forests having been proved to be reservoirs and retainers of moisture, and being known to exercise an important influence upon the climate of a country, they can not fail to exert a sanitary influence. Where they occupy extensive tracts of low and level land, their retention of superabundant moisture, by obstructing its free escape by evaporation or by the natural channels, and causing it to be retained among the accumulated remains of vegetation, may undoubtedly produce disease, and in such cases their influence upon the sanitary conditions is unquestionably bad. On the other hand, and in other situations, the admitted influence of forests upon the continuous supply of pure and healthful water, produces the most happy and important hygienic effects upon all animal life.

To a certain extent, also, and in particular localities, masses of forests, and even belts of trees, may exert a most happy hygienic effect by cutting off the malarious exhalations arising from marshy districts that would otherwise prove very injurious to the health of neighboring communities.

The natural respiration of the trees when in leaf may also exert important influence in purifying the atmosphere by their powers of absorption and digestion, or assimilation.

Especially in tropical countries, and even in sub-tropical and lower temperate regions, the usual forestal condition of moisture and decaying vegetable matter, accompanied by heat, are believed to give rise to that enigmatical but universally accepted condition called malaria—a most unsatisfactory term, and a more unsatisfactory condition of our atmosphere.

The rich low lands of these Western States, which were once heavily timbered, were found to be very sickly and to abound in fevers when the hardy pioneers first opened their farms, though these lands, since being cleared and drained, have become entirely salubrious, their sanitary conditions have been changed by the complete removal of the forests.

The unhealthfulness of the dense forests, especially on the lower levels within the tropics, is too well known to need a reference to localities by way of illustration.

It has been supposed that certain trees gave forth exhalations that were insalubrious. The fabled Upas tree is familiar to every school boy, but the reports of modern travelers and the lights of modern science have united to dispel the fable. There is such a tree as the Upas, known to botanists as the *Antiaris toxicaria,* and it belongs to a family many of which contain a poisonous principle, chiefly found in their milky juices, but there is no evidence of poisonous exhalations from the tree that could affect the atmosphere, as set forth in the fable. Many trees exhale carbonic acid at night, and unpleasant effects might be produced by exposure to a confined atmosphere surcharged with such a gas.

Many trees exhale a heavy perfume when in blossom that has been found prejudicial to the health of delicate persons, and some are really poisonous in their aura, as the *Rhus venenata* of our Northern swamps. The noble and valuable *Ailanthus glandulosa,* from the Farther East, which may yet play an important role in our Western forestry, just now bears the weight of odium on account of its exhalations. True, it belongs to a poisonous family, and does affect some sensitive persons injuriously. This. however, is exceptional, and is rather a matter to be referred to the peculiar idiosyncrasy of individuals. To most persons this tree, though unpleasant, is not poisonous nor injurious.

The opportunity can not be permitted to pass without the remark that in this country the prevailing haste of our people has induced them to adopt this, and some other trees, for planting in their streets and avenues, on account of their rapid growth, without duly considering their compatibility or otherwise for such a purpose. The ailanthus has, indeed, an important place to fill, where it will prove eminently satisfactory, but that place may, perhaps, not be as a shade tree in city or village.

The various species of *Eucalyptus* that have been introduced from Australia, though unfitted for our latitudes, have proved valuable acquisitions in hotter regions, especially on account of their rapid growth and valuable timber, but they have a strong claim, also, on the score of their reputed hygienic relations.

They have been largely planted in the swampy regions of Algeria, where they are reported to have produced marked effects upon the health of the country bordering upon the marshy districts. The question arises, however, whether the happy effect be due to their pleasant balsamic exhalations, or perhaps more probably to their power of absorbing and assimilating immense quantities of water from the swamps that were formerly so very unwholesome there.

Here we must forego the advantages of the *eucalypti,* but it is not at all improbable that in the miasmatic regions of our temperate zone, where the extremes of cold will not permit the introduction of the *eucalypti,* we may find a valuable substitute for them in the stronger growing species of poplars and willows. The *Populus monilifera* and *angulata,* and the *Salix alba* have great powers of absorbing moisture, and may rival the Australian trees as swamp-drainers.

HEALTH RESORTS.

Pine forests have been highly recommended as health resorts, and some virtue has been claimed for their resinous exhalations. These may possibly exert a favorable influence in certain classes of disease, but it should also be remembered that the hygienic conditions of any country depend largely upon the geological character of the soil and its elevation above the sea-level, with the attendant purity of the atmosphere and its hygroscopic condition. Thus we find the most famous health resorts are usually situated upon land that is well drained by a porous subsoil of sands, gravels and sandstones, or underlaid by metamorphic rocks; or they are found in elevated and mountainous regions that are proverbial for absence of malaria; or, again, they are well exposed to the salt air of the ocean, and, at the same time, away from the exhalations of swamps and marshes.

At the close of a valuable paper by Dr. G. L. Andrew, of Laporte, Indiana, read before the American Health Association, appears the following summary of his argument, which is gladly reproduced:

1. Forests increase the amount of condensation over their own areas, but by reason of the amount intercepted by their leaves and stems the annual rain-fall at the earth's surface is not, perhaps, materially affected by their presence or absence in regions well covered with other vegetation and thoroughly cultivated.

2. By means of their interlaced roots, mosses, lichens and humus, they check the efflux of superfluous rain-fall, thus regulating the water supply in streams and springs, and decreasing the proportion of the annual precipitation that is borne to the sea by the natural drainage of the country.

3. Forests diminish the evaporation from the earth's surface, but this hygrometric deficiency is much more than compensated by the increased evaporation from their leaves. Forests may thus become beneficial, or otherwise,

according to circumstances. The change which tree-planting has already produced upon our western plains is an unmixed good, but, by increasing the humidity of the climate of certain health resorts, valued mainly for their dryness—as Denver, for example—is not unaccompanied with evil.

4. Trees modify temperature—wooded countries being warmer in winter and cooler in summer. This they do by radiation, but, owing to their slow conducting power, the times of their daily maximum and minimum do not occur until some hours after the same phases in the temperature of the air, thus distributing the heat of the day more equally over .the twenty-four hours. The special significance of this effect lies in the fact that, as relating to human health, the daily range of the thermometer is of more importance than the mean temperature of whole seasons.

5. Trees radiate and evaporate through a stratum of air equaling in thickness their height, whilst the radiation and evaporation from grasses, plants and shrubs is confined to a stratum limited to the comparatively lesser planes which they occupy.

6. From the preceding it may be fairly inferred that they modify climate to the extent of influencing the amount and character of the diseases in their vicinity. (In this inquiry residence in forests is not considered, universal experience having shown those situations which are permanently shaded to be insalubrious.)

7. Forests and tree belts are of undoubted value in preventing the dissemination of malaria.

8. Trees are of positive sanitary value in affording shelter from the excessive heat of the sun, from the violence of winds, and in promoting æsthetic culture.

9. The importance of devoting to forests all regions unfit for profitable culture, and of protecting them by an enlightened public sentiment, as well as by legal enactment, may be fairly assumed as a sanitary as well as an economical necessity.

Fourth Day—Saturday.

FORENOON SESSION.

At 10 o'clock A. M. President Earle called the Society to order.

Mr. F. P. Baker, of Kansas, from the Committee on Excursion to Mobile, reported that near one hundred members had expressed a desire to make the excursion, and that Tuesday A. M. had been agreed upon as the time of leaving this city for Mobile.

On motion by Mr. E. H. Williams, of Indiana, a committee,

consisting of Williams, Smith and Nowlin, was appointed for the purpose of reporting a plan for raising the necessary funds for the support of the Society.

Mr. Galusha, of Illinois, from the committee to whom the report on Experimental Stations was recommitted, reported the following, which was adopted:

REPORT OF THE COMMITTEE ON EXPERIMENTAL STATIONS.

WHEREAS, The attention of the Congress of the United States has been so often called to the importance of fostering the interests of agriculture, horticulture and the mechanic arts, as to induce them to provide for the establishment in the several States of the Union of agricultural colleges for the special work of teaching those sciences relating to agriculture and the mechanic arts; and,

WHEREAS, In the opinion of the members of the Mississippi Valley Horticultural Society these institutions generally devote an undue proportion of the instructions in these colleges to literary studies, and thus, in so far, fall short of accomplishing in the best manner and to the fullest extent the special objects for which they were created;

Resolved, That we urge upon the trustees of the various agricultural colleges the importance of giving prominence to the science and practice of agriculture, horticulture and the mechanic arts; and,

WHEREAS, A bill has been introduced into Congress for the establishment in each of the several States one or more Experimental Stations in connection with these agricultural colleges, for the testing of trees, plants and seeds, and different breeds of animals, etc.; therefore,

Resolved, That we urge upon the Representatives and Senators in Congress from the several States represented in this convention, attention to the importance of the objects named in said bill, and earnestly request them to adopt this bill, or another equivalent in its provisions.

Resolved, That a sufficient number of copies of these resolutions be printed by the Secretary and distributed among the members of this Society for their use in carrying out the objects sought.   .

Mr. *Baker,* of Kansas, a member of the same committee, asked leave to add the following supplemental resolution, which the Society granted:

Resolved, That in view of the rapid extinction of the forests of the country, the time has arrived when all government timber lands should be withdrawn from market, and the timber thereupon only should be sold, and in such a manner as to protect the forests from extinction. To do this effectually the forest lands should be divided into districts of reasonable extent, each under care of a government inspector, whose duty it shall be to supervise the forest growth, to bring trespassers to justice, and to see that only such trees are sold as can be spared without detriment, or whose removal would be advantageous, or that no trees below a certain size shall be cut on tracts designated. It should also be made his duty to exercise oversight of tracts from which the merchantable timber has already been removed, to see that the young growth is not injured, and especially that it be protected from fire. To this end there should be a body of young, energetic and practical men educated by the government, and standing in the same relation to it that the graduates of West Point and Annapolis do, competent, faithful, and fond of their work. To raise up this class there should be established such a number of national schools of forestry as may be found necessary, care being taken that the schools are distributed in the different sections of the Union according to climatic division and the character of their natural forests, as, for instance, the white pine regions, the southern pine and cypress country, the regions where the walnut, maple, elm and deciduous trees are the prevalent growth, and the high prairies and treeless plains and mountain slopes. Attached to each of these schools there should be an experimental farm, where every tree known to the United States should be planted, and in certain localities, as determined by their natural dryness and altitude, the methods of irrigation as applied to forest culture should be thoroughly tested.

The President appointed Mr. T. T. Lyon, of Michigan, a substitute for Mr. P. J. Berckmans, of Georgia, as chairman of the Committee on Fruits on Exhibition

Mr. Smith, of Wisconsin, then read the following

REPORT OF THE COMMITTEE ON TRANSPORTATION OF FRUITS AND VEGETABLES:

Refrigerator cars may be and are good where they can be governed by one person in an intelligent manner—our President does this.

But for general use we do not deem it practical. Well ventilated cars, both for express and freight, should be provided by transportation companies wherever fruit is to be carried during warm weather. The free circulation of air through the whole load is indispensable to its keeping in good condition. Instance—strawberries from Mississippi, Tennessee and Southern Illinois, by express, reach Chicago often so thoroughly heated as to be entirely unfit for shipment, and of little value to any one.

The cause—cars packed solid with fruit and vegetables, generate sufficient heat to seriously damage them at any time; but packed in tight cars, often loaded to the roof, shut up tight, no chance for any air to circulate through the car, makes it suffocating to breathe and melts the fruit. To avoid this, express cars, particularly, should be so constructed as to admit all the air possible; if it were possible, they should be piled with inch strips between each tier of cases. Railroad men may say that ventilation admits cinders. This is true; but the openings can be covered with wire screens fine enough to admit air plentifully and keep out cinders; and all openings can easily be fitted with slides, to close when cold weather requires.

The enormous increase in growth of fruits and vegetables has made a corresponding increase of transportation, often taxing it to its utmost capacity, and crowding it far beyond the power of companies to properly handle it. It is a matter that should interest every grower to such an extent that, individually and collectively, they will make such demands as will bring the remedy. The shipments from the South to the North are large enough to warrant us in demanding of railroad and express companies—

1. Cars properly constructed for the preservation of perishable property confided to their care.

2. Enough of such cars to properly load and carry it.

3. Asking that proper time be given at such stations as need it for careful handling, etc.

4. That such cars be run through from the point of loading to Chicago, or other distributing points, without breaking bulk or transferring.

Most of the above refers to express transportation. Railroad companies supply their customers with such cars and facilities much better than the express companies.

At certain seasons of the year the fruit carriage has now become a large part of the revenue of the express companies. It is right, it is just, that we, the growers and shippers of this produce, should have the best facilities afforded us to properly lay our products at the doors of our consumers, thereby stimulating our industry and increase the revenue of the transportation companies, and give the consumers all over the country sounder and more palatable fruit, thus making all "more happy."

One illustration, showing the value of currents of air through fruit for long carriage : Strawberries grown in Florida and South Carolina come North on steamers to New York. They pack in quart baskets, not tight boxes, in open slat crates holding four layers of baskets, layers separated by light racks. On board steamer they are placed in what they call a fan refrigerator, the air being forced through the piles of crates by a fan run by the steamer's engine. This fruit, after several days' voyage to New York, comes to Chicago by express, and if the weather is cool the seller need not hasten to sell. If out of order, by turning out, the spoiled fruit is easily picked out, the decay seeming to be in individual berries, not in masses. You say this fruit coming early, and the weather cool, it ought to keep. Very true, but by our present means of transportation can you pack and ship strawberries in any quantity and at any time, and have them in salable shape two weeks off the vines ? They do.

Upon motion of Dr. McKay, of Mississippi, the report was amended as follows :

Be it further Resolved, That a standing committee of six members of this Society, exclusive of the President, who shall be chairman of said committee, three of said committee to reside north of the Ohio river, and three south of the same, be appointed. It shall be the duty of this committee to make every honorable effort within their power to secure such improvements in transportation as shall be most advantageous to grower and consumer alike, and will, as we believe, be advantageous to all concerned in this very important interest.

DISCUSSION ON THE REPORT.

Mr. Baldwin, of Michigan—I consider this one of the most important subjects yet presented to this Society. I feel a personal interest in it. The railroads should give us cheaper rates and better handling than they are now doing.

Mr. Porter, of Tennessee—I second Dr. McKay's motion. I think we should have two good committees, with the President as chairman, on a subject of such great importance. Let us bring all the force we can to bear on the railroads

The report as amended was adopted.

President Earle—Our next paper is a practical one by a practical man, and that on a subject second in importance to none heretofore presented to this convention. Many of us succeed better in raising fruit than we do in marketing it. The subject that Capt. Hollister, of Alton, Ill., will now present you is, "Markets and Marketing." Ladies and gentlemen, I now call your attention to Capt. Hollister's paper:

MARKETS AND MARKETING.

BY E. HOLLISTER, OF ILLINOIS.

Referring to your programme, I find myself distributed among those horticulturists who can tell you all about raising fruits and vegetables, and I am expected to furnish the market and tell you how to dispose of your products to the best advantage. This seems to me a one-sided affair. I came here to learn about this very thing, as well as have a good time.

Some of my experience has been bought at a very heavy price, the value of the goods being taken into consideration, and if any hints thrown out will be of value to others I shall feel much gratified.

The field is a broad and widening one, as we shall find, and I shall not, were I able, go over the whole of it, but here and there sketch a few salient points.

The question of latitude and railroad facilities are the chief factors for determining the market for your horticultural products. This mighty valley of the Mississippi, with soil practically exhaustless in its fertility and productiveness, capable of supplying the wants of much of the old world and the new, is most favorably situated, and the great question here, as with us, is how to prepare, in the best manner, the products for the Northern markets so as to obtain the prices adequate to the outlay, with fair margins.

The distance you may send any given product is very much under each shipper's control; while one may succeed in sending strawberries from New Orleans to Chicago, others may not have their goods arrive in even, fair condition at either Louisville, Cincinnati or St. Louis. Much, very much, depends on the manner the fruit is handled before the express takes it.

If it were possible for each shipper to be at the end of the route and see his fruit there, some degree of light would fall upon his vision, which, without it, he would emphatically deny the paternity, and insist that his neighbor's fruit had been substituted. Much, then, depends upon the handling of the fruit, especially berries.

The first requisite in this direction is the condition of the berries before picking. The strawberry should be clean, dry and free from dirt or sand. Never pick for a distant market wet or over-ripe berries. If you have no local or near market, pick and throw away; much less loss will come by heroic treatment, and your plantation will be in much better condition for the next picking, with few or no over-ripe or soft berries.

Watch the pickers' hands, when berries are in condition to travel. If any one has stained hands, discard at once, unless reform is sure. Each berry with the half-inch stem should be picked and put in the quart box before another is taken hold of. Do not allow the pickers of strawberries or red raspberries to retain in the hands more than two or three berries at a time at the utmost. Pick less and pay more for it. Insist upon great care on this point.

Each picker should have a case holding four to six quarts and provided with some covering to shade the berries from the sun while the picker is at work. Much damage is caused by neglect in this direction. If no natural shade is convenient, you must provide one, as indicated. While on the stem or twig the fruit can withstand a great degree of direct heat from the sun, but when once taken off a much less heat will cause serious damage. Fill the quart box full and round up; press with the hand slightly but firmly so as to leave the box full and firm, but do not press enough to bruise or break the fruit. Use the twenty-four quart case and put double bottoms to the quart boxes, well fastened with tacks to the four sides, sufficient for one-half the top layer of every case—one-half a bottom will do for the double. The reason for this is obvious. Should the bottoms of the quarts become unfastened, as usually made, they sink down upon the berries beneath and the consequent result of the " jam " manufactured in this way is to find no market, they are absolutely worthless; besides the stains of the bleeding fruit deface not only the poor sufferer, but all with which it may come in contact, especially those beneath, and when unloaded from the car the appearance is more that of the slaughter house than the clean, dry looking conveyance in which they were placed. The verdict at the inquest will be " murdered in the house of its friends." This is no fancy picture. Such results are seen daily during the berry season, and the wonder is that such fruit sells as well as it often does.

As the managing of the pickers and packers is distinct from my subject, I will only suggest that women are employed to good advantage, and some of the most efficient and reliable help comes from this source. A daughter of a representative in the State legislature is quite a proficient in the packing of peaches and enjoys it. The wife and others of the family of a neighbor take charge of the packing of entire and large crops of berries, peaches and grapes, than which no others have been so uniformly successful. If without such help, educate for this purpose, and success will surely follow.

What is the capacity of the quart box or measure named? It is well to know what we are talking about. There are two standard units of measures. The United States standard unit of liquid measure is the old English wine gallon of two hundred and thirty-one cubic inches. The United States standard unit of dry measure is the British Winchester bushel, which is eighteen and one-half inches in diameter and eight inches deep and contains 2,150.42 cubic inches.

	Gallon.	Quart.	Pint.
Wine Measure	231 cu. in.	57¾ cu. in.	28⅞ cu. in.
Dry Measure	268⅘ " "	67¼ " "	33⅗ " "

There is a little over five and one-fourth quarts in a gallon wine measure than dry measure. A quart box, then, five inches square and two and one-half inches deep, will hold sixty-two and one-half cubic inches level full; when properly filled for shipment or retail, rounded up, will hold a full, honest quart, standard measurement, while the measure used by too many, called a quart inside of four and one-half inches square and two and three-fourths inches deep, contains only 55.68 cubic inches, or when properly rounded, may hold 57¾ cubic inches, or a liquid quart only.

To the shame of some it is the custom to improve (?) on even this measure by so shortening the bottoms that it might be difficult for the uninitiated to know which is the top and which is the bottom, as it has much the appearance of all bottom.

Sometimes the consumer, more inquisitive than wise, raises the question of the amount of the contents of the inside quart, before alluded to; the dealer has only to empty the berries into a tin or liquid quart measure, when he triumphantly demonstrates before his customer how easy it is to sell him five quarts less to the bushel, by his simple legerdemanic art of "heads I win and tails you lose."

It is the custom of some of the Northern shipp'ng points to send in stands, containing two to four half-bushel drawers, and, when sent short distances, find ready sale with the retailer, who, with deft hands, manipulates with a light wooden paddle into the measure, be it liquid or dry; if in the latter, he counts on twenty quarts to each half-bushel drawer; if in the dry quart, his bushel will make at least thirty-five quarts. In St. Louis, the market regulations are such that the standard dry measure quart is only used for berries and such; yet, with the dexterity acquired by long practice, even with the berries sent from the South in the standard quart, which they empty in drawers for that purpose, they seldom make less than two quarts from each twenty-four quart case.

Of course, all the berries shipped do not arrive in such order as to justify much rehandling, but the good and firm berries seldom reach the consumer in the original package.

To sum up, then, the question of package best suited for strawberries, raspberries and blackberries, is a full standard quart in cases of twenty-four each—with the exception of red raspberries, which should always be picked and shipped in pint boxes, in crates containing twenty-four each, of the same standard capacity with quarts. Use the broad or flat quart and pint. Do not be tempted to use the deep and small measures. Fill the measure full and rounding. Have the cases made squarely and neatly, just large enough to hold the quarts and pints in their proper places, with the covers not to exceed half an inch above the quart boxes. With the covers fasten on each end on the top a half-inch strip, one inch wide. This will permit ventilation, to some extent, when loaded into the car. The square quart box alluded to, known to manufacturers as the " Halleck," is, in my judgment, the best. In some parts of Missouri, Arkansas and elsewhere, the long quart with a single straight piece for the bottom, known as the " Leslie," is used ; and, being quicker made, for one thing, and holding rather over a full quart measure for another, finds favor with both shipper and consignee. Yet the fact remains that a great many of the bottoms slip out from the corner fastenings, the weight and juice of the berries softening the wood so as to make it bend itself out of shape, and then comes the mischief to the poor berries and all concerned.

Use your own brand, or consignee's stencil and number, put carefully on the top and also on both ends ; note on any box not full the number empty ; always send a bill or statement—put in an envelope, and nail under the lid, projecting an inch or so to be readily seen by the consignee—giving the amount of the shipment, and noting the quality by some private mark on the box ; give in a brief way what you expect to send next day. Saturdays are considered the poorest market days ; but few re-shipments can be made by the consignee to advantage, and the local market with him has to be crowded with arrivals of that day ; make no shipments to arrive on Sunday.

Within a month your shipments of strawberries will begin, and for six weeks or so, we of the North will be depending on you for strawberries. We expect you will send us good fruit, and that it will reach us in good condition, and we do not hesitate to say that the prices will be satisfactory.

In this connection, the safe and speedy transportation of our perishable products becomes one of the leading questions. Where it is possible, let one or more growers combine to load a car, and see to the handling and loading, that it be done carefully, and so stowed away as to secure ventilation throughout. Brace and protect the cases, so that they shall not move or be disturbed ; by adopting this plan you will relieve the express companies of much abuse, the employes who are so unmercifully scored for lack of care in handling ; and while I would not relieve them of one iota of blame, the greatest cause of complaint comes from the necessity of handling large quantities of fruit in a very limited time. Another idea in advance of this plan is found in the use of the refrigerator car; as in the former case, you have the handling of your own fruit to load, and can see that each package is stowed right side up. I trust some discussion will be brought out at our meeting on this subject, by those practically acquainted with all the requirements.

The peach crop is one of large importance to the rapily growing North and Northwest, to which we are to look for our markets—for, with good No 1 fruit, honestly packed, our markets have not been over-supplied for some years. In this direction there is room at the top of the horticultural ladder. The varieties one should grow must be determined by the locality, and the markets to supply.

In the Southern part of Illinois, Alton district, for a continuous supply from the earliest to the end of the season begin with Alexander, Beatrice, Hale (very limited number), Mountain Rose, Reeve's Favorite, Crawford's Late, Old Mixon Free, Stump, White Heath Cling (limited), Smock, Bileyus' October.

For long shipments by rail the one-third bushel box seems best adapted, protecting the fruit from pillage and from being bruised. When the loading in cars can be controlled, I prefer a box with six laths to cover; the heads used for this box are five by eight inches; then, instead of one lath to cover of say seven and a half inches use two of three inches, leaving a space between for show and ventilation; when the loading has to be done by the average expressman, make your box nearly tight, and as strong as wood and iron will do it. Peaches were sent in car-lots, in good condition in peck baskets, a trip of thirty-six hours, into Minnesota, while in smaller lots, by usual express, and shorter distance, they invariably arrived in bad order, though specially packed for such shipment.

The best condition of the fruit for shipment is only acquired by practice. As a rule, much of it is packed too green and hard. When such is the case it will not ripen, but rots very quickly. A fully matured peach, not soft, is in the best condition for transit, and should be uniform in size, as nearly as possible. Never wedge in the little ones to make them tight in the box, rather leave the space for ventilation: yet the boxes must be filled, and when nailed up, so firmly packed as not to shake in the box. When loading into the car, have strips of boards or lath placed between each layer, and see that the car has proper ventilation. For short distances, by rail, the peck peach basket is a favorite, and good fruit always sells to advantage thus packed. The peaches may be riper for such markets and go safely in such packages, provided the baskets are full and rounded up, then covered with tarleton, which sometimes is thought to heighten the color of the peach; this to be securely sewed to the basket, then over all a cover or cross tops to prevent bruising when handled.

Time will not permit, or I should enumerate all fruits and vegetables, the manner of packing, etc. I will mention the grape as one very likely to be found profitable to our Southern growers wherever they may succeed. The Ives and Concord are generally considered the most productive, at least as far South as Cairo, perhaps farther. The best package is one not exceeding ten pounds; the shape and material a matter of choice with the shipper, yet often it is controlled by the usage in the selling markets, of which your commission merchant will better inform you.

I refer to a few vegetables which need special care in packing and transportation to secure "paying prices." Green peas bring the best prices in boxes not exceeding a half bushel, fairly ventilated, but not too open to let the contents waste out. To bring the best prices and quick sales, they must be fresh and of good green color; when wilted or discolored they sell very slow, if at all. If in larger packages, and on the road two or three days, they become heated and worthless.

String beans also occupy a similar place in our list as the pea, and usually reach the Northern markets in fair condition. The round bean commands the best price.

I shall say but little about tomatoes; but of one thing be assured, that crooked, knotty and rough specimens should not be packed at all. The third-bushel box is generally considered the best, and is used almost to the exclusion of all other packages.

Potatoes, for the Southern grower, have become a crop of very large proportions and remunerative. For the earliest, the third-bushel box may be used, and, when so fully matured that the skin will not peel or bruise, then the barrel, holding three bushels (the empty flour barrel is used to advantage), and well ventilated, will prove satisfactory. Early Ohio, Beauty of Hebron and Early Rose best suit the trade.

Cucumbers are a crop of no small importance, are easily raised and bear transportation better than some vegetables. They must be of uniform, fair size, smooth, and green in color; if at all yellow when they reach market they are not sought after. The White Spine variety, above all others for use in the green state, is most largely grown. The earliest may be sent in small packages. For the crop, the same package as for potatoes, well ventilated, will prove good and economical.

It seems needless to add that *absolute honesty* in packing all your fruits and vegetables is essential to success with no small or inferior specimens; but rather make three grades. First, the best end of the crop; second, that of fair quality and size; and, lastly, the inferior, which is to be discarded entirely from your shipping packages.

Mark your two shipping grades so your commission merchant will know at a glance the contents, and be able to secure you full market prices, and frequently a little more.

Never pack fruit or vegetables you would not be willing to buy. With absolute honesty we must combine an inherent love for horticulture, together with a reasonable share of regard for the " root of all evil," not omitting your good name, which is more to be desired than great riches. With such guides to your work, the result will be that men will arise and call you blessed; your name will be treasured as household words, standing high on the roll of horticultural fame, perhaps, next to him whose natal day was so recently celebrated here and all over this broad land. He, first in peace, first in war, and first in the hearts of his countrymen.

DISCUSSION ON MARKETING FRUITS.

Mr. Webb, of Kentucky—I wish to inquire of the gentleman, which is the best strawberry box?

Mr. Hollister, of Illinois—The Halleck box is the best we have tried.

Mr. E. T. Hollister, of St. Louis—The most important matter connected with the production of fruits and vegetables, is to get them into market in such a condition as to enable the producer to realize the greatest amount of revenue from them. To do so he should become familiar with the requirements of the markets in which he intends to dispose of them. Articles that sell readily in some markets are not wanted in others, and a style of package that is popular in one locality is not desirable in another. This should always be considered in preparing your products for shipment.

If you are not familiar with these matters, a letter to any respectable dealer will always receive a courteous reply. with the desired information. We can speak for no market but our own, where the most desirable package for strawberries, and that class of fruit, is the twenty-four quart case. For peaches, plums, pears and that class of products, the one-third bushel box is the popular package. String beans and green peas should be shipped in bushel boxes. For apples, the barrel should be the size of the flour barrel. Never send your fruits to market in second-hand boxes or barrels, but always in bright, new packages, which, being more inviting, will sell more readily, and at a sufficient advance upon the price to be obtained for the old packages to more than pay for themselves.

Nothing is gained by giving short weights or measures, or by shipping in odd sized or shaped packages, as they are always the last to sell on a quick market, and it is impossible to sell them on a dull market, except at a greatly reduced price. The quality of the article you are about to place upon the market is also a very important matter, and should receive very careful consideration.

12

In packing any article for shipment, whenever you come to a specimen about which you have any doubt, give the pig-pen or evaporator the benefit of that doubt, as it will pay you much better there than in the box.

A good rule to be governed by in packing fruit is, never to put an article into the box that you would not place upon your own table, and the buyers will soon become acquainted with your brand, and your goods will always be the first to sell, and will generally bring you good prices.

Evaporators are now furnished at prices that place them within the reach of almost every one, and are about the best friends the fruit raisers have found, because they enable them to utilize a large portion of their crop that would otherwise either be wasted or placed in the center of the box, to depreciate its value and cause the purchaser to make remarks that would grate harshly upon the ear of the packer should he happen to be present when it was opened, and to avoid that brand when making future purchases.

Honesty, in packing fruit, is the best policy, and the man who furnishes honest goods and gives sixteen ounces for a pound, four pecks for a bushel, and four quarts for a gallon, is the one who makes the most substantial friends, and achieves the greatest success in business.

Mr. Williams, of Indiana—There is no doubt that the interests of the commission men and growers are identical. The commission man that understands his business certainly has the interest of the grower at heart. I indorse what has been said here in regard to the manner of putting up fruit. The reputation of some commission men has, perhaps, brought about this feeling. The idea that a man can go into the commission business without capital has often caused better houses to suffer very materially. It is not a very hard matter for the person shipping to find out the honesty of those to whom he is shipping. He ought to satisfy himself on that point; it is a thing he can do very easily. The commission men are not all the most dishonest men in the world, by any means. You take off the top berries of the boxes of some growers, and you have a lot of little, green, insignificant berries that are not fit for the chickens to eat. I will grant you that there is a great deal of this snide fruit that comes through middle hands; men who buy your good fruit, mix it with the bad, and sell it to commission men, in which case the fault does not rest with the grower.

The President—I indorse very highly what has been said about the best kind of packages; and I want to commend to our friends in the East our packages as being more suited to the grower and dealer in every respect. I use the square Halleck boxes. I put in eight or nine tacks and the bottoms never drop out. I don't think we have had one bottom to drop out in an average of fifty cases. Now I would recommend that particular package as the best one that ever has been used. I have often seen the old style of packages, both the crates of baskets and " stands " of drawers, used over and over again until they were very dirty and offensive. But the first cost of these packages was considerable, and economy dictated their continued use as long as possible. I am glad that this practice is becoming unpopular. The gift package is the cheapest, and, when well made, is the best, and should come into universal use.

Mr. Williams, of Indiana—I see no reason why the package referred to by the President should not take the place of the others, and there might be a little improvement on that. This trouble of dropping down is something we have to contend with very largely, and the cases might be made so as to be ventilated a little more.

The President—You don't want any ventilation in the packages; but you don't want to shut them up tight when it is hot. If your cars are not cool, then you want ventilation through and among the cases.

Mr. Williams—In regard to return packages; it used to cost us from $400 to $500 a year to collect the packages. I would be glad to see that arrangement done away with. We have a great deal of trouble hunting them up.

Mr. Kiely—I indorse what Mr. Williams has said. I want to see the return package abolished. They create a great deal of trouble because producers don't get them back promptly. It gives a great deal of labor and extra expense. Packages should always go with the fruit and give the purchaser no further trouble. I think the Halleck box is, perhaps, the best we can get.

Mr. Galusha, of Illinois, offered a resolution that it is the sense of the members of the convention that all fruits should be sold by weight, and that the net weight and the variety of fruit contained should be plainly marked upon each package, with the name of the grower or shipper. Laid over till the next general meeting. He said: No legislature can make any law saying in what kind of a package I shall sell my fruit. It can't be done. I have a right to go into Chicago or anywhere else, with any kind of package, and sell it at what I can get. No statute of man can keep me from doing it so long as we have a supreme court and a principle of law which enables a man to sell as he pleases. But it is an easy thing to put the number of pounds upon the package. I believe that this is the only feasible way out of the trouble.

Mr. Presley, of Minnesota—We find that the fruit gets very hot on account of not having ventilation in the boxes. I am certainly in favor of the square box. I think it is the best box we can get for the strawberry. If it could be so arranged that the cases could have air, it would be a good thing.

Upon motion of Mr. E. T. Hollister, of Missouri, it was

Resolved, That the Society recommend the use by strawberry shippers of the full quart box and 24 quart case, and that they be very careful to use sufficient tacks to prevent the bottoms of the boxes from falling down, and that return packages be entirely discarded and that we further recommend the use of full one-third bushel boxes for peaches and that class of fruits.

Mr. Kiely, of Missouri—In long shipments I think the Excelsior is very desirable.

Dr. Hape, of Georgia—That is my experience; they would invariably reach their destination in good condition.

Mr. Signaigo, of St. Louis—As far as I know about peaches, I think they ought to be shipped without any packing. If they are put up properly they are not liable to heat, having more ventilation.

Dr. Hape, of Georgia—I am in the habit of packing my pears wrapped in tissue-paper, and nailed down tightly. They generally reach their destination in good condition

Mr. Kiely, of St. Louis—As to baskets, I think the question depends upon the destination you have to ship to. For a long distance, they are not good; but they are for a short distance. They demoralize the trade, as you never know what quantity you have.

Dr. Hape, of Georgia—They are very popular in Atlanta. I use them for peaches, and sell them to families without any handling. For short distances I don't think they could be better. But gen--tlemen who ship to Cincinnati don't find them so good ; the distance is too long.

The President read a telegram from Mr. F. Chandler, General Passenger Agent of the Missouri Pacific Railroad system, offering reduced rates for the next annual convention if held in California, of one fare to Los Angeles and return, provided no less than one hundred members go.

The Society then adjourned until 2:30 o'clock P. M.

Fourth Day—Saturday.

AFTERNOON SESSION.

The Society met at half past three, President Earle in the chair, who said : My friends, we have been reserving the best of the wine to near the last of the feast. I believe that no society and no institution worth preserving can long maintain its usefulness without the cordial and active co-operation of woman. Hence I have gladly embraced the opportunity to engage several of our most accomplished ladies, who are also zealous horticulturists, to prepare us papers for this meeting. Two of these ladies are present, and I now invite your attention, first, to a paper by Mrs. H. M. Lewis, of Madison, Wisconsin, to be followed by one by Mrs. D. Huntley, of Appleton, Wisconsin :

BIRDS IN HORTICULTURE.

BY MRS. H. M. LEWIS, OF WISCONSIN.

The day was going—yes, 'twas gone. I was reclining upon the lounge thinking it over, for it had been a busy, happy day. A book was lying before me. I picked it up and languidly read for a half hour. The last words I remember reading were these : " Arcadia, a realm where sunshine never scorches, and yet shade is sweet, where simple pleasures please, where the blue sky, the bright water and the green fields satisfy." With these words my eyes closed, and the sweet goddess, sleep, allured me into her own chosen realm—the mystical dreamland. She transported me over sea and land to a celestial island, a new world. "In this home," she says, "you are to be remote from care, master of yourself—no sorrow or deformity shall ever enter here, for this is a world of happiness, truth, love and beauty." Never before had we seen Nature's dear face so beautiful—never before known such holy rest and peace. Weeks passed thus, but at last a longing for something more was felt. We inquired after our feathered songsters, the birds, but no one had ever heard of such strange bright-colored singing animals as we described, that had wings like fins that could swim in the air. Alas! alas! the charm was now broken for us forever. We could be happy in no home— not even Heaven itself—where the singing of birds was unknown, and we implored our good genii to take us back again to our Wisconsin home of summer's heat and winter's cold. As we neared our native land we discovered spring approaching. In the far dim distance, on the Pacific slope, over Alaska's borders, the western prairies, eastern mountain tops and meadow lands, we heard millions of voices which were recognized as those of the robin—the same dear old robin redbreast song that delighted us so much in childhood—that will delight us ever while we live. The sweets of summer are compressed in that old song, and it kindles anew the fires of youth. This sweet song has been sung for ages, and, perhaps, will be sung for all time. Who can tell? Thoreau says: "I heard a robin in the distance, the first I had heard for many a thousand years, methought, whose notes I shall not forget for many a thousand more."

When I awoke from this eventful dream I could but exclaim, what would summer be without birds! What if the birds should refuse or forget to obey Nature's calling for a year and pass us by! How much of the cheer, gladness and beauty of summer would be gone! Let us awaken our slumbering faculties to the contemplation of the blessings, joys and beauties surrounding us. Let us enjoy the flowers of the field and the birds of the woods; seek to know much of their habits, haunts and language, for the birds' language is as easily learned as that of the little child's, for every want is expressed by cry, song or chirp.

A true bird lover, by constant observation, will with little difficulty learn to name the great majority of our birds, for each class has its own individuality. The flight, the walk, the shape of the bill, feet and wings, enable the student to distinguish and name them. It is a rare delight to know and properly name the birds as they appear among us in the spring.

We who are interested in ornithology, in botany, and in horticulture, should insist upon having natural history introduced into our schools. The young in our primary schools should be taught to name the animals and flowers, and to know them intimately in their homes, to name the birds of the air, and upon turning over the soil to know of what it is composed, and able to tell at a glance whether the rocks dug out of it were formed by the action of fire or water; this is giving to the child a glorious education, good for all countries, all times, and all seasons. We go to school to learn something of ancient•Greece and Rome, of Alexander and Napoleon, but of ourselves and of the wonderful life around us we know nothing, or but little

Thomas Carlyle says: "For many years it has been one of my constant regrets that no schoolmaster of mine had a knowledge of natural history; so far at least as to have taught me the names and habits of the little winged and wingless neighbors that are constantly meeting me with a salutation which I can not answer, as things are." Who will deny that if this knowledge had been Carlyle's, his life had not been sweeter, and better and the world, as well as he, been the gainer?

People living in towns and cities should make friends with Nature, for, by doing so, a new, fresh fountain of life is ever near. But to the people of the country, who sometimes are burdened with a feeling of oppression and isolation, she comes most near, for to them she whispers her secrets and mysteries, that are so old, yet ever new. Dear Mother Earth, from her we came, and to her at last we shall go. It is from the bright things of earth that music and poetry are born, and who so much a teacher of the poet as the robin and blue bird, just out of the sky—where he-came from is a mystery, for he brings no reporter with him, and his secrets we can never know. The blue bird is one of the earliest, sweetest and most familiar birds of the garden. Burrough says, "when Nature made the blue bird, she wished to propitiate both the sky and the earth, so she gave him the color of one on his back, and the hue of the other on his breast." The first breath of spring brings him among us. His song is a sweet, melodious warble, all harmony, for his notes are so pure that he is incapable of making a discord. The song is continuous through the summer; wherever we go, in town or country, it is heard. The western blue bird is said to sing a more sweet and tender song than the eastern bird, also to have a more brilliant and showy color.

The robin's song has not a great variety of notes, therefore naturalists do not regard him as a first-class minstrel. He ranks about as third rate; but for a song that wears like the old home melodies, give us first and last the robin's song, with its sweet, simple melody, that always cheers and refreshes but never tires. No bird sings at dawn like the robin. He is most assuredly the favorite bird of our land, the bird of poetry and song. He has even been regarded as the bird having a soul, probably from the many tales and legends that have been told of him in past ages. The ancient legend of the robin that came to us ages ago is this: The dear bird saw Jesus upon the cross; he plucked a thorn from his brow, and the blood stains which tinged the breast of that faithful bird have been upon every robin since. One other legend is:

> " Of the fiery pit,
> And how, drop by drop, this merciful bird
> Carries the water that quenches it.

> " He brings cool dew in his little bill
> And lets it fall on the souls of sin ;
> You can see the mark on his red breast still
> Of the fires that scorch as he drops it in."

The blackbird comes soon after the robin. He is not a favorite bird, but he has a mission to perform, and he does it well. He devours myriads of insects. His food consists largely of spiders, beetles and larvæ. They are very social birds, and the only polygamists, I believe among our Northern birds. They build poor nests, and as they dislike the cares of life, sometimes deposit eggs in the nests of other birds.

Of sparrows we have many varieties. They are a very interesting family of birds. Most of them are early comers. The chipping sparrow, or hair bird, is the most common. They are so familiar that we can nearly approach them on the ground, but if we take a look at the beautiful speckled eggs when the old ones are in sight the nest is deserted and the eggs destroyed. The only exceptional case I have ever known was at the home of President J. M. Smith, of Wisconsin. In the vines that covered his porch a pair of sparrows had chosen their home. The old birds came in and out of the vines with perfect freedom, although busy feet were passing to and fro all day. Many times we were within a yard of the nest, but the mother bird showed not the least sign of disquietude. I found birds' nests abounding in this charmed spot. A phebe bird had built under a little bridge; ground birds were hatching in the strawberry beds, and over them shields constructed to keep the berry pickers from treading upon the young birds. Other nests had been transferred by the men to more favorable quarters, and from a nest in the eaves an old bird looked complacently down upon us among the pines, and while attending to her maternal duties seemed to be listening with us to the eloquent words spoken on that eventful day. These birds paid daily for their keeping, not only by destroying obnoxious and injurious insects, but by giving sweet song, grace and beauty to the world about them. Perhaps St. Guthlac meant such as these when he said, " Know ye not that he who hath his life according to God's will, to him the wild beasts and wild birds draw most near."

No bird is so strongly associated with my early childhood as the song sparrow. That sweet religious song, I seem to hear it now, as I heard it those years ago on the banks of a swift flowing river; sometimes the song will be repeated the same for a hundred times, then will begin variations most numerous. These birds dress alike in russet and gray, and come to us very early in the spring.

The white-throated sparrow calls upon us for about two weeks in the early spring, and again in the autumn, and while they remain are brim full of frolic and song. Many of their notes are like the song sparrows. They nest in the far North.

The vesper sparrow has a song never to be forgotten by the bird lover. The notes are soft, sweet, plaintive and flute-like, and it ends with trills and quivers. This bird sings most sweetly after sunset—hence the name of vesper sparrow. One night, as the shades began to gather in the pine woods of the far North, a vesper sparrow began to sing, another answered, then the song was taken up by voices far and near over hill and valley. Just at this time a misty rain came noiselessly down. The scene was a weird, unearthly one, and it took but little fancy to bring the music down from the clouds. This evening song held us willing captives for a good half hour.

The English sparrows are bright, blustering little fellows, and in the heart of a large city, where the wild birds are seldom or never seen, are not objectionable; but this I fear is the only place in America for him. All bird lovers must deprecate his advent into our new country; but he is here and multiplying, and the momentous question for us to answer, is this: How shall we keep him under, or rid ourselves of him? The mature bird eats grain, the very young ones are said to eat worms. They are so pugnacious that native birds fear them. A few robins are wintering in Madison, Wis. this season. The sparrows, to my certain knowledge, have given them but little rest and peace. I have seen these saucy little birds attacking woodpeckers and blue jays many times during the past winter. If Dame Fashion would decree that the English sparrow was the coming bird for the ladies' head-wear, and for parlor decorations, as the sunflower has been of late, it would be a boon to the country.

The beautiful golden robin, or Baltimore oriole, is well known from Canada to the Gulf. The name Baltimore was given because of the resemblance of his coat to that of Lord Baltimore. The song is strange, sweet and powerful. He is apt to confine himself to but few notes, but he is capable of singing an exhaustive melody of great variety and beauty. The deep hanging nest is usually suspended from a tall tree. The city nests are not so beautiful and symmetrical as the country ones. It exhibits in this nest workmanship most rare and wonderful. In the South the nests are made of Spanish moss, which is attached at both ends to the forks in a branch, then the moss is woven in opposite directions until a hammock-like nest is produced. The oriole takes his food largely from the tree, and while looking on the under side of the leaf for the worm, hangs with his head downward.

The orchard oriole is a sweet singer—not well enough known—color dingy yellow and olive. The nest is a tree-hanging one. The rose-breasted grosbeak comes with the oriole and cat-bird. They are beautiful birds. In some parts of Wisconsin and Minnesota they are the birds most commonly seen, but about Madison not common. Perhaps in the near future we shall see more of them, for they are said to be changing their location. Audubon places this bird very high in his list of minstrels. The song begins like the cat-bird's, then rises and falls in waves, and ends with warblings, echoes and trills that are indescribably sweet. This bird will probably be the bird of poetry and song in future years. They make valuable cage birds, and the young are successfully raised in captivity. They show remarkable skill in nest building—will bend twigs by biting the innerside from end to end.

The cat-bird, or northern mocking bird, frequents both town and country. When he first comes he is shy, but should you desire it you can be on delightfully intimate terms with him, for he will hover round you, sing to you and bathe in the wooden bowl with the robin at your feet.

A pair of cat-birds have built nests in our garden for several years. A dead limb in the upper part of the tree has been the chosen spot for song. When our minstrel returns in the spring and sings again from his own favorite spot, we feel that the absent member of the family has returned, and we greet him with great joy, which I hope he returns. He often sings with such rapture and abandon that the song continues as he takes flight from one tree to another. Many parts of the cat-bird's song are wonderfully sweet and melodious, for he imitates many other birds, besides singing his own sweet song. But alas! alas! for the imperfect life of bird and flower; the thorn must appear with the rose, and discord with melody, for he often gives in place of his sunny song, only the cry of the cat, and the filng of the saw, when the love making is over.

The brown thrush, or mavis, is a bird occasionally seen in our garden, but he takes most naturally to fields and woods. He is related to the robin. When he sings he flies upon the highest limb of a tree and then pours forth a strong, sweet, rich, intricate warble, that not uncommonly lasts an hour. His notes—

> "They melt upon the ear, they float away,
> They rise, they sink, they hasten thy delay,
> And hold the listener with bewitching song
> Like sounds from heaven,"

For he ranks as singer first among our northern birds.

The bobolink is the great song bird of the east, where it is heard constantly in orchard and field. With us he seams to take naturally to low lands. His song is very musical and merry. He is the great solo singer among birds. He has no relatives in this country. Washington Irving addresses him in the words of Logan:

> "Sweet bird; thy bower is ever green,
> Thy sky is ever clear;
> Thou hast no sorrow in thy note,
> No winter in thy year.

> "Oh! could I fly, I'd fly with thee;
> We'd make, on joyful wing,
> Our annual visit round the globe—
> Companions of the spring.

The red-eyed vireo and warbling vireo are small, interesting birds. They are to be found over the entire North in summer. The sweet little warbling song begins with the dawn and continues through the day. I scarcely remember a day or an hour last summer that I did not hear that song under my window. Many times these birds pursued flies so eagerly and so near that we would feel the rustle of their wings as they passed by. The nests are beautifully constructed. The white-eyed vireo is called the politician, because in the texture of its nest it uses pieces of newspaper. A nest in my possession has a penny postage stamp on one side.

The scarlet tanager is the most beautiful bird seen in the North. His body is of the most brilliant scarlet. His preference is for woods and fields, but sometimes he hovers near our towns and cities. His song is a whistle, both strong and musical.

The American goldfinch is a true wood warbler, known from the Arctic to the Gulf.

The wren frequents both country and town. It is a favorite everwhere. Very little is known of its habits. A small box or hollow is the chosen place for its nest. They are ever ready to accept a home with us if we prepare a place for them—and they are very valuable birds for the garden. The song is sweet and strong for so small a bird. It begins on a high, sharp key, then suddenly falls to a sweet murmuring song that ascends again and ends with a rapid trill.

The fly-catcher pewee, or Phebe, is well known. It is a small, brown bird that prefers solitude, or dark, shady places, where it repeats the song "Phebe" from dawn to dark. Some writer has said: "So plainly expressive of sadness is this peculiar note, that it is difficult to believe that the little being that utters it can be free from sorrow."

Even winter, with its desolate ice and snow, is made more endurable and pleasant by the bright and merry birds. Troops of cedar birds, titmice, woodpeckers, snow birds, cross-bills, blue-jays, snow buntings, pine finches, red polls, and others, come among us at different times during the season. All the varieties of woodpeckers, but one, winter in this latitude, I believe.

The chickadee, or titmice, are well-known winter birds that come in flocks during the cold weather, a pair of woodpeckers, called brown creepers, always accompanying them. The little chickadee chatters and sings in the most happy manner, even though the cold be biting, and zero reigns around him. The one we are most familiar with is the black-capped titmouse.

Every winter we expect to entertain one of these little black-throated visitors in our living rooms. He delights and entertains us with his cunning ways all winter; often, as we write, he will walk upon the paper, and perch upon the inkstand, crack the hemp seed on the arm of the chair, and, while hopping about on the table, sing and whistle right merrily. This dear little creature is a stranger from a land almost unknown, and we know but little of his haunts and habits. He weighs no more than an ounce, but he has as much individuality as the mammoth elephant. Reason, or instinct, has taught him to husband his food, for winter consumes rather than produces, and in the folds of a curtain, behind a leaf, or in a book, choice bits of food are prepared for the future. He holds the hemp seed firmly between his feet, and pounds away until the shell is broken; in this way he also cracks a hazel nut. He eats no sweets, prefers butter, tallow and rich nuts, frolics in a pan of snow, sings three songs, not strong but sweet, and whistles divinely; and when evening comes his reason prompts him to creep for shelter and protection into a little hollow, or under a leaf, and then he hides his head under his wing, in a bed of downy feathers, until morning.

In the spring, with sad hearts, we say adieu to the little Esquimaux of the winter, for we open the window and liberty is his. Sometimes he returns to his roost in the bay-window several times before taking his final departure, for we allow him to go out and come in as he pleases; at last he goes away into the great world. Our hearts always go out in gratitude to the little stranger of the winter that has brought nothing but sunshine, grace and beauty into a household. The black-throated titmice are exclusively Northern birds. They range from the Arctic to Maryland—no further South I believe. The titmice are diligent workers when looking for food. They live largely upon the larva and eggs of insects.

I would like to call the attention of the horticulturist to this bird; if we are to have foreign birds introduced into our country, let birds of this family find a place, for they are entirely beneficial. The birds of which I have made mention·are insectiverous with the exception, perhaps, of the English sparrow. They destroy myriads of insects, worms, and flies that are doing great harm to our fruits, flowers, and vegetables. The good that a single pair of these birds confers upon the country in a single year is incalculable.

The American shrike, or butcher bird, should be well known to the horticulturist, for it is the great destroyer of our birds. It is said to possess the faculty of imitating the notes of other birds for the purpose of decoying them within its reach, then dart suddenly into the thicket and bear off the body of some deluded victim. It is said to eat only the brain. It then impales its victim upon a thorn or other sharp point. Probably the victim is thus preserved to appease hunger in case of an emergency; but this part of their history is not known. The shrike nests in the far North, but inhabits Eastern, Middle, and Southern States. They are birds of good size, color mostly gray, wings and head coal black, breast light gray and white.

The blue jay is a well-known bird. It belongs exclusively to North America, and is cousin to the shrike. Its brilliant plumage, large size, attractive form, and shrill cry, render it prominent over the Northern States. We can but admire this beautiful bird in winter when other birds are gone, for he gives a bit of color and life to the landscape that is most delightful. But away with him, we say, for he is a pirate and marauder. He delights in breaking the eggs of other birds, and picking the bones of the young. He cares not for the severity of winter, and is seldom found frozen. In autumn he deposits in the thickets, fence corners, and other convenient places, food for winter.

Horticulturists who are interested in the birds should be guardians of them, and do what can be done for their preservation and protection, for they are "fellow citizens of our farms and hamlets;" therefore if it be necessary to make laws protecting them, let that be done. Let us prevent the wholesale slaughter of our valuable birds and water fowls by heedless men and boys, who care but little for the future good of our country.

I fancy I hear a voice saying, you dwell upon the the bird's uses and beauties, but not upon his defects and vices. This we certainly would do unless it be clearly proven that the birds have more vices than virtues.

> "You slay them! and wherefore? For the gain
> Of a scant handful more or less of wheat."

When we plant our fruit trees, our berry bushes, and our strawberry vines, plant a few extra ones for the birds. Lowell says, " For a' that and twice as muckle as that, I would not exchange him (the robin) for all the cherries that ever came out of Asia Minor."

Let us educate our children to protect, study and love the birds, and if specimens of eggs are desired, to take a part of them without robbing the nests. Teach them that to kill a bird with a sling shot, or in sport, is a sin. Let the farmer when guiding the plow, the farmer's son while driving the cattle to pasture and meadow; the mother and children while working among the flowers, fruits and vegetables, or when abroad in the cool of the evening, listen to the voices of the birds, and before the summer is over I assure you, that new life-long friends will be yours that will be well worth knowing.

> "And there's never a leaf nor a blade too mean
> To be some happy creature's palace ;·
> The little bird sits at his door in the sun,
> Atilt like a blossom among the leaves,
> And lets his illumined being o'errun
> With the deluge of summer it receives ;
> His mate feels the eggs beneath her wings,
> And the heart in her dumb breast flutters and sings,
> He sings to the wide world and she to her nest—
> In the nice ear of Nature, which song is the best ?

ADORNING RURAL HOMES.

BY MRS. D. HUNTLEY, OF WISCONSIN.

The outward surroundings of the homes of any people are the truest indications of the prosperity of the country and the intelligence of its inhabitants. It matters little whether the dwelling is a mansion or a cottage: it is the taste and skill displayed in the adornment of the grounds, the planting of trees, the care of the flowers and the lawn which indicate the culture and refinement of the owner The costly dwelling may be the perfection of architectural beauty, but the embellishments of art become effaced by sunshine and storm, while the more humble dwelling, adorned with nature's treasures, is continually increasing in beauty. The educating influence of pleasant surroundings upon the minds of the young can not be overestimated.

Children reared in rural homes take their first object lessons from the great book of nature. The love of the beautiful, which all possess in a greater or less degree, is strengthened by association till it becomes a safeguard from evil, and the grand incentives for labor which are constantly presented in rural life create habits of industry, and young men and young women go out from country homes fitted for usefulness in any vocation, and with a love for the beautiful in nature so strong and so lasting that, in later years, they turn from any and every calling to secure a home somewhere in the country. In all the hurry and worry of business life they sigh for the clover-scented fields, the daisied slopes, the green hills and valleys of childhood, and the accumulations of years are expended to purchase a rural home, where the evening of life can be passed among the beauties of nature.

Besides the benefits of delightful surroundings to the young and the example and incentive which a beautiful home presents to every beholder, the pleasure of adorning and beautifying a place for ourselves and our loved ones is beyond all computation. We do not appreciate as we ought, the fact that if we choose, we can possess a portion of this beautiful earth; our government is most generous. Somewhere in our vast country we can have, almost for the asking, a part of the footstool of God for our inheritance; Nature is lavish with her gifts; we can select from her storehouse the best of her treasures; we can surround ourselves and our children with excellence and purity, with grand incentive and high example, and with all that can be expressed in those thrilling words, the comforts of life; we can make our homes lovely if we choose; we can shade them with trees, decorate them with vines, and adorn them with flowers. Wherever we dwell nature has something delightful for those who love her. The artist spends years of labor upon a bit of canvass which is only a picture of some of nature's lovliness. We who grow her beauties in field and garden can make a living landscape, more glorious than an artist's picture, or a poet's dream.

In writing of the rural homes of our land it must be remembered that we tell you of the simplest of nature's beauties.

It is folly to expect that the people of the country can attempt the care and culture of the wonderful beauties of the greenhouse and conservatory.

Hundreds of new homes are constantly springing up all over our land, and it is a question for the owners to decide, whether these shall be all bleak, and bare and desolate. with nothing to shelter or shade them, or shall they be adorned with the beauties of nature till they become ornaments to the landscape, a second Eden in which to dwell? For the new home on a Western prairie, or among the forests of the Northwest, or here in the South, it matters not where, so there is great love for the work, we will make some prudent suggestions that can be safely followed and which will give the most pleasure for the labor bestowed.

Just here it must be remarked that it should not be expected that the entire work of ornamenting the lawn and garden should be done by the male members of the family. That would be an unequal division of the pleasures

of the household. Women can find no more delightful or healthful employment than the care and culture of flowers and fruits in the garden.

The first and most essential requisite for the adornment of a rural home
is, that the owner should possess an unconquerable love for the beautiful in
nature—a love for trees and plants and fruits so great that he can not be
happy without them. This will remove all difficulties, and success will follow. Then the arrangement of the buildings should receive due attention.
Each one should be so placed as to invite ornamentation by tree or vine, and
also so situated as to increase this beauty when planted.

The dwelling should be some rods from the public road, and also from the
other buildings, to give room for a spacious lawn, which should be covered
with grass in any climate where nature spreads this lovely carpet; where
she does not, there is more abundant room for carpet gardening and bedding
plants. Then the fruit and vegetable garden should be located a pleasant
distance from the house—near enough to be seen and enjoyed and cared for
by the family. A garden on each side of the lawn, wherever this is practicable, will be found very satisfactory. To secure a certain growth of trees
and shrubs, begin with such as can be found growing in the same locality.
This will insure success in the first efforts.

Many very desirable trees, and some very beautiful ones, can easily be found
growing in their native wilds. To these should be added such new varieties
as have been tested and found hardy; with these should be set the hardy
fruit trees, a few at a time, if necessary, and with great carefulness. Do not
say, " I can not plant a large orchard, so I will plant none at all." A few
trees set each year will give you a growing interest and a better orchard in
the end, especially when trees are short lived, than a large number that may
leave you, en masse, suddenly, as they come. The fruit bearing shrubs should
be grown in every garden; they will furnish berries for the table a longer
time than any of the other small fruits.

The vegetable garden, also, with its long list of edibles, and its annual
fruits, is an ornament as well as a necessity to any home.

First in this garden we will plant the strawberry; it grows so rapidly, bears
so abundantly, and will grow in any climate from Greenland to the Gulf;
all can have the strawberry. We can not recall the time when we did not
know and prize this fine old fruit. We all have pleasant memories of the
sunny hillsides and green meadows where we gathered the earliest wild
strawberries. How faithfully we hunted every berry from its hiding place,
and how eagerly we hastened homeward to show our treasurers to the loved
mother who waited our coming. Yes, we will plant the strawberry, and we
will care for it well, and with every returning season we will gather the delicious fruit, with happiest memories of the wild berries of our childhood, and with unnumbered thanks and blessings for those who, by careful
culture, have given us the magnificent berries of the present day. Then we
must find a place for that royal old fruit, the grape. This, too, was one of the
wild fruits we gathered in the long ago. Then we thought the little purple

clusters the best in all the world; now we have grapes so large and so delicious, they remind us of those that were brought from the " promised land." All should have this most delicious fruit in their garden.

We have mentioned trees and shrubs first, for the adornment of the home, because they are of slower growth than the flowers, and in a work so important and so fraught with pleasure to the home as the planting of fruit, shrubbery and trees, the growth of one season should not be lost by delay.

And now, lastly, we mention the flowers, not because they are least, but because we love them best.

> " Flowers, bright, beautiful flowers,
> They are linked with life's sweetest and happiest hours."

They comfort us when lonely; they cheer us when sad; we can gather them in field and garden; we can brighten the dreariest room with their presence; we crown the fair maiden for her bridal, and with sweet, sad memories we place them in the folded hands of our loved dead. O, beautiful flowers, we will love you always; we can take you with us, but the lovely trees and the green grass beneath them we must leave in our fields and gardens, till we can come again to admire their grandeur and their beauty.

> " There is a lesson in each flower,
> A story in each grove and bower,
> On every herb on which you tread
> Are written words which rightly read,
> Will lead you from earth's fragrant sod
> To hope and holiness and God."

The true flower lover can not long remain contented in a flowerless home. If there are many difficulties to contend with, begin with kinds of easiest culture. Shrubs and perennials are easily grown. Many of them require but little care, and some will live and blossom many years when wholly neglected. Shrubbery should be selected with due regard to the climate in which it is grown. In the North and West the lilac, syringa, snowball, spirea, honeysuckle, and many others are entirely hardy, and with age increase in beauty, both of foliage and flowers. In the South the treasures of the floral world are at your command.

But more desirable than all these, are the hardy roses. No flower is so universally loved and admired as the rose. Thousands of new roses are offered in catalogues, but we dare not try these in the new home; a few of the old ones we loved in childhood, like the " hundred leaf," the blush rose, or the little white Scotch rose, with some of the lotus kinds, like Giant of Battles and Madam Planters, that we know will not die, will give us roses all the summer.

After roses and other shrubbery, we would grow dahlias, because they will do more in the way of ornament for a new home than any flower we know. They grow very rapidly, often attaining ten feet in height, and bloom profusely with large conspicuous flowers of brilliant colors of every shade, from deepest red, nearly black, to purest white. In form and size a well-grown dahlia resembles a miniature tree,and where shrubbery is small, or where there is none, the dahlias fill an important place. The most satisfactory colors are white, yellow, red, dark maroon and the light shade of purple. Names of dahlias are often unreliable. The finest white dahlia we have ever grown is the white aster. This is a bouquet dahlia, with pen-bristled petals—very handsome among cut flowers. Besides this, there should be one of the large "show" dahlias in every collection, however small. Another very fine dahlia is white Bartlett: flowers are small, rose colored, and form a lovely contrast when grown with darker shades. All lovers of flowers will admire this magnificent flower when properly grown and trained to sticks or trellis. To many this is delightful work. Those who find it a task should never grow dahlias.

Among perennial plants there are many that are hardy, of easy culture, that will give a succession of bloom from the time the snow-drop and crocus unfold their tiny buds in spring till the frosts of autumn send all our floral treasures to their wintry beds. The tulip is the most brilliant of all the spring flowers, and wherever planted will live for years with but little care. There are many more of this class of plants that are very showy in the garden, but among them all there are none so hardy and so easily grown as the herbaceous peonies. In the days of our grandmothers a group of the crimson peonies was the pride of every door-yard. Now we have them of many colors and various shades, from crimson to pure white, and of delicious fragrance. A bed of these upon the lawn will delight all lovers of brilliant colored flowers. But, of all the herbaceous plants, none can exceed the splendor of the lilies. Those of the olden time were thought more glorious than the raiment of kings. Now we may grow in our simple gardens "lilies all rugged with rubies and garnets and sparkling with crystal points." Their culture is not difficult. Plenty of moisture, drainage and good soil is all that is required. The Japan lilies are now offered in great variety. If you can have only two of these magnificent flowers get *Lilium longiflorum*, and that queen of Japan lilies, *Lilium auratum*, and you have an ornament for your garden which can not be excelled. For those who have transient homes, or for that large number who will find themselves the coming spring in new homes without one flower, the annuals are the most precious of all the floral gifts of God to men.

With these, in one brief summer, you can make your home the delight of your family and the admiration of your friends. A great number are not necessary for a fine display. If we could have but four annuals, we would choose the pansies first. The name pansy is from the French word, *pensee*, indicating thought. We fancy they are thoughtful flowers, their bright faces look up to us as though curious of our admiration. We must grow the pansies.

"O beautiful pansies, whatever betide,
Come smile in thy beauty my threshold beside.'

13

Next the pinks for their spicy perfume, the verbenas for their varied colors and constant bloom, and the old sweet peas for their memories of home.

> " Why better than the primrose
> Love I this little flower?
> Because its fragrant leaves are those
> I loved in childhood's hour."

But trees and flowers are not enough with which to ornament our homes; we must have vines for our porches and doors. A house without a vine is like a bird without a mate; it has a look of desolation; but decorate it with vines, train them over the doors and windows, and the dwelling soon takes on a look of cheerfulness and contentment. "Every summer's morning it presents fresh beauty and glory, which the products of art can not surpass." Vines grow rapidly, and many of them bloom so profusely, there is no good reason why any home should be without its drapery of green.

The climbing roses are lovely when in blossom, but they are not desirable for doors or windows. If we grow the climbing roses it must be on a trellis or some support in the garden.

There are many hardy perennial vines that can be found growing in their native wilds, that when transplanted to our gardens will need no further care, unless it should be necessary to cut back their rampant growth. The best of these is *ampelopsis quinquefolia,* or Virginia creeper, also called Woodbine, and is now widely known in our own country and in Europe as the American ivy. Its growth is very rapid, its foliage very handsome. It will grow in any soil or situation, and if once planted you will always have this beautiful vine. The wild clematis, known as Traveler's Joy. can be found in great abundance in all our forests. It is a strong grower, and in August is covered with clusters of small, white, sweet-scented flowers. We have grown this for several years, and for posts or pillars it is one of the prettiest vines we have ever seen. *Celastrus Scandens,* or climbing bittersweet, is another very desirable native vine.

Among the annual climbers there are many that will give a wonderful growth of foliage in a few weeks. *Cobea Scandens* Canary bird flower (*Tropæolum*) and cypress vine will all grow well in the open ground. The latter is somewhat delicate, but south of 38° it grows in great luxuriance. But better than any of these are the dear old morning glories. We must always grow them for their memories of childhood. Any one of the vines, or any of the shrubs or flowers before mentioned, will make your home to you. and your loved ones the sweetest place on earth.

Besides these, every flower lover desires some of the rare, beautiful plants now seen in all large collections. Many of these will grow in any garden. A bed of foliage plants upon the lawn is a delightful ornament to any home. A box of Coleus upon the piazza or window-shelf, with hanging baskets above them, filled with vines, will make you glad continually. A few geraniums and fuchsias may be added to give brightness, and trailing plants to add grace to boxes and brackets. Grow all you can of these lovely things. From experience, we assure you, the more of them you have the happier you will be.

But says one, "I could never ornament my home in this way; it would require the skill of a landscape gardener to keep such grounds in order."

Say not this, dear friend; do not you know, that not till it verges upon the impossible do we reach the limit to what love and labor will do, with only a little portion of this beautiful earth ? We plant the tiny seeds, we set the trees, then turn to other labors; and lo! the great, grand mystery of plant life rises up before us, and foliage, and bloom, and fruit are our reward; we plant the seed and protect it from harm, and nature does the rest. No worker in all this busy world has so many helpers as the horticulturist of to-day. Nurserymen, seedsmen and florists are constantly investigating, experimenting, and communicating useful information. Books, papers and catalogues will keep the amateur posted in his work.

But, says the working woman, I have so few flowers, and only the common kinds; I can not adorn my home with them. Say not so, my sister. Do not you know that every tiny flower holds in its bosom the great secrets of nature ? That the humble plant is as perfect as the oak ? " The violet is as fragrant as the palm, and the roses of Sharon are as beautiful as Lebanon's majestic cedars."

If you can have but few of the growing beauties of nature, plant a vine by your door-way, and it will cover the side of your dwelling with its drapery of green; plant one tree and it will spread out its leafy banners above your head, and ever make you grateful for its shelter and shade; plant one packet of seeds, if you can no more, and care for them well, and your flowers will expand in colors more royal than the purple of Tyre, and give you fragrance more sweet than the spices of Arabia

I have not the time, says another. Say not this, my friend. Every one of us has all the time which God has given to mortal man, and our mental and moral status is determined by what we do with it. Thousands of rural homes tell us most unmistakably what their owners have not done with their time, in the years that are past.

If we spend the passing hours in idleness or useless work, or in fictitious reading, and leave our gardens and dooryards uncultivated and uncared for, we have taken our choice in the use of our time, and must accept the result. If we neglect to adorn our homes with natures' jewels and thus leave the love of the beautiful undeveloped in our children, the loss to them and to the world is irreparable. Our homes are the nurseries of our children; their education begins in the home; the foundation of character is laid there, and when our children go from us the world receives the product of our homes. We attach great importance to the productions of our country; we have a national pride in her manufactures, her mechanics, her works of art. Let us remember that the best production of any country is its people.

But I am growing old, says another; it is now too late. No, 'tis never too late to begin to do well; plant some green tree, or some sweet flower, that will make the world more beautiful because you have lived in it; they will brighten the evening of your life, and if you do not see the fruit of your labors those who come after you will bless your memory. We do not expect a harvest in spring time.

> " The year grows rich as it groweth old,
> And life's latest sands are its sands of gold."

Many who meet here to-day have passed the meridian of life. The whitened locks and " silver threads " betoken years of labor and experience, but our work is not yet done. With life's latest sands we will add wisdom and skill to our labors; and here in this sunny land, where summer lingers long, where nature decks the groves and fields with the fairest of Pomona's pearls, and the sweetest of Flora's gems, you of the South will multiply your orange groves, and beautify your gardens and make lovely your homes, while we of the North, on hillside and valley, where winter reigns one half the year, will battle for success amid frost and snow, till each returning season shall bring more excellent fruits, more lovely flowers. The East with its busy workers, the West with its hardy sons, will join in the work, till our whole vast country shall be known and honored among the nations of the earth for the intelligence and integrity of her people, the excellence of her fruits, the loveliness of her flowers, and the beauty of her rural homes.

At the close of Mrs. Huntley's paper, President Smith, of Wisconsin, explained the active part which the ladies of his State had long taken in practical horticulture, and their participation in all their horticultural meetings. He said that with the help of the ladies they were able to hold both useful and attractive meetings; " and," said he, " we are very proud of our lady members."

The President—And I wish to say, Mr. Smith, that *we*, of this Society, are very proud of *our* horticultural ladies, too! (Applause.)

Mr. Galusha, of Illinois—We have listened to two most charming and instructive essays, which call from us something more than the cheers and encore of a delighted audience. The topics upon which these beautiful papers were written are in the thoughts and very near the hearts of all true lovers of rural life. It is a good omen for the future usefulness of this and kindred societies where the talent and the skill of the ladies are enlisted in the advocacy of the cause of the feathered songsters and the beautifying of our rural homes. I offer the following resolution :

Resolved, That the heartfelt thanks of the members of this Society be, and are, tendered to the ladies who have been so kind as to favor us with the valuable and interesting papers to which we have just listened.

The resolution was, by a rising vote, unanimously adopted:

Mr. Ragan, of Indiana—The lady has spoken of the blackbird. This bird has been badly abused. I regard it as one of our best friends. How it may be in Wisconsin I do not know. In our State it has but few friends, which, I think, is on the same principle that the English sparrow is so universally abused, viz., because "somebody" says he is bad. Neither of them are admired as pleasant songsters, yet they are noisy fellows. The blackbird, with us, is largely insectiverous. The paper on home adornments is a charming one. Our homes are truly what we make them, and a *home* is all we can have in this world; therefore, we should make our homes as pleasant and happy as possible. Anything that encourages the beautifying and adorning of our homes should be encouraged by societies like this.

Mr. Ragan then proceeded (with a few words of apology) to read his paper on insect enemies of the orchard:

CAN WE MASTER THE INSECT ENEMIES OF THE ORCHARD?

BY W. H. RAGAN, OF INDIANA.

In its individual capacity, an insect is an insignificant thing, truly one unworthy of the earnest attention of intelligent ladies and gentlemen, such as compose this Society; not so, when the subject is viewed collectively, as the topic assigned me would indicate.

"Can we Master the Insect Enemies of the Orchard?" at first glance might seem to be a problem of easy solution, and when originally proposed to the writer, at a time when "distance lent enchantment to the view" was accepted rather rejoicingly.

As the time draws near, the duty seems to rest more and more heavily upon me, until now, that I am forced into action, I begin to realize how hard, indeed, is cruel fate, that has bequeathed to me such luck!

The only consolation left me is in the fact that the extreme length of the programme of this meeting, and the known ability of others who can better entertain, will fully warrant me in appropriating that jewel of literary consistency, brevity!

To the question, therefore, I might give either an affirmative or a negative answer; affirmative, if orchardists, large and small, would act in concert with the sole object in view of winning; negative, if otherwise.

And here I might express the fear that *otherwise* will prevail, at least until we have more nearly approached the millenium of earthly bliss.

But seriously, Mr. President, I have viewed with no small degree of alarm, the steady and onward march of our orchard pests; in spite of our science; in spite of our boasted progress, until I have almost despaired. Entomology has enlightened us on the subject of bugs and beetles; it has clearly defined the differences that distinguish these two subdivisions of the insect tribes; it has assured us that one sucks its food, while the other bites it; it has explained to us in high-sounding terms the metamorphosis of insects; it has shed a brilliant ray of light on *coleoptera*, and *orthoptera*, and *lepidoptera;* yet, sir, the beautiful things have steadily encroached on our chosen domain, until, like the Irishman, when the mule put his foot in the stirrup, I am almost ready to exclaim, "be jabbers, if you are going to git up I'll git down."

But when we retrospect the history of our race, and read the story of the

GARDEN AND THE ORIGINAL PAIR,

With the anathema pronounced upon us, for their sake, we fail to find that insects were to figure in our everlasting torment, and hence we conclude that quiet resignation to their ravages is no part of Christian virtue, so we will, at least, take the matter of "unconditional surrender" under advisement before giving up the ship.

We have great consolation in knowing that the orchard that receives careful culture and attention, like the well-fed flock, suffers least from insect depredations.

The scaly aphis, the borer, the canker worm, the codling moth, and their kind, find but little comfort under the vigilant eye of the careful orchardist, while they literally revel in the orchard of the sluggard.

Unfortunately, as we must to some extent share the sins of each other, and as the sluggard predominates, we must help feed the hungry hosts of our careless neighbor, since insects are endowed by nature with the powers of locomotion. Here lies the chief difficulty in the way of effectual success.

If we, as fruit-growers, can, by moral suasion, or through the terrors of the law, possibly devise a way of enforcing the necessary diligence in this cause, we will certainly have taken an important step in the direction of a solution of the important question that stands at the head of this paper. Until then we are destined to be goaded and harrassed, like Pharoah of old, by insect pests.

But insects are not all pests. Many of the tribes that infest our orchards are friendly in their operations, and greatly aid us in our efforts to conquer those of a noxious character. Upon these we must rely for assistance in waging war on the pests.

To know and to protect our friends, therefore, becomes a duty. Entomology, as a science, must aid us in recognizing our friends and our enemies. It is to this science that we must look for information in regard to the effects of wholesale applications of poisonous insecticides; whether they are not more destructive to friends than to foes; whether, in our poisons, traps and lanterns we are not killing the "goose that lays the golden egg." This is the part that science must perform in the solution of this great problem, though scientific knowledge alone will never rid our orchards and gardens of insect pests.

DISCUSSION ON INSECTS.

Mr. Stofflebeam, of Illinois—We try in my country to raise plums, but we find the curculio very injurious. If it is not out of place I would, if there is any lady or gentleman in this audience that has had any success in raising plums, like to hear from them.

Mr. Holsinger, of Kansas—In answer to the gentleman's inquiry, I will say that I had hoped that this question had been settled. To my mind it certainly is. Plum growing, through the knowledge disseminated by our advanced horticulturists, is a certainty to all those who may follow the methods for trapping and destroying the curculio. It is but little expense to secure a crop annually of this most delicious fruit. To be successful, you must begin in time. As soon as the blossoms are shed secure some wide muslin, sufficient to cover the surface occupied by the largest tree. Cut in two equal lengths; sew up one-half the length, joining the two together in one broad sheet. You are now ready for work. With the aid of three boys, ages from eight to twelve, I have been able, in a few hours, to clean two hundred trees. The boys run under the trees, spreading the cloth, the tree in the middle of the sheet through the part not sewed together. Now, with the ball of the foot, give a few quick, energetic kicks. (I never injured more than one tree in this way.) A rubber mallet might be better. An open-mouthed bottle will be found serviceable to drop them into; or, they can be crushed between the thumb and forefinger. All fallen fruit should be picked up and destroyed, and in this way the crop materially lessened. The plum gouger, *Anthonomus prunicida,* Walsh, has been, of late years, more deleterious to plum culture than the curculio. "It may be easily distinguished from other weevils by its ochre-yellow throat and legs, and its darker wing covers, which are dun colored or brown, with a leaden gray tint, and has no humps." I do not agree with most entomologists that it is more difficult to capture than the curculio. I think it drops as readily with a slight jarring, but I admit it takes wing more readily. I have caught them, even while mated, in mid air. The greater necessity for destroying the fallen, imperfect fruit is the fact that the gouger frequently makes its transformation within the pits of both the plum and peach.

Mr. Galusha, of Illinois—It is understood with us in Illinois, that no one man can rid himself of curculio, unless his neighbors all do the same thing, because they will go from orchard to orchard.

Mr. Hudson, of Louisiana—We in the South have attempted to raise peaches, and when we have succeeded in making good crops, the season having been favorable, we have found our efforts destroyed by the curculio. I have read a gread deal on the subject, and while I agree fully with Mr. Galusha, that the extermination of this pest can only be brought about by co-operation, I wish to say that it is not so easy a thing in this section of the country where our population is very much scattered. We are separated from each other by small pieces of timber land, and when the curculio is driven out from an orchard it takes refuge in the pine lands and is preserved there. In consequence, you will perceive that there is no method of destroying them here. I desire to ask one question, and if there is any practical pear grower here who knows, of his own knowledge, I ask him, as a special favor to the South, whether there be actually any method of applying coal gas tar that is worth the trouble?

Mr. Baldwin, of Michigan—I will say that I can not tell which of the remedies I have used that has succeeded; perhaps all. This year I began with sulphur, but I did not use a great deal of it. Then I used the coal gas tar, and then at night I burnt lights standing in vessels of water. In the morning I found a great many curculios, attracted by the light, that were drowned. I burnt lights for about four weeks. The curculio is a night-flying insect, and you catch a great many. I think we have got to catch and kill them in some way, and I am satisfied that we can raise plums by using these methods.

Mr. Sambola, of Louisiana—I desire to give to the convention my views on this subject. I now possess a place in this city, where my father has devoted fully twenty years in destroying the insects which have prevented the successful cultivation of the grape   He had upon his place fully eight thousand grape vines. He protected them from the ants by the use of coal gas tar, which prevented the ants from creeping up the vines. He was successful in that way.

Mr. Wiggins, of Louisiana—A gentleman, with whom I am acquainted, in the neighborhood of Crystal Springs, Mississippi, informed me that in selecting ground for his peach orchard he would clear off ground surrounded by trees. Planting out his trees there, it was his custom, when the trees came to bear, to keep it well cultivated and clean. He would send his children to gather the peaches every morning that had fallen, and put them in barrels for the purpose. He told me it was eminently successful, and that he never was successful until he kept his peach orchard perfectly clean. When the peaches would drop on the ground he would carry them off immediately. He was the only man in that neighborhood who had a majority of sound fruit. They have noticed up there that if they should happen to have two peach seasons in succession, that the second year they have always had unsound peaches. This country is peculiarly adapted to the curculio, to an extent that I hardly think you can realize in the North; and I am satisfied, from personal observation, that, as far as the South is concerned, the only true method of preventing damage from the curculio is to keep the orchard well cultivated, and to keep it well cleaned up.

Mr. Kendel, of Ohio—Our peaches are very little troubled with the curculio. We raise them very well along the lakes, but plums we can not get on account of the curculio. Why they should attack the plums and not the peaches I don't understand. The only way I have known plums to be kept is by gathering the fruit as fast as it falls.

Mr. Nowlin, of Arkansas—I have probably one hundred Wild Goose plum trees. I think last year it was the prettiest sight I ever saw, about a bushel to the tree; large, handsome fellows. I also had a few young Green Gage trees bearing their first crop. They all matured without any evidence of curculio. There was some evidence of curculio in the peach crop, but not very extensive.

Mr. Hudson, of Louisiana—I am satisfied that a diligent use of the sheet under the trees will successfully prevent the ravages of the curculio.   I think there are two kinds of curculios—one that attacks the peaches and one the plums.

Mr. Nowlin, of Arkansas—If any country is the home of the Wild Goose plum, Arkansas is, but we are troubled with the curculio also.   I have saved the crop, however, by sowing powdered slacked lime upon the trees.

Mr. Beatty, of Kentucky—I have had considerable experience in this matter, and I find that the use of the sheet in catching curculios will save the fruit.

Mr. Hollister, of Illinois, spoke of the difference between the curculio and the plum gouger.   The first makes a crescent-shaped incision in the fruit, and the gouger only makes a simple perforation.

Mr. Galusha, of Illinois—The curculio does less damage to the Wild Goose plum than to any other variety, because the eggs laid in the plum are killed by the acid juices of the fruit.

The following paper, by one of the most justly noted scientists of the West, although present at the meeting, in the absence of the author, was not read.   The topic, "An Orchard Scourge," seems appropriate to come in at this juncture.   The name of Prof. T. J. Burrill is, in the opinion of the Secretary, a sufficient *passport* to *position* in the body of this report:

AN ORCHARD SCOURGE.
(*Fusicladium deudriticum.*)

BY PROF. T. J. BURRILL, OF ILLINOIS.

Every one must have noticed last year (1882) a peculiar shriveling and curling of the leaves of apple trees, beginning, in many cases, soon after the bursting of the buds in springtime and continuing, more or less, during the season.   Many trees really never gained full foliage during the summer, but throughout the year looked starved and ragged.   On closer examination, the stunted and injured leaves appeared dark-colored, or, perhaps, sooty-black, in spots and irregular lines.   The young twigs, too, presented a similar appearance, being blackened, and often distorted in growth.   In some localities, especially southward, pear trees suffered in the same way, but the leaves more generally attained full size, however much they were discolored and distorted.

The fruit, too, of both these orchard trees was unusually badly injured by what people call the "scab."   The apples have been, in numerous instances, so scarred and spotted as to be practically worthless, except for stock or cider. Pears, after having gained considerable size, were seen to have been affected over great areas of their surface by the injuries received, while still quite young, the later appearance being a rough, discolored surface, though "scabs" similar to those on the apple were plentiful enough. In the case of both fruits, the unyielding coating of destroyed tissues gave way to the internal forces of expansion, and cracks, more or less deep, occurred. In Champaign county the Early Harvest apples, among others, were divided half way to the core, or even deeper, by several irregular fissures, leaving knobby lobes, more or less covered by a layer of blackened, corky tissues.

It is well known that "scabby" fruit, besides being injured in appearance, much sooner decays, at least in a great majority of instances. Rot begins at the "scab," and proceeds inward and around. Often this occurs while the fruit still hangs on the tree, and almost certainly takes place if scabby apples or pears are gathered and stored in a moist place.

Appealing to the microscope, we find all these injured parts of the trees and fruit bear the vegetative threads (mycelium) and spores of a fungus, specifically the same whether on the leaves, the twigs, or the surface of the fruit. However different the appearance to the unaided eye the injury may be on these different parts, there is no appreciable difference in the microscopical characteristics either of the fungus or in the real destruction of the cells and tissues. However different the appearance to the unaided eye the diseased spots or patches were, occurring on the leaves, twigs or fruit, anyone competent to judge in such matters would, upon microscopical examination, pronounce the fungus specifically the same in all cases. Its mode of growth and development is essentially the same on all parts of the tree, save such modifications as, evidently enough, arise from the difference in the parts themselves. On the fruit, the epidermis and perhaps a few layers of cells are destroyed, while the deeper tissues continue to live and grow. On the leaves, the epidermis is similarly destroyed, but, on account of the thinness of the leaf, the whole structure goes with it. The scars on the twigs somewhat resemble those on the fruit, but instead of being circular, or nearly so, they are elongated in the direction of the fibers; usually, also. they are much smaller.

By proper manipulations it is easy to make out that the mycelium of the fungus consists of a few colorless, frequently branched, inconspicuous threads, woven loosely through and through the cells of the supporting plant. This poorly developed mycelium neither wanders far nor penetrates deeply. On the fruit, it is confined to the spot which eventually shows the characteristics of the disease, and to the surface layers of cells. From the white threads there arise short, erect, tinted portions, which, from their density, form a velvet-like mat covering the affected spot. On the outer ends of these minute stalks the multitude of spores is borne, and these being dark olive-brown, or in the mass almost black, give to the spot the color observed. The spores are usually about four times as long as wide, often somewhat club-

204 Mississippi Valley Horticultural Society.

shaped, i. e., thicker towards the apex, and consist of a single cell, or have a transverse partition making two cells.

In the early condition of the affected spot, the mycelium and spores occupy a small central area; but as growth continues the mycelium gradually spreads into the surrounding tissues, and soon dies in the center, so that the fungus is found in a ring at the outer edge of the affected spot. Sometimes this spreading continues for months from the same initial point, and a large part of the surface of a fruit may be involved, or, for some reason, the fungus soon perishes, and the spot remains small. Frequently, numerous small spots near together coalesce, and thus, in another way, cover the surface.

Spores are produced by the fungus in a similar manner when it inhabits the leaves and young stems, only they are never found in such luxuriance of number, on account, no doubt, of the less available nutriment. There seems to be no special season for their maturity—they form and ripen throughout June, July, August, and September, and as soon as mature, germinate whenever suitable conditions of moisture, etc., are present. If in this condition the spores reach the living surfaces of the leaves, twigs, or fruit. the filament produced by the germinating tube, penetrates the tissues and a new crop of mycelium and spores results, together with the injured condition of the host.

There are those who, admitting the presence of the fungus in this destructive disease, deny its agency as the cause of the difficulty. With them it is a secondary result, a mere accompaniment or follower of the real destroyer. In the majority of such cases we are asked to seek for the latter in the conditions of the climate or the inherent peculiarities of the affected plants. It is true the exact connections and the special processes by which heat or cold, wet or dry, starvation, over-cropping, etc., produces the effects just as they are observed in time and space are never explained by anyone who pretends to be informed upon the subjects of vegetable physiology and pathology; but talk is cheap, and never easier than in general speculations by those who do not care to be exact and definite, and especially by those who do not look close enough to see the obstacles in the way. It is often easier to get a full account of what exists in the center of the earth than what there may be behind a picture hanging upon the wall of a room occupied by the informant. In the former case he does not feel restrained by the possibilities of proof, and does feel that his notion is as good, at least, as that of his auditor can be. The two may disagree, but that does not hurt anything.

So, in these apparently difficult problems of disease in plants, it not unfrequently happens that opinions are the more tenaciously held the less the real knowledge possessed upon the subject. When the bark of an apple tree is found after a snow-storm to be freshly gnawed, and when the well-known track of a rabbit is seen about it, no one thinks of saying, " I admit the presence of the rabbit and the quality of its teeth for this work, but contend that we should not account it the cause of this wound. If the snow had not fallen the animal would not have touched the tree, hence the snow is the real gnawer of this bark." Or, " if the bark had not been palatable and nutri-

tious, it would not have been injured, so its own condition is the first cause
of the mutilation. The rabbit is only a secondary thing." I say no one in
such a case tries to indulge in such metaphysics. All admit the direct
agency of the animal in causing the mischief, because all are familiar with
the possibilities of those well-sharpened teeth, and all can clearly see their
imprint in the wound. There is no use of argument in this case. But of
these hypothetical fungi, of which nothing is known, whether good or evil, it
is not strange that people leave them out of the premises altogether in reaching a conclusion. Without the compound microscope we are hardly aware
of their existence, and certainly must remain ignorant of their direct effects
and their methods of producing them. But, fortified and prepared with this
marvelous instrument and the proper ability to use it, these things disappear. Then there is no important difference in what can be known, and
thoroughly known, between the methods and effects of these minute but
real, specific, self-nourishing and self-propagating things known under the
general name of *Fungi,* and that other specifically characterized thing called
rabbit.

Having had abundant opportunity to observe, I have no hesitation in saying that a certain fungus is the direct cause of the disastrous malady which
has so seriously injured the apple and pear orchards of our whole Northwest
during the last year. The rabbit itself is subject to conditions; its depredations in summer amount to nothing, so far as trees are concerned, and certain conditions of winter ruefully reduces their numbers. Our fungus is no
less, perhaps not more, subject to varying conditions of temperature, moisture, etc., or in a word of environment. Its vigorous growth is impossible un- .
der one set of these co :ditions; it unduly develops under another combina-
tion of influences. But in the sense that the rabbit, and not the peculiarities
of the weather, is the direct cause of the gnawing, so the fungus, which has
been described, and not the rain, or the dew, or the sun, or the frost, is the
immediate agent of this scab and rust.

It is, however, no new thing. It has neither come into existence in our
time nor has it recently been introduced in our part of the country. Its
dispersion over the world seems to be as wide as that of the apple itself, and
records now exist in the books of its occasional prolific development and injuries over nearly a century of time. Botanists have baptised it with several
names, hard enough of course, and collectors of specimens count it in the
make-up of herbaria, sometimes more than once, on account of the synony-
mical names under which it is known. Now, however, the authorities are
quite generally agreed that henceforth *Fusicladium dendriticum,* Fhl., shall be
its true and only title in scientific parlance.

Turning now to the supposed conditions which have of late influenced the
increased injuries of the fungus, nothing can be asserted with positiveness,
but all indications seem to point to atmospheric and climatic causes rather
than any special physiological changes in the trees themselves. Some kinds
of trees are much worse affected than others, and this may be generally true

of special varieties, or only during certain seasons, or at certain ages of the stock. But nearly all varieties of apples and pears have unusually suffered, at least in places, during the last year. Even nursery stock has been singed and stunted.

It seems to me, we are first to look to the open and humid autumn of 1881 as an important contribution to the severe result. During this time the fungus certainly did vigorously develop on the fading leaves, and especially on the unripened shoots of the year's growth. As the spores very readily germinate when moistened, it is not probable that any of them survive the winter on the fallen leaves. When once germinated, winter's vicissitudes soon put an end to them as they do to sprouting seeds. But on the twigs, in the dry air, both spores and mycelium successfully pass the winter and freely grow in the spring.

Having thus an unusual start last spring (1882), and unusually favored by the remarkable lateness and wetness of the season, the fungus became immensely developed, and, as we know, did immense damage. The outlook for next year (1883), as at present indicated, is not encouraging, but no one can certainly predict the results. Certain it is that the trees are now badly infested, and with similar conditions a similar development may be expected.

The important question is, "Can anything be done to reduce the damage?" I can not, with assurance, say "yes." But some experiments on a small scale seem to be sufficiently encouraging to plan for further and more extended trials. The thing to do, of course, is to kill the fungus and prevent its reappearance. From what has been said the most favorable time for treatment is in the winter when the leaves are off, and the applications should be made to the young wood.

The suggested trials are, first, pruning away any unnecessary young growth and especially that most affected, then syringing the tree with an emulsion of kerosene oil made with soap and water. To prepare this, mix equal quantities of soft soap, or hard soap softened with water and heat, and common coal oil; stir vigorously and for at least five minutes, then add ten to twenty times the quantity of water, and again stir. The result should be a uniform milky fluid. Apply in any way so as to wet the bark of the last year's growth, or, for thoroughness, that of two years' production. No fears need be entertained of injury to the tenderest part of the tree if the emulsion is well made. It can be applied, if desirable, to the leaves, but there is much less surface to wet before these appear, and it is much easier to reach it.

Coal oil of itself is injurious to vegetation, but when made into an emulsion, and thus diluted, no fears need be entertained about its use. Still it may be in this state quite destructive to such fungus growths as that of which we write.

Sulphur has been recommended for similar use, but in this case little good can be anticipated from it, at any rate, if applied in winter. The sulphur itself does not kill fungi, because it is insoluble, but the beneficial effect comes from the gases, products of which it forms a part. In the winter these are not formed, while the rains wash away the solid material. Kerosene, on the other hand, is as effectual in cold as in warm weather, and kills by direct action.

There is another thing that may be mentioned in favor of the oil emulsion : it is also destructive to insects, and, wherever they may be reached, to their eggs. It is probable that the eggs of the apple aphis, which are deposited in autumn on the twigs, may be destroyed in this way. If so, we can kill two birds with one stone.

Upon motion of Prof. S. M. Tracy, of Missouri, Mr. John T. Hardie was unanimously elected to the Vice Presidency for the State of Louisiana.

Mr. Williams, of Indiana, chairman of the committee to devise ways and means to pay for the expense of collecting statistics by the Secretary, etc., read the following report :

Resolved, That for the purpose of procuring sufficient means for the payment of the Secretary and the publishing of the annual proceedings and statistical matter of the Society, we recommend—

1. That at every exhibition made by this Society, when premiums are offered, an entry fee of 10 per cent. of the amount of the premiums competed for shall be required and collected in advance.

2. That we recommend the preparation of a scale of fees where diplomas or medals are awarded instead of money.

3. That the collection of 10 per cent. and other fees shall be placed in the hands of the Treasurer, subject to an order from the Secretary, signed by the President.

4. That the proceeds from the sale of our publications be devoted to the expenses of the statistical department.

5. That a Directory of nurserymen, commissionmen, florists, seedsmen and manufacturers of horticultural wares, etc., be published as advertising matter in our annual proceedings, and that a fee of two dollars be charged for each name so published, when accompanied by satisfactory references.

6. And that we also recommend that the Executive Committee be instructed to fix the salary of the Secretary and set apart such an amount from the premium fund as, in their judgment, will cover any deficit in meeting all expenses.

On motion of Prof. Colmant, of Mississippi, amended by Mr. Evans, of Missouri, the report was referred to the Executive Committee.

The Society then adjourned to 8 o'clock P. M.

Fourth Day—Saturday.

EVENING SESSION.

President Earle called the Society to order at 8 o'clock P. M. and proceeded to announce, as per resolution adopted in the afternoon, the following

COMMITTEE ON TRANSPORTATION.

Northern Section—F. A. Thomas, of Illinois, J. M. Smith, of Wisconsin, and Captain E. Hollister, of Illinois.

Southern Section—Dr. H. E. McKay, of Mississippi, Major A. W. Rountree, of Louisiana, and Major S. H. Nowlin, of Arkansas.

The President—Our first subject this evening is that of raspberries and their management. Our excellent friend, the Treasurer of this Society—may the responsibilities of this office be larger in the future than they have been in the past—who is one of the most successful fruit growers of the West, will read us a paper upon that topic. I take pleasure in inviting you to hear Major J. C Evans, of Missouri.

RASPBERRY MANAGEMENT AND THE NEW RASPBERRIES.

BY J. C. EVANS, OF MISSOURI.

It has been said that successful farming is much more complex than any trade, and demands more constant thought than most branches of professional life, together with the executive ability equal to the management of any business. This will apply to the growing of small fruits as well as to farming. A very small per cent. of those engaged in farming are making it a success, and of the large number who have embarked in the business of growing small fruits, perhaps just as few have succeeded. The chances for success are few, while those for failure are many.

What is meant by success is that the acre of raspberries has paid for planting, pruning, cultivating, picking, marketing, and the interest on the money invested in land, tools, etc., and has a fair per cent. left for net profit. And if this continues for a series of years, then we call it a success.

I would not discourage any one from engaging in this pleasant and interesting occupation, but I ask the question, how many of us are making the growing of raspberries a success, and why the many failures? If the question were asked, do raspberries do well in your section? you would say yes. Any farmer may plant a patch in the corner of the garden or along the fence and just let them alone, and he will have plenty of berries for the family; but suppose he tries two or three acres in this way and undertakes to market them for profit; he would certainly fail. But the intelligent fruit-grower who has learned all the conditions necessary to success may select the varieties known to do well in his soil and climate and apply these conditions, and reasonably good profits will accrue. The object in growing raspberries, after we have plenty for the family, is the money we can make out of the business.

If we wish to go right, then we must start right; we must learn (and that is our object in coming together here). Is our soil adapted? If we have that that will produce a good crop of corn, we consider it good for raspberries What exposure is best, and why? Land sloping gently to any point, except south, or southwest, because not so liable to shorten the crop of fruit in ripening. or the growth of canes later in the season by drought; besides, the sun has less power on the canes before and after sudden freezing, which is the principal cause of what is c lled winter-killing. The preparation of the land before planting is a matter of great importance, for on this depends the growth of canes the first year and the crop of fruit the second, as well as for years after. The land should be ploughed deep, the deeper the better, and well pulverized, then marked off in rows seven feet (most growers say six, but seven gives more room to cultivate and pick), with shovel plow, and the plants placed three feet apart in the furrow, and a little dirt drawn around them to hold them in place until the furrow is filled from each side with the same kind of plow.

The middles should not be planted in any other crop, as is the custom of some growers, especially new beginners, and where land is valuable, as a matter of economy. I question the economy in any case. The land should be thoroughly cultivated through the growing season, and the plants topped at a foot high to cause laterals to push out. In the following spring these laterals should be cut back to six inches long, and the land cultivated before the buds start, and again after the fruit is picked. The yearly after-treatment will be the same, except that the topping will naturally be a little higher each year. I would say here that the great mistake of most growers is in leaving too much wood. Better have fewer berries in number and more in measurement.

The above applies to both red and black varieties, with the exception that red is seldom pruned at all and is almost always allowed to grow in a mass or hedge row. Some growers, however, have practiced summer pinching to a limited extent and claim that it works well. Others cut back to one-third or one-half of the cane early in spring and say that it is right. I have practiced this on the Thwack for several years and find it works well.

When we come to talk about varieties we have a long list to consider, both red and black, but my experience being limited to a few of the leading varieties, I shall name only such, and would say to those who wish to plant, if

14

you know of a variety, either new or old, that has given satisfaction in your vicinity with the treatment you expect to give it, that is the one for you to plant.

We used to be satisfied to grow Doolittle and Mammoth Cluster, but many growers in our section are now discarding them and planting Hopkins as the best black-cap. Gregg is also doing well in·some sections. Turner is a fine red one, and has done well over a large section of country, but some growers are giving it up and planting Thwack as a better shipping berry, though not so good in quality as the Turner and some others, but a much better berry to send a long distance. Its large size and ability to retain its fine color make it sell readily at good prices.

There are no doubt many among the long list of candidates for public favor that will prove·themselves good in certain localities, and some of them may come to the front and take the place of those now considered best; but we must test them in a small way first. In conclusion let me repeat, never plant extensively any variety until it has been well tested in your section, no matter how well it has done elsewhere.

The President announced the arrangements that had been made for the excursion to Mobile. The party will leave here Tuesday morning at 7·o'clock, and, arriving in Mobile at 12 o'clock, will be received by Mobile and Ohio Railroad officials, who have provided carriages for the entire party. Tuesday evening, and the greater portion of Wednesday, will be devoted to sight-seeing, and then the excursionists will take their departure either for home or return to New Orleans. The latter will leave Mobile at 4 o'clock Wednesday evening.

Upon motion of Mr. Holsinger, of Kansas, it was unanimously resolved to remain in Mobile until Wednesday evening.

The President having been requested by some of the delegates to make inquiries as to the cost of an excursion to San Antonio, Texas, announced that the Morgan Railroad had offered to take excursionists, if a sufficient number went, at twenty-five dollars for the round trip and give them two weeks time.

Mr. Baker, of Kansas, announced that as he was to leave in the morning, he had turned over the matter of transportation to Prof. Colmant, of Mississippi.

The President—Among the new fruits which are attracting our attention, perhaps none are more inviting and excellent, or more promising of commercial value than the Japanese persimmon. Our old friend D. B. Wier, well remembered by all Illinois fruit men, has found "the promised land" hidden away among the prairies and forests of Arkansas. He will tell us what he knows about

THE JAPANESE PERSIMMON IN ARKANSAS.

BY D. B. WIER OF ARKANSAS.

Arkansas, by reason of its geographical position and magnificent climate, should be. and will be, the early fruit and vegetable garden of the great Northwest. Her northern half, the upland, or hill region, is the home of the apple, the peach, the plum, and perhaps the pear, as well as of all the small fruits, including the grape and cherry. Nowhere, I think, are the trees and plants o these fruits more healthy or longer lived, and certainly nowhere are they of finer flavor, size and color. The northwestern third of the State is peculiarly adapted for the apple. This standard fruit is there grown of the finest size, color and quality, the tree exceedingly healthy and long lived. It is also finely adapted to all other hardy fruits. This region having now direct railroad connection with West Missouri, Kansas and Nebraska and the whole Northwest, it is worthy of the attention of fruit-growers. The region is very healthy, water the very best, and land cheap. It is settling up fast with first-class, energetic people.

The northwest center of the State, with all its mineral riches and splendid scenery, is also one of the finest of fruit regions. It is also soon to be opened up by a line of railroad, North and South, opening up to it the splendid markets of Memphis and cities beyond on the South, and Kansas City and other fine markets North.

The south line of the hill country from Newport, on White river, to Little Rock, is already developed to some extent as a fruit producing region. With an outlet to markets North and South by the great Iron Mountain railroad route, it sends vast amounts of fine, early fruits to the great St. Louis market and also to Texas. This railroad, stretching from the northeast to the southwest corner of the State, gives the fruit-grower along its line a choice of either the Northern or Texas market. This road is bordered on both sides of its entire length by splendid fruit lands. The same is true of the Little Rock and Fort Smith railroad. The climate of all this northern portion of the State is exceedingly healthy, except in the lowest bottom lands along the streams. There is room for tens of thousands of energetic fruit-growers.

But I was to write of the persimmon. Well, I will come to it in due time.

The greater portion of Southern Arkansas and all its eastern side is well nigh a level plain, with a soil composed of either alluvium or clayey silt, generally covered with a heavy growth of timber. Nearly all of the eastern portion of the State, except Crowley's ridge, which reaches from Helena to the Missouri line, overflows to some extent in times of extreme high water.

This Crowley's ridge is an exceeding fine fruit region. The pear especially seems to thrive there wonderfully when compared with its very general failure every where West.

Then we have the whole northeastern part of the State almost a level plain covered with heavy timber, except parts of three counties lying between the lower White and Arkansas rivers, with a soil on the uplands made up of a very fine, clayey silt, finely adapted to nearly every kind of fruit in its natural condition, and when thoroughly underdrained with tile will most certainly be one of the finest fruit soils in the world. Easily cleared, and easily tilled, without a rock or a pebble to interfere with the plow, hoe or cultivator. The prairies are healthy, and exceedingly level, yet, generally, with slope enough so as to be readily tile-drained. Nearly all fruits grow on the better surface-drained portions of these prairies in great perfection and abundance, with scarcely any care given them by the settlers, showing plainly what could be done there with proper orchard cuture.

The timber lands of this region are generally very much better surface and under-drained than the prairies; therefore, the different fruits on them do measureably better. But the timbered lands are very unhealthy, especially along the streams, to unacclimated people, particularly Northern people; and as it costs about as much to free the land of trees, stumps and roots as it would to under-drain the prairies, and considering the better health of the prairies, they, the prairies, would be my choice, first, last and all the time. Land is wonderfully cheap in all this region. It is not a corn nor a wheat country, but nearly every other known crop does well, some of them giving enormous crops. For instance, all the leguminous plants, such as peas and beans, in all their species and varieties, sweet and Irish potatoes, vines of all kinds, and the sorghums and millets.

We are now ready to consider the persimmons. The native persimmon (*Diospyros Virginiana*), grows plentifully all over the State, but in the hill region it is not generally found, except in the bottom lands along streams. But in the more level portions of the State it abounds everywhere, even on prairies, and is, perhaps, the most plentiful of arboreal plants, except it be the sassafras (*S. officinale*). It is found on all kinds of soils, from the wettest to the dryest, but attains its maximum growth on the overflowed lands, on the margins of rivers, where it may often be found two to three feet in diameter at its base, and stretching upward as straight as an arrow, sixty to eighty feet, without a branch, producing, irregularly, immense crops of large, luscious fruit, ripening from July on through the fall and winter, many varieties hanging on the tree nearly the winter through.

Strange as it may seem, I have found everywhere, where the persimmon is plentifully indigenous, that the great majority of the people insist that this fruit is not ripe nor edible until after frosts. While the reverse is true, many of the finest varieties ripen, and are exceedingly luscious, early in August. Our botany tells us that the flowers of the persimmon are "diœciously polygamous," while the truth is, as I see it, they are monœcious, diœcious and polygamous, or, in other words, we find individual trees that are strictly staminate, others pistilate, others with perfect flowers, and also others of every grade between. Therefore, I should say that its flowers are not more diœciously than monœciously polygamous. They are simply and exactly polygamous. This being the fact, as a natural consequence trees of it grown from seed will have many entirely barren individuals amongst them, and many individuals prove barren when isolated from others that would prove productive if not so isolated; yet, pistillate individuals, seemingly strictly so, produce, some of them, very fine, seedless fruit, when so isolated. Two of the finest flavored and largest fruited (as we incorrectly call the edible part, the seeds being the fruit proper) varieties I have ever observed were entirely without perfect seeds, and had scarcely observable rudiments of seeds.

The fruiting of the persimmon as a mass is very irregular, with generally only a small portion of the great mass of trees fruiting each year. But occasional seasons nearly every tree gives an abundant crop of fruit. When such a season happens, every living thing in a persimmon country is happy, for nearly every animal and bird is very fond of them, and what few living creatures there are that do not feed on them, feed, as a rule, on such as do. They are a very rich, fattening food for all.

Again, there are varieties that seldom, if ever, fail to produce a heavy crop each year; others that bear every other year; others that give an immense crop one year and a light crop the next. So we see the fruiting is like the flowering—very diverse. This tells us that if we wish to grow persimmons with good fruit, and yearly productive, we must bud or graft, or grow our trees from root-cuttings, from such varieties as suit us in these respects.

The varieties among our native persimmons are endless, ranging in quality from those inedible at any time of year to those exceedingly large and luscious, rivaling, I think, in size and edible qualities, the finest of the Japanese persimmons.

The commercial value of the fruit of the native persimmon is, as yet, very little, but I think it has great future prospects. It can not be well sent to distant markets, owing to its want of consistency when ripe, for all varieties of it that have come under my notice are very soft when ripe enough to be edible. But I have thought that it could be cured and dried with sugar, and make in this way a very nutritious food or sweetmeat. When properly handled the fruit makes a very palatable, wholesome, exhilarating beer, or drink It should also, if fermented and distilled, make a very fine fruit ·brandy. As a food it is very valuable for man or beast. All kinds of stock fatten on it quickly. The vast amount of overflowed waste lands of the South, if planted with yearly productive varieties of native persimmons, ripening in succession, would make a range for fattening hogs, surpassing by far the cornfields of Illinois and Iowa.

The tree belongs to the Ebony family (*Ebenacea*), and will, in time, as fashions roll around, become of great commercial value. It is a most beautiful wood, hard, fine-grained, fine dark color, receiving a splendid polish, and said to be fine for wood engraving. It would make most beautiful furniture and pannelings. As we have now skilled horticulturists looking up and propagating the finer varieties of this valuable but long-neglected fruit, we will leave it in their hands for the present. But all lovers of fruit, where it is indigenous, should give it attention and seek out the finest varieties and perpetuate them. It seems to be a fruit without an enemy in the insect world, its astringent, acrid pulp protecting it from all enemies until ripe.

THE JAPANESE PERSIMMON—(*Dicspyros kaki*).

The Japan persimmon was introduced into this country some ten or twelve years ago, if I recollect rightly, by Thomas Hogg, of New York, and by him disseminated with great liberality. I tried to grow trees of it of his importation in Northern Illinois, but found that it would not withstand our winters, the trees killing down to the surface of the soil each and every winter, but springing up in the spring. It will probably prove a very valuable fruit everywhere south of Memphis, Tenn. In Southern Arkansas the experience so far shows it to be everywhere reliable, the climate and soil both suiting it admirably, so far as known. But right here I must call a halt, for I have not seen enough of this fruit growing in garden and orchard to pass an opinion on it from personal observation. I have seen the trees growing in many places South with fine health and vigor; have seen and eaten of the fruit and know it to be both very handsome and very good. The indications are that its Northern limit will equal or surpass that of the very hardiest figs. That thorough horticulturist, Mr. Berckmans, of Georgia, should be able to tell you all about the Japan persimmon; therefore I pass—I mean that I pass the subject over to him.

I am very, very sorry, for the reason that I was informed in the first place that my subject was to be "Ar-kan-saw; its Great Diversity of Fruits." But my good friend, the Major, who runs the *Spirit* of Ar-kan-saw, or lets it run him, I forget which, after seeing me place myself outside of about a peck of fine, ripe persimmons, thought, I suppose, that I had laid the foundation for a good solid paper on the persimmon subject, so he switched me off. If he had let me have the other subject I would have spread myself out big. I would have told you how she of the tropics and he of the North each spring made love "Over the garden wall" in Arkansas, and brought with them all the knick-knacks and finest fruits and flowers of two zones, even figs. You should have seen what magnificent yearly crops of figs we have on the Arkansas prairies. But what has all this got to do with persimmons?

The President—We have now come to the last paper which our too limited time will permit us to hear read at this meeting. And as the apple is our longest keeping fruit, we have kept this subject in reserve to the last of the meeting. Mr. W. M. Samuels, of

Kentucky, is one of our most careful and experienced pomologists, and his judgment upon the new varieties will be of value to apple planters everywhere. I invite your attention to Mr. Samuels' paper upon

THE NEW APPLES OF VALUE FOR MARKET.

BY WILLIAM M. SAMUELS, OF KENTUCKY.

I am requested, by your honorable Society, to tell what I know about new apples of value for market.

In naming them it is impossible to mention varieties adapted to all parts of our vast country. While some varieties succeed in one locality or latitude, they become entirely worthless in others. Some require the genial influence of the South to fully develop and ripen their fruits; while the colder North seems better adapted to others. Many varieties flourish on limestone soils, while others are equally at home on clay or sandy lands. Some varieties require to fully mature on the trees, others, as the Baldwin and Greenings, suffer little from the effects of premature picking. Fruits commonly attain to perfection when permitted to fully mature on the trees. This is notably the case with the orange.

Unfortunately, however, many of our fruits must be gathered before ripe, in order to reach market in good condition. An apple that is a favorite for a near market may become worthless for a distant one. A variety that would be pronounced first-class in every respect, except in color, by the horticulturist, might be entirely ignored by the average city buyer. There seems to be little or no improvement in the public taste as time advances.

It has been but a few year since the Ben Davis, with its brilliant colors and large size, was sold in the South, while Northern dealers ridiculed a taste that sought an apple of such inferior qualities. But it has gradually advanced in notoriety, until it has reached the front as the leading market variety; and during the past season, when New York and other Eastern buyers bought the fine fruit grown in Kentucky, Missouri and Illinois, the Ben Davis became the favorite export apple. The London papers referred to it as the favorite table fruit.

The apple attains to a greater perfection in the United States than in any other country. It is grown over a larger extent of territory than any other fruit, and is the only fruit we have in its natural or fresh state the year round. It is in more general use than any other fruit. It is utilized in many ways, and is the great health-giving luxury, relished alike by all classes.

From a commercial standpoint it rivals many of our important field crops. While we are importing many varieties of fruits in common use, the apple has become an important article of export.

We find, however, that other fruits of less importance have attracted the attention of our pomologists, who have made rapid strides in developing and introducing new and valuable varieties.

The same skill and attention devoted to the discovery and production of new apples, would, no doubt, have given us a fruit far superior in size, color, flavor and keeping qualities to any now in existence. For want of proper attention but few new varieties of importance have been brought to notice during the last decade.

Many years ago I sent South for new varieties that were highly recommended for testing in our latitude, hoping to get something that would improve the keeping qualities of our fruit. I have fruited most of them and find many identical with our old sorts. Nickajack proved to be our old Carolina Red, or Blue Pearmain; Buncome, Lady Finger, Buckingham and Equinetley, so highly eulogized, produced our Fall Queen, that has been grown from sprouts, in Kentucky, for more than half a century. I got some good keepers, however, but deficient in size and color necessary to make a valuable market apple. Some of them may be grown profitably for home market.

This question of introducing new varieties is one of vital importance to the fruit-grower, and should be handled with great caution. What we want in the South is an apple of good size and handsome appearance, that will hang on the tree till frost, and not speck.

In giving the following list it is difficult to determine how far back I should go, in naming new varieties; some of them may have been long familiar in certain localities, while they are unknown at other places. I shall first name those not generally grown, and as they are described in our fruit books, I will only give their value as a market fruit; and in naming this catalogue of apples valued for their market qualities, I shall regard size and appearance as the main requisites, rather than the cultivated taste of the amateur or pomologist.

I have nothing new to offer in the extra early sorts superior or equal to Red June, Early Harvest, and Red Astrachan. The Red Astrachan has not been profitable with us.

Hames is a few days later, larger and much more sightly. We have the best of authority for this valuable apple in P. J. Berckmans, of Augusta, Georgia.

Summer King—Received from A. D. Webb, Bowling Green, Kentucky. This is a beautiful apple, of good size and excellent quality; an old variety, but not known much out of its native locality; tree, a good grower, erect or spreading when of bearing age; an early and good bearer alternate years: season, 10th of July.

We have a large list of varieties not in general cultivation, that are fine market sorts, and ought to be tested in different latitudes. They would, no doubt, improve our present stock in many localities; but as they are all described in the books, I will merely name them.

Hagloe—A large, yellow sort, an improvement on the Horse, which seems to be on the decline.

Carolina Watson—The same season, red.

Summer Queen —Magnificent, large, red-striped.

Ragan's Yellow—Larger and earlier than Horse.

Taunton or Trotter—Large, red.

Huntsman's Favorite—A large apple of good quality.

Kinnard's Choice—Large, dark red, valuable in Middle Tennessee.

Western Beauty—Large, red, very promising.

Stark's Seedling—Large, beautifully splashed and striped with red.

Ducket—Large, yellow, with crimson cheek.

Ben Davis Seedling.

Santa—Good size and a long keeper, South.

Shannon—A large, beautiful yellow apple, from Arkansas, very highly prized there.

This list is mostly cultivated only in its native locality.

But something new is what we want; this is the theme that excites the curiosity of every one.

Maxey—A seedling from Hart county, Ky. A. D. Webb, Bowling Green, Ky., who is the best of authority, says: "It is doing remarkably well; a long keeper; will ship any distance; good size; a thrifty grower; attains to a large size; color, rather dull. Fifty bushels have been taken from the original tree in one season." Specimens here for examination.

Saunder's Seedling—A chance seedling, near George P. Murrell's, Austin, Ark., from whom I quote: "Size, medium; nearly a solid red; flesh, white, tender and crisp. The pecularities of this apple are that it was never known to speck on the tree, and has not failed to bear a crop for twenty-five years; will keep until January in Arkansas."

Filiquah—Concerning this valuable variety, I quote from the same authority. He says: "I can hardly describe this variety and do it justice. It is necessary to see an orchard in bearing to approximate an idea of their uniformity in size and their perfect symmetry in shape and appearance. Tree, a rapid, erect grower."

Salome—Being introduced by E. C. Hathaway, of LaSalle county, Ill. It is fully described by him, with the highest commendations from nearly all our best pomologists. I received a letter from O. B. Galusha, the highest authority, who says: "This apple stands alone in its long season of use; is excellent for dessert and cooking, out-keeping any other good apple; is of red cheek (good color), of good medium size, no small or defective ones; holding on tree until ready to be picked; better than any other sort here. It combines more good points as a variety for market than any other." Samples of this apple are here for inspection.

Jones' Seedling—This fine, long keeper is introduced by William Henry Smith, of Leeper's Fork, Williamson county, Tennessee. Fruit, rather large, round, oblate, slightly conical; skin, smooth, greenish yellow, shaded with brownish red, almost covered with minute brown dots; stalk, short, slender; cavity, medium, smooth, partially russeted. The size and long keeping qualities of this variety will make it a valuable market sort. Specimens here for examination.

Glendale—This beautiful, large apple is furnished by J. W. Smith, Glendale, Hardin county, Kentucky. Mr. Smith informs me that it has never been propagated except from sprouts. He set an orchard of sprouts, taken from fourteen trees, and about two hundred fruited in 1882: all true to the original type. Origin unknown. Many years ago some sprouts were brought from Virginia to Hardin county and planted. Others have been planted in the neighborhood and produced the very same fruit. This is certainly a very great acquisition, and must be a valuable market sort, rivaling the Ben Davis, which it resembles in its large size and beautiful appearance, being a better keeper, and does not speck on the tree. Tree, a compact, upright, thrifty grower; wood, hard; young shoots, very dark; leaves, very large, dark green; fruit, large, conical, or roundish conical; color, yellow, shaded all over with red and sprinkled with light dots; stalk, short, slender; cavity, medium; calyx, open. Specimens are here for inspection.

McCawley's Favorite—I quote from A. J. Trout, an extensive fruit grower in Trimble county, Kentucky, well posted and good authority. He says of it: " A new Seedling of the Bellflower, is a fac-simile of it in appearance, but far better flavored. Tree, thrifty, bears young, and more regularly than any apple I know; hangs on well, and keeps longer than Ben Davis or Rome Beauty; should be named Perfection." This is different from the apple of the same name in the books. We have some seedlings of merit in Western Kentucky.

Picket—A seedling of rare value, from Ballard county, Kentucky. Being of good, uniform size and fine appearance; red striped; excellent in quality; keeps well; a thrifty, erect grower, and good bearer; having all the requisites necessary to make it popular with the amateur or market man during its season, which is until March. Described in Downing's revised work.

Watwood—Also a seedling from Ballard county, Kentucky. The great value of this variety is its uniform good crops and long keeping; size, medium; color, dull red. Orchards are grown here from sprouts taken from the original tree; which is a thrifty grower. I have specimens for inspection.

Pebles—Another Ballard county variety; unsightly; color, green; size, medium, but the best keeper I have found; combining as many good qualities, perhaps, as Brother Galusha's Salome, except in appearance. Specimens here for inspection.

The last three mentioned are not fruiting, except in Western Kentucky. I introduced them after having them examined by some of our best fruit men. The first described being very highly commended by the Hon. Charles Downing; also having taken the first premium at the great St. Louis Fair.

Although entirely out of place, I can not refrain from calling attention to the red crab. It is certainly the most valuable of all crabs for cider. Cider for testing, and specimens are here for inspection.

As far as my limited knowledge extends, I have in this report endeavored to notice only such new varieties as I hope may improve on the old sorts, at least, in some localities, and be a benefit to the fruit grower. I have also called attention to the value and importance of the apple, and its neglect by our scientific pomologists. Wonderful results may be accomplished by hybridization. Since I left home my attention has been called to Rainey's Choice. This beautiful, large apple, exhibited at Nashville in 1882, was awarded the first prize as the finest apple ever exhibited in that city. This must be a grand acquisition.

My attention has been attracted, since I came here. by the fine display of apples from the Northwest; many varieties new, or new to me, of fine size and appearance, and, I am informed, of great merit. I would suggest to every grower of apples to examine them, and test them on the different soils and in the different latitudes.

If I have given any information that will advance the interest of fruit growing, I shall have accomplished what I desire.

At the conclusion of Mr. Samuels' paper, Mr. T. T. Lyon, of Michigan, chairman of the Commmittee on Fruits on Exhibition, reported the following :

REPORT OF THE COMMITTEE ON FRUITS EXHIBITED.

Mr. President, your Committee on Fruits respectfully report, that they find on exhibition, by George P. Peffer, of Wisconsin, sixty varieties of apples, four of crabs, and three of pears. Several of the apples are seedlings, of which nearly all are so far past season that a safe judgment as to their value can hardly be arrived at. Among the named varieties we observe many of comparatively recent origin in the Northwest, which are assuming importance for their ability to bear the climate of the prairie States. The specimens, though past their season in very many cases, and more or less injured in transportation, have evidently, as the rule, been well grown.

We also find an exceedingly fine and well preserved collection of 145 plates, by the Missouri Valley Horticultural Society, many of them, however, being duplicates. The varieties exhibited. are : Romanite, Fulton, Ross Greening, McAfee's Non-such, Winter May, Stannard, Fink, Ragan's Red, Janet, Seeknofurther, Clayton, Ewalt, Shawnee, Rome Beauty, Ben Davis, Newtown Pippin, Wine Sap, Cannon Pearmain, Lady, Nickajack, Jonathan, Roman Stem, Missouri Pippin, W. W. Pearmain, Grimes' Golden, York Imperial, Peck's Pleasant, Strawberry, Golden Russet, Huntsman's Favorite, Danvers Winter Sweet, Lawver, Lady's Sweet, Swaar, White Bellflower, Dutch Mignone, White Bell, Autumn Swaar, Yellow Bellflower, Sops of Wine, Fameuse, Roxbury Russet, Pennock, Porter, Kansas Blush, R. I. Greening, Maiden's Blush, King of Tompkins County, Gano's Seedling, Norton's Melon, Fallawater, English Russet, Lowell, Hewes' Crab, Hyslop Crab, Soulard Crab, Superior Cider, Esopus Spitzenberg, Smith's Cider, Gloria Mundi, Willow Twig, North Carolina Red, Bucks County Pippin, Penn. Red Streak, Striped Gilliflower, Chronical, Gano's Red, Newtown Spitzenberg, Missouri Pippin, English Golden

Russet, Baldwin, Northern Spy, Limber Twig, Rambo, Milam, Peck's Pleasant, Wagstaff's Seedling, Lansingburg, Jersey Black, American Golden Russet. It also includes one plate of pears and six plates of crabs, and a dish of native nuts, which, from their peculiar appearance give indications of a possible hybridization between the Pecan and the Shell-bark Hickory, which, if the fact, is to us a matter of much surprise.

We also find upon the tables the Salome, a recent seedling of Illinois, shown, as we understand, by President O. B. Galusha, of the Illinois Horticultural Society. It is a fine looking, medium-sized fruit, in perfect condition and of fair, sprightly flavor; fine grained and tender and crisp in texture, juicy and agreeable. It is represented to remain in good eating condition from autumn to late spring with only ordinary care. If valuable it will probably be on account of qualities of tree or fruit that are peculiarly fitted for the climate of that region.

We also find one plate of seedling apples from Dr. J. A. Briggs, of Hart county, Kentucky, named Maxey, which does not give evidence of special value, so far as the fruit is concerned.

Also, four plates of a seedling from J. W. Smith, of Hardin county, Kentucky; fine looking specimens, but of little value, so far as appears from the fruit shown. Season, January to April; regular bearer every year; always free from specks; origin, sprouts brought many years since.

A plate of apples named "Jones' Seedling," from William H. Smith, of Williamson county, Tennessee, which, although much discolored by fungus, is of fine size, very good flavor, and shows, in the specimens, evidences of its long keeping qualities.

A plate of Pebles' Seedling, from W. M. Samuels, of Kentucky, although very distinct from the foregoing and not its equal in quality, has apparently desirable characteristics as a market variety, though lacking color.

Specimens from W. M. Samuels, of Kentucky, under the name of Watwood Seedling, are of medium size and beautiful color; in form very similar to the Rambo; of good or very good quality; apparently nearly past its season.

We find three plates of the Prentiss grape exhibited by the propagator and disseminator of this variety, T. S. Hubbard, of New York, which, though so long past their natural season, yet remain but slightly affected in flavor, holding perfectly to the peduncle and generally in unexpectedly good condition.

Several specimens of the Japanese persimmon are shown by P. J. Berckmans, of Georgia, which, although long past their season, are in unexpectedly good condition, and to the surprise of your committee yet in eatable condition and of very agreeable flavor.

A seedling cider apple shown by A. D. Webb, of Kentucky, is in size below medium; overspread with dark red; white, firm flesh; juice moderate in quantity, very rich, sprightly and high flavored. Said to be a very superior cider apple; origin unknown.

We find a large and fine collection of canned and pickled figs and other articles, from Mrs. Margaret Wetmore, of Ponchatoula, La., all of which are beautifully put up and apparently in excellent condition.

We find a small lot of dried or desiccated apples upon the tables, said to come from Battle Creek, Michigan, but without a label, and the exhibitor is to us unknown. The fruit is well prepared and in excellent condition.

We also find upon the tables, credited to Captain A. Sambola, of Louisiana, branches of *Spirea prunifolia*, under the name of Bridal Wreath; the Tabasco orange, the paper mulberry, the variety of *Mespilus*, commonly known as Japanese plum; sour orange; fig trees, either in bloom or developing their foliage; also, wood of the orange, intended to show its great weight and its useful qualities for mechanical purposes.

We also find three or four dishes of oranges—the last of the past season's crop—and a large lot of sour oranges, both picked and upon the branch; together with a large bouquet of roses and flowers, with ferns and other foliage; and ears of corn and seeds of okra, all of which we understand to be the contribution of Mrs. A. G. Brice, corner of Burdette and Second streets, Carrollton, Seventh District, New Orleans.

Perhaps your committee should also state that, although not fruits, they find upon the tables two yearling trees of the new "Teas' Hybrid Catalpa," about eight or nine feet in height, of one year's growth from the seed. It is claimed to be as hardy as *speciosa*, and is apparently fully as vigorous.

All of which is respectfully submitted,

T. T. Lyon, Chairman.

J. J. Colmant.

Mr. George Davies, of Ohio, chairman of the committee appointed to suggest a suitable testimonial to the retiring Secretary, Prof. S. M. Tracy, of Missouri, reported the following, which was unanimously concurred in by the Society:

REPORT OF THE COMMITTEE ON TESTIMONIAL TO PROF. TRACY.

Mr. President, as chairman of the committee appointed to attend to the case of our retiring Secretary, I am pained to inform you that, after due deliberation, we find him guilty of faithfully serving this Society as Secretary since its organization, four years ago, until now, for which this committee request that you pass sentence upon him and present him with this fine gold watch, upon which is elegantly engraved his monogram, and, on the inner case, the words, "Mississippi Valley Horticultural Society to S. M. Tracy, New Orleans, February 24, 1883."

The President, requested Prof. Tracy to step forward, and, in a very solemn manner, addressed him thus: "It is my sad duty to announce that you have been found guilty of faithfully serving the Mississippi Valley Horticultural Society, for four years, without asking pay, a thing that no secretary of a well-regulated horticultural society was ever known to do, and as you have done so unconstitutional an act, I hereby sentence you to wear this badge of servitude to the Society to the end of your life—and I hope that you will always be on time."

Prof. Tracy was overcome by the evidence of esteem shown him by the Society, and accepted the valued testimonial, responding in feeling terms.

Miss Mathilde Rodriguez, of New Orleans, and Miss Stella Daigre, of Metairie Ridge, Jefferson parish, in behalf of the ladies of Louisiana, supplemented this valued gift by presenting to Prof. Tracy and to President Earle two beautiful bouquets.

Prof. Tracy, as Chairman of the Committee on Resolutions, offered the following, which was unanimously adopted by a rising vote:

MR. PRESIDENT—In the gathering of the members of this Society from the snows at the North, the prairies of the West, and the plains and mountains of the "Great American Desert" of our schoolboy days, and in assembling them in this Crescent City, with its balmy breezes, budding flowers and ripening fruits, commingled in delightful confusion, we might be excusable if there arose in our minds some anxiety as to the sufficiency of the arrangements that should be found needful for the convenience of our deliberations; and even as to the success of our efforts to interest its people in the object of our gathering; to say nothing of our desire to visit and acquaint ourselves with the, to us, curiosities of this almost tropical region.

We are confident that we speak the unanimous sentiment of this Society when we say that our fears in this respect have proved groundless, and our anticipations have been more than realized.

In view of these facts, Mr. President, we submit the following:

Resolved, That our most hearty thanks are due and are hereby tendered to the N. O. Liedertaffel, to the Continental Guards, to the N. O. Cold Storage Co., to the President of Leland University, and to Mrs. Dr. Richardson, for their kind invitations; and also to Major A. W. Rountree for his cordial welcome to his most attractive orange plantation; to the various railroads for courtesies extended, especially to the Louisville and Nashville, and the Mobile and Ohio roads; to *The Times–Democrat* and *Picayune* for unusually full and accurate reports of our discussions; to the reporters who have labored so untiringly to catch our every whisper; to the proprietor of the St. James Hotel, who has spared no pains to make our stay agreeable; and lastly, and more heartily than words can express, do we thank the Gulf States Fruit Growers' Association, which, with such unbounded hospitality and princely liberality, has paved the way for the most successful and enjoyable meeting which we have ever held. Especially do we thank the ladies of New Orleans for kind attentions shown our visiting ladies, and we feel that our deepest gratitude is due to Messrs. Hudson, Mellon, Wiggins, Marx and Sambola for untiring individual labors in our behalf.

Upon motion it was resolved to leave the selection of the time and place of the next meeting of the Society to the Executive Committee.

Mr. Goodman, Secretary of the Missouri State Horticultural Society, extended an invitation to hold the next meeting in Kansas
City, Mo., and Mr. Evans, of Missouri, thought it a very good
place of meeting, as the contemplated excursion to California would
be rendered feasible thence.

President Earle returned his sincere thanks to the Society for the
patience and good temper shown in the course of the session, and
expressed his pleasure in having visited the Crescent City.

After receiving, amid great applause, a most cordial invitation
from Judge E. M. Hudson, Vice President of the Gulf States
Fruit Grower's Association, to revisit New Orleans, the Society
adjourned.

MEETING OF THE EXECUTIVE COMMITTEE.

The Executive Committee met in the St. James Hotel, New Orleans, February 25, 1883; present Messrs. Earle, President; Evans, Treasurer; Ragan, Secretary, and Galusha, Hollister, Colmant, Nowlin, Smith, Holsinger, Furnas and Tracy.

On motion of Major Evans, of Missouri, the Mississippi Valley Horticultural Society will hold an exhibition of fruits in the city of Louisville, Kentucky, in connection with the Southern Exposition, in September next, provided that the sum of five thousand dollars ($5,000) is guaranteed for the purpose of paying premiums and defraying the other expenses of the same; also, that accommodations shall be furnished, such as space, tabling, etc.

On motion of Prof. Tracy, the President and Secretary were directed to confer with the Southern Exposition Company and make such arrangements with said company as may be, in their judgment, fair and honorable, provided that they shall have first secured the guarantee of the sum of $5,000.

Prof. Tracy moved that the Exhibition be held the first week in September, 1883, and that the President and Secretary are directed to prepare the premium list and rules and regulations, which was adopted.

President Earle called attention to the fact that the receipts from membership fees would not be sufficient to publish the Transactions of the Society and pay other necessary expenses.

Secretary Ragan moved that a Business Directory be published in the Transactions of the Society, for which the sum of three dollars ($3) will be charged, in addition to the fee of membership, which motion was adopted.

The Treasurer (Maj. Evans), the President, and several members, entered into a written agreement to furnish the necessary funds for the publication of the Transactions of the Society beyond what may be received from the fees of membership.

On motion, the price of additional reports to members was fixed at $1.

On motion of Mr. Smith all competitors for premiums at the fruit show in Louisville shall be members of the Society.

Hon. A. W. Campbell of West Virginia, was made Vice President for that State.

On motion of Prof. Tracy, the President, Vice Presidents, Secretary and Treasurer were authorized to fix the time and place of the next meeting of the Society, after which the committee adjourned *sine die.*

15

ADDITIONAL PAPERS.

The following papers were prepared for the meeting, but in the absence of the writers and for want of time, were only read by title and filed for publication. They will doubtless be read with interest by all who are so fortunate as to secure copies of this volume.

SECRETARY.

MANAGEMENT OF PEACH ORCHARDS.

BY GEORGE W. ENDICOTT, OF ILLINOIS.

I submit the following as some of the most practical points to be considered in the successful management of peach orchards in this part of the great Mississippi Valley. And I want to say right here that no part of this paper has been written from theory, unless the theory had been tested and found practical; neither was it written to cover every locality in this valley.

In writing of orchards, the soil should be considered first, and the soil for different varieties of peaches should vary as much as the peaches. The red and white-colored fruit does better on soil not over-rich in humus or mould: while the yellow-fleshed fruit will do well in a very strong soil, if it has a good subsoil and perfect drainage. But all kinds of peaches require a good clay subsoil to be long-lived, and exempt from the attacks of the yellows. Any deficiency of the surface soil can be helped by the liberal use of ashes and barnyard manure, with an occasional dressing of phosphate of lime. The preparation of the soil should be deep and thorough before the trees are planted.

The location of a peach orchard is a very important point to be considered. Perhaps the surest location is south and east of large bodies of water, and the next choice would be the summit of the highest hills, with a free exposure to the north and west.

AGE AND SIZE OF TREES TO PLANT.

For a long-lived and thoroughly profitable orchard the young seedlings should be planted where they are to remain when they are three or four inches high, and pushed by good cultivation till time to bud them. After they are budded they should not be cultivated deeply, as the overgrowth would tend to drown the buds

But, as most orchardists claim that the above method scatters the work over so much ground, they prefer to plant trees one year from the bud, and, if the trees are well grown, and well dug, and well planted, success will be reasonably sure, provided the trees are mulched if a drought sets in immediately after they are planted.

DISTANCE TO PLANT.

In planting peach trees the distance apart to plant has been a stumbling block to many, and the theories set forth by some writers are so contradictory and unreasonable that experience alone can determine what is best. A little thought will convince any planter that different varieties will do better at different distances. For instance, the Amsden and Alexander are enormous fruiters when young, and are short lived, and should therefore be set closer than Mountain Rose or May Beauty, which are a little tardy when young and are long lived, strong growers, and good bearers for many years when they do begin to fruit.

A good rule would be to plant the early bearing sorts sixteen by twenty feet, and the large growing, long-lived varieties twenty by twenty-four feet. This distance lets the sun in on the ground to dry it out during the rainy spells we have during the summer, and prevents rot to a great extent. In fact, an orchard of peaches planted twelve by twelve feet on our strong soil here would be nothing but a hot-bed for rot and curculios. I have an example of that near me. Not one basket of good, sound peaches has been gathered from it in five years.

WHAT VARIETIES TO PLANT.

What varieties to plant is a question for each orchardist to decide for his own locality, and a list that would be satisfactory at this point would not serve at some other place. But with our railroad transportation the safest list would reach through the season from June to October.

The following list of well tried varieties will give a succession, and, by adding local varieties of known excellence, will be good through the whole valley: Alexander or Amsden. Early Rivers, Hoynes' Surprise, Yellow St. John, Mountain Rose, Large Early York, Old Mixon, New Thurber, Reeve's Favorite, Christiana, Steadley, Picquet's Late, Salway and Henrietta for a cling. This list would have to be curtailed at the North and some of the fine Southern varieties added at the South.

There are many other good peaches, but the list named covers the season with fruit and combines as many good points as any I could name to plant for profit.

After the varieties are settled on and the trees planted, the cultivation of a young orchard is an item to be well considered by the planter. Almost every one will plant some crop in a young peach orchard, and if the proper crops are chosen there can be no harm in it, provided the soil is well fed for the extra crop.

But no crop should be planted that has to be cultivated after midsummer; therefore, corn is the best crop. and potatoes the worst, as digging the potatoes prolongs the growing season too late for the wood to ripen properly. This applies only to young trees till they begin to bear ; after the trees begin to bear heavily they must be cultivated all summer, to keep up a good growth till fall, so the leaves will not fall prematurely; if this happens, the warm weather late in the fall will advance the buds so much that they will be likely to get killed with the cold of winter, especially all the Crawford type of peaches.   I don't know of a better way to treat an old orchard than to cultivate well till about September 1, and then sow two bushels of rye per acre, and turn it under when in bloom the next spring The growing rye will keep the soil from washing away in the winter and early spring, and a heavy crop turned under puts the ground in the best possible condition for a good, healthy growth of wood and fruit.

INSECT ENEMIES TO TREES.

The insect enemies of peach trees are the two species of borers. Without using any scientific names, I will call them root and trunk borers. The first named is the most to be dreaded, and the injury done by either can not be cured.

Therefore the peach grower must depend on prevention for permanent results. If the borers have got a start, they must be cut out, every one of them, and destroyed, and the wounds induced to heal as soon as possible ; but the injury they can do in a short time will be more or less permanent; but it is much easier and cheaper to prevent than to cure.

The following treatment, if thoroughly done, will be successful: Take two gallons of strong (country) lye soap and add one pint of crude carbolic acid; set the mixture in the sun for four or five days, or till the soap and acid are thoroughly mixed; then add six gallons of warm rainwater, and keep the mixture thoroughly stirred, and apply to every part of the trunk, crotches of limbs, and crown or upper roots (first remove the earth from base of tree) with a brush or mop of old cloth; then apply one-half peck of leached ashes to the crown of tree. This treatment annually has been a sure remedy with me, and answers for all the borer family. It should be applied about May, in this latitude.

PRUNING.

The pruning of peach orchards has run so much to theory in the minds of horticultural writers in the last few years that common sense has had to give way, and will only come to the front again when the folly of these paper orchardists perishes with the lives of the trees they have mutilated.

The head of a peach tree should be started about four and one-half feet from the ground, and a leader trained up straight three or four feet with side branches radiating from this main stem ; and none of these main radiating branches should ever be allowed to exceed five feet in length. This will necessitate summer pruning, without which no peach tree is well trained. When the trees are young the suckers or sprouts may be allowed to grow on the trunks to some extent, and kept shortened in, so the trunk will be protected from the hot sun and the attacks of the trunk-borers. These side shoots should all be removed as soon as the top of the tree will shade the trunk.

A number of limbs should be allowed to grow a little lower than the head is wanted till the tree comes into bearing; then they should be sawed off, with stumps about five inches long (the use of these stumps will be explained in another chapter), and the whole top of the tree must be thinned out and shortened in so the sun and air can reach every peach on the tree some time in the day.

THINNING THE FRUIT.

Thinning the fruit of a peach tree has never received the attention of our growers as it should. There are many varieties of peaches that are such heavy fruiters that you seldom see a specimen of first-class fruit on a tree that has 4,000 peaches on it (and that is about an average crop on a full-grown tree), and the whole crop will not bring money enough to pay for packages and freight; while, if 3,500 of the number had been thinned off, the 500 would have filled ten boxes or baskets that would net $1.00 each. This is no theory; it is the actual result from alternate trees in the same row. Thinning is not only a success financially as to the fruit, but the health of the tree is greatly promoted. In fact, I believe that over-fruiting shortens the lives of our peach trees more than one-half. To properly thin fruit on a full-grown tree, there should always be a space of four to six inches between each two specimens. Dr. Hull, of Alton, said, eight inches, but I think that distance ought to be modified to conform to the different conditions of tree and soil. But there is one very important point to be considered right here. If peaches are to be thinned they must be bugged, and if they are bugged they must be thinned ; and, with a few isolated exceptions, there can be no first-class peaches marketed in this valley without both. Any man who can not accept these two last conditions had better not go into peaches for profit.

CURCULIOS.

Catching the curculios, or " bugging" peach trees, is a subject that will be indorsed by some growers and sneered at by others, and both parties will contend they are solid in their positions. But the one solid argument on the side of bugging is that the fruit always sells at the outside price, and there is always a demand for it, when the wormy stock is a drug on the market, and it don't require a philosopher to tell a peach shipper what that means.

The cost of bugging I have found to be about seven cents per bushel, by careful account kept for six years. I have found the most convenient catcher to be a light circular frame covered with cheap muslin, with an opening in the center to admit the operator and suspended to the shoulders with wide straps, and a slit or opening in front to admit the tree. Armed with a broad brimed hat, a two pound hammer and the catcher, you can walk up to and straddle the trunk of the tree with the slit in the catcher until the tree is near the center, then strike one of the stumps (never strike any part of trunk with anything) spoken of in the chapter on pruning, a sharp blow, back out and repeat at each tree. At the end of each bout sweep the catcher and souse the bugs into a pail of water that has had a gill of coal oil poured in it. Bugging should be done each morning, early. A catcher twelve feet in diameter will be large enough for an old tree if well pruned, and a smaller one will do for young trees.

MARKETING, ETC.

The package to be used will be a matter governed by the tastes of shippers. Consumers prefer baskets, but dealers say the boxes are best to handle. Let the package be what it may, always be sure it holds just what it purports to, and that the fruit in sight is a fair index to the whole contents, and then put your name or trade mark on every package and take your chances on the market, always remembering that buyers keep a black book and are not slow to put your name in it if your fruit don't come to the proper standard.

And now, to sum up the whole matter of peach growing, if you have a good location and soil, with plenty of muscle and vim, you can go into peach growing with a fair show of success. But if you expect to plant trees and harvest the enormous imaginary crops you often read about, without hard work and plenty of it, you will be sadly mistaken.

GRAPE CULTURE AND CIVILIZATION.

BY ISIDOR BUSH, OF MISSOURI.

The history of grape culture is as old as history itself; we might say, it is pre-historic. Egyptian tradition makes Osiris the founder of the culture of the vine; and grape seeds are found with the oldest Egyptian mummies. The myths of Greece claim the honor of planting the vine for Bacchus, the son of Zeus. Holy Writ tells us that father Noah planted the vine which, according to legend, God himself had given him from Paradise, as a reward after suffering the cares and pangs of the flood, commanding him to "take good care of it." And, truly, this one command of the Lord the descendants of Noah have well obeyed up to this day. History tells us that kings, emperors, and even bishops, the princes of the church, fostered and promoted the culture of the grape Emperor Carolus, the Great, sent vines from Orleans (France) to be transplanted on the "Heights of Ingolsheim," and, according to a popular legend, preserved in songs, the great emperor arises annually, when the vines are in bloom, from his grave to bless the vines along the river Rhine. In fact, the history of all times and all civilized nations records the introduction and progress of grape culture, keeping pace with the progress of culture and civilization. In this country of ours, exactly two hundred years ago, William Penn, the founder of Pennsylvania, gave to that place, now part of Philadelphia, which was then first settled by Germans from the Rhine and called Germantown, a town seal with the inscription: " *Vinum, Linum et Dextrinum,*" to indicate the approval of their special industries, "viticulture, flax culture and weaving." The United States Government, by its Department of Agriculture, has always given a fostering care—such as it could give—to this important branch of horticulture. In 1861 the Legislature of California appointed a commission with a view to promote the culture of the grape-vine, and Mr. Haraszty was sent by the Governor to Europe, from where he brought hundreds of valuable varieties, including the now famous Zinfindel, to the Golden Gate, and made the Pacific coast one of the great wine-producing countries of the world. Republics are ungrateful, and Mr. Haraszty's noble and successful efforts were never paid by the State; but now, when the *phylloxera* threatens to destroy the very valuable industry, the Legislature of California appropriated $10,000 for the use of the State Viticultural Commission for the year 1881, and $10,000 more for the year 1882. France has spent for the same purpose, to save her vineyards from the ravages of the phylloxera, hundreds of thousands of francs; and, since it was discovered that certain American vines were the best, if not the only practical means of reconstituting grape culture in Europe, the governments of Italy, Spain and Portugal have also planted and encouraged the planting of American grape-vines in their States.

Where is, or was, "the original home of the grape-vine?" This question has, from time immemorial, been a matter of dispute. The honor was claimed for Mount Nysa, the cradle of Bacchus; for father Noah's Ararat; for Persia and Colchis. Nearly all writers on grape culture, however, placed it somewhere in Asia. The French even to-day call it the Asiatic grape, and naturalists generally designate that species as the " *Vitis Vinifera,*" the only "true grape." All cultivated grapes are supposed to be varieties of that species, and the *V. Labrusca* and other wild grapes merely degenerated or retrograded seedlings of the same. It is but quite lately that the incorrectness of that assumption has been recognized; that scientific researches have established the important truth: that nature herself has brought forth or developed different species of grapes in various climates and soils, from which human skill and industry should produce and cultivate the noblest of fruit adapted to its surroundings. Geological discoveries have proven that it is the indigenous wild grape of the Rhine, from which the celebrated Riesling of Germany originated, and not the Orleans grape, transplanted by Emperor Charlemagne. It now seems incredible that we could so long be blinded by authority when it was known that the grapes of Persia, which Hafiz mentions in his songs (translated into all European languages), and which Sir

Kerr Porter, the celebrated English traveler, describes as the " Kishmish and Samarcand grapes," had bunches weighing ten to twelve pounds, with berries too large for a small mouth; nor is this peculiar and very different class of grapes a thing of the past; it still exists and is cultivated in Persia and Georgia (Transcanasia). The Parsee and some other Asiatic sects are not guided in this respect by the Koran; and in some provinces, as in Kacheth, viniculture is the principal agricultural pursuit. The travelers, Dandini and Schulz, have seen vines on the Lebanon which are said to continue in bloom from March to July and to bear ripe grapes from June to December, whose berries are as large as small plums, in clusters weighing from ten to twelve pounds.

And who of us does not know the legend of the first discovery of America by the Northmen (Wheaton: History of the Northmen); that Leif, the son of Erick (Erikson), who landed in the year 1002 in Narragansett Bay, named it "Vinland," because his German man, "Tycker," had there found many wild grapes. So, also, Columbus, when he discovered Hispania (now Cuba), sent large grapes (probably of the Scuppernong class) to Queen Isabella of Spain, and another island was even called Martha's Vineyard. The Pilgrim Fathers saw vines in abundance when they landed at Plymouth. "Here are grapes, white and red, and very sweet and strong, also," wrote Governor Edward Winslow, in 1621.

Botanists are now studying and classifying the different kinds of original wild vines, and from their seed and intercrossings are produced beautiful, exquisite new grapes, best adapted to the respective home of each species. I do not wish to be understood as denying that grape-vines can also be successfully transplanted to localities where their parent species can not be found; the successful introduction of the European grapes in California proves that they can be successfully transplanted; but I do believe that such is the exception, and that, as a rule, varieties of a native species are surer of enduring success. Most of you know that all attempts to transplant and cultivate the grapes of Europe, the *V. Vinifera,* to the Atlantic coast and to the Mississippi Valley, proved failures; even when grafted on American phylloxera-resisting roots, they mostly failed, as far as tried, either from climatic causes, or from the attacks of cryptogamic diseases, mildew (*Peronospora*) and rot. Nor is the process of grafting European vines on American roots, now practiced on a very large scale in France, as easy or safe an operation in our variable climate as it is there. Hybrids, produced by crossing the foreign on our native grape, though at first deemed to be highly promising, have also generally given unsatisfactory results in this country. Though superior in quality and beauty to our purely native grapes, they lack in hardiness, vigor and productiveness. It is a remarkable fact that some of these hybrids are very successful in Europe; more especially the Triumph, a cross between Concord and Chasselas Mosquee, by Mr. Campbell; the Othello, a cross between *V. Riparia* and Black Hamburg, by Mr. Arnold, and the Black Eagle and Black Defiance, crosses between Concord and Black St. Peter, by Mr. Underhill.

It seems, therefore, that these and some other hybrids have inherited, from the American parent, the phylloxera-resisting root, but also from the European parent the non-resistance to climatic influences—the great sensibility to rot and mildew. European horticulturist are now largely engaged in producing these new hybrids, but it is doubtful that these will prove a great gain for American grape culture.

In our country the efforts of hybridizers to produce new crosses between foreign and native varieties have been wisely abandoned, or rather directed to the producing of crosses between the native varieties. Among the new grapes thus produced I will name Mr. Rickett's Jefferson (Concord and Iona cross); Lady Washington (Concord with Allen's Hybrid, the latter having partly Vinifera parentage), and Mr. Caywood's Duchesse (white Concord seedling with Delaware or Walter). The great expectations which are attached to these crosses between native American varieties are best shown by the circumstance that Mr. Rickett's, the originator of the largest and finest collection of hybrids ever produced by one man, has lately sold to Mr. Stone, of Rochester, the stock of his new grape, the Empire State (a seedling of Hartford Prolific fertilized with the Clinton), for $4,000, or for more than its weight in gold. Some grape growers, however, have more confidence in pure seedlings, as those varieties are called, which are produced from the seed of a native grape, supposed not to have been fertilized by the pollen of another vine. Of these the following, among others, are considered promising : The Lady, Moore's Early, Early Victor, Noah, Prentiss, and, above all, the Golden Pocklington. But I believe that these are also crosses. Some of them, at least, are so dissimilar to their supposed parent that my belief seems sufficiently justified. The question only remains, how can grapes be cross-fertilized by nature without the aid of man ? By insects seems scarcely a sufficient explanation, as the flower of our fruit-bearing grape-vines contains both the stamen and the pistil within the same calyx. I am inclined to believe that the stigma of the grape flower does not receive the pollen of its own individual blossom, as the two are probably not ready for fecundation at the same moment; thus the mere breeze of the air may be sufficient to bring about cross-fertilization where different varieties, blooming at the same time, are growing in proximity to each other. This would explain the dissimilarity of seedlings from cultivated varieties with their parent. Where wild vines of the same species, and none others, grow near together, there the seed is pure and will invariably reproduce the same kind. This hypothesis, should it prove correct, would be of great practical value.

Most grape growers, however, care very little whether these fine, new varieties are hybrids, or accidental crosses, or pure seedlings. They deem it of little importance to know which varieties were the parents. They ask only, can they be successfully grown in this or that locality? I think that, although this question can be decided only by practical tests, we may be somewhat guided in advance by knowing the parentage. The fine, large, showy table grapes, the Pocklington for instance, originating from seed of the Concord, will probably be successfully grown where the Concord does well and is free from rot. The Prentiss, a splendid seedling of Isabella, seems to me of doubtful success, where this old variety generally fails, as it does in the Mississippi Valley. Here the Bacchus, a Clinton seedling, and the Taylor seedlings, Elvira, Noah, etc., may have a better prospect of success.

I frankly confess my serious doubts, my fears, that rot and mildew, so prevalent and increasing of late in many parts of this rich Mississippi Valley, will prevent the success of most of the large, fine table grapes, which nearly all belong to the Labrusca class in this, our territory. As long as those pests do not either disappear or can not be·checked by some means; as long as no remedy or preventive against them is discovered, I have but faint hopes for the success of these new table or market varieties in the West, except in some peculiar spots mysteriously exempt from these fungoid diseases.

But the grape was never grown for its use as a table fruit only; nor could its culture be profitable on a large scale for that use alone. The markets would soon be overstocked and its value reduced below the cost of production. The main purpose for which grapes are grown is for wine, the fermented juice of the grape, that universal oldest remedy against human afflictions, that elixir which enhances our pleasures, dispels our sorrows, invigorates and rejuvenates man as no other stimulant can. Noah and Bacchus already made wine of the grape, and its use as a beverage is almost as old as the grape itself. In ancient Greece the time of grape-gathering and that of drinking the new wine was the occasion of great festivities, consisting of public dinners, theatrical representations, music, sacrifices for the prosperity of the state and for the souls of the dead. True, a licentious Roman people converted those festivities into nocturnal orgies and called them "Bacchanalia," but the wisest men of that time said: " Let us not ascribe these orgies to the God of Wine; let the excesses be punished and suppressed; but prize and use properly the divine gift and it will embellish our life with flowers and fruits, as whose protector Bacchus is revered; it will foster poetry, fine arts and all social pleasures."

Thus, from time immemorial to this day, the art of making wine and its uses have existed and spread and grown all over the world, and nowhere has it been entirely suppressed except in China, where, five hundred years before our era, an imperial mandate ordered the uprooting of all the grapevines in the vast empire, and where the refusal to do so was punished by death. Has this made the Chinese better, more virtuous or civilized? No, indeed! But the use of enervating opiates has taken the place of invigorating wine. And this will be the consequence wherever wine is prohibited. In all civilized countries there is scarcely a festive board without wine. The church uses it in its sacred service as the symbol of God's noblest gifts; the physician prescribes it as a health-restoring tonic to the sick and convalescing.

The wine production has reached hundreds of millions of gallons, it forms the wealth and pride of many nations, and its failure in one year is considered a great calamity where and when ever it occurs.

How small a proportion of the grape production is utilized for the table compared to what it is for wine-making may be seen from the official figures of the State Viticultural Commission of California for 1880, which are, in brief, as follows :

> 10,200,000 gallons of wine; value in producers' hands...$2,795,000 00
> 450,000 gallons of brandy. at $1.15 (in bond)........... 517,500 00
> To this should be added for value of raisins................. 100,000 00
> And for grapes used for table, preserving, etc., less than 150,000 00

Thus, you will see, that but five per cent. of the entire grape production of California is used for market and table purposes, although it produces the finest table grapes, of which car-loads are sent to Eastern markets.

We grape-growers of the Mississippi Valley can not produce as showy table grapes as California, nor can we, as already stated, grow the table grapes of the Eastern or Atlantic States with general success; the native grapes of the Mississippi Valley are emphatically wine grapes.

I do not claim that they are the best wine grapes the world produces ; and while we may excuse the poetic effusion of a Longfellow, who sang :

> There grows no vine
> By the haunted Rhine,
> By Danube or Guadalquivir,
> Nor an island or cape
> That bears such a grape
> As grows by the beautiful river (the Ohio).

Or that

> Catawba wine
> Has a taste more divine—etc.

Yet I can not indorse such presumptuous, unscientific assertions as I find, for instance, in the "American Wine and Fruit Grower," August number, 1882, page 75, " that only from these (our true wine grapes from the Æstivalis and Riparia class) can we make wine which will rival and surpass the best wines of France, Germany and Spain." I do claim, however, that we possess in the Nortons', the Cynthiana, and perhaps in some black Taylor seedlings, very good red wine grapes, free from rot and mildew; in the Noah, Elvira, Missouri Riesling and others, some very promising white wine grapes; still better kinds, further South, is the Lenoir (Black Spanish) and Herbemont and that we shall, before many years, by the production of new, superior varieties, and by improving and progressing in the art of wine making, fully equal the average productions of the wine countries of Europe, and make grape growing one of the leading branches of horticulture.

This may not seem desirable to some. I am aware that many would rather, like that Chinese emperor, uproot every vine, from a desire to pre‍vent intoxication. But wine is itself an apostle of temperance. The best medical authorities, such as Dr. Lunier, medical inspector of the insane asylums and prisons of France, and at the same time Secretary of the Temperance Society there, has shown, by able researches, that the ratio of percentages of disease and crime attributable to alcoholic excesses decreases in proportion as in each district the consumption of wine and beer increases; that natural wine and beer cures the thirst for distilled spirits instead of exciting it. The French Temperance Society aims to repress entirely the circulation and sale of bad spirits—discovering modes of detecting them, punishing adulterators of wines, beers, etc., and encouraging the use of pure, cheap wine, beer, tea and coffee, as the best means of curing the public thirst for distilled alcohol.

American travelers returning from Europe, who were strong opponents of wine before they visited these countries, now testify that where wine is most abundant, cheap, and generally used by the people, drunkenness does not exist.

But I am requested not to discuss the temperance question, and I have no desire to do it. I simply stated a few facts. I do not deny that wine is intoxicating if used to excess, but not more harmful, aye, even less so, than drinking ice water to excess. I am sure that to every one who has been killed by wine, a thousand have been killed by ice water; and I may certainly be permitted to quote the New Testament, which teaches (1 Tim., v. 23), "Drink no longer water, but use a little wine for thy stomach's sake." Or to quote the greatest poet, Shakespeare, saying: "Good wine is a good, familiar creature, if it be well used." I could quote for hours, for, next to love, wine was most and best sang by poets of all tongues. I shall, however, quote one verse only, beautifully rendered in English by a dear lady friend of mine:

> From the wine-cup's red and fiery fountain,
> From the goblet's depths, enchanted gleaming,
> Deadly poison and a sweet refreshment,
> Beauty and vulgarity are streaming.
> 'Tis according to the drinker's pleasure,
> 'Tis his will that qualifies the measure.
> Thus the fool, by coarsest slumber fettered,
> Lies enchained—the slave of his desires;
> And the cup that robs him of his manhood,
> At our lips but strengthens and inspires;
> Kindles sparks of wit about us gleaming,
> Lends our speech an angel's inspiration,
> Sends a glow through every vein, and beauty
> Wraps us in her sweet intoxication.
> For is wine not like unto the rain-drop
> Which is filth itself when filth it reaches,
> But on fruitful ground it proves a blessing,
> And its hidden worth to mankind teaches.

THE PECAN TREE.

BY DR. CHARLES MOHR, OF ALABAMA.

Among the trees of the forest region of Eastern North America the pecan tree recommends itself above all others to the attention of the fruit-grower, and particularly to the horticulturist of the Mississippi Valley, its range being largely determined by the course of the Mississippi river and its larger tributaries east and west. With every year its cultivation is attracting more attention in the Southern States, by the constantly increasing demand for its nuts, not only to supply home markets, but as an article of export. Wherever the thin-shelled varieties, with their plump-sweet kernel of unsurpassed richness, find their way, they take the first rank among all others of similar kind. The high prices obtained of late years offer better inducements for the propagation of these better varieties, and tend generally to the future preservation of the natural groves

It is needless to dwell on the botanical character of the *Carya oliviaformis,* as it is called by the botanists. It is found described in almost every descriptive botany of the country. It shall only be mentioned that among its congeners, the hickories, it is distinguished by its elongated fruit, tapering at both ends, with a cylindrical, smooth nut with a thin shell, separating easily from the deeply-lobed seed.

The pecan tree prefers, naturally, the cool, damp bottom lands of a deep, rich soil, not subject to long-continued overflows, or constantly wet. The area of its distribution follows, in the mean, the course of the Mississippi river, with an extent largely prevailing in a southwestern direction. Its boundaries, within the United States, have been accurately ascertained, in the course of the investigations of the forest growth of our country, in connection with the tenth census.

Starting from its southern extremity in the United States, on the Rio Grande near Loredo, under the 28° of latitude, its western boundary follows, in Texas, nearly the 100 meridian; with an eastern trend it traverses the center of the Indian Territory, follows the eastern border of Kansas, and reaches, with a strong deflection at the 97° of longitude, its most northern limit on the Mississippi river, near the 42° of latitude, embracing Southern Iowa, Southeastern Kansas, almost the whole of Missouri, all of Arkansas, the eastern half of Indian Territory, the larger part of Texas, and of Louisiana, above the low alluvial plain in the eastern, in the low-grass savannas and drift hills in the western, part of that State. East of the Mississippi its area is confined to the bottom of that river in the northern part of Illinois, and, stretching through the lower portion as far east as the meridian of Louisville, Kentucky, it embraces the lower basin of the Wabash river, of the White river, and the bottom of the Ohio river. Scarce in the northern part of Kentucky, it is abundant in the lower Green River Valley, and that of the Cumberland, to the lower basin of the Tennessee river.

In the State of Mississippi it is confined to the lands of the Yazoo and Mississippi delta. Beyond the limits of the United States the tree extends into Northeastern Mexico. Prof. Buckley found it seventy-five miles west of the Rio Grande, at Lampasas Springs, in Mexico.

East of the Mississippi bottom the pecan tree is not found in the Southern States. As indicated by the measurements recorded by Prof. Ridgeway, in his account of the lower Wabash region, it appears to arrive there at its best development. There it takes the first place amongst the largest of timber trees. Several individuals standing within sight, were, by actual measurement, found one hundred and seventy-five feet in height by a circumference of fifteen feet, the trunk clear of limbs to a length of seventy-five feet. Farther south, in the forests of the Mississippi and Yazoo rivers, it does not attain such dimensions; trees exceeding three feet in diameter were scarcely observed. Beyond the Brazos river, in Texas, in the dry atmosphere of the West, it is of lower, more sturdy growth. Its massive trunk, with an average diameter of three feet, spreads horizontally its mighty limbs at a distance from fifteen to twenty feet above the ground, and covering by its shade an area from eighty to one hundred feet in diameter. In regard to the quality of its fruit, it reaches, in the South, to far greater perfection than throughout the Northern range, and consequently the Southern nuts are more highly valued.

The nut of Western Texas is of a fine quality, and the crop of the native pecan groves grows, with every year, more in importance as one of the valuable productions of the soil. It can be considered as almost never-failing. The ease with which it is gathered, handled and disposed of, its resistance to external influences and to decay, render it the most remunerative of all the fruit crops of that country. Keeping its richness and sweetness for a longer time unimpaired than any other of the oleaginous seeds, the pecan nut is valued as one of the most desirable among all the dessert nuts.

Full cause for regret have those who, in their hasty greed for gain, sacrificed, at the beginning of their settlements, their pecan groves to King Cotton. They find themselves deprived of a constantly increasing source of income, which requires no expense of time and means, and their posterity of an inheritance to have benefited coming generations. The traffic in pecan nuts forms quite an interesting item in the trade of Western Texas. In the cities of Austin and San Antonio, during the fall, wagon-load after wagon-load, hauled for hundreds of miles, can be seen to arrive. On my inquiries among the principal merchants in San Antonio, the most important center of that trade, I found that, in the season of 1880, 1,250,000 pounds were received at that place alone. The price paid by the wagon-load varied from five to six cents per pound.

To the cultivation of this tree has, so far, scarcely any attention been paid in Texas. In Louisiana, throughout the so-called Mississippi coast, the Opelousas and Atchafalaya region and that of the Bayou Teche, it succeeds exceedingly well and produces fruit unsurpassed in quality. The early French

settlers planted the tree around their habitations, and avenues of magnificence, of the age of many scores of years, are found, bearing testimony to the
long duration of the productive stage of its life.

In the lighter soils of the coast region of the Eastern Gulf States, across to
the Atlantic slope, its cultivation, wherever undertaken, with proper care and
under proper conditions of soil, has proved a success. In South Carolina
Prof. Buckley observed large trees on the plantations of the Santee river,
planted by the Huguenots from seed brought from Louisiana. Mr. Berckmans states that the tree succeeds well in Georgia, near Augusta. In the coast
plain of Alabama and Mississippi the pecan is found to grow well, and by repeated application of the proper fertilizers, to produce nuts of very fine
quality. In that region all the lands of a good surface drainage with a deep
clay subsoil retention of moisture, such as is favorable to the growth of the
live oak, loblolly pine, Cuba pine, and covered with the inkberry bush
(*Ilexglabra*), can be considered as well adapted to its cultivation. Many thousands of acres of land of that description can be obtained at low prices, con-
tiguous to rairoad lines, which, covered with pecan trees, can be made to
yield a revenue which can not fail to place them among the more valuable
lands in these States. In the undertaking of such an enterprise one has only
to keep in its extent the resources in sight required to provide his trees with
the needed supply of plant food. It can not be too strongly stated that only
by the liberal application of fertilizers he can meet with success in a soil
naturally deficient in the needed elements of nutrition. Failing in this custom, the trees will remain of stunted growth, and either entirely barren or
produce a worthless, thick-shelled and badly filled nut. In soil as indicated,
sufficiently manured and under the observation of due care in transplanting,
there can be no failure. The success achieved of late years in Mobile county
has given great encouragement to the cultivation of the pecan tree; groves of
several hundred trees have been started and many are following the same
example. The nuts are planted in the fall in drills, well filled with rotten
stable manure, the plants thinned out in the course of the following season,
during which they grow to the height of eight or ten inches. Between the
second and third year the seedlings are transplanted to the grove. After the
third year the transfer is connected with great risk to the life of the young
tree. The fall season after the first good frost is considered as the best time
for transplanting. The trees are placed at a distance from thirty-five to forty
feet. Holes are dug about three feet in diameter and one and a half feet
deep. The ground is thoroughly mixed with an abundance of a compost of
rotten stable manure, fine bone dust and potash. Many clip the long tap-
root slightly to induce the production of laterals. The very few rootlets of
the tap root must be prevented from drying up, and consequently the transfer from the nursery to the grove has to be effected with as little delay as
possible, and best during damp weather.

Under these precautions scarcely any loss of plants, in transplanting, will
be incurred, and during the winter months the tree has ample time to es-

tablish itself firmly in the well prepared and enriched soil. The young tree makes a rapid growth, and will, by repeated manuring, with the advent of each succeeding spring, bear after the sixth or seventh year of its transplanting. In 1873, I planted in my garden trees not quite three years old; they began to bear six years after, and this season their branchlets were bending under the heavy clusters of fruit of fine quality. They measure from twenty-eight to thirty-two inches in circumference, and are over fifty feet high. To show how quickly this tree responds, in the quality and quantity of its crop, to the application of fertilizing agents, I will state that the season before last, when the manuring of the trees was neglected, the crop was an entire failure; the largest part of the nuts were badly filled or entirely empty; whereas, in the present season, under a generous supply of the compost mentioned, the fruit was abundant and the nuts excellent. With the fifteenth year the tree begins to yield profitable returns. The following instance will serve as an illustration of this fact. A tree, planted in my immediate neighborhood from the seed in October, 1867, yielded, this fall, two and one-half bushels of nuts, which were of a high grade, and sold at the best market price throughout, at twenty cents per pound, to a dealer. This is a return of thirty dollars from one tree. This tree I found to measure sixty inches in circumference, and sixty-five feet in height. Mr. Vail, one of our principal dealers, who is doing his best to encourage the cultivation of the pecan tree in the vicinity of Mobile, paid, this winter, $125 for the product of five trees of the same age, at the average price of eighteen cents per pound for the nuts. They were of the fine, thin-shelled kind, of good size and fine flavor. The demand for such qualities is large, and hundreds of barrels would have found a ready market at the same rates, to meet the inquiries· Isolated as these instances might appear, they can not fail to serve as a proof of the profit to be derived from the cultivation of the pecan tree, and its importance as a resource of the low-priced lands along the Gulf shore in that section.

Among the insects injurious to the pecan tree only the tent caterpillar has so far been observed, which seems to infest it before all others; pains must be taken for its destruction as soon as it shows itself.

The attempts to raise the pecan, with any degree of success, on the rolling, sandy pinelands have all resulted in failure. The want of retentiveness of their thirsty, silicious soil renders the application of fertilizers of no benefit. It fails, also, in soils with a rocky substratum, impeding the deeply penetrating tap-root in its growth.

This tree varies greatly in the size and quality of its fruit. These variations are produced by different conditions of climate and soil, but seem principally to depend on the amount of nutritive elements of the soil. The way for the improvement of the nut is chiefly to be found in the liberal application of the proper fertilizing agents already indicated. The propagation of the best varieties is most easily effected through the seeds, whose offspring remains true to its kind, if properly treated. The experiments in grafting have not led to results encouraging the propagation of improved kinds. I have no knowl-edge of instances proving the budding or grafting of older trees a success. The grafting of stocks of young trees offers no diffculties, but offers no advan-tages; the seedling being of a more rapid growth, and not remaining constant in its character, bears its fruit as soon, if not sooner, than the graft. Mr. Dele-hamps, a fruit-grower of Mobile county, informs me that, nine years ago, he grafted scions of the pecan tree upon some young stalks of the Mockernut hickory, *Carya tomentosa,* some at the collar, others two to three feet above the ground; several of these trees are now twenty feet high, blossomed last year, and are expected to bear fruit this coming season.

THE SCIENTIFIC PRODUCTION OF NEW FRUITS.

BY DR. J. STAYMAN, OF KANSAS.

As this Society is composed of persons living over a very wide range of country and a diversified climate, it would appear that the subject of this pa-per should be the production of fruits adapted to general cultivation, or at least to cover the districts represented.

If this is the case, we fear some of you will be very much disappointed, for there are very few, if any, such fruits, as they are not within the ability of man or the effort of nature to produce. Therefore, all we expect to do is to give what we believe to be the best methods to approximate these results.

There is not, and can not be, a universal variety, any more than there can be a universal panacea. It is not nature's method—she produces variety.

We have the hills and dales, the groves and the prairies, the cold North, the temperate East, and the mild and balmy South, the deserts of the West, the Italy of the Pacific, with the blizzards of the Northwest and the siroccos of the Southwest. She has furnished us with many species and numerous varieties of fruits growing wild over these districts: it is our province to cul-tivate, improve and make use of them. There are some varieties of these wild species that will not succeed, where others of the same species do. In fact the same species will not always succeed within its own geographical boundary. Some species and varieties have a very limited range, while others have not. But every plant, vegetable and fruit must have a certain amount of heat, light and moisture to fully develop and bring it to perfec-tion, and if restrained in these requisitions it will become debilitated and dis-eased or of deficient quality. And if it were not for the vicissitudes of climate, every plant would succeed wherever these conditions were found; but as it is, they will succeed in different locations.

The production of new fruits is no difficult problem, as all of you under-stand it; neither is it difficult to produce those of excellent quality, as that

16

has often been done. But to produce desirable varieties for general cultivation or for a given location, is a problem not yet fully solved.

This is what I understand to be the subject under consideration, and, to more fully illustrate it, I will have to show what will or what will not succeed in a locality or district, for this appears to be the foundation upon which we have to work to accomplish anything. For if we have no clear conception before us of what we want and where we will have to go to find it, we will be groping our way in the dark and have nothing but conjecture and uncertainty in our work.

Take the apple, for instance, our most staple fruit, that has, perhaps, as wide a range as any species; we find many of its varieties confined to a very limitad range.

There is, perhaps, no winter apple in cultivation that will succeed as such two hundred miles south of its place of origin. There is a geographical boundary for every variety. Take an apple, for instance, that matures in Massachusetts on the 27th of October; it will mature in Pennsylvania the 19th, New Jersey the 18th, Ohio the 16th, Illinois the 15th, Indiana and Maryland the 11th, Delaware the 7th, Virginia and Missouri the 5th, Kansas the 4th, Kentucky the 3d, Tennessee the 2d, and North Carolina the 1st. In these extremes we have very nearly a month's difference in season, and in the mean temperature a difference of 8.6 degrees. This fact has been either disregarded or overlooked in procuring and producing new varieties.

In our eager desire to get hardy sorts, we have exhausted the resources of the North, and have gone to Russia in the hope of meeting with better success; but what is the result of our labor? We have got scarcely anything but acid summer and fall cooking apples. This might have been anticipated, as it is not in the natural order of development.

Neither can we hope for much better from the seedlings of such. We might as well go to Minnesota or the North, and endeavor to raise corn adapted to the South from the seed of Northern corn.

Nature's method is always to perpetuate a variety under the conditions in which it is grown. All of its energies are concentrated to that end, and if grown there uninterruptedly for generations it would become a marked type of that location, and the fittest of its seedlings only would survive and continue their existence. Such varieties could not be expected to be adapted to any great range of latitude except by gradual development. This being the case, there must be a meteorological zone of adaptibility for a variety as well as for a species.

While we admit that hardy varieties may be procured in the North, it does not follow that they can not be found anywhere else; for we have had as hardy varieties, from the South and on our own grounds, as the Duchesse of Oldenburg, one of the most hardy of the Russian type, and some of the wild grapes of Arkansas are as hardy as those of New England.

Neither does it follow because a variety will endure the cold of the North that it is healthy, and will also endure the heat of the South; for the crab-apples, that are among the most hardy, are the most subject to sun-scald and blight.

Having given you the hardy side of our question, I will now call your attention to the opposite, or tender side.

That tender or diseased varieties can produce healthy and hardy seedlings, we think few will maintain; yet that has been the general method resorted to.

Take, for instance, the grape, such as the Iona, Diana, Isabella, and others that succeed scarcely anywhere, and hybridize them with the European grape, which does well nowhere in the Atlantic States, and how could we expect the seedlings from those to succeed, when our most hardy and healthy native species hybridized with the foreign grape has not done so?

While we might admit the propriety of using the European grape under some particular circumstances, we believe the indiscriminate use of it to be not only detrimental to the interest of fruit growers, but to the progress of horticulture. If our resources were exhausted there might be some reason for it, but while there is such an ample field before us not yet explored, of richer and more hardy grapes, there is neither reason nor propriety in it.

Having shown that we need not go to Russia for hardy apples or to Europe for tender grapes to improve our fruits, we now shall endeavor to show where we should go and how to improve them. It is an admitted fact that a species growing wild will remain and continue to produce its kind until brought under domestication; then it will change and sport into varieties.

Herein lies the principle almost unobserved that produces all the improvement in our fruit. For it follows as a corollary that if a species improves under domestication, a variety of the species will improve by cultivation. It therefore follows that the location where a variety can be grown to the very highest state of perfection is the place where the best specimens are grown and they must produce the best seed for improvement.

This agrees with facts as far as observations go, for nearly all our improvements in cereals and vegetables have been produced by the judicious selection of seeds from the best developed and most perfect specimens in accordance with the objects we have had in view.

This corresponds with our own observation, for in the selection of seeds from the best specimens of a number of varieties, very many of the seedlings showed a marked improvement.

The success of Mr. John Burr, of this place, in his native seedling grapes, warrants the same conclusion, for it is a remarkable fact that nearly all his seedlings are an improvement upon their parents. Why should this not be the case, when all the energies of nature are exerted, under favorable circumstances and cultivation, to unfold and develop the saccharine principle and quality of the fruit, which, in some instances, amounts to as much as twenty-five per cent. of increase? And why should not the seed that contains the most active living principle also unfold and develop?

That it does develop, we have many examples. The Concord grape is, perhaps, one of the most marked instances, as it came directly from the wild grape ; but why has Mr. Bull, the originator of it, been unable to produce another grape its equal out of the thousands of seedlings from it ?

The simple fact that so very few grapes of value have been produced from the Concord shows clearly that the efforts of nature are about exhausted in the improvement of that variety. Once admit the fact that improved varieties are produced with certainty in exact proportion to the perfection of our fruit, and we then have an object in view and a stimulus to encourage us in the production of new fruits, where the enterprising and ambitious genius will have ample room to develop his skill.

From what we have already said it is evident that to produce desirable varieties for a given locality we must take the seeds from varieties that suc-ceed best in that location, and, for general cultivation, from those which generally succeed.

If we desire early maturing varieties, we should choose those that have that tendency, and we may go North for those ; but if we wish late maturing varieties, choose from those that mature late, and, if we can not find them at home, go South for them.

As hardiness and productiveness are indispensable to success, and size, color and quality are important considerations, we should select seeds only from varieties possessing these qualities in some marked degree, upon the principle of " like producing like." Where this can not be done, we should resort to cross-fertilization, and perhaps this would be the most certain and expedient method, as we are more likely to find some of the qualities in several varieties than to find them all in one.

For instance, suppose we were to select a winter apple for the Middle States, to include Kansas, Missouri, Southern Illinois, Arkansas, Kentucky, Southern Indiana, Ohio, Pennsylvania and New Jersey, including Delaware, Maryland and Virginia, which have very nearly the same mean temperature throughout the growing and maturing seasons, we would take the Winesap as the parent stock, either naturally fertilized or crossed with some other desirable variety, as Boyd, Lawver, Hoover, Cullawhee and Rawles' Janet, for winter sorts. For hardiness, productiveness and early bearing, such as Ben Davis and Missouri Pippin. For hardy summer and fall varieties, such as Oldenburg, Kansas Queen, Pewaukee, Wealthy, Fameuse and St. Lawrence. For extra quality, such as Early Joe, Benoni, Jonathan and Muster. For cooking, large size and fine color, such as Red Astrachan, Alexander and Early Queening. These would generally produce colored apples of fair size and good quality.

The reason we would select the Winesap for our parent stock is because it loses little, if any, in shrinkage, and is the farthest advance in all the desirable qualities of any winter apple in cultivation. It is so marked in its constitution that it produces, by its own fertilization from selected seeds under favorable conditions and cultivation, seedlings equal to most of our grafted varieties, nearly all of which are colored winter varieties, as Leavenworth Beauty and Stayman's Winesap. These can be equaled, if not excelled, by the methods herein indicated.

What we have here said in respect to the apple applies to other species of fruit, except that, perhaps, small fruits have a greater range of latitude, and yield more readily to the influences of domestication, as may be seen in the raspberry and strawberry.

The grape, that is at present exciting so much attention and that has had so much labor bestowed upon it, appears to require something more than the passing notice we gave it.

There is perhaps no species of fruit that has a wider range; that is more healthy and hardy; that bears more profusely and with more certainty than the wild grape, yet we have very few improved varieties in cultivation that are free from rot and disease. This would not be the case if there were not something wrong in the production of these varieties. They must have originated from diseased or local varities not adapted to general cultivation, or we would have made some improvement over Delaware, Catawba and Concord. To overcome these difficulties effectually and with certainty, we will have to commence anew and produce a new race of grapes entirely exempt from disease.

That this can be done we have no doubt, for nature has most generously done her part, and if we do our part according to our ability, the work will soon be accomplished. Neither need we go far off or put ourselves to any great inconvenience, for the material is at hand.

It is, however, true that we must go into a new field and clear the way, but the soil is so rich and fertile that it will amply repay us for all the labor bestowed upon it.

To commence this work we would take a wild variety of the pure *æstivalis* species, that is perfectly healthy and hardy, like the Cynthiana and Avilla. These are not only very vigorous and productive, but perhaps the richest grapes in existence, containing one-third more sugar than the Concord, being pure, sprightly, without pulp and of excellent quality, with very small seeds.

There has been no condition of weather or season that we have yet seen but they have succeeded. They are not only phylloxera and gall-louse proof, but almost hard-pan and drought proof. We doubt if there is a location where these grapes will not succeed within the boundary of their maturity, and at a place where a grape can grow.

Here we have grapes without fault, except they mature late and are of rather small size. To overcome these difficulties we have other wild grapes of the pure *labrusca* species that are equally as healthy, hardy and productive as the other, that will mature as far North as Canada, some of which are larger than any grape in cultivation. They possess all the qualities to make them succeed wherever they will mature, and they are as thoroughly proof against the weather as the other species.

In these two wild species we have all the requisites to produce healthy, hardy seedlings of the very highest quality and of the largest size, maturing either early or late. All that is required is to place these two species under thorough cultivation in a good location and hybridize the one with the other. Save the seeds of these and plant them, and they will produce a new race of grapes that will succeed.

This is the new and fertile field that we referred to; it is now yours to possess. That you will occupy it and prove worthy of your trust, is our sincere desire.

THE GRAPES OF THE SOUTHWEST.

BY GILBERT ONDERDONK, OF TEXAS.

To whatever purpose we may apply the products of the vineyard, the viticulture of a region is a matter of no small importance to its people. While grape culture has not taken its place among the leading industries, except in a few localities, yet, if the products of the vineyard were to be stricken from among our resources it would reveal a void that would be seriously felt by the nation.

Such is the extent of our national domain, such the variety of our climate, such the diversity among our population, and so various the degrees of development in the different sections of our widespread country in every other department of human industry, that it is, after all, not a matter of wonder that such different degrees of advancement in different sections have been made in the culture of the grape. While the horticulturists of some sections feel as though they have made vast strides toward perfection in their list of grapes, yet in other regions it is clearly realized that there is yet much to be done before reaching the standard of excellence demanded by the times.

We have been slow in recognizing the fact that while in some favored regions varieties are practicable, that yet, after all, each section must have its peculiar type of grapes. We may choose this or that variety or class, because we are informed of its results in some other region; still, questions of soil, altitude, temperature, humidity, and even conditions which we have been unable to detect, all take their part in the matter of results. We may invent contrivances to gain the effect of local modifications of climate, we may multiply every effort of human skill and wisdom, and yet, if we are attempting to succeed with a certain variety in a region hostile to its existence, we are fighting against nature, and must meet with practical failure. While we all recognize this principle in every other department, yet many of us have most singularly ignored it in our horticulture.

Perhaps I ought to beg pardon for such a lengthy introduction, but I must excuse myself by pleading the general disposition on the part of cultivators to each think that the special favorite in his own grounds ought to prove the sum of perfection everywhere. Again, there are so many who seem to believe that every variety can be made to succeed anywhere, and, as the title of this paper indicates. I very distinctly claim that the Southwest (I mean the

·extreme Southwest), as far as information is settled, is practically confined to certain types·of grapes.

·We have not been able to profit by the vast improvements of the North and Northeast. Their varieties are of no general practical value to the extreme Southeast. Their fruits, generally, are not worth planting in our climate, and their grapes are decided failures with us. We are sorry—but we have to deal with facts. In Northern Texas, four hundred miles north of us, the case seems to be different. There, both northern and southern *Æstivalis* seem at home, and even *Labrusca* varieties are reported successful. I well remember when we, too, thought we were successful with the Catawba, Diana and Concord. But after obtaining two or three crops our vines failed. I remember when my Goethe, Agawam and Wilder were the admiration of all who saw them; but six years after planting all were either dead or fruitless. We await with interest the final result in North Texas. But, judging from their success with Northern varieties of peaches and other fruits which are a failure in Southern Texas, we must concede to North Texas a larger variety in grape culture than we can claim in the more extreme Southwest.

Some experiments in the mountains of Texas seem to prove the practicability of profitably preserving some of the *Vinifera* varieties upon *Rupestrsi* ·stocks. In the dry mountain air some of these varieties ripen well, and it is hoped that wherever the *Rupestris* stocks will flourish, and the atmospheric conditions favor the proper maturity of these varieties, that the *Viniferas*, so valuable as raisin grapes, may yet furnish a valuable industry. But in the lower portions of Texas these varieties rot during a majority of the seasons. Below Matagorda Bay, on the sterile sands of the sea shore, these varieties seem exempt from phylloxera, and much less liable to rot than away from the immediate coast.

With the exceptions which I have named, our profitable grapes must undoubtedly come from the Southern *Æstivalis* species. The Cynthiana, Norton, Neosho, and their type, although valuable in extreme North Texas, fail in the South. On the other hand, the varieties of the Herbemont type are perfectly at home all over the State. They are our grapes of the present. In this group I include the Herbemont and Lenoir, with their seedlings. They are eminently the wine grapes of the extreme Southwest. The type represented by the Black July, Louisiana and Cunningham seem too far south at Victoria; yet only eighty miles northward they are valuable, and as far north as Hot Springs, Arkansas, I learn of their value and success. Thus we seem to have something like an indication of the northern and southern boundaries, or the proper zone for this branch of the *Æstivalis* family, while the southern limit of the Herbemont division seems to lie somewhere entirely below the State of Texas.

While we are quite satisfied with the wine·grapes of the Southwest, yet we are not so concerning the supply of table and market grapes. They have not the fleshy pulp so much prized for market purposes.

There is a popular demand all over the Southwest for a white grape on something like a Herbemont vine. This end seems to be attained by the production of the Medora from the seed of the Lenoir. The Medora will be carefully tested before it is disseminated. If it comes up to its very high promises, then, indeed, have we found a rare treasure to Southwestern viti-culture.

In conclusion, we of the Southwest would beg the representatives of a much older horticulture to judge us and our present results, not by what we are to-day, nor by what we have done to the present hour. Northern culti-vators have the benefit of generations of experience. They have gained no-ble victories. But so different from their climate is our own, that those tri-umphs are not for us. We must fight our own battles; we ask a remem-brance that we are in the infancy of our existence; we can appeal to the ex-perience of no former age; we inhabit a region with a climate so different from that of any other that has been occupied by our countrymen, and then we have but just emerged from a semi-nomadic state. If we are to take the past fifteen years of progress as a guide in estimating future improvement, then, indeed, is there a bright prospect for the great Southwest.

THE BEST APPLES FOR SOUTHERN MARKETS.

BY A. C. HAMMOND, OF ILLINOIS.

Early in the winter I received a communication from your worthy Presi-dent requesting me to prepare a paper for this meeting, " The Best Apples for Southern Markets," which, without duly weighing the difficulties of the sub-ject, I consented to do. I shall, therefore, without preface or apology, proceed to the discussion of the question.

To do so intelligently, it becomes necessary to understand something of the requirements of this market and the changes that have and are con-stantly taking place in it.

The demand has always been for a large, bright red apple, and this require-ment is more positive now than twenty years ago.

Christmas is the great holiday of the South, and alike in the mansion of the rich and the cabin of the poor, great preparation is made for the festivities of the occasion, and one of the requisites is a supply, whether it be a peck or ten barrels, of brilliant, red apples, that can only be grown to perfection in our Northern clime; and the shrewd grower or dealer who depends on this market will always be prepared to meet this demand.

Thirty years ago the orchardists of Southern Ohio and Indiana and North-ern Kentucky shipped the products of their orchards down the river in flat boats, selling at the various cities and plantations along the route, and finally landing what was left at New Orleans. For many years the Pennock or Big Romanite was the popular apple for this trade, being large, red and a good keeper, but not up to the standard in quality. Something better was therefore demanded, which induced the orchardists of the above-mentioned section to grow the Pryor's Red, which, notwithstanding its homely, russet coat, soon became popular on account of its superior quality. But in course of time the fruit of the Pennock fell a victim to disease that destroyed its value; the Pryor's Red was attacked by a leaf rust, or blight, that made its production unprofitable; the flat-boat trade was also abandoned, and this market was compelled to look to other sources for its supply.

By this time Chicago, St. Louis, Cincinnati and Louisville had become important fruit markets, and the dealers of the South naturally turned to these cities for their supplies.

Baldwin, Rome Beauty, Ben Davis, Willow Twig, Spitzenberg, Northern Spy, Winesap and Janet, were sent forward in large quantities. Baldwin, for a time, promised well, as it was large, red, and good; but under the influence of the sunny Southern skies rapidly decayed, unless grown as far north as Michigan, and is now less sought for than formerly. Rome Beauty was satisfactory in all but keeping qualities. It will not endure the climate. Willow Twig lacked color, a bright red being indispensible to popularity. Spitzenberg and Northern Spy were subject to the same objections as Baldwin and Rome Beauty. Winesap, in color, quality and general appearance, was all that could be desired, but was too small. Janet lacked both color and size, and was not, therefore, much sought for. Ben Davis was found to be large, bright red, and of fine form and appearance, and, when grown north of the 39° of latitude, to keep better than any other variety. True, the quality was not altogether satisfactory, but one objection weighs but little against so may good points.

Assuming that the Ben Davis is one of the best—if not the best—apple for Southern markets, it may not be uninteresting to the horticulturists of the Mississippi Valley to know something of its origin and history. I therefore quote from a report made by myself to the Warsaw (Ill.) Horticultural Society, several years ago.

"In 1830, Charles Hill emigrated from Kentucky to Illinois, and settled near the the Mississippi river, in Hancock county, a few miles north of the 40th parallel of latitude, bringing with him a number of small seedling apple trees, which he planted at the foot of the bluff. Some of these trees lived, and in course of time produced fruit, all but one, however, proving to be of little value. This one was a rapid-growing, symmetrical tree, and produced a large, red, handsome apple, of remarkable keeping qualities. This apple attracted the attention of a local nurseryman, who procured scions, and propagated a few hundred trees, selling them under the name of Red Pippin. About 1850, Henry Kent, an extensive nurseryman of Quincy, Illinois, began to propagate it, and from that time its dissemination was rapid, being sent out under the name of New York Pippin, Red Pippin, Baltimore Red, etc. In 1865 the Illinois State Horticultural Society named it Ben Davis, and by that name it is now known throughout the length and breadth of the land.

Thus it will be seen that this popular apple originated near the fortieth parallel, and observation proves that it is more perfectly at home there than anywhere else. During recent travels among the orchards of Illinois, Iowa, Kansas and Missouri, I have carefully observed it, and find that, after passing the forty-first parallel, it becomes smaller and less perfect, and, turning southward, after passing the thirty-ninth parallel, it ripens early, and loses its keeping qualities. So well is its value understood in the section of country referred to, that, in many places, nine-tenths of the late planting is of this variety.

While we claim that this is the best apple that we now have for Southern markets, we do not wish to leave the impression that it is entirely satisfactory. We accept it as the best we can do for the present, but with the confident expectation that the skill and indomitable energy of the horticulturists of the Northwest will, in time, bring out something possessing the good points of this variety combined with the delicious flavor of the Spitzenberg, Jonathan or Grimes' Golden.

We have, during the past season, frequently met with the Missouri Pippin, an apple resembling the Ben Davis in some particulars, but not quite so large, and apparently a little better quality. It is an apple of much promise, and may take a prominent place in this market.

During the past three years we have frequently met with the "Salome," an accidental seedling grown by E. C. Hathaway, of Ottawa, Illinois, which we consider one of the most promising new apples. Since the original tree came into bearing, ten or twelve years ago, it has not failed of a crop. The fruit is of medium size, smooth and uniform in appearance, of fair quality, and a remarkably good keeper. Hon. O. B. Galusha, President of the Illinois State Horticultural Society, has watched it carefully for several years, and gives it as his opinion that it is the coming apple, and peculiarly adapted to Southern markets on account of its wonderful keeping qualities. Our present opinion is, that in a few years, it will be one of the popular apples in this market.

We, of the North, want the luscious fruits that grow only in this sunny land, and in return we desire to send you our green apples and canned and evaporated fruits; and at this meeting hope to learn more definitely your requirements, that we may be able to furnish that which will give the most perfect satisfaction.

When, more than three centuries ago, Juan Ponce De Leon, after a fruitless search for the fountain of youth among the islands of the sea, turned his face westward, pushing, day after day, through swamps, jungles and brakes, finally stood upon the bank of the mighty river that flows at our feet, was it only a beautiful fancy that said to him that, if he had not discovered the fountain of youth he had found the Eldorado of which he was equally in quest? For where does the sun, in all its course, shine upon so fruitful a land as this wonderful valley of the Father of Waters? Who can estimate ts wealth of cotton and sugar, of wheat and corn and fruits?

The little stream, that issues from the unpretentious lake (Itasca) nestling in the wilderness, gives no promise of its coming grandeur, but glides quietly onward, through forests and marshes, past the cabin of the pioneer and the camp of the lumberman, until, upon its banks, the crimson apple and tempting pear appear. Still ownward it flows, past noisy towns and pretentious cities, gaining force and volume at every step, until the blushing peach and purple grape tempt the voyager upon its turbid waters. Onward, still onward, as if anxious to meet its destiny, it rushes, and now upon its bosom floats the commerce of a nation, and upon its banks flourish the orange, lemon and fig. Is it not evident that the great variety of products, especially, fruits growing in this great valley, ranging from the cranberry of the North to the orange of the South, through nearly twenty degrees of latitude, and that have become a necessity in every well ordered household, not only in our own, but in many other lands, will bring such wealth as will finally make it the Eldorado which the intrepid Spaniard so eagerly sought. Was it not an inspiration, rather a fancy, that whispered in his ear the wonderful destiny of this newly-discovered land?

> " Know ye the land of the cedar and vine,
>   Where the flowers ever blossom, the beams ever shine ;
>   Where the light-winged zephyr oppressed with perfume,
>   Wax faint o'er the garden of Gul in her bloom ;
>   Where the citron and olive are fairest of fruit,
>   And the voice of the nightingale never is mute ;
>   Where the tints of the earth, and the hue of the sky
>   In color, though varied, in beauty may vie,
>   And the purple of ocean is deepest in dye? "

In conclusion, permit me to say, that to us who left our ice-bound homes but a few days ago, this wonderful transformation to advancing vegetation, vernal fields and sunny skies seems like a miracle. To say that we are enjoying our visit but feebly expresses the thought we desire to convey ; but the many pleasant incidents connected with it will ever be treasured among the pleasant memories of our lives.

THE ADAPTATION OF FRUITS TO CLIMATE AND SOIL.

BY J. C. PLUMB, OF WISCONSIN.

This subject, which I can here but briefly outline, is the one central topic around which cluster all theory and practice, all experience and observation; that which underlies all the art and science of fruit growing.

Climate and soil are natural conditions which may be modified, but never materially changed in a given locality, except by very expensive processes, which forbid general use, nor which can materially and permanently affect local conditions. Thus, shade and shelter may modify the extremes and rapid transitions of temperature, but not to change the mean annual temperature. Extensive forests conserve moisture and rainfall, giving it a more equal and extended distribution; but this prolongs growth, and thus makes the plant more sensitive to the inevitable changes which must follow. And so the rich prairies of the Northwest do not want close protection, but must have a free circulation of air, to secure mature and hardy wood. Large bodies of water, which admit of a free passage of air over them, are of greater value in modifying climate than forests, and are permanent.

Artificial soil drainage is of great value in adjusting the little balance of temperature which favors or prevents an untimely frost, also to promote an early growth as well as early maturity. But a good natural drainage, from a porous subsoil, is much more desirable and economical to the commercial fruit-grower. The first attainable only at a great outlay, while the latter is "free soil."

In all countries where a "short, warm summer" necessitates rapid growth, only sheltered valleys and warm hillsides are chosen for the growth of all the crops; but where the heat of summer is prolonged into late autumn, the fruit-grower chooses the hill-top or the cool northern slope for his orchard. So we find everywhere that while art may modify and assist, it is first and best to recognize and accept nature's provisions for the successful growth of desirable fruits.

In this work we have the experience of practical men, as well as the re-researches of science, and even nature herself points unerringly to her adaptation, as seen in the natural distribution of plant life; a most wonderful and instructive school, and free to all.

But here comes in this insatiable desire to grow everything, so to speak; to enlarge the list of varieties and species beyond the bounds of economy or certainty. This is laudable when one can afford it, but too often indulged in at the expense of both profit and ultimate pleasure. There is often much pleasure in a growing plant, but there should be more in its flower and fruit. Natural adaptation says "thus far and no farther," and we do well to heed the admonition.

Says an anonymous writer: "Common sense teaches us the impossibility of finding in one spot all the requirements of successful culture of fruit for which we may crave; geology is, therefore, not to be blamed for the failure of finding it. But common sense, independent of abstract science, goes even further, and teaches that certain districts of the country are more favorable to fruit culture, and especially to the highest perfection of certain kinds of fruits, than the generality of the country. And here geology comes in quite handy to teach us where those districts are to be found and for what reason their superiority exists, quite independently of any difference in the climate."

Colonel J. H. Stevens, one of the pioneers of Minnesota, says: "There is nothing so instructive and useful to the fruit grower as a study of our own native forests. Certain varieties grow and thrive best in low, moist grounds of the river bottoms. Other varieties are found only on the dryer soils of the uplands, and these all have been .thus growing for an hundred years or more and seem good for as many years to come."

The growth of these trees from the first has been in harmony with nature's plan; first, in the selection of the soil; second, in the culture. Their first years of slow progress saved only the fittest, and mulch their only culture. They knew no scorching suns nor wasting droughts, and in the lapse of years have become the giants of the forest.

This lesson of adaptation we may learn in the natural growths of every region of our country, nor can the growing of fruit trees form an exception to the law of natural conditions of success.

Following the severe winter of 1855–6 I made extensive observations in our State, and became fully satisfied that the injuries we had experienced were traceable to certain natural causes and conditions which could be avoided by a more careful selection of hardier varieties, and by planting in soils and locations which would produce the highest conditions of hardiness or self-resistance to the extremes of climate. I found that certain soils and aspects would produce a heavy, hard wood, which would ripen as fast as made, while in other soils and aspects the same variety would be soft and immature at the advent of winter. Hence, in my earlier writings on this subject, I made prominent the necessity of planting the orchard upon firm, dry soils, comparatively elevated, and with a cool, open exposure; because I found, invariably, the best conditions of a tree of any given variety in such locations. Subsequent observations confirmed this view, and they have been extended to nearly every county in our State, and the rules then given are found even more applicable in the central and northern regions; for as the cold increases with the higher latitude and with the more variable soils of the North, the necessity of greater hardiness is more apparent.

But I found other natural conditions coming in as factors in this problem of fruit growing; such as the constituent elements of the soil and subsoil and amount of water it contained at different periods of the year; also, the atmospheric temperature and degree of saturation as modified by large bodies of water. This led me to a careful study of the superficial geology and topography of our State, where I found a rich field of investigation and the foundation for a most hopeful system of practice in tree growing. Much that before was uncertain now became clear and certain in theory and practice, and I came to believe that the adaptation of a variety need not necessarily be subject to the results of long years of trial in each given locality, and to confidently claim that where the natural conditions of soil and subsoil, elevation and aspect of any location are given, it is within the province of scientific horticulture to as clearly give the varieties and treatment best for that locality, or to say if those natural conditions render success doubtful without extraordinary expense in preparation for the success of the tree.

The principles upon which adaptation rests may be classed:

1. Organic—Structural, including variety and manner of growth.
2. Geological—Soil formation.
3. Climatic—Temperature, saturation, moisture.
4. Location—Including aspect and elevation.
5. Culture—Including pruning and general care.

That woody growths differ in their organic structure is a matter of common observation. But to show the relation between such differences and capacity for enduring climatic changes has been too generally overlooked by scientific observers. Woody structure is made up of vegetable fiber, which holds the sap in various stages of development towards organized matter. This vegetable fiber contracts with cold, while the sap expands with any degree of cold sufficient to congeal it (pure water expands below 39° F.). This contraction and expansion is a severe strain upon the cellular structure of a tree, and a rupture of its cells produce some form of disease. Now, the capacity of a tree or plant for enduring repeated extremes of temperature, or, in common terms, hardiness, is measured by its toughness or strength of fibre, and the size of its sap vessels.

Thus a section of Rhode Island Greening shows a much larger proportion of porus wood than the native crab, and equal sized sections of each variety, dry, will show a difference of twenty (20) per cent. in weight in favor of the crab wood. The same will hold good with all wood growth of a given species and climate. There will be found a corresponding difference in their capacity to resist the changes of temperature as indicated in this test, allowing something for the operation of the vital force in all cases.

The question of " vital force " is one on which science is at variance. Some claim that there is no inherent vitality, but that organized matter is built up and lives by a general law of growth, or " matter in motion." Whatever may be the true theory of life or action in organized matter, we know that, while individuals differ largely in their native vigor and endurance, the variety or species show much greater variation in this respect.

Thus, we have the hard woods of the South, of which the live oaks, the *Citrus* family and the *Maclura* are examples of extremely close-grained wood, yet very sensitive to cold, and for still another reason, because they never get ready for it, but prolong their growth indefinitely. I believe we may measure the enduring powers of a given species by the size of its capillary cells, the toughness of its fiber and its natural season of growth.

On the question of soils, our State Geologist remarks: " The most reliable natural indications of the agricultural capabilities of a district are to be found in its native vegetation. The natural flora may be regarded as the result of nature's experiments in crop-raising through the thousands of years that have elapsed since the region became covered with vegetation."

Science as well as experience shows that lime and magnesia are indispensable elements in the production of fruit. And so we see that our whole series of limestone soils are well adapted to the healthy development of the apple-tree and the production of the finest fruit; and they are, in these respects, so nearly alike that no distinction need be made in them, where they hold true to the series.

Geology tells us where we will find the limestone in its native beds, and the general character of the soil, with the topography and hydrology of the several districts. Meteorology gives us the relative temperature, and locates the greatest extremes; while vegetable physiology unfolds to us the natural forces of the tree, and enables us to understand its requirements.

All these helps thus become invaluable to the fruit-grower who would be master of his profession, and would stand upon a sure foundation.

Taking the country at large, there are other factors in this question of soil formations which we have not time to here discuss, but will again present the views of our anonymous writer (who is he ?), who says:

" Drawing an imaginary line on the map of the United States from Sandusky, Ohio, to Knoxville, Tennessee, and from there at about right-angles to the westward, we divide the land east of the Rocky Mountains into two sections. East and south of this line is a formation created by volcanic action, whose layers are upturned at almost any angle of inclination, whose interior is in consequence loosened up and rent into innumerable crevices. The other section, lying west and north of the division line, embraces the rich agricultural States of the land, and is formed by horizontal layers or strata, deposited in the ages of the past. This formation is the deluvial and calcarious or limestone formations. The former is, geologically speaking, of the metamorphic age, to which is joined the tertiary formations which make up the shores of the Atlantic Ocean.

" The rich soils of the North and West produce, in consequence, the fruits indigenous to their climate to the highest perfection. Any one wishing to raise apples is, therefore, here in the place designed by nature for the genus apple. The grower of pears will find his proper home on the eastern side of the line, on the slopes of the Eastern States, which offer a soil less rich in rampant plant food, but thoroughly drained by volcanic action. The grape-grower and speculator in extensive peach orchards will find the southern side of the line—the slopes of the Alleghenies in Virginia, the Carolinas, Georgia, Alabama, clear on to the Ozark Mountains in Arkansas—the most advantageous location for his enterprise.

"Geology, together with meteorology, teaches this, and infinitely more, and has pointed out, for many years, that the southern slopes of the continent correspond more closely to the leading vine and fruit-producing countries of Europe than any other portion of the United States, the Pacific States excepted."

That the above limitations are subject to criticism we admit, but, as a whole, it outlines the grand natural division of the Mississippi Valley very truthfully in horticultural adaptation.

Professor Swallow, of the Missouri Agricultural College, has found that ridges and steep declivities filled with flints give the best apples, pears, peaches, cherries, plums and grapes on that farm. Of course this is due to something else, probably, than the presence of solid flints in the soil. It shows, however, the value of observation,. and that the same results do not always follow from the same apparent causes.

The climatic conditions of the Mississippi Valley are remarkable and varied. Here the waters of the Gulf create a sub-tropical climate, and the same Gulf winds sweeping up the western slope of the valley give it the mild winter weather so prevalent from Nebraska south, and reaching often into Iowa, Minnesota and Dakota. In fact, to this influence we are indebted for our let-up from the boreal blasts which come to us almost unbroken from the ice fields of the polar regions. In summer and early autumn we have the counter trade-winds from the great plains to the southwest. which give us our fine grapes and well ripened dent corn.

The Northwest has peculiar natural conditions, climatic, which have,. and always will be great factors in this question of fruit growing, and my own State of Wisconsin may be said to have been an "undiscovered country" prior to our experiences of 1855–6.

We then awoke to the fact of peculiar conditions of climate as well-as of soil, and the next ten years was a period of much study, experiment and observation of natural conditions affecting hardiness and our capacity for fruit growing. We found our new soils rich in humus, producing a late growth of wood unfit to bear the extremes of winter. This tendency was enhanced by the prolonged autumn heats characteristic of the Northwest.

We also found the mean summer temperature of Pittsburg, Pa., with the winter of Montreal, Canada. The former, 72°, enters our State near the southeast corner and leaves it near the northwest border 2½° to the north. The winter mean of 20° entering our State on the latitude of Green Bay and leaving it near the southwest corner. These lines, so adverse in all the Eastern States, here, for the first, cross each other in the central southern portion of the State, each pursuing its westward way, but diverging more widely at the West.

These peculiar climatic conditions we were the first to experience, and we trust other States, West and North, profited by our reverses in learning the lessons they taught us.

In giving advice to fruit growers we inquire, 1st, the natural conditions of soil and climate; and, 2d, what change may be made in natural conditions and care, so that the list of varieties may be extended; and, 3d, we advise a careful examination of growing orchards and to plant mostly of most successful varieties. The questions of variety and culture must be considered for each locality and be adapted to the local conditions. These are certain principles of growth which everywhere apply to a given species. The apple thrives best in a cool, moist climate where there is sufficient summer heat to mature its growth and a firm, calcareous, retentive soil, while the peach thrives best in a dryer climate and more porous soil several degrees further South, exempt from extreme cold.

The question of protection is a never ending source of trouble to all fruit-growers, except those who by choice or necessity plant upon the bleak hill-tops, or cool northern slopes. We find these locations growing varieties with great success, that on the reverse side, or in sunny sheltered locations, are a total failure. And we find the warmer these locations and soil, the more hopeless the case. This is not accident, but in conformity to law as plain as anything in the realm of nature.

The skillful balancing of the temperature and moisture of the air, in culti-vating different kinds of plants, and the just adaptation of them to the vari-ous seasons of growth, constitute the most complicated and difficult part of a gardener's art.

Prof. Lindley gives the following rules:

" 1. Most moisture in the air is demanded by plants when they first begin to grow, and least when their periodical growth is completed.

" 2. The quantity of atmospheric moisture required by plants is in inverse proportion to the distance from the equator of the countries which they nat-urally inhabit.

"3. Plants with annual stems require more than those with ligneous stems.

"4. The amount of moisture in the air most suitable to plants at rest is in inverse proportion to the quantity of aqueous matter they at the time con-tain. (Hence the dryness of the air required by succulent plants when at rest.)"

The *Pyrus Malus*, of which the Baldwin, Greening and Pippins are of an exalted pattern, do the best in New York and Michigan, while *Pyrus As-trachana*, of which our Russias, Duchesse, Alexander and Astrachan are types, do much their best in Vermont, Canada and Wisconsin, and the *Pyrus Bacata*, or Siberian family, are vastly better grown in the latitude of Green Bay, Wisconsin, and in Minnesota, than further south.

The same may be noted of the oaks and pines which extend over a wide belt of our country, from the Gulf of Mexico to Lake Superior, but require many and widely different varieties to cover the different conditions of soil and climate.

This law of natural selection or adaptation is so uniform in its application, that we draw the line of separation of species and varieties for each locality with great certainty, and a more definite knowledge of, and obedience to the law would save much money and time now wasted in planting without any settled rule of practice. It would also give faith to plant more largely and further north than is now considered safe.

From the foregoing outlines we conclude:

1. That the limits of adaptation of a variety should be more sharply de-fined and more rigidly insisted upon. The American people are a race of experimenters, which is all right for those who choose; but the commercial planter wants positive data and every reasonable assurance of success when he plants. Individual interests may induce the nurseryman and salesman

17

to extend their lists into the region of the unknown, and too often unknowable, varieties, "far fetched and dear bought," but the commercial planter will not venture much beyond the old and well proven list.

2. Indivduals and societies have done a grand work in furnishing positive data for the guidance of fruit-growers. We point with pride to the living and written works of our Downings, Warder, and Thomas. We honor our Wilder in his devotion to the great American society, and the long array of lesser lights, but as devoted and useful to the pomology of the West; may the number of them never be less.

3. Every locality, which has its own naturally distinct features of soil and climate, should also have its local pomology, with its corps of observers and its experimental stations, its local societies, and published records. Our public and private schools should teach elementary horticulture, and our State and national goverment should give substantial aid to this increasing interest of our country.

Members and friends of the Mississippi Valley Horticultural Society, gathered from twenty different States of our Union, and from twenty degrees of latitude, representing the great valley from Superior to the Gulf, bearing the fruit productions of great extremes of climate, and great variations of soil, gathered with one accord, but of many minds (a fair type of our horticulture, greatly diversified, but an ultimate unit), to us the question comes, what will we do in this great work of placing the horticulture of the Mississippi Valley upon an enduring foundation, and that each locality may have a more definite and practical knowledge of the laws of adaptation?

PLANTING FRUIT TREES.

BY G W. MINIER, OF ILLINOIS.

The fruit supply of the country has become a practical question. Years gone by fruit was esteemed a luxury. now it is deemed a necessity. That the usual supply has been cut off in the last few years, in many portions of the country, is patent to every observing man. The cause and the remedy belong to the thoughtful. It has, somehow, got into the minds of the people that fruit trees are everlasting, instead of being only perennial. Our first orchards are not merely growing old—they have become practically worthless. In almost every other pursuit men are thoughtful, careful and wise.

To insure a flock of sheep they know lambs must be raised; pigs are the forerunner of hogs, and calves the harbingers of cattle. But our old orchards stand, year after year, with blasted limbs, dead tops and decayed bodies, and yet we complain of the seasons and arraign Providence for not giving us fruit. This is certainly unwise, and from a religious standpoint it looks impious. If, as the Apostle Paul says, "the gospel is the power of God to salvation," may we not say that trees are God's power to give us fruit. If heaven can not be gained without the first, neither can fruit be had without the latter. Now. what shall be done? Shall we have our farms and lawns disfigured with old, worthless and scraggy trees because they once bore good fruit? Nay, verily. Cut them down and turn them into fuel. Plant another orchard, not on the same plat of ground; but seek a new site and turn the old one into pasture. It will pay as well, and better than those miserable old, tumbledown trees. God planted a garden eastward in Eden. Go thou, farmer, and humbly imitate your Creator.

Geologists tell us that God swept the earth eons of ages since, with ice—the glacial period. We have had a slight specimen this winter. But a good ax and strong muscles will answer your purpose. "Turn the old trees into ashes and original elements and plant young ones. With wise culture all this dread of a dearth of fruit will vanish, for 'tis made of such stuff as dreams are," and coming generations will rise up and call you blessed.

In selecting trees for planting get only vigorous ones. Those two years old are best. No one should be allowed to give us three years old trees if we can buy two years old ones. Don't purchase trees from tree peddlers. Go yourself to the nursery. Give tree peddlers a wide birth. If there be no other remedy, train a big black dog to go for them.

Prepare the ground by deep plowing; set your trees one inch deeper only than they were in the nursery; tend the orchard for years, as in hoed crops; see them every day, as you would your lambs, pigs and calves. Follow the above directions, and should you fail to have plenty of fruit, call on me and I'll divide.

HISTORICAL SKETCH.

Desiring to preserve in permanent form the early history of the Mississippi Valley Horticultural Society, the Secretary has secured, from the pen of ex-Secretary Prof. Tracy, the following sketch; also, the awards of premiums made at the exhibition in St. Louis September, 1880.

This sketch, with Major Nowlin's paper on the " Origin and Importance of the Society," preserves its records down to the present time, when it becomes one of the permanent institutions of the country, with a *future* in prospect that will guarantee the preservation of its subsequent history. SECRETARY.

HISTORICAL.

BY PROF. S. M. TRACY, OF MISSOURI.

At a meeting of the Missouri State Horticultural Society, held in St. Louis, January, 1880, delegates from the Arkansas and Illinois State Societies were present, and the subject of forming a "Mississippi Valley Horticultural Society" was introduced by Mr. Nowlin, one of the Arkansas delegates. After considerable discussion, the matter was referred to a committee of nine, three from each of the State societies represented at the meeting, as follows: S. H. Nowlin, C. C. Smith and J. B. Hoag, of Arkansas; Parker Earle, O. B. Galusha and J. E. Starr, of Illinois; Norman J. Colman, J. C. Evans and S. M. Tracy, of Missouri. After a thorough canvass of the subject, and correspondence with the presidents and secretaries of the various State societies in the Mississippi Valley, it was thought best to take steps for the formation of a society which should be more especially suited to the wants of Western Horticulturists than is any society now in existence. The presidents and secretaries of the State societies interested were made members of the committee, and the following call was issued :

. MISSISSIPPI VALLEY HORTICULTURAL SOCIETY.

To the Horticulturists of the Mississippi Valley:

In pursuance of action taken at the late meeting of the Missouri Horticultural Society, which embraced delegates from several other State societies, a committee was appointed to invite the horticulturists of the Western and Southwestern States to meet in convention, for the purpose of effecting the organization of a Mississippi Valley Horticultural Society, and also to arrange for an extensive exhibition of fruits and flowers during the coming autumn. After consultation with horticulturists in several States, the undersigned have decided to call a convention for that purpose, to meet in St. Louis on Wednesday, the 8th day of September next, at 9 o'clock A. M., the particular place and programme of meeting to be hereafter published.

We are also pleased to be able to announce that the Merchants' Exchange of St. Louis has, with characteristic courtesy and liberality, granted us the use of their great hall for the purpose of a horticultural exhibition; and they also guarantee the funds necessary to enable us to offer a schedule of prizes, amounting in all to nearly $3,000, which is herewith published. This exhibition will be held on September 7, 8 and 9, 1880.

We offer a very liberal list of premiums, and have encouragement to believe that we can secure the largest and best arranged display of horticultural products ever made in our country. Certainly there has never been an opportunity for making so magnificent a display, as the hall of the St. Louis Merchants' Exchange is the largest and finest in America.

While the purpose of the proposers of this organization is to serve more immediately the interests of pomology, forestry and floriculture in this great Mississippi Valley, yet we invite the co-operation, both in the convention and in the exhibition, of all persons interested in the horticultural growth of the country, without regard to locality.

We confidently hope that lovers of pomology and rural art in all these States will join us, with the enthusiasm and energy of the Western men, in the effort to make such an organization and such an exposition of our horticultural resources as shall be worthy of the great country in which we live:

NORMAN J. COLMAN, President Missouri State Horticultural Society.
J. C. EVANS, Missouri State Horticultural Society.
S. M. TRACY, Secretary Missouri State Horticultural Society.
S. H. NOWLIN, Secretary Arkansas State Horticultural Society.
C. C. SMITH, Arkansas State Horticultural Society.
J. B. HOAG, Arkansas State Horticultural Society.
PARKER EARLE, President Illinois State Horticultural Society.
O. B. GALUSHA, Secretary Illinois State Horticultural Society.
J. E. STARR, Illinois State Horticultural Society.
H. TONE, President North Texas Horticultural Society.
T. V. MUNSON, Secretary North Texas Horticultural Society.
W. H. RAGAN, Secretary Indiana Horticultural Society.
T. T. LYON, President Michigan Pomological Society.
C. W. GARFIELD, Secretary Michigan Pomological Society.
J. M. SMITH, President Wisconsin State Horticultural Society.
C. L. WATROUS, President Iowa State Horticultural Society.

J. L. BUDD, Secretary Iowa State Horticultural Society.

M. W. PHILLIPS, Oxford, Mississippi.

R. W. FURNAS, President Nebraska State Horticultural Society.

D. H. WHEELER, Secretary Nebraska State Horticultural Society.

J. M. MORTON, Secretary Tennessee State Horticultural Society.

E. GALE, President Kansas State Horticultural Society.

G. C. BRACKETT, Secretary Kansas State Horticultural Society.

H. W. L. LEWIS, President Gulf States Fruit Growers' Association (Miss.)

S. M. WIGGINS, Secretary Gulf States Fruit Growers' Association. (La.)

J. T. GRIMES, President Minnesota State Horticultural Society.

J. DECKER, Secretary Kentucky State Horticultural Society.

A. WHITTAKER, President Texas States Horticultural Society.

E. N. FIELDING, Secretary Texas State Horticultural Society.

J. A. WARDER, President Ohio State Horticultural Society.

On April 13, the committee met in St. Louis, and organized by electing Parker Earle, of Illinois, Chairman, and S. M. Tracy, of Missouri, Secretary. The details of the proposed organization and of the exhibition were considered at some length; regulations were adopted, and a premium list was arranged aggregating, $2,675, which was divided as follows: Apples, $600; pears, $300; peaches and plums, $360; grapes, $295; miscellaneous—sweepstakes, etc., $1,120.

The exhibition was held on September 7, 8 and 9, in the Merchants' Exchange, and although the attendance of visitors was small the exhibit was, with the exception of the one made in Philadelphia during the Centennial, the largest ever made in America. Something over eight thousand plates of fruit were shown, coming from nineteen different States. One thousand and thirty-eight entries were made by one hundred and thirty-two exhibitors.

In number of plates exhibited Missouri ranked first, Michigan second, Illinois third, and New York fourth. In apples there were four hundred and twenty-three entries; in pears, two hundred and eighty-nine; in peaches, eighty-eight; in grapes, one hundred and sixty; and in the miscellaneous class, seventy-eight. The tables were so arranged that competing exhibits were placed together, and each plate had a label giving the name of the variety, and the name and address of the grower.

On Wednesday, September 8, a meeting of horticulturists was called in the parlor of the Laclede Hotel, and a permanent organization effected by the adoption of a constitution and the election of the following officers:

President—Parker Earle, of Cobden, Illinois.

First Vice President—Ex-Gov. R. W. Furnas, of Brownville, Nebraska.

Secretary—S. M. Tracy, of Columbia, Missouri.

Treasurer—H. G. McPike, of Alton, Illinois.

Arrangements for future meetings were left with the Executive Committee.

The second annual meeting of the Society was held in Cincinnati, Ohio, on

September 7, 8 and 9, 1881. This meeting was mainly for the reading of papers and discussions, but a small exhibition of fruits was made at the Cincinnati Exposition, then in progress.

The Society having no funds at its disposal for printing purposes, a full report of this meeting was published with the report of the Missouri State Horticultural Society for 1880–81.

At this meeting the following officers were elected:

President—Parker Earle, of Cobden, Illinois.
First Vice President—G. W. Campbell, of Delaware, Ohio.
Secretary—S. M. Tracy, of Columbia. Missouri.
Treasurer—J. C. Evans, of Harlem, Missouri.

During the next year the Society had full assurances that arrangements could be made for holding a meeting and exhibition in connection with that of the Chicago Fair Association, and these assurances were continued as late as August—too late for making any other arrangements—when the Fair Association failed to secure its grounds, and the meeting called for September, 1882, was adjourned to meet in New Orleans, La., February 21, 1883.

LIST OF PREMIUMS

Awarded at the First Exhibition of the Mississippi Valley Horticultural Society, held in St. Louis, September 7, 8 and 9, 1880.

APPLES.

Best collection by any State or local society or individual (not more than one hundred varieties), Missouri Valley Horticultural Society; second premium, Warsaw Horticultural Society, Illinois.

Best forty varieties—First premium, A. C. Hammond, Warsaw, Illinois; second premium, W. G. Gano, Parkville, Missouri.

Best ten varieties from south of 37th parallel—First premium, W. M. Samuels, Clinton, Kentucky; second premium, S. H. Nowlin, Little Rock, Arkansas.

Best ten varieties raised between 37th and 41st parallels—First premium, S. E. Willetts, Brussels, Illinois; second premium, Z. S. Ragan, Independence, Missouri.

Best ten varieties raised north of the 41st parallel—First premium, Grand River Valley Horticultural Society, Grand Rapids, Michigan; second premium, J. H. Ricketts, Newburg, New York.

Best plate Sweet Bough—Wm. Rowe, Grand Rapids, Michigan.
Best plate Bailey's Sweet—A. C. Hammond, Warsaw, Illinois.
Best plate Porter—J. T. Hubbard, St. Joseph, Missouri.
Best plate Maiden's Blush—J. T. Johnson, Warsaw, Illinois.
Best plate Lowell—Wm. Rowe, Grand Rapids, Michigan.

Best plate Rambo—Z. S. Ragan, Independence, Missouri.
Best plate Pennsylvania Red Streak—W. M. Samuels, Clinton, Kentucky.
Best plate Jonathan—A. H. Worthen, Jr., Warsaw, Illinois.
Best plate Winesap—A. H. Worthen, Jr.
Best plate Willow Twig—S. E. Willetts, Brussels, Illinois.
Best plate Rawles' Janet—J. T. Johnson.
Best plate Ben Davis—W. M. Samuels.
Best plate Huntsman's Favorite—Z. S. Ragan.
Best plate Lawver—W. G. Gano, Parkville, Missouri.
Best plate Shannon—E. F. Babcock, Little Rock, Arkansas.
Best plate Red Canada—A. C. Hammond.
Best plate Baldwin—W. M. Samuels.
Best plate Yellow Newtown Pippin—R. Degarmo, Assumption, Illinois.
Best plate Shockley—W. M. Samuels.
Best plate Rome Beauty—W. M. Samuels.
Best plate Smith's Cider—E. F. Babcock.
Best plate Yellow Bellflower—Calhoun Horticultural Society, Illinois.
Best plate Seedling—J. C. Evans, Harlem, Missouri.
Best plate any variety—W. G. Gano.
Best collection of Crab Apples—First premium, Minnesota Horticultural Society ; second premium, J. C. Plumb, Milton, Wisconsin.

PEARS.

Best collection, not more than fifty varieties—First premium, Ellwanger & Barry, Rochester, New York ; second premium, J. H. Ricketts, Newburg, New York.
Best collection of twenty-five varieties—First premium, P. Earle & Sons, Cobden Illinois ; second premium, Bush & Son, Bushberg, Missouri.
Best five varieties for market—First premium, Z. S. Ragan, Independence, Missouri; second premium, P. Earle & Sons, Cobden, Illinois.
Best plate Bartlett—J. Rhodes, Bridgeton, Missouri.
Best plate Howell—A. H. Worthen, Jr., Warsaw, Illinois.
Best plate Louise Bonne of Jersey—S. H. Nowlin, Little Rock, Arkansas.
Best plate Seckel—G. Green, Louisville, Kentucky.
Best plate Flemish Beauty—Ellwanger & Barry.
Best plate Beurre Superfin—Ellwanger & Barry.
Best plate White Doyenne—Ellwanger & Barry.
Best plate Onondaga—J. H. Ricketts.
Best plate Beurre Bosc—Ellwanger & Barry.
Best plate Winter Nellis—J. Menifee, St. Joseph, Missouri.
Best plate Duchesse d'Angouleme—P. Earle & Sons.
Best plate Beurre Clairgeau—G. H. Baker, Cobden, Illinois.
Best plate Beurre d'Anjou—P. Earle & Sons.
Best plate Dana's Hovey—P. Earle & Sons.
Best plate Lawrence—Ellwanger & Barry.
Best plate Beurre Easter—P. Earle & Sons.
Best plate any variety—To a plate of Sheldon, exhibited by P. Earle and Sons.

PEACHES AND PLUMS.

Best collection of peaches, by any State or local society or individual (not more than twenty-five varieties)—First premium, Murray Bros., Elm Grove, Missouri; second premium, Grand River Valley Horticultural Society, Grand Rapids, Michigan.

Best collection of peaches, by any State or local society or individual, preserved whole in solution (not more than twenty-five varieties)—First premium, Allegan County Horticultural Society, Allegan, Michigan.

Best collection of peaches, by any individual (not more than ten varieties)—First premium, Z. S. Ragan, Independence, Missouri; second premium, J. H. Ricketts, Newburg, New York.

Best plate Amsden—Z. S. Ragan.

Best plate Crawford's Late—J. H. Ricketts.

Best plate Smock—J. Decker, Fern Creek, Kentucky.

Best plate Heath Cling—A. Lavelle, St. Joseph, Missouri.

Best plate New Seedling—J. H. Ricketts.

Best plate any variety—J. H. Ricketts.

Best collection of plums—Ellwanger & Barry, Rochester, New York.

Best plate of plums—Ellwanger & Barry.

GRAPES.

Best collection of grapes, by any State or local society or individual—First premium, T. S. Hubbard, Fredonia, New York; second, Bush & Son and Meissner, Bushberg, Jefferson county, Missouri.

Best ten varieties of grapes for wine—First premium, Bush & Son, Bushberg, Missouri; second premium, Rommel & Sobhe, Morrison, Missouri.

Best ten varieties of grapes for table—First premium, J. H. Ricketts, Newburg, New York. (Most of these ten varieties are unknown to the committee as to habit of growth and character for general cultivation. Premium awarded for quality and fine appearance.) Second premium, Bush & Son, Bushberg, Missouri.

Best plate Salem—B. H. Young, Louisville, Kentucky.

Best plate Telegraph—Bush & Son and Meissner, Bushberg, Missouri.

Best plate Delaware—J. H. Ricketts, Newburg, New York.

Best plate Iona—J. H. Ricketts, Newburg, New York.

Best plate Herbemont—G. Muhm, Augusta, Missouri.

Best plate Massasoit—A. Engleman, Shiloh, Illinois.

Best plate Lindley—A. Engleman, Shiloh, Illinois.

Best plate Hermann—A. H. Worthen, Jr., Warsaw, Illinois.

Best plate Scuppernong—J. J. Colmant, Columbus, Mississippi.

Best plate Thomas—J. J. Colmant.

Best plate Flowers—J. J. Colmant.

Best plate grapes for table (Triumph)—Rommel & Sobhe, Morrison, Missouri.

Best plate grapes for wine (Cynthiana)—Rommel & Sobhe.

Best plate Concord—N. Bensing, Hermann, Missouri.

Best plate Catawba—Isaac Wells, Villa Ridge, Illinois.

Best plate Goethe—Bush & Son and Meissner.
Best plate Martha—A. Engleman.
Best plate Elvira—Bush & Son and Meissner.
Best plate Wilder – B. H. Young, Louisville, Kentucky.
Best plate Norton's Virginia—J. Rinderer, Augusta, Missouri.
Best plate Cynthiana—H. Jaeger, Neosho, Missouri.
Best plate Lady—G. W. Campbell, Delaware, Ohio.
Best plate Amber—Rommel & Sobbe.
Best bearing cane of new seedling for table and market, quality and productiveness to rule—T. S. Hubbard, Fredonia, New York—Prentiss.
Best bearing cane of new seedling for wine, quality and productiveness to rule—Rommel & Sobbe, Morrison, Missouri—Elvira Seedling No. 3.
The Committee on Grapes recommended a discretionary premium for collection of seedlings from Nicholas Grein, of Hermann, Missouri.

SEMI-TROPICAL FRUITS.

Best display—Gulf States Fruit Growers' Association, New Orleans, Louisiana.
Best display California fruit—George C. Swan, San Diego, California.
Best plate pomegranates—J. J. Colmant, Columbus, Mississippi.
Best plate Mandarin oranges—A. Sambola, New Orleans.
Best plate shaddocks—S. M. Wiggins, New Orleans.
Best plate lemons—George C. Swan.
Best collection green-house plants—First premium, H. Michel & Co., St. Louis; third premium, W. A. Syred, St. Louis. No second premium awarded.
Best specimen plant—Henry Michel & Co.
Best display cut flowers—Henry Michel & Co.
Best floral design—Henry Michel & Co.
Best display preserved (whole) fruit—St. Louis, Iron Mountain and Southern Railway.

SWEEPSTAKES.

Best collection of horticultural products by any State horticultural society—First premium, Missouri Valley Horticultural Society; second premium, Michigan Pomological Society; third premium, Illinois Horticultural Society; fourth premium, Western New York Horticultural Society.

APPENDIX.

ROSTER OF OFFICERS

Of National, State and Important Local Horticultural and Kindred Societies, for the Year 1883.

AMERICAN POMOLOGICAL SOCIETY.

Hon. MARSHALL P. WILDER, President, Boston, Massachusetts.
PATRICK BARRY, First Vice President, Rochester, New York.
Prof. W. J. BEAL, Secretary, Lansing, Michigan.
BENJAMIN G. SMITH, Treasurer, Cambridge, Massachusetts.

AMERICAN FORESTRY CONGRESS.

Dr. GEORGE B. LORING, President, Washington, District of Columbia.
Hon. H. G. JOLLY, First Vice President, Quebec.
Dr. J. A. WARDER, Second Vice President, North Bend, Ohio.
Dr. F. B. HOUGH, Recording Secretary, Lowville, New York.
WILLIAM LITTLE, Corresponding Secretary, Montreal.
JAMES S. FAY, Treasurer, Wood's Hall, Massachusetts.

AMERICAN ASSOCIATION OF NURSERYMEN.

Col. NORMAN J. COLMAN, President, St. Louis, Missouri.
A. W. WEBBER, Vice President, Nashville, Tennessee.
D. WILMOT SCOTT, Secretary, Galena, Illinois.
A. R. WHITNEY, Treasurer, Franklin Grove, Illinois.

MISSISSIPPI VALLEY HORTICULTURAL SOCIETY.

PARKER EARLE, President, Cobden, Illinois.
Major S. H. NOWLIN, First Vice President, Little Rock, Arkansas.
W. H. RAGAN, Secretary, Clayton, Indiana.
Major J. C. EVANS, Treasurer, Harlem, Missouri.

GULF STATES FRUIT GROWERS' ASSOCIATION.

H. W. L. LEWIS, President, Osyka, Mississippi.
E. M. HUDSON, Vice President, New Orleans, Louisiana.
S. M. WIGGINS, Secretary, New Orleans, Louisiana.
J. C. POTTS, Treasurer, New Orleans, Louisiana.

FRUIT GROWERS' ASSOCIATION OF ONTARIO.

WILLIAM SAUNDERS, President, London.
WILLIAM ROY, Vice President, Owen Sound.
D. W. BEADLE, Secretary and Treasurer, St. Catharines.

ARKANSAS HORTICULTURAL SOCIETY.

W. K. TIPTON, President, Little Rock.
GEORGE P. MURRILL, Vice President, Austin.
E. H. CHAMBERLAIN, Secretary, Little Rock.
S. H. NOWLIN, Corresponding Secretary, Little Rock.

COLORADO STATE HORTICULTURAL SOCIETY.

Dr. ALEXANDER SHAW, President, Denver.
J. M. CLARK, Secretary, Denver.
WILLIAM DAVIS, Treasurer, Denver.

GEORGIA STATE HORTICULTURAL SOCIETY.

P. J. BERCKMANS, President, Augusta.
Dr. W. R. JONES, First Vice President, Herndon.
T. L. KINSEY, Secretary and Treasurer, Savannah.

INDIANA HORTICULTURAL SOCIETY.

SYLVESTER JOHNSON, President, Irvington.
C. M. HOBBS, First Vice President, Bridgeport.
W. H. RAGAN, Secretary, Clayton.
DANIEL COX, Treasurer, Cartersburg.

ILLINOIS STATE HORTICULTURAL SOCIETY.

O. B. GALUSHA, President, Morris.
MILO BARNARD, Vice President, Mantino.
LEN SMALL, Secretary, Kankakee.
A. C. HAMMOND, Assistant Secretary, Warsaw.
S. G. MINKLER, Treasurer, Oswego.

IOWA HORTICULTURAL SOCIETY.

R. C. SPEER, President, Cedar Falls.
Prof. J. L. BUDD, Secretary, Ames.
HENRY STROHM, Treasurer, Iowa City.

KANSAS STATE HORTICULTURAL SOCIETY.

Prof. E. GALE, President, Manhattan.
M. B. NEWMAN, Vice President, Wyandotte.

G. C. BRACKETT, Secretary, Lawrence.
FRED. WELLHOUSE, Treasurer, Fairmount.
GEORGE Y. JOHNSON, Lawrence,   ⎫
Dr. CHARLES WILLIAMS, Washington,   ⎬ Trustees.
L. A. SIMMONS, Wellington,   ⎭

KENTUCKY HORTICULTURAL SOCIETY.

J. S. BEATTY, President, Simpsonville.
D. L. STALLARD, Vice President, Woodburn.
J. L. CLARK, Recording Secretary, High Grove.
A. P. FARNSLEY, Corresponding Secretary, Louisville.
A. D. WEBB, Treasurer, Bowling Green.

MINNESOTA STATE HORTICULTURAL SOCIETY.

JOHN S. HARRIS, President, La Crescent.
OLIVER GIBBS, Secretary, Lake City.
J. T. GRIMES, Treasurer, Minneapolis.
JAMES BOWEN, Librarian, Minneapolis (deceased).

MISSISSIPPI HORTICULTURAL SOCIETY.

DR. H. E. McKAY, President, Madison.
C. W. GALLAGHER, First Vice President, Meridian.
PROF. J. J. COLMANT, Second Vice President, Agricultural College.
S. H. STACKHOUSE, Secretary, Crystal Springs.
J. D. SIDWAY, Treasurer, Jackson.

MICHIGAN HORTICULTURAL SOCIETY.

T. T. LYON, President, South Haven.
CHARLES W. GARFIELD, Secretary, Grand Rapids.
S. M. PEARSALL, Treasurer, Grand Rapids.
T. H. FORSTER, Librarian, Lansing.

MISSOURI HORTICULTURAL SOCIETY.

PROF. S. M. TRACY, President, Columbia.
L. A. GOODMAN, Secretary, Westport.
J. C. EVANS, Treasurer, Harlem.

NEBRASKA HORTICULTURAL SOCIETY.

SAMUEL BARNARD, President, Table Rock.
J. H. MASTERS, 1st Vice President, Nebraska City.
MISS M. A. STRATTON, 2d Vice President, Lincoln.
J. T. ALLAN, Secretary, Omaha.
CHRIS. HARTMAN, Treasurer, Omaha.

OHIO HORTICULTURAL SOCIETY.

DR. J A. WARDER, President, North Bend.
NICHOLAS OHMER, Vice President, Dayton.
GEORGE W. CAMPBELL, Secretary, Delaware.
LEO WELTZ, Treasurer, Wilmington.

WISCONSIN HORTICLLTURAL SOCIETY.

J. M. SMITH, President, Green Bay.
J. C. PLUMB, Vice President, Milton.
WM. TRELEASE, Secretary, Madison.
B. S. HOXIE, Corresponding Secretary, Cookville.
MATT. ANDERSON, Treasurer, Pine Bluff.

WEST TENNESSEE FRUIT AND VEGETABLE GROWERS' ASSOCIATION.

JOHN W. RANSOM, President, Gadsden.
J. E. PORTER, Secretary, Humboldt.
B. F. TRANSOU, Treasurer, Humboldt.

HORTICULTURAL SOCIETY OF NORTHERN ILLINOIS.

S. N. SLADE, President, Elgin.
ARTHUR BRYANT, 1st Vice President, Princeton.
E. W. GRAVES, Recording Secretary, Sandwich.
D. WILMOT SCOTT, Corresponding Secretary, Galena.
L. WOODARD, Treasurer, Marengo.

HORTICULTURAL SOCIETY OF CENTRAL ILLINOIS.

A. C. HAMMOND, President, Warsaw.
DR. A. G. HUMPHREY, Vice President, Galesburg.
F. M. DOAN, Secretary, Jacksonville.
H. M. DUNLAP, Treasurer, Savoy.

HORTICULTURAL SOCIETY OF SOUTHERN ILLINOIS.

EDWARD ROGERS, President, Upper Alton.
W. H. FULKERSON, Vice President, Jerseyville.
E. A. RIEHL, Secretary and Treasurer, Alton.

MISSOURI VALLEY HORTICULTURAL SOCIETY.

J. C. EVANS, President, Harlem, Missouri.
GEORGE W. HOPKINS, Secretary, Kansas City, Missouri.
FRANK HOLSINGER. Treasurer, Rosedale, Kansas.

DIRECTORY

OF

HORTICULTURAL BUSINESS.

NURSERYMEN AND FLORISTS.

ALBERTSON & HOBBS, Bridgeport, Indiana. General Nursery Stock. Small Fruits a specialty. Experimental Fruit Farm near Indianapolis.

HENRY AVERY, Burlington, Iowa. General assortment of Trees and small Fruit Plants. Varieties adapted to the climate.

BUSH & SON & MEISSNER, Grape Nurseries, Bushberg, Jefferson county, Missouri (Isador Bush & Co., St. Louis). Vineyards and Orchards.

BLOOMINGTON NURSERY CO., Bloomington, Ill. Nurserymen and Florists. Established 1852. Inccrporated 1883. Successors to F. K. Phœnix.

CADWALLADER BROS., Louisburg, Kansas. Specialties, Apple, Cherry and Peach Trees. Osage Orange Plants and Apple Seedlings in quantities.

MATTHEW CRAWFORD, Horticulturist, Cuyahoga Falls, Ohio. The Strawberry a specialty. Send for catalogue.

JOHN S. COLLINS. Moorestown, N. J. All the new and choice sorts of Berries and Fruits. Specialty, Kieffer's Hybrid Pear.

GRANVILLE COWING, Muncie, Indiana. Special attention to small Fruits and new Potatoes. Experimental Plantations. Fruits for Market.

GEO. W. CAMPBELL, Delaware, O., Grower of Grapevines for amateurs and planters. Choice New Varieties a specialty. Established in 1857.

JAMES EDGERTON, Barnesville, Ohio. Small Fruits for market and Plants for sale. Promising new sorts tested.

18

O. B. GALUSHA, Pres. State Hort. Society, Morris, Ill., Nurseryman. Small Fruit Plants a specialty. Fruits for market in season. Send for catalogue.

C. H. GREGORY, Altus, Arkansas. Nurseryman, Fruit Grower and Market Gardener. Varieties for the South tested.

G H. & J. H. HALE, South Glastonbury, Conn., Nurserymen and Fruit Growers. New and choice Berry Plants by mail a specialty. Catalogue free.

HUNTSVILLE NURSERIES, Huntsville, Alabama. W. F. Heikes, manager. Specialties, LeConte and Kieffer Pears, Fruit Trees and Plants.

HEIKES NURSERY CO, North Main street, city limits, Dayton, Ohio. General assortment of Nursery stock. Orders carefully filled.

HAMMOND NURSERIES, Geneva, N. Y. Standard and Dwarf Pears, Keiffer Pears, Pocklington Grapes, Cut-leaf Weeping Birch, Champion Quince.

Z. K. JEWETT, Sparta, Wisconsin. General Nursery. Baled Packing Moss, Forest Evergreens.

A. W. & J. S. KERR, Collins Nurseries, McKinney, Texas, Growers and Dealers in Nursery Stock. Experimental Farm, devoted to testing varieties.

GEORGE J. KELLOGG, Janesville, Wisconsin. Fifty varieties Strawberries, Raspberries, Grapes, etc., etc., for the North.

D. W. LANGDON, Langdon Nurseries, Mobile, Ala. Fruit Trees, open ground Roses, Evergreens and Ornamental Shrubs adapted to the South.

JOHN T. LOVETT, Little Silver, New Jersey. General Nursery business. Small Fruits a specialty.

T. V. MUNSON, Denison, Texas. Peaches, Grapes and Plums specialties. Largest stock of Triumph Grape grown.

J. H. PRIEST, Greencastle, Indiana. Specialty Raspberries and other Small Fruits. Twelve acres in experimental grounds, near the city.

WM. PARRY, Parry P. O. New Jersey. Specialties Kieffer's Hybrid Pear and Small Fruit Plants. Express office, Riverton.

ROSE BANK NURSERIES, Nashville, Tenn. Oldest in the South. A. W. Webber, Secretary. Everything true to name and exactly as represented.

RUMSON NURSERIES, Hance & Borden, m'gers, Red Bank, N. J. Specialties, Peach, Ornamental and Silk Food Trees, including Eggs and reqisites.

SIMPSON & HOGUE, Vincennes, Indiana. Proprietors of Knox Nurseries, established in 1851. Small Fruit Plants a specialty.

STATE AGRICULTURAL COLLEGE, Columbia, Missouri. Grape Vines a specialty. Cared for by a member of the Faculty.

SAMUEL SMITH, Carbondale, Illinois, Horticulturist and Dealer in General Nursery Stock.

DR. H. SCHROEDER, Bloomington, Illinois. Specialty, Grapevines and small Fruits, Mulberry Trees and Silk culture.

W. M. SAMUELS & CO., Clinton, Kentucky. Fruit and Ornamental Trees. Grapevines and small Fruits. Newest Peaches, Apples and Pears.

I. N. STONE, Fort Atkinson, Wisconsin. Headquarters Stone's Hardy Blackberry and other Small Fruit Plants.

DR. A. L. SMALL & SON (Len. Small, Secretary State Hort. Society), Kankakee, Illinois, Nurserymen. Specialty, Plum Trees.

W. K. TIPTON & CO., Little Rock, Arkansas. General Nursery stock, Small Fruit and Market Gardeners. Fruits for the North.

E. Y. TEAS, Dunreith, Indiana. Lucretia Dewberry, best Hardy Blackberries, Raspberries, Strawberries, Catalpa Seedlings, New Blight-proof Pears.

A. R. WHITNEY, Franklin Grove, Illinois. Established in 1843. General Stock. Whitney's No. 20 Crab a specialty.

ANTHONY WIEGAND, Florist, Indianapolis, Ind. Largest Stock of Plants and Cut Flowers in the city. Established over twenty years.

LEO WELTZ & SONS, Wilmington, Ohio. Proprietors Wilmington Nurseries, established in 1858. General stock. Small Fruits a Specialty.

A. D. WEBB, Bowling Green, Ky., Fruit and Plant Grower. Originator of Warren and Longfellow Strawberries.

COMMISSION MEN AND DEALERS IN FRUITS.

THOMAS MASON, 183 S. Water street, Chicago, Illinois. Special attention to the sale of Fruits and Produce.

HAGER & SPIES, 101 S. Water street, Chicago, Illinois. Foreign, and Domestic Fruits. Wholesale.

F. A. THOMAS, 104 S. Water street, Chicago, Illinois. Fruit Shipping and Commission. Special attention to Sale of Fruits.

BARNETT BROS., 147 S. Water street, Chicago, Illinois. Specialties Fruits and early Vegetables. Consignments Solicited.

M. BAKER & CO., 93 S. Water street, Chicago, Illinois. Domestic Fruits given special attention.

A. L. McCLAY & CO., 95 S. Water street, Chicago, Illinois. Special attention to Fruits and early Vegetables from the South.

C. H. WEAVER & CO., 129 S. Water street, Chicago, Illinois. Commission Dealers in Green and Dried Fruits and Country Produce.

BARRON & BERMINGHAM, 131 S. Water street, Chicago, Illinois. Green and Dried Fruits and Produce.

A. L. TUCKER, 167 S. Water street, Chicago, Illinois. Green Fruits and Vegetables. Promptness guaranteed.

LOVE & BOOTH, 113 S. Water street, Chicago, Illinois. Wholesale Fruit and Produce. References good.

M. GEORGE & CO., 95 S. Water street, Chicago, Illinois. General Fruit and Produce Commission.

F. NICKERSON & SON, Chicago, Illinois. Fruit and Produce Commission. Prompt attention to business.

E. C. REICHWALD, 165 South Water street, Chicago, Illinois. Specialties, Fruits, Vegetables and Melons.

T. D. RANDALL & CO., Chicago, Illinois. Oldest Fruit and Produce house. Special attention to Fruits and Produce.

STEWART & WLOCOTT, 115 South Water street, Chicago, Illinois. Wholesale Fruits and General Commission Merchants.

L. F. ADAMS & CO., corner Maryland and Pennsylvania streets, Indianapolis, Indiana. Fruit Commission. Small Fruits a specialty.

A. A. BARNES & CO., cor. Maryland and Delaware Sts., Indianapolis, Indiana. Fruits and Vegetables a specialty. Oldest Fruit House in the city

HENRY SYERUP & SON, Indianapolis, Indiana. Fruits, Vegetables, Country Produce. Consignments solicited. Stencils furnished free.

MUMMENHOFF & CO. (E. H. Williams), 23 South Delaware street, Indianapolis, Indiana. Special attention to sale of all kinds of Fruits.

GEORGE HITZ & CO., 31 South Delaware street, Indianapolis, Indiana. General Fruit and Produce Commission.

VOORHEES & CO., Detroit, Michigan. General Commission. Special attention to Fruits and Country Produce.

GEORGE DAVIES, Cleveland, Ohio. Fruits and Vegetables a specialty. All orders receive prompt and personal attention.

A. C. KENDEL, Cleveland, Ohio. Special attention to Fruits, Farm and Garden Seeds and Florists' Wares. Promptness guaranteed.

E. T. HOLLISTER & CO., 809 Broadway, St. Louis, Missouri. Domestic Fruits and Vegetables, specialties.

JACOB SCHOPP & BROS., corner Broadway and Morgan streets, St. Louis, Mo. Wholesale Fruits and Vegetables.

GERBER & SIGNAIGO, 818 Broadway, St. Louis, Missouri. Special attention given to the sale of Fruits and Vegetables.

P. M. KIELY, 719 Broadway, St. Louis. Sixteen years experience. Fruits and Early Vegetables a specialty.

B. PRESLEY & CO., St. Paul, Minnesota. Foreign, Domestic and California Fruits, Berries, Nuts, and Country Produce.

W. H. BRYAN & CO., 12 and 14 Walnut street, Cincinnati, Ohio. Specialties, Fruits, Produce and Vegetables.

THOMAS JOANNES, Green Bay, Wisconsin. Dealer in Fresh Vegetables and Green Fruits, Garden and Farm Seeds.

MANUFACTURERS OF HORTICULTURAL IMPLEMENTS AND MACHINERY.

C G. HAMILTON, Detroit, Mich. Dealer in Cider, Sorghum and Jelly Machinery. Agent for Boomer & Boschert Cider and Wine Press.

EWALD OVER, Indianapolis, Ind. Ragan's Power Cider Press, Apple Grinders, One-horse Grain Drills, Binder Trucks and other Implements.

N. A. WHITNEY, Franklin Grove, Ill. Manufacturer and sole proprietor of . Whitney's Western Tree Digger.

MANUFACTURERS OF FRUIT AND VEGETABLE PACKAGES AND COLORED PLATES.

A. W. WELLS & CO., St. Joseph, Mich. Manufacturers of Peach, Grape and Bushel Baskets, Berry Boxes and Shipping Packages of all kinds.

W. P. MESLER & CO., Cobden, Ill. Manufacturers of Fruit Packages. Send for price-list. Reference, Parker Earle, Pres. M. V. H. Society.

D. M. DEWEY, Rochester, N Y. Original Colored Fruit Plate Manufacturer. Nurserymen furnished catalogues free on application.

FRUIT GROWERS.

ABNER ALLEN, Wabaunsee, Kansas. Fruits and Sweet Potatoes for market. Special attention to Seed Sweet Potatoes.

W. G. GANO, Parkville, ten miles north of Kansas City, Missouri. Large Orchardist. Apples a Specialty. Correspondence solicited.

J. M. SMITH, Green Bay, Wisconsin, Gardener. Dealer in Fruits, Vegetables and Plants. Large grower of Small Fruits for Market.

W. R. STUART, Ocean Springs, Mississippi. Orange Groves. Early Vegetables. Orange Lands for sale. Imports Jersey Cattle.

MALVERN VINEYARD, Malvern, Arkansas. Sixty acres in vineyards. Manufacturers of native Wines, Brandies, Cider and Vinegar.

A. W. ROUNTREE, 309 Josephine street, New Orleans, Louisiana. Commercial grower of Oranges and early Vegetables.

SEEDSMEN AND DEALERS IN FLORISTS' WARES.

E. SCHAPER & CO., 612 North Fifth street, St. Louis, Missouri. Dealers in Seeds, Plants, Bulbs, Garden Tools, etc.

PLANT SEED CO., 812-14 North Fourth street, St. Louis, Missouri. Field, Garden, Grass and Flower Seeds.

J. F. MENDENHALL & CO., Indianapolis, Indiana. Farm, Field and Garden Seeds. Horticultural Implements. Florists' Wares.

AGRICULTURAL AND HORTICULTURAL PRESS.

AMERICAN AGRICULTURIST, New York. Monthly. Orange Judd Co., Publishers. Byron D. Halsted, Managing Editor.

AMERICAN RURAL HOME, Rochester, New York. Weekly. One dollar per year.

CANADA HORTICULTURIST, St. Catharines. Monthly. D. W. Beadle, Editor. Published by the Fruit Growers' Association of Ontario.

COLMAN'S RURAL WORLD, St. Louis, Missouri. Thirty-sixth year. Weekly. One dollar per annum.

COUNTRY GENTLEMAN, Albany, New York. Weekly. Devoted to Agriculture and Horticulture.

DRAINAGE AND FARM JOURNAL, Indianapolis, Indiana. Monthly. Published by J. J. W. Billingsley & Son.

FARM, HERD AND HOME, Indianapolis, Indiana. Monthly, Published by Brown & Abromet.

FARMER AND FRUIT GROWER, Anna, Illinois. Weekly. "The best Horticultural paper in the West." H. C. Bouton, editor and proprietor.

FARMERS' HOME JOURNAL, Louisville, Ky. Weekly. $1.50 per annum. Agriculture, Horticulture and Live Stock. Th. S. Kennedy, Hort. editor.

FARMERS' REVIEW, Chicago, Illinois. The business farmers' paper. Weekly. One dollar and a half per year. Best market reports.

GREENE'S FRUIT GROWER. C. A. Green, Editor, Rochester, N. Y. Illustrated Quarterly. Twenty-five cents per annum.

INDIANA FARMER, Indianapolis, Indiana. Published weekly by the Farmer Company. $2 per year. Liberal horticultural department.

INDUSTRIAL TIMES, Indianapolis, Indiana. Weekly. Devoted to Agriculture, Horticulture and general news. One dollar per year.

JOURNAL OF AGRICULTURE. Phil Chew, Proprietor, St. Louis, Mo. A weekly, eight-page agricultural paper. $1 per year.

KANSAS FARMER, Topeka Kansas. Weekly. Devoted to Western Agriculture and Horticulture.

PRAIRIE FARMER, Chicago, Illinois. Weekly. Published by the Prairie Farmer Company. Oldest agricultural paper in the West.

RURAL CALIFORNIAN, Los Angeles, California. Illustrated monthly. One dollar and a half per year.

RURAL NEW YORKER, New York. Weekly. New Fruits and experimental work a specialty.

THE COMMONWEALTH, Topeka, Kansas. Weekly. One dollar per year. Commonwealth Company, Publishers. F. P. Baker, editor.

THE AGRICULTURAL PRESS, Indianapolis, Indiana. Monthly. One dollar and twenty-five cents per year. Cyrus T. Nixon, Editor and Publisher.

WESTERN FARMER, Madison, Wisconsin. T. D. Plumb & Son, Publishers; J. C. Plumb, editor horticultural department.

INDEX.

Lightning Source UK Ltd.
Milton Keynes UK
UKHW022148181218
334232UK00011B/658/P